Community Economics

Community

ECONOMIC STRUCTURE AND CHANGE

IOWA STATE UNIVERSITY PRESS / AMES

Economics

N SMALLER COMMUNITIES

RON SHAFFER

To Claire, Monica, and David

Ron Shaffer is Professor of Agricultural Economics at the University of Wisconsin—Madison.

Composed by Iowa State University Press
Printed in the United States of America

First edition, 1989

Library of Congress Cataloging-in-Publication Data

Shaffer, Ron, 1945–
    Community economics.

    Bibliography: p.
    Includes index.
    1. Regional economics.   2. Economic development.   3. Geography, Economic.   I. Title.
HT388.S5   1989   330.9   88–6149
ISBN 0–8138–0031–5

Contents

Preface   xi

1. Defining Community Economic Analysis   3

Community   3
Resources   5
Development   5
Community Economic Analysis   8
What Community Economic Development Is Not   9
An Outline of Things to Come   10
Summary   10
Study Questions   11

2. Community Economic Development Theories   12

Supply-Oriented Development Theories   13
   The Basic Growth Function   13
   Equilibrium Growth   14
   Less Restrictive Equilibrium Growth Conditions   16
   Productivity Theory   17
   Resource Endowment Theory   19
   Technological Adoption   20
   Market Failure   22
   Summary   25
Demand-Oriented Development Theories   27
   Export Base Theory   28
   Summary   34
Institutions and Community Economic Development   35
   Institutions Affecting Community Economic Development   36
   Institutional Change   37
   Entrepreneurship   38
   Summary   40
A Synthesis   41
   Critical Elements of the Model   43
Study Questions   44

3. Location Theory and Community Economic Development   46

Significance of Location Theory to Community Economic Analysis   46
Least Cost Approach   47
  Transport Costs   48
  Labor Costs   49
  Agglomeration Costs   50
  Transport vs. Nontransport Costs   52
  Space Cost Curves   53
  Institutional and Physical Factors   53
  Summary   55
Demand Maximization Approach   56
  Basic Market Areas   58
  Delineation of Market Boundaries   60
  Distortions in Hexagonal Market Areas   63
  Summary   63
Profit Maximization Approach   63
Behavioral Approach   66
  Objective Functions   66
  Uncertainty   66
  Information   68
  Summary   69
Critique of Classical Location Theory   69
Summary of Location Theory   69
The Location Decision Process   70
Location Factors   72
Summary   77
Study Questions   79

**4. Community Economic Development Policies,
    Goals, and Objectives   80**

Basic Policy Questions   80
Creating a Strategy   81
Goals or Objectives   82
  Hierarchy of Goals   84
  Relationship among Community Goals and Objectives   84
  Goals and Objectives through Time   88
Policy Model   89
  Socioeconomic Welfare Function   89
  Selection of Policy   91
  Philosophy of Community Economic Development Policy   92
Community Economic Development Strategies   94
  Attract New Basic Employers   94
  Improve Efficiency of Existing Firms   95
  Improve Ability to Capture Dollars   96
  Encourage New Business Formation   96
  Increase Aids/Transfers Received   96
Policy Evaluation   97
  Components   97
  Methods   99
Are Community Economic Development Programs Zero Sum?   102
  Forms of Zero Sum   103
  Conditions for Zero Sum   104
Summary   107
Study Questions   108

5. Implementing Community Economic Development Programs 110

    Starting an Economic Development Program   110
      Preparing   111
      Organizing   117
      Prospecting   119
      Targeting   119
      Diversifying   123
    Summary   124
    Study Questions   124

6. Central Place Theory and Market Analysis 125

    Central Place Theory   125
      Terminology   126
      Central Place Hierarchy   126
      Range of a Good or Service   133
      Demand Threshold   133
      Estimates of Demand Thresholds   136
      Irregularities in Central Places   139
      Limitations of Central Place Theory   139
      Summary   141
    Market Area Analysis   142
      Trade Area   143
      Delineating Trade Areas   143
      Gravity Models   144
      Reilly's Law of Retail Gravitation   147
      Other Determinants of Trade Area Boundaries   149
      Trade Environment   150
      Sales Potential and Retention   151
      Trade Area Capture   152
      Introducing New Goods and Services   153
      Summary   156
    Study Questions   157

7. Capital Markets and Community Economic Development 158

    Capital Markets   159
      Nonhomogeneity of Capital Markets   161
    Community Capital Markets   162
      Secondary Markets   164
      Correspondent Banking   165
    Capital Market Failures   166
      Mobility   167
      Information   169
      Risk   170
      Regulation   171
    The Role of Banks in Community Economic Development   172
    Policy Responses to Capital Market Failures   174
    Summary   175
    Study Questions   176

8. Labor Markets and Community Economic Development   178

Labor Markets   178
Demand for Labor   181
Supply of Labor   184
Institutions   188
Labor Market Theories   189
  Supply-Oriented Theories   190
  Demand-Oriented Theories   192
    Signaling/Screening or Credentialing Theory   192
    Job Competition Theory   193
    Dual Labor Market Theory   194
  Summary   195
Community Labor Market Issues   195
  Job/Worker Matching   195
  Unemployment   197
  Information   198
  Labor Mobility and Wage Differentials   199
Community Actions   200
Summary   201
Study Questions   201

9. Government Involvement in Community Economic Development   203

Public Sector Involvement   203
Public Response   205
  Demand for Goods and Services   205
  Supply of Factors of Production   207
Basic Approaches   209
Incentives/Subsidies   212
  Types of Subsidies   216
  Which Type of Subsidy?   218
Reservations about Subsidies   221
Summary   226
Study Questions   227

10. The Impacts of Community Economic Development   228

Economic Development Impacts   229
  Local and Nonlocal Impacts   231
  Monetary and Nonmonetary Impacts   232
  Primary and Secondary Impacts   234
  Private and Public Impacts   236
  Positive and Negative Impacts   240
Community Impacts   241
Multipliers   242
  Factors Influencing Multipliers   242
  Warnings about the Use of Multipliers   250
Summary   253
Study Questions   254

11. Economic Base and Input-Output 256

Economic Base Studies 256
  Social Accounts of the Community 257
  Sectoral Composition of the Community's Economy 259
  Measuring a Community's Economy 260
  Economic Base Multipliers 263
  Delineating the Economic Base 267
  Summary 273
Input-Output Analysis 274
  Crucial Assumptions 275
  Transactions Table 275
  Direct Requirements Table 279
  Total Requirements Table 279
  Input-Output Multipliers 281
  Uses of Input-Output 283
  Summary 284
Study Questions 285

Notes 287
References 297
Index 317

Preface

THIS TEXT EMERGED FROM TEACHING an advanced undergraduate/beginning graduate course in community economics at the University of Wisconsin—Madison. The course arose out of a concern that students of agricultural economics, rural sociology, and planning needed a more comprehensive understanding of the multitude of nonfarm economic activities affecting rural America.

The text reviews the economics of smaller communities, which has traditionally not been part of the main body of economic literature. We have extensive publications on macro- and microeconomics, and a substantial body of research on regional economics is emerging, but the literature in community economics is more scattered. My teaching, applied research, and work in extension community economics convinced me of the need to organize the community economics literature in a fashion demonstrating that there is a body of community economics theory or to give way to our harshest critics' claim of its absence.

Only a moment's reflection is needed to recognize that regional and national economies are aggregations of households and businesses within a common space, but there has been little work on how those economic units function, interact, and change through time. This text proposes to fill that void. The unit of analysis is small, open, multi-actor economic systems and how they function and more toward explicit and implicit goals.

No undertaking of this nature is the result of a single person's efforts, despite the title page of this book. I have been blessed with colleagues who encouraged and challenged me to organize my thoughts. At the risk of overlooking many of them, I wish here to give special mention to a few. Glen Pulver, Gene Summers, Marv Johnson, Ed Blakley, Mary McCarthy, and Richard Barrows read portions of the manuscript and served as sounding boards for ideas. In many cases, their direct contributions are significant; in some cases I garbled their ideas. The students in my community economics analysis course over the last thirteen years also contributed by their numerous questions that forced me to delve into the literature; they signaled that there is an interest in the economics of communities.

There are many citizens in Wisconsin and county extension community development agents whose interest in community economics continually reminded me that universities must help them improve their collective economic conditions. Finally, I want to thank Arne Selvik, president of the Institute of Industrial Economics, for the wonderful year in Bergen, Norway, that gave me the opportunity to assemble the scraps of paper (that previously passed for lecture notes) into the essence of this manuscript.

To Kity Notø, Dawn Danz-Hale, and Karen Denk, who received so many chapters more than once because a paragraph needed to be moved or did not convey its desired message, a special thank you. Marsha Cannon's understanding and fresh insights into the early draft saved me many frustrating hours. To Monica, thanks for your artistic gifts.

The quiet encouragement and support of Claire, Monica, and David are gratefully acknowledged. Their patience during the gestation of this book was far greater than could have been expected.

Community Economics

Defining Community Economic Analysis

1

A DESIRE TO CREATE JOBS for high school graduates, or improve access to consumer goods and services, or support new small business start-ups, or identify the types of training which should be provided young workers—these are some of the concerns raised by community residents every day. These matters are partially determined by national and regional economic conditions, but the circumstances of a given community can be manipulated to some extent by local residents. These concerns condense into three central issues: What is the economic situation now? What could it be in the future? How can desired changes be brought about?

Community economic analysis requires an understanding of a community and its economy. Economic theory must be called upon to provide insight into what is happening in the community's economy and how local and nonlocal decisions influence local economic change.

Community economic analysis (CEA) derives from community resource development (CRD) and is the subset of community resource development emphasizing the economic rather than the social-political-environmental dimensions of the community. Since community economic analysis is a direct descendant of community resource development, it is appropriate to define community resource development first. Then community economic analysis will be defined.

Community

Most definitions of community contain some reference to area, commonality, and social interaction. *Community* as used here is a group of people in a physical setting with geographic, political, and social boundaries and with discernible communication linkages. These communication linkages need not always be active, but must be present. People or groups

3

interact in the defined area to attain shared goals (Clark 1973; Freilich 1963; Hillery 1955; Koneya 1975).

There are at least five different approaches to studying a community (Long et al. 1973; Sanders 1966). They are: qualitative, ecological, ethnographic, sociological, and economic. The qualitative approach is a perspective of a community as a place to live. This approach looks at the housing, schools, neighborhoods, and attitudes of individuals in the community. The ecological approach is a study of the community as a spatial unit (i.e., the spatial distribution of groups of people and their activities and interactions within the community and among communities). The ethnographic approach is the study of the community as a way of life. The emphasis is on the total cultural dimensions of the community, not just its demography, economics, or geography. The sociological approach views the community as a social system and concentrates on its social relationships, which are patterned into groups and larger social systems, both inside and outside it. The economic approach examines the linkages between economic sectors, such as agriculture, Main Street merchants, and households, and the types of jobs and skills present in the community. This approach considers the sources of income, the distribution of income, and the change in income over time. Finally, this approach considers the resources (e.g., natural, financial, human, and managerial) found in the community.

A comprehensive study of a community requires a blend of each of these approaches. Community goals and decisions involve more than just economic dimensions. Failure to recognize the linkages among the dimensions reduces the prospect of successful action. These alternative approaches to the study of a community highlight different ways to delineate its boundaries. Regardless of the approach, common interests and concerns define community boundaries, and they generate a series of functional sub-communities (Kimball 1978). A functional sub-community is contained within the boundaries of a larger, more general community, and is defined by a single issue or function. The boundaries of the trade area or the boundaries of the labor shed define some economic boundaries of a community. The trade area is the geographic area from which the community draws a significant portion of its retail trade customers. The labor shed is the geographic area from which people commute into the community for employment.

Political interests define different community boundaries. The municipal limits of the village represent one set of political boundaries. The county in which that village exists represents another. School attendance boundaries, or school district boundaries, also define a community. A river basin or watershed or even an air quality shed define a community based on common physical interests.

Communications networks also define community boundaries. The people in a newspaper circulation or television or radio coverage area are part of a community because they receive news and other information from a "single" source. A community can also be defined by the source of its supportive services (e.g., smaller rural communities dependent upon a larger regional medical center for specialized medical services are linked by that service).

Any definition of a community's boundaries must select those associations or common interests most important for the concern being examined. Regardless of how general or specific the criteria used to identify community boundaries, there will be some residents excluded from the interest group—for example, people without children in school are less concerned about the prospect of a neighborhood school being closed.

Defining a community generally involves identifying a geographic area, some kind of communications or social linkages, and a commonality of mutual interest. Regardless of the criteria used to circumscribe the community, use of another set of criteria will generate a different arrangement of people and will redefine the community border. The commonality of interest offered in this book is the current and future economic condition of the community.

Resources

Economists define resources as the inputs or commodities that enter the production process to become transformed into an output. This definition is appropriate here, if used with care. The community is an economic system containing within its boundaries a bundle of resources available to generate an output, typically called welfare, for its residents. These resources include the political, social, economic, and physical inputs which support or have potential to support community decisions. Resources are the local and nonlocal natural, financial, human or cultural factors used to attain community goals. As explained in Chapter 2, mobility and accessibility of resources are as important as simple quantity because many resources are locationally specific and not ubiquitous (e.g., mineral deposits vs. air). The technology existing in the community affects the supply of community resources. The community's culture conditions (i.e., its ability and willingness to exploit resources) affect the public perception of what resources are available. For example, if the political culture of the community discourages the use of intergovernmental aids, then that external resource will not be exploited in local efforts to create jobs and income.

Development

Development is a concept, somewhat like community, that almost defies definition. It relates to the present resource base of the community, for this is used to produce change. It is an ongoing event, which may progress at different rates over time but which is continuous. At times and in some places the rate of development approaches zero. While development frequently implies the creation of something more, it can also mean less. For example, development occurs if a community replaces a large "dirty" industry with a smaller "clean" industry, even though total employment declines. Development implies greater equity. Equity is not the same as equality. Equality suggests that the "economic pie" is divided by the number of people in the population and distributed equally. Equity emphasizes access to opportunity.

Development involves structural change in the community. Some structural changes include: (a) modification of factors of production, (b) better utilization of existing resources, (c) changes in the structure and function of existing institutions, and (d) changes in attitudes and values of the population. Finally, a characteristic of development that is assuming increased importance is "reduced vulnerability to sudden shifts in production technology and in the market environment" (Pryde 1981, p. 523). This means a resilient, diverse, and innovative economy.

Development can be initiated by external shocks (e.g., changing energy prices or technological changes) that create disequilibrium and disruption in the economy requiring some type of institutional or structural adjustment. The goal of development policy is less to prevent such impacts, than to enhance the economy's capacity to respond. As part of the process, it may be necessary to provide compensation for those parties who bear a disproportionate share of the adjustment. Shapero (1981, p. 26) argues that development means that an area or the people in an area

achieve a state denoted by resilience—the ability to respond to changes in the environment effectively; creativity and innovativeness—the ability and willingness to experiment and innovate; initiative taking—the ability, desire and power to begin and carry through useful projects. In conjunction with this is the need for diversity, which offers an area some measure of invulnerability to the effects of many unforeseen events and decisions. With diversity there is always part of a local economy relatively unaffected by the changes in a single industry or market place or by legal constraints on a given product. Diversity provides a favorable environment for creativity and innovativeness.

This makes clear the concept of community economic vitality. The terms "vitality" and "development" are thus almost synonymous.

The concept of *vitality* relates to the policy goal of reducing community vulnerability to sudden shifts in production technology and the marketing environment. It is a concern about transitions and dynamic adjustment of resources to different and more valued uses. Vitality is anticipation of emerging needs and associated changes. Vitality means that the community is prepared to make the adjustments necessary to assure or improve the economic standards of the community. Change is fundamental to the concept of vitality, and the way in which the community adjusts to or deflects external or internal change is the mechanism. The concept does not mean that the community is totally at the mercy of external changes but that it recognizes that what may have worked yesterday may not be appropriate today or tomorrow.

Economic development is the sustained, progressive attempt to attain individual and group interests through expanded, intensified, and adjusted use of available resources. Important elements in development include: (1) setting of goals (2) identification of individuals and groups and their interrelationships, (3) understanding of the present and future effect of decisions made now, and (4) the attempt to form new combinations of existing resources or the pursuit of new resources. Economic development can also be defined as those activities which lead to greater resource productivity, a wider range of real choices for consumers and producers, and broader clientele participation in policy formation. Economic development is goal-oriented change, not change for the purpose of change.

Human welfare (well-being) is the end product of the development process. It is a value-laden concept that affects the economic efficiency and equity (social justice) dimensions that pervade definitions of economic development. Human well-being includes health, interpersonal relationships, physical environment, housing, education, the arts, and numerous other aspects of life. The significance of these different dimensions of human well-being is that frequently achieving desired goals in one dimension limits actions or achievement in other dimensions. This potential conflict and the need to make trade-offs will be examined in greater detail in Chapter 4.

While not the major focus of our efforts in this text, it must be remembered that economic development is a human/social phenomena. How it is achieved, or even the form of development sought, is conditioned by the behavioral/institutional framework of society. The participants in the development process operate within a behavioral framework that defines acceptable and unacceptable activities. ("Process" is used throughout this book to denote change over time rather than social interaction per se.) They attempt to coordinate the various dimensions of development so that they complement each other. The behavioral framework and the participants' actions are linked by the resource base available to the community to bring about desired development patterns.

Discussions of economic development are sometimes clouded because it is used as a synonym for economic growth. The concepts are closely related but are not identical. Economic growth can occur without development, and development can occur without growth. Growth means more economic activity, while development can be achieved through less economic activity. Growth does not imply some form of improved equity or restructuring of a community's economy. Development is a larger concept, but in reality the distinction is seldom clear. When growth is occurring, there may be small changes in institutions, behavior, and technology, but development requires major changes in all these areas.

The nonstandardized definition of economic development leaves a multitude of partial measures of community economic development — changes in the volume and type of economic activity in the community, changes in productivity, and changes in economic stability. No single measure completely encompasses the multifaceted nature of economic development.

The yardstick used to measure development depends on the goals of the community. For example, if it desires to improve the status of individuals currently outside the economic mainstream, development could be measured by the responses to such questions as: what has happened to people in poverty, what has happened to the unemployed, or what has happened to inequity? The simplicity of these questions belies the difficulties of an accurate response, or how people will judge a given response.

Development is a multi-dimensional concept that incorporates more than just market values; it includes concern about equity and well-being and the community's ability to adapt to change.

Community Economic Analysis

Community economic analysis occurs when people in a community analyze its economic conditions, determine its economic needs and unfulfilled opportunities, decide what can and should be done to improve economic conditions, and then move toward agreed-upon economic goals and objectives. Stated in a simpler fashion, *community economic analysis* examines how a community is put together economically and how it responds to external and internal stimuli. It is not a rationale for maintaining the status quo but is a comprehensive effort to change the economic situation within the community. Throughout this book the terms "community economic analysis" and "community economic development" are used interchangeably. The former has a more technical connotation, the latter a stronger policy orientation.

There are several common elements in community economic analysis and the community resource development process (Cary 1970, pp. 2–4). First, the community, rather than some smaller (firm, household) or larger (nation) economic entity, is viewed as the body which makes and implements decisions. Second, the community's initiative and leadership, rather than externally imposed mandates, is a source of change. Local citizens assume the leadership position, and the identification, encouragement, and training of local leadership is a basic objective. Third, the community can use both internal and external resources to achieve change, drawing on its own strengths and capabilities and looking beyond its boundaries for supplemental resources. Fourth, the participation of citizens within the community should be as inclusive as possible; all will not participate, but all should be given an opportunity to do so. (Community resource development and community economic analysis implicitly assume a democratic political system in which people have an opportunity to express their preferences.) Fifth, community resource development and community economic analysis are holistic in that they comprehensively examine the different dimensions of the community. Sixth, changed attitudes in people are as important as the material achievements of community projects during the initial stages of economic development.

What Community Economic Development Is Not[1]

It is important to distinguish between community economic development and other related activities. Community economic development is not a poverty program. Poverty programs are concerned with the activities of a specific portion of the population. Conditions of poverty typically arise from a lack of job skills, a lack of consumer skills, physical or mental disabilities, discrimination, poor health, and improper education. Poverty programs need not lead to economic development (i.e., they may provide no long-term solution for people in poverty). If a community chooses to pursue an economic development program, people in poverty need not be a specific target.

Community economic development is not synonymous with industrial development. Community economic development is much broader and more comprehensive than industrial development. In Chapter 4, five basic strategies for pursuing community economic development are reviewed. Briefly, they are: attracting new basic employers (in both manufacturing and nonmanufacturing), improving the efficiency of existing firms within the community, improving the community's ability to capture existing dollars, encouraging the formation of new businesses, and increasing the aid received from broader levels of government. Industrial development is only part of one of these five strategies.

Community economic development is not an attempt to exploit resources to yield the maximum economic return. If resources are nonrenewable, the short-run gains obtained contribute little to achieving the human welfare goals of community economic development. A historical example is the exploitation of northern Wisconsin forests at the turn of this century. A current example of natural resource exploitation with a long-run goal is

Norwegian North Sea oil development policy. The Norwegian government chose to limit the rate of exploitation of these hydrocarbon resources to reduce the strains on the economic and social fabric of the country.

Community economic development, poverty programs, industrial development, and resource use are therefore neither mutually exclusive nor identical.

An Outline of Things to Con

This book seeks to examine theories applicable to the questions of the economic development of small open economies (communities). The ideas and theories put forth here can also be applied to metropolitan areas and neighborhoods, but they are more appropriate for the small, freestanding community.

The next chapter reviews economic development theories for their applicability to such economies. Understanding these theories permits judgments as to the fundamental forces affecting community economic development and as to whether proposed corrective actions will accomplish the outcomes desired.

Chapter 3, on location theory, represents a particularly significant aspect of community economic analysis because of the importance of space to economic activity and relationships among economic units. Chapter 4 addresses the delineation of community economic development goals and objectives, the first step in setting community economic development policy. The organizing and implementing of community efforts to encourage economic development activities is the subject of Chapter 5. Chapter 6 reports the economics of providing consumer goods and services and the analysis of consumer markets from the community's perspective. Chapters 7 and 8 review the economics of capital and labor markets and how their functioning affects community economic development. Chapter 9 gives a justification for government actions in community economic development efforts and reviews some attempts to promote economic change. Chapter 10 discusses the economic changes likely to occur in a community as a result of an economic development event and the effect of community and project characteristics on its impact. The final chapter examines some of the tools used to analyze economic conditions of a community.

Summa

The general purpose of community economic analysis is to improve economic opportunity and quality of life through group decisions and actions. Community economic analysis is an action-oriented study of how a community is put together economically and how it responds to internal and external stimuli. Specific problems, resources, and alternative actions must be identified. Essentially, community economic analysis is problem-solving applied to community economic problems. The steps in the process, simply enumerated, are:

Where are we now?
Where do we want to be?
Why aren't we there now?
What needs to be done to get us there?
Who is going to do it?
When is it going to be done?
How will we know we got there?

Community economic analysis represents a conscious attempt to improve the decision-making associated with community economic development. The emphasis is on the technical and structural analysis of community versus individual decisions. This means consideration of the interaction of the economic, political, social, and institutional components of a community. Community economic development is a dynamic concept concerned with movement and change—with overcoming obstacles and capturing opportunities.

Study Questions

1. Communities are unique social phenomena. How can they be defined?
2. What is a sub-community?
3. Development is often used interchangeably with growth. How are they similar or different?
4. What is community economic analysis?
5. What do community resource development and community economic analysis have in common?
6. How are the scientific method and community economic analysis linked?
7. Why is the concept of equity important in discussion of community economic development?
8. In defining community boundaries, why are political boundaries important for community economic development?
9. Some suggest that community economic development is simply a change in job patterns and income levels. Is this sufficient given the discussion of development in this chapter? Explain your answer.
10. The idea of community economic vitality was mentioned in the discussion of community economic development. Are the concepts identical? If not, how are they distinguishable?
11. Why do you believe it is important that the community economic development concept places so much emphasis on group decisions, participation, and indigenous leadership?

Community Economic
Development Theories

2

EACH COMMUNITY IS ECONOMICALLY UNIQUE and performs some specific economic functions for a given group of people more economically than can be provided from any other source. Each community responds differently to external and internal stimuli. This chapter will review the reasons why communities are at different levels of development and some theories about how their development can be influenced.

The choice of economic development theories to be reviewed here is based on two criteria. First, the theory should offer some guidelines for intervention by either community or outside political forces. This criterion excludes theories such as cumulative causation and stages of development because they suggest that the development process, once started, is immutable. Second, the theory should have some relevance to the community situation. Theories that require modification of the money supply and other policy tools beyond the control of a community are excluded.

While our understanding of community economic development is inadequate for formulation of a general theory, we know the elemental concepts that need to be included. Community economic development produces community welfare, measured by wages, income distribution, stability, and the like. The community uses its resource base (infrastructure, capital, entrepreneurship, and labor) in conjunction with its current economic structure to achieve development. A general theory must recognize the interaction between demand and supply forces and how that dynamic changes the economic conditions and structure of the community in ways that stimulate or hamper development.

If the community is perceived as an economic decision-making unit wishing to maximize profits or utility or reward from the use of its resources, the parallelism between theory of the firm, resource owners, consumer behavior, and community economic analysis becomes apparent. A community's output, or real income, or employment is a function of what it can supply and what is being demanded. What it can supply depends upon the types of resources it has, how many it has, and how they are used. Demand refers to how much of what is produced can be sold, at what price, where the markets are located, and how they are changing. Acceptable economic actions and decision-making set the framework for demand and supply decisions. Furthermore, these actions occur among spatially separate economic units, adding another dimension to the decisions.

The discussion of community economic development theories will be organized around supply-oriented development theory, particularly the neoclassical model, and demand-oriented development theory, particularly export-based theory. Then institutions and the role they play in community economic development will be reviewed. The chapter will close with a synthesis of the different theories.

Supply-Oriented Development Theories

Supply-oriented development theories emphasize the importance of capital, labor, and other factors of production in creating more output and income (Borts and Stein 1964; Borts and Stein 1968; Carlburg 1981; Richardson 1969b, pp. 331–36; Richardson 1978a, pp. 135–44; Siebert 1969). These theories presume that what is produced can be sold (i.e., there is no concern about markets). The following discussion (based on Richardson 1969b, pp. 331–36) starts with a generic presentation of the neoclassical growth model, and then moves to specific theories.

THE BASIC GROWTH FUNCTION. The neoclassical model assumes a continuous relationship linking the output of the area to the capital and labor available. This relationship, referred to as a production function, is defined as:

$$Y = f(K, L, T) \tag{2.1}$$

where Y is level of real income or output; K is stock of capital (capital is used in the generic sense here and refers to natural, manmade, public, private, and social capital); L is stock of labor; and T is technology, which is assumed to be constant among regions and represented by the passage of time.

If the factors of production are paid their marginal product and a perfectly competitive market exists, or at least behaves in a perfectly competitive manner, then the production function in (2.1) can be used to understand the causes of community economic growth. The neoclassical competitive market model assumes that factors of production will move in response to market signals to equalize factor prices. This implies that transportation costs are zero; that there are no economies of scale or agglomeration; that resources are mobile, homogeneous, and divisible; and that information flows freely and costlessly.

Assuming a Cobb-Douglass production function (for simplicity, because other forms of the production function would also work) and constant returns to scale, we get the following production function:

$$y = tk^a l^{1 - a}. \tag{2.2}$$

Equation (2.2) can be differentiated completely, as shown in (2.3) below, with respect to time to represent the growth function for community i. (note that lowercase letters denote change and uppercase letters denote level or stock):

$$y_i = a_i k_i + (1 - a_i) l_i + t_i \tag{2.3}$$

where y is the growth rate of community output or real income, k is the rate of change in capital, t is the annual growth rate in technological progress, l is the growth rate of labor, and a is capital's share of income. Capital's share of income is the marginal product of capital times the capital-output ratio, $MP_K(K/Y)$. With constant returns to scale, $1 - a$ becomes labor's share of income, or the marginal product of labor times the labor-output ratio, $MP_L(L/Y)$.

EQUILIBRIUM GROWTH. A basic assumption of neoclassical growth theory is that capital will be fully employed when savings and investment are equal. The market mechanism creating equality of investment and full employment savings is the interest rate. If there is no risk and uncertainty, the interest rate equals the profit rate. For equilibrium growth to occur among communities, the marginal product of capital must equal the nationally determined interest rate. Furthermore, the marginal product of capital equals capital's share of income times the output-capital ratio (i.e., the change in output divided by the change in capital times the output-capital ratio):

$$MP_k = a\frac{Y}{K} = \frac{\Delta Y}{\Delta K} \frac{K}{Y} \frac{Y}{K} = r \tag{2.4}$$

$$= \text{ where } a = \frac{\Delta Y}{\Delta K} \frac{K}{Y}.$$

In other words, the last unit of capital employed in every community yields the same marginal product. This requires that the rate of change in output (Y) equals the rate of change in capital (k) if capital maintains a constant share of output (a). This equilibrium rate of growth is affected by the growth of the labor force, labor's share of income, and technological progress in the following fashion. If

$$y_i = k_i \text{ or } \% \Delta Y = \% \Delta K$$

and

$$y_i = a_i k_i + (1 - a_i)l_i + t_i$$

then

$$y_i = a_i y_i + (1 - a_i)l_i + t_i$$
$$y_i(1 - a_i) = (1 - a_i)l_i + t_i$$
$$y_i = l_i + \frac{t_i}{1 - a_i} = k_i. \tag{2.5}$$

For equilibrium growth to occur in a system of communities (in the state, region, or nation) the growth rate in every community must be equal and constant:[1]

$$y_i = y_j = y_m = \ldots = c.$$

Using the relationship developed in (2.5), the neoclassical model therefore requires that the rate of capital accumulation among communities be equal and constant:

$$k_i = k_j = k_m = \ldots = c.$$

Extending this even further, the relationship of technological progress, labor's share, and labor-force growth among communities must be equal and constant:

$$\frac{t_i}{1 - a_i} + l_i = \frac{t_j}{1 - a_j} + l_j = \frac{t_m}{1 - a_m} + l_m = \ldots = c.$$

The end result is that the equilibrium growth rate of a region or a state or the nation depends upon the equality of the output growth rates (y_i) among communities in the system, which in turn depends upon equality of the capital accumulation rate (k_i) among the communities. Furthermore, the equilibrium output growth rate (i.e., capital accumulation rate) among communities depends upon technological progress, the growth rate of labor, and capital's share of output. This leads to the conclusion that capital's share, technological progress, and labor-force growth are equal among communities and will remain constant over time:

$$a_i = a_j = a_m = \ldots = c_a$$
$$t_i = t_j = t_m = \ldots = c_t$$
$$l_i = l_j = l_m = \ldots = c_n$$
$$c_a \neq c_t \neq c_n.$$

For capital's share of output within a community to remain constant requires that technology be neutral in its effect upon the use of both capital and labor. Neutral technology alters the production function but not the marginal rate of substitution between capital and labor. Nonneutral technology alters the production function and the marginal rate of substitution between capital and labor. Thus, either capital and labor must be perfect substitutes for each other or nonneutral technological change must be offset by changes in the capital-output ratio, $\Delta(K/Y)$. A significant element of the neoclassical growth model is that the flexibility of the capital-output ratio allows the economy to maintain an equilibrium growth path.

LESS RESTRICTIVE EQUILIBRIUM GROWTH CONDITIONS. The equilibrium conditions stated above are very restrictive. The assumptions lead to an equality of all the elements in the growth function (2.5) among communities. However, relaxing these restrictive assumptions permits differences in capital's share, technological progress, and labor force growth among communities while still maintaining equality of growth rates among communities. A flexible capital-output ratio is the key element for less restrictive equilibrium conditions. For example, if labor force growth rates vary among communities, and capital's share of income remains constant, then communities with slower labor force growth can maintain an output growth rate equal to other communities by substituting technology for labor (i.e., more technological progress). Scenarios can be constructed that permit some elements of the growth equations to be unequal among communities. But as long as all communities are required to have an equal output growth rate ($y_i = y_j = \ldots$), other elements of the equations must adjust.

The growth in per capita output is equal to the difference in the rate of output growth and the rate of population growth ($y_i - n_i$). Thus increases in per capita output depend upon technological progress and labor's share of output, represented by the following simple algebraic manipulation of (2.5). If

$$y_i = \frac{t_i}{1 - a_i} + n_i$$

then

$$y_i - n_i = \frac{t_i}{1 - a_i}.$$

Here n represents population growth and equals labor force growth (l) if constant labor force participation rates are assumed.

If population growth rates do not vary among communities, $n_i = n_j$, any differences in technological progress among communities ($t_i \neq t_j$) would cause the rate of growth among communities to be unequal. However, the capital-output ratio adjusts to permit equality of growth rates among communities. When technological progress in one community exceeds that of another ($t_i > t_j$), dynamic equilibrium ($y_i = y_j$) can be maintained if capital's share in the community with the slower technological progress exceeds capital's share in the community with the faster technological progress ($a_j > a_i$). This occurs because the marginal product of capital in the two communities must be equal ($MP_{ki} = MP_{kj} = r$). This can occur only if the capital-output ratio in the community with the slower technological progress exceeds the capital-output ratio in the community with the faster technological progress ($K_j/Y_j > K_i/Y_i$). In other words, more is capital used per unit of output in the community with less technological progress.

In summary, the neoclassical model suggests that sources of output or income growth for communities arise from any of the following economic actions: (1) an increased supply of capital or capital accumulation; (2) an increased supply of labor or population growth; (3) some form of technological change; or (4) some form of increased economic efficiency because of shifting resources from lower- to higher-productivity uses. The ability to adjust the capital-output ratio by substituting capital for labor or vice versa permits an equilibrium growth rate even though there may be differences in the rate of growth of labor (population) or capital accumulation or technological progress among communities.

Now two specific forms of neoclassical development theory, sometimes labeled productivity/investment-stimulated development theory and natural resource endowment theory, will be discussed.

PRODUCTIVITY THEORY. Productivity theory argues that a deficiency of capital—private, public, or human—causes the lack of community economic development (Leven 1965, 1966). Indicators of private capital deficiency include low rates of return or profits and plant obsolescence. A poor road system or an antiquated sewer system indicate a public capital deficiency. Low educational attainment, below average health levels, and a poor-quality work force indicate a human capital deficiency.

Productivity theory contends that changes in the goods and services a community sells elsewhere (exports) result from, but do not cause, economic development. The export base theory, discussed later in this chapter, and productivity theory represent contrasting views of development stimuli. Subscribers to the productivity theory attempt to improve the real income or output of a community by removing capital deficiencies. Advocates of this perspective believe that the emphasis on capital reduces the potential risk of cyclical fluctuations arising from an overly heavy dependence on exports.

For development to occur, productivity theory argues that a community must generate and finance the investments necessary to increase its productive capacity. The theory presumes that relatively mobile capital funds among communities respond to market signals. Savings move from communities with a savings surplus (local savings exceeding local investment) to communities with a savings deficit. Thus national, not local, savings are critical for a community to generate the investments necessary. Capital mobility means that less developed communities need not finance their development themselves.

Productivity theory assumes that all resources (except natural resources) respond to market signals by moving toward communities with higher returns until the last unit of capital yields no greater return whether used in another community or for another purpose (i.e., when the marginal product of capital is equal to the national interest rate). This is the pure competition equilibrium in a spatial context. Since factors of production must move spatially, it becomes obvious why natural resources are not considered part of the capital base.

The policy prescriptions of productivity theory contend that investing large amounts of time, energy, and money in the capital base of the community improves its rate of economic development. In many cases, this investment must come from external public or private capital.

Productivity theory makes the following simplifying assumptions: (1) the existing institutional framework allows all nonnatural resources to adjust freely to market signals; (2) the value of resources is fixed over time; and (3) technology does not change over time. Assumptions (2) and (3) prevent changes in factor prices and technology from disrupting the equilibrium.

These simplifying assumptions make the theory somewhat less than satisfactory for policy guidance. First, the institutional framework does not ensure the total resource mobility implied by the theory. Even in a relatively developed economy such as the United States, savings tend not to move into depressed or less developed communities (the capital gap argument). Second, the theory assumes away some of the major reasons for disequilibrium among communities, including differences in capital-labor ratios, differences in product and factor prices, and differences in technology. Third, the reliance of less developed communities upon external capital to make necessary investments means that they become dependent upon these external sources. Fourth, and probably most significant, the theory gives no guidance about where capital should be invested to yield the type of development desired. Should it be invested in private, public, or human resources?

The productivity theory contends that nonnatural resources and their ability to produce externally desired goods and services, along with the associated local economic linkages, determine the level of community economic development. Resource mobility among uses and places plus attracting investment in the capital base of the community become the major policy suggestions of this approach.

RESOURCE ENDOWMENT THEORY. A second supply-oriented development theory is the resource endowment theory, which argues that a community's economic development depends upon the natural resources the community has and the demand for the products produced from those resources (Ciriacy-Wantrup 1969; Perloff and Wingo 1961). A community's resource endowment, in the short run at least, is the inventory of natural materials used to produce goods and services required. It is important to remember that the value of a resource is a derived value, and the demand for a resource is a derived demand. A resource is worthless unless used in some form of production. A liberal definition of production includes extraction of minerals, buildings, labor, and the recreational use of a wild river. Since the value of a resource derives from the final demand for the products produced, variables that affect final demand concern the community. The level of income, the distribution of income, tastes, and preferences, foreign trade, and the organization of production (whether it is competitive or monopolistic) affect final demand. These variables can change and alter a community's relative advantage in supplying inputs required by the national economy. The resource endowment theory implicitly assumes that over time a community can respond to changing demand by shifting resources to the production of different goods and services.

The theory contends that a community develops through the use of its resource base, and that the growth of supportive businesses and activities reinforces and sustains that development. This need for linkages permits distinguishing "good" and "bad" resources for the community. A good resource produces a stream of nationally desired goods and services. It has economic ties with additional processing (forward linkages) and input suppliers (backward linkages) in the community. An example might be a dairy farmer's use of land good for nothing more than forage and pasture production. The backward linkages of his production into the local economy are to dairy equipment dealers, feed mills, veterinarians, and labor. The forward linkage includes milk haulers and processors of milk into cheese and other products. Another desirable characteristic of a good resource is that a high proportion of the returns from using it generate an active demand for locally produced goods and services (i.e., the resource is owned locally). A bad resource would not possess these characteristics.

A community choosing to follow the policy prescriptions of the resource endowment theory must avoid overdependency upon a narrow range of resources. It can become vulnerable to forces beyond its control. Technological change can shift the relative production advantages among communities (less of a local resource may be needed, or other local resources may become more productive). For example, the development of new cotton varieties, fertilizers, and irrigation methods led to a shift of cotton production from the southeastern to the southwestern United States. There could also be a depletion of the resource base itself (e.g., the exhaustion of gold and silver deposits in the West, leaving ghost towns). Furthermore, over time substitutes may be found for a key resource, as artificial rubber replaced natural rubber.

While the resource endowment theory focuses on the community's ability to supply a good or service relative to other communities, not on the level of or change in external demand, demand does play a role. The demand for the product being produced should be income-elastic so that demand will grow over time with income. The community's economic future could be affected by a shift in the national demand for its output (e.g., consumers' preference for the convenience of artificial fibers over cotton in clothing).

A major limitation of resource endowment theory is the long-run shift of the economy away from the direct use of natural resources toward more processing of semifinished goods and the provision of services. This relative decline of the importance of raw material in the final value of products weakens the link between the resource base of a community and its economic development.

In summary, natural resources perform a significant role in community economic development. While resource endowment theory incorporates final demand into its analysis, it is a supply-oriented theory because the point of analysis is the availability of resources, not the availability of external demand. In many cases, natural resources can be an obstacle to achieving community economic development. The surrounding economic and social structures play an important role in the use of resources. The important issue is how the existing natural resources interact with capital, labor, and technology to produce a product desired by some market.

TECHNOLOGICAL ADOPTION. A community can grow by importing capital and labor or by making better use of its existing capital and labor through technological improvement. The capital and labor portions of a community's production function will be discussed in Chapters 7 and 8. The spatial diffusion of technology or innovation significantly affects the rate of development among communities. The neoclassical model assumes distribution of technology instantly over space and uniformly over time. But technological change does not occur at a constant pace, nor is it uniformly adopted everywhere (Borts and Stein 1964, pp. 7–10; Thompson 1978; Molle 1982). The neoclassical model suggests that innovation creates higher profits for adopters by reducing their average costs. These excess profits create an incentive for technological adoption and lead to diffusion. The question remains: what causes differences, if any, among communities in the type of technology used?

Technological change separates into two phases, invention and innovation (Lloyd and Dicken 1977, p. 409). *Invention* is the flash of insight that provides new understanding of basic questions. It tends to be a physical-biological-chemical phenomenon related to production processes. It can be either autonomous (largely a random event) or induced (arrived at through research and development expenditures). Inventions need not be used immediately and can remain dormant for considerable periods of time. *Innovation* is the adoption of inventions and their application to production, marketing, or organizational problems. While also dependent upon flashes of insight, it is more likely to be influenced by entrepreneurial attitudes (typified by a willingness to seek different solutions to problems), economic conditions, and availability of investment funds. Another way to distinguish between invention and innovation is to say that invention is an ongoing process somewhat independent of economic conditions, and depends upon the inherent curiosity of the population. Innovation is much more dependent upon economic conditions (e.g., growth rates and competitiveness in the market) and the ability to generate investment funds to capitalize on a new development.

A variety of forces retards the transmission of technology over space (Malecki 1983; Thorngren 1970). The most important obstacle is differences in the rate at which management accepts and adopts technology. Mere receipt of information about an invention does not ensure adoption. Management reduces risk by requiring repeated and redundant messages about the invention coupled with information about how it has preformed for similar firms. The transmission costs of technology are not zero. They include becoming aware of the new technology, figuring out how it can be applied, and disrupting production and training workers in its use. In some cases, a completely new production process is required, which means that the technology will not be adopted until the present capital stock is fully depreciated. New technology requiring only minor change is adopted more quickly.

Communities are composed of different industrial sectors, and the rate of technological progress varies among sectors. Communities containing sectors experiencing rapid technological change themselves change more rapidly than other communities, but patents, restrictive union agreements, and secrecy in the use of the technology impede its transmission among communities.

Technological change moves through the economy in two different manners, called the neighborhood effect and the hierarchical effect (Hagerstrand 1966). The *neighborhood effect* means that innovation is quicker if the adopter is physically close to the inventor or to a previous adopter. The ultimate neighborhood effect is when inventor and adopter are one and the same. Social communication and interaction influence the spread of an idea, while adoption results from learning, accepting, and making a decision. The spread of new ideas occurs through public media, such as trade magazines, or, most influential, through personal communication among individuals. The volume of social and professional contacts directly enhances the technology adoption rate. The neighborhood effect stems from the logic of seeing new technology applied and being profitable (Robson 1973).

The *hierarchical effect* means that inventions and innovations occur first in larger communities, then spread out and down through the urban hierarchy (see Chapter 6 for further discussion of urban hierarchies). New technology tends to appear in spatial concentrations due to agglomeration and communication. Much research and development occurs in urban centers, stimulated by the frequency and intensity of personal contacts.[2] The hierarchical spread of inventions from larger to smaller areas derives from the logic of the volume of interpersonal contacts and the presence of sufficient markets, reducing risk when adopted. In a strict interpretation of the hierarchical effect, innovation would flow down and out from the larger centers to the smaller centers, not laterally among similar-sized centers nor in reverse, from smaller centers to larger ones. Evidence strongly suggests, however, that diffusion of innovation flows both up and down the urban hierarchy and also laterally (Pred 1967).

These hindrances to the instantaneous spread of technology contribute to a market imperfection preventing every community from equal or instantaneous access to the same technology. The end result is that communities develop at different rates because they use different technology.

MARKET FAILURE. A market brings together demanders and suppliers of products and resources and permits them to negotiate a mutually agreeable transaction. However, if the actors cannot reach an agreement, the market must send a signal to demanders or suppliers to change their behavior. Furthermore, that signal must indicate the type of change required, and the actors within the market must receive, respond, and adjust appropriately to it.

However, uncertainty, imperfect information, relocation costs, etc., impede the adjustments associated with smooth and perfect operation of a market. Any economic development strategy must reduce barriers to economic development or market imperfections. Many of the assumptions of the neoclassical, perfectly competitive market model are violated consistently. When they are, the model no longer predicts behavior or reflects real-world experience.

Market failure takes two forms: structural failure and performance failure. *Structural market failure* occurs when the market economy does not exhibit the welfare-maximizing characteristics assumed in the neoclassical model. By welfare-maximizing characteristics we mean that as individuals seek to maximize their profits or utility, they also maximize community welfare. Structural market failure arises from imperfect information, immobility of labor or capital among communities and uses, and externalities causing a misallocation of capital or labor among uses and places. *Performance market failure* occurs when the market economy, while functioning well in the structural sense of the neoclassical model, fails to yield a socially desirable distribution of income and output. Performance market failure arises from a disagreement about the proper distribution of ownership of and income from resources.

Either form of market failure often justifies government intervention. The policies discussed in the last half of this book (manpower and industrial development programs) reflect dissatisfaction with the movement of resources or the distribution of resources and income among communities and, implicitly, among groups of people.[3]

The pure competition market model posits the following equilibrium conditions: (1) equal factor prices, net of transportation cost differentials among communities or over space; (2) equal marginal products for each factor in the production of all goods and services among communities or over space; (3) equal product prices among communities or over space, net of transportation cost differentials; and (4) technology uniformly distributed and available.

Factor prices, product prices, and profits are not equal over space for several reasons, the most obvious being differences in transportation costs. Transportation costs are not uniform in every direction or among commodities, which distorts the factor and product prices and sends an unintended market signal. Other causes of market failure include resource immobility, imperfect information, transaction costs, increasing returns to scale, externalities, concentrated market power, second best, and public intervention (Vaughan and Bearse 1981, pp. 314–16).

Some immobility of natural resources such as land, minerals, and forests is acceptable, but immobility of other resources such as capital, labor, technology, and management prevents equalization of factor and product prices over space or among products. There are two forms of *resource immobility*. The first occurs when external resources fail to perceive and respond to long-run economic signals from the community, represented by the failure of capital and labor to move into a community that offers a higher return. The second form of immobility occurs when community resources are not used in their most productive manner, for example, when labor or capital in a community continues to be used to produce something of lower value to society. This could occur when labor remains unemployed or the price of other outputs increases.

Beyond the general question of type of resource immobility is recognition that the propensity to move in response to market signals varies among resources (Richardson 1973). For one resource, people, factors that influence the rate of migration (mobility) include distance, information flows, psychic forces, age, occupation, and family status. For another, capital, the rate of migration varies with the form of the capital (e.g., land vs. money), information flows, historical investment patterns, and uncertainty.

Let us now return to the suggested causes of market failure and take as an example labor markets. *Imperfect information* prevents the unemployed worker from being aware of job opportunities or the types of skills to acquire. *Transaction costs* are the unemployed worker's cost of finding out about job opportunities or acquiring an appropriate skill. *Increasing returns to scale* become evident in the efficiencies gained by having the federal and state governments provide a job information service rather than having each worker attempt to obtain job information. *Externalities* mean that if the individuals making the investment expenditure cannot capture sufficient returns, they will underinvest (e.g., in education). *Concentrated market power* affects the labor market by reducing the incentive for product innovation and development, either through altered behavioral response to market signals or because resources are unavailable to smaller economic units. The concept of *second best* means that an imperfection in one market, such as the capital market, causes less than optimal conditions in a second market, such as employment for certain individuals. *Public intervention,* while designed to improve the functioning of the market, can also generate perverse signals. For example, the regulation of financial institutions to protect depositors can discourage high-risk investments even when they have high growth potential.

While the importance of these factors must be recognized, they can be overemphasized (Vaughan and Bearse 1981, pp. 316–21). Specifically, in a dynamic context, these "sources of market failure" create opportunities for entrepreneurs. Thus, if the community fails to develop, the cause may be less market failure than failure to encourage entrepreneurs to exploit opportunities. Also, public intervention to overcome market failure may actually act as a barrier to development (see above and Chapter 9).

In a dynamic economy, some additional barriers to development include the following: lack of entrepreneurship; the high cost of adjustment (the cost of creating additional highly skilled labor or sophisticated machinery); uncertainty about such things as governmental fiscal and monetary policy; institutional rigidity (e.g., bureaucratic behavior); a lack of capacity, both institutional and human; a lack of key resources or key organizations to support the development process; and a lack of integration or coordination between key parts of the economy and political systems (e.g., an adversarial relationship between the public and private sectors). These may be more important than the traditional, quasi-static market failure concepts already listed. The failure of capital and labor to respond to market signals or the failure to send appropriate market signals awaits fuller discussion in Chapters 7 and 8.

SUMMARY. Supply-oriented development theory derives from the neoclassical production function concept in which output is a function of capital, labor, and technology. This theory assumes a perfectly competitive market economy or a market behaving like a perfectly competitive economy. Equilibrium within the system of communities occurs when the growth rate among all communities is equal.

The growth of output or income in a community comes from an increase in the quantity of labor and/or capital used, adoption of new technology, and reallocation of capital or labor to more productive uses within the community.

The elemental assumptions of the neoclassical model of the perfectly competitive market include continuous full employment of both capital and labor; constant returns to scale; perfect information and no uncertainty about current or future conditions; no externalities; and a homogeneous and perfectly mobile stock of capital and labor (Richardson 1973; Richardson 1978b). The use of an aggregated community production function requires the implicit assumption of no differences among places or sectors in the type of output produced or technology used. Furthermore, the failure to include space explicitly in the analysis does not allow examination of how phenomena like spatial oligopoly affect community economic development.

Relaxing the assumptions of the neoclassical model permits analysis of the sources of market failure. The two major types of market failure are structural and performance failure. The market imperfections of concern here are the immobility of factors of production among communities and imperfect information among communities.

The neoclassical approach to community economic development suffers from several general limitations that must be noted in using the theory for policy prescriptions (Richardson 1973). To some extent the limitations appear as causes of market failures. The neoclassical model presumes that there will be an equilibrium solution driven by prices causing an appropriate allocation of resources among places and uses. This quest for an equilibrium requires resources to make marginal adjustments; the model ignores the inertia of locational change or discontinuous adjustments of labor and capital. It also ignores the spatial diffusion of information and technology so important in determining economic activity in a given place. It presumes negative feedbacks, where "nonequilibrating" actions will self-correct rather than reinforce (i.e., cumulative causation). These limitations result in the general policy philosophy that manipulation of prices will yield the appropriate outcome.

Much of the preceding discussion has used comparative statics, where all factors are in equilibrium or in search of equilibrium. But in a dynamic economy the equal factor or product prices or marginal products required for equilibrium may not occur among communities, for a variety of reasons: (1) discovery of new resources or depletion of existing ones; (2) differing diffusion and acceptance of technology among communities and industries; (3) changes in consumer tastes and preferences and associated shifts in demand; (4) varying accumulation of capital and differing rates of growth of labor among communities, causing continued factor price differentials; and (5) differing managerial abilities and efficiencies among communities. All of these variables can cause continuing factor price differences among communities, in contrast with the suggestion made by comparative static analysis that there is an equalizing of growth rates among communities.

However, even if factor prices equalize among communities over time, that does not necessarily mean equal per capita incomes. The reasons for this include an unequal distribution of the ownership of productive resources among communities, differences in labor force participation rates among communities, and heterogeneous labor force(s) among communities.

The justification for using the neoclassical theory of the firm for community economic development rests on the analogy that communities use resources (capital, labor, and technology) to produce outputs (jobs and income). Furthermore, the community's need to make decisions to allocate resources among competing uses appears similar to a firm's need to allocate its resources among competing uses. Yet the analogy is a limited one. Some of its limitations, market failures, were discussed above. Space represents another limitation and will be discussed in detail in the next chapter; briefly, space confounds the application of the neoclassical theory of the firm to community economic development because the theory fails to incorporate phenomena like the decay of information over distance, spatial oligopolies, the need to internalize spatial externalities, and spatial agglomeration (Richardson 1973, p. 69). These forces create situations where the forces of convergence (equilibrium requirements) of returns and per capita income fail to operate. Rather, differences in capital-labor ratios (technology) cause continuing differences in wages among communities. In this situation the high-wage area continues to attract both labor and capital and to grow faster than the low-wage area (i.e., the wage levels will not converge).

Despite these shortcomings, neoclassical development theory does provide us a basis on which to make judgments about development activities, particularly the movement of factors of production.

Demand-Oriented Development Theories

Demand-oriented development theories suggest that local development results from an external or national demand for locally produced goods and services. If a community has a comparative cost advantage in the production and distribution of a good or service demanded in the external market, then the community will attract the capital and labor necessary to produce the good or service.

Over the long run, competitive market forces create an optimal spatial distribution of economic activity by selecting those production sites most cost-efficient for the market served. Local unemployment, low income, and slow growth represent short-run symptoms of a decline or shift in demand for the community's output. The market responds to this decline in demand by shifting capital and labor to alternative production (more productive uses) within the community or in other communities. The presence of lower-cost factors of production, particularly unemployed labor, attracts other lines of production to the community. Persistent symptoms of distress (unemployment, low income, lack of growth) indicate that national economic development might be improved if an absolute decline (i.e., out-migration of resources) occurred in the community.

The types of capital and labor adjustments mentioned above suggest a continuing discussion of the supply-oriented approach to development. But there is no supply problem, since the community has unemployed factors of production (e.g., capital and labor). The community needs to pursue a strategy of creating demand for the goods and services it produces and thus employment for local capital and labor.

Depressed local economic conditions uncorrected by market forces continue for several reasons. First, the low wages for labor in the community reflect the efficiency wage of labor (i.e., its marginal product is low). Second, the excess of social overhead capital in the community is illusory (water, sewer, and street systems are obsolete and cannot accommodate growth). Third, a limited population base prevents the community from achieving thresholds (sufficient local markets) for a wider mix of goods and services. Finally, a community failure to offer adequate returns to factors of production results from excessive transportation costs.

The policy implications of the demand-oriented approach to community economic development are straightforward. The community's continued economic development depends upon external demand and upon cost differences with other communities. This leads to three policy alternatives for the community: (1) create adequate external demand for locally produced goods and services, which is typically beyond the means of a single community; (2) shift local labor and capital to the production of goods and services experiencing demand growth; or (3) subsidize the total costs of producing a good or service within the community to make it competitive with other communities. While alternative (3) might make the community competitive, a subsidization program may become a continuing effort that is not self-correcting (see Chapter 9). Any attempt to subsidize production in a community distorts the market, that is, the factors of production do not receive the correct market signals and resources remain committed to less efficient uses. Demand-oriented development theory supports the subsidization of specific communities only in order to redistribute income geographically (see Chapter 9).

Demand-oriented community economic development theories study the forces that affect the demand for the goods and services the community produces and the way in which that demand is translated into community income or employment. The most explicit demand-oriented community economic development theory is the export base theory, discussed next.

EXPORT BASE THEORY. Export base theory or economic base theory argues that a community's economy can be divided into two sectors (Andrews 1970d; Andrews 1970c; Andrews 1970a; Blumenfeld 1955; North 1955; North 1956; Sirkin 1959; Tiebout 1956a; Tiebout 1956b). The first is the export or basic sector, that portion of the economy which trades with other areas. The export sector brings dollars into the community because someone outside the community purchases goods and services produced in the community. The second sector (the nonexport, nonbasic, or residentiary sector) sells its product within the boundaries of the community and exists to support the export sector.[4]

Export base theory contends that the development of a community depends on the vigor of its export industries. The critical force in the community's economic development is external demand, not its ability to supply capital and labor or to use technology. The timing and pace of the community's economic development depends upon the success of its export sector, the characteristics of that sector, and the disposition of income received from export sales (North 1961, p. 1).

The characteristics of the export sector and the disposition of its income translate external forces into community economic development. How changes in this sector affect the rest of the community depends upon the number and strength of the linkages between the export and nonexport sectors (i.e., upon the characteristics of the export sector). Furthermore, the distribution of income from the export sector and the ownership of resources used in it assist in translating export sector changes into community economic development. For example, if the ownership of export base resources is external to the community, then changes in the export sector have a minimal impact on the community because the income is not recirculated or reinvested in the community. Finally, the availability of skills that permit the local labor force to work in the export sector also determine whether external demand can be translated into local economic change.

The traditional export industries are agriculture, forestry, mining, and manufacturing. However, current versions of the theory recognize that exports need not be limited to these sectors. Wilbur Thompson (1975 p. 211) suggests that the intellectual ability of the community is its true export:

The economic base of the larger metropolitan area is, then, the creativity of its universities and research parks, the sophistication of its engineering firms and financial institutions, the persuasiveness of its public relations and advertising agencies, the flexibility of its transportation networks and utility systems, and all the other dimensions of infrastructure that facilitate the quick and orderly transfer from old dying bases to new growing ones. A diversified set of current export— "breadth"—softens the shock of exogenous change, while a rich infrastructure— "depth"—facilitates the adjustment to change by providing the socioeconomic institutions and physical facilities needed to initiate new enterprises, transfer capital from old to new forms, and retain labor.

The real criterion in determining the export function is whether the activity brings income into the community. Exports occur when an economic transaction (a sale) occurs across the community's economic boundaries, either as the movement of a good, service, or capital to the purchaser or the movement of the purchaser to the good, service, or capital (Andrews 1970c, pp. 52–58; Andrews 1970b, pp. 98–115). The *movement of goods* to the consumer or purchaser is the most commonly perceived type of export transaction. Goods that move to the purchaser could be consumer or capital goods, raw materials, or semifinished products. The identifying characteristic of this form of export is the physical movement of the good across the community's economic boundary. The *movement of services* occurs when the service is used or consumed beyond community boundaries. Examples include commuters from the community transporting their labor to another area, insurance protection being sold to entities located elsewhere, or state and federal government facilities being located in the community. The *movement of capital* to the consumer or purchaser occurs when a community household or business makes a nonlocal investment on its own initiative, for example, purchasing life insurance or stocks and bonds or starting an outside branch of a local business.

The *movement of the consumer or purchaser* to the good occurs when nonresidents purchase local goods. The movement of the consumer to services occurs when nonresidents enter the community and consume a service within the community; some examples are recreation, regional medical services, and university education. The movement of the consumer to capital occurs when the initiative to export capital comes from a nonresident of the community; an example is the local banker approving a loan to finance a nonlocal investment.

The export base theory requires several assumptions which are often not explicitly recognized (Conroy 1975a; Pfister 1976; Richardson 1973; Tiebout 1956a): (1) income and employment changes in a community are totally dependent upon changes in the level of exports, with no other stimulus for local change; (2) the marginal propensity to consume locally (the amount of local income spent for local products) is stable over time and over a relatively wide range of income change (see "Multipliers" in Chapter 10 for more detail); (3) the amount of local income generated by each dollar of local spending does not change and thus the local labor content does not vary over time for locally consumed goods and services; (4) there are no changes in the relative prices of capital or labor as their use increases or decreases (no shift from labor to capital, or vice versa, in response to changes in export demand) (Muth 1968); (5) the additional capital and labor required to expand production is available immediately and without any increase in wages or profits, since the community has a perfectly elastic supply of capital and labor to meet increases in demand; (6) the economic structure of a community at any one time will predict its future economic structure; (7) the homogeneous export sector implies that earnings from jobs, backward linkages, etc., in separate subsectors of the export sector are roughly equivalent; and (8) none of the local consumption of the goods and services sold for export comes from importing those goods and services (i.e., no cross-hauling).

The volume of exports from a community can either increase or decrease over time. There may be a rightward shift in the external demand curve or the good or service exported may have a high income elasticity; or income levels of nearby areas may increase; or the comparative advantage in the community may improve. An example of the shift in external demand which affected some communities is the growth in the use of coal in the United States during the 1970s. A service with a high income elasticity is the hospitality and recreation industry. The income level of nearby areas is important because most communities sell more to nearby than to distant communities. The improvement of a community's comparative advantage increases its exports because it permits lowering prices relative to other communities. Changes in technology or prices affect the profitability of using the community's factor endowment for exports; for example, the exploitation of tar sands in northern Alberta, Canada, was profitable as crude oil prices increased and new technology became available. A change in tastes and preferences that increases the demand for specific products favorably impacts on some communities because they have the resources (factor endowment) to produce that good or service.

A community could also experience a decline in the volume of its exports over time because of a leftward shift in external demand; or because of depletion of its natural resource base; or because of a relative decline in its comparative advantage through an increase in the costs of land, labor, and capital; or because technological changes alter input combinations for which this community previously had an advantage. If a community does not adjust to the forces decreasing its volume of exports, it will find itself stranded outside the economic mainstream with a relatively or even absolutely worsening economic position.

Just as communities experience increases or declines in their existing export base, they experience the creation of new export sectors. The factors causing an increase in exports can cause new export activity. Two additional forces of particular significance are government investments and new technology. Government investments in social overhead capital (water and sewer systems, industrial parks, transportation systems) can eventually lead to new export businesses. New technology has a differential effect among communities. Some communities gain a competitive advantage through adopting it early. An example is the parallel growth of the microprocessor industry and of communities capable of supporting such businesses.

Four points support the use of export base theory: (1) the theory focuses attention on one of the more important sources of independent demand in the community, exports; (2) export demand is more critical in smaller, less self-sufficient communities; (3) the theory is relatively simple and easy to understand; and (4) it is more appropriate for forecasting community income or employment in the short run than in the long run.

There are six major weak points to export base theory (Blumenfeld 1955; Hirsch 1973, pp. 192–94; Lewis 1972; North 1955; Richardson 1969b, pp. 328–30; Stewart 1959; Thomas 1964, pp. 427–30; Tiebout

1956a; Tiebout 1956b; Williamson 1975). First and foremost, export base theory is not a general theory of community economic development but is more appropriate for smaller communities, simpler economies, and the short run than for larger communities, complex economies, and the long run. Second, a theory that argues that a simple exogenous shift in export demand is the source of economic development borders on naiveté because community economic development is also affected by other forces, some of which will now be examined. The theory does not explain changes in the marginal propensity to consume locally as income changes (marginal propensity to consume locally is assumed constant; see "Multipliers" in Chapter 10). The export sector is not homogenous, and changes in different parts of it have dissimilar multiplier effects within the local economy; for example, think of the different linkages that agriculture has with the local economy, compared with manufacturing or the recreation industry. The changes in the export sector also depend on nonexport or supporting economic activities which help create the comparative cost advantage for the export sector. For example, a change in export activities partially depends on the efficiency of the transportation system. Two other factors affecting the community's economic development are the size and location of the market (the nearer it is, the more the impact) and the initial factor endowment of the community (its ability to produce different goods and services for export).

A third shortcoming of the export base approach for community economic development is its failure to explain how development can occur despite a decline in exports. A community experiencing a decline in its exports can still grow because nonexport businesses can grow enough to offset the decline. An improvement in the community's terms of trade (i.e., it is getting a better deal for the goods it sells) means that it is exporting fewer goods yet still maintaining or improving its total income.

Fourth, export base theory is only a partial theory. In the strictest sense, the level of export sales in a community is not independent of intercommunity relations or intercommunity feedbacks (Lewis 1972, pp. 19–20). In Figure 2.1 we see that as income falls in one community, it reduces imports from another community, which means an income decline in the second community (i.e., its exports decline, as do its imports from the third community), and reduces the third community's exports and income. The change in community income is a function of the change in community exports, and the level of exports from any community is a function of income levels in all other communities.

If a system of communities makes up the world, the question becomes: How do you have an initial change in exports which is autonomous to every community and initiates the change in income? One way to interrupt this cycle is to initialize the change in exports through a technological advance,

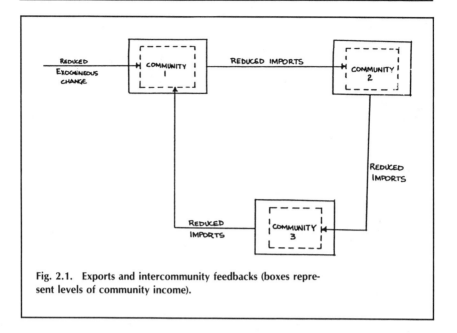

Fig. 2.1. Exports and intercommunity feedbacks (boxes represent levels of community income).

or to change the supply of capital and labor, or to reallocate capital and labor within the community, or possibly even to change institutions to improve comparative advantages. So for a system of communities, export base theory fails to explain the initial export changes, which are conveniently and justifiably assumed to be exogenous for the individual community.

Fifth, the export base approach to community economic development does not account for structural changes in a community. It argues that a community's economy will forever depend on its export sector. However, as communities grow they become less dependent upon exports; at some point in their development, some nonbasic sectors become "self-sufficient" and maintain themselves without heavy reliance on export activities, which the theory does not explain.

Sixth, while export base theory argues that nonbasic activities are a passive component of the community's economy, they need not be. In many cases, such activities change without a change in the basic sector, in direct violation of the fundamental premise of export base theory that all local economic changes are initiated by changes in the export sector. The source of growth can flow from the nonexport to the export sector, in direct contradiction to export base theory. Some examples of this type of change are as follows: (1) the nonbasic sector becomes self-sustaining and is no longer dependent upon the export sector because the local market has become large enough to support the business and there is sufficient local trade among businesses and/or households (import substitution, the replacement of an imported good or service with a similar or identical locally produced good or service); (2) local government investments change the amount and the character of the social overhead capital base of the community and stimulate new export activities; (3) noneconomic stimulated in-migration (in-migration stimulated by the presence of amenities or by retirement) causes nonexport activities to increase without an increase in exports; (4) improved efficiency in the nonbasic sector induces growth in the basic sector by making the export sector even more competitive relative to other areas; and (5) the nonbasic sector experiences a higher rate of technological change than the basic sector. In example (5) a shift of resources into the nonbasic sector increases community growth more than if the resources continue to be allocated to the export sector. The basic sector need not grow in this situation, in contrast to example (4).

In summary, export base theory has intuitive appeal and simplicity. It also has a relatively sound theoretical foundation, based on the concept that some local economic sectors transmit external economic forces into the community to stimulate further change. Changes in community income depend upon changes in export demand. Exports increase because of a rightward shift in demand or an improvement in the competitive position of the community; they decline because of a leftward shift in demand or a loss of competitive position. New export sectors appear in the community because of changes in tastes and preferences and technological changes.

Export base theory is more appropriately applied to smaller economic areas that are relatively more dependent upon external trade and to simpler, less diverse economies. The importance of the export sector to the community declines with increases in the diversity and completeness (self-sufficiency) of the local economy.

A community has an export sector because it has a cost advantage in producing a good or service, it has a unique resource for the production of that good or service, it has a unique marketing location, and it has some type of transportation advantage. Over time, the economy of a community tends to create supporting activities that enhance the competitive position of the community's export sector. These activities can take several forms: (1) specialized marketing organizations, (2) specialized credit institutions, (3) specialized transportation facilities, and (4) a trained labor force with specialized skills. The most obvious example of this support specialization is the relationship of an agricultural community to production agriculture (farming).

SUMMARY. Demand-oriented development theories argue that the lack of long-run economic development is not the result of inadequate productive capacity because there is unemployment, unused capital and out-migration from the community. Rather, they attribute the lack of development to inadequate demand. What needs to be done is to increase the demand for goods and services produced by the community or to shift the goods and services produced in the community to types for which demand exists— essentially a structural question. This expanding export sector should have good internal linkages with the rest of the community so that external economic forces are transmitted effectively to the local economy. The export sector brings income into the community. The nonexport sector serves markets within the community and generally supports the export sector, although it can lead development.

Institutions and Community Economic Development

Institutions are basic to any form of social interaction, although their importance is not usually recognized except when changes in them are proposed or when they are not performing satisfactorily. Here we are interested only in institutions that facilitate or impede community economic development. Institutional forms that affect communities are those that govern how market forces interact and those influencing the capacity to make decisions, specifically, institutions that influence entrepreneurship, capital accumulation, technological change, labor supply, and resource use (Parsons 1964; Ruttan 1978; Schultz 1968).

Institutions are the rights and obligations or social, political, and legal rules that govern the use of a community's resources (production), exchange, and the distribution of rewards (Davis and North 1971). Traditions, customs, attitudes, and governmental arrangements set the framework in which economic units (households, businesses) make consumption and production decisions. Institutions are concerned with decisions and with decision-making; they can be formal or informal (how and when the power structure meets, resolves differences, and reaches a consensus is an important institutional arrangement in community decision-making). The role institutions play in community economic development can possibly be ignored in the short run, but not in the long run (Schmid 1972; Shaffer 1969).

Beyond rules and regulations, another institutional factor affecting community economic development is the capacity to perceive and accommodate change (Ruttan 1984, p. 549). The ability of the local community to distinguish problems and symptoms and to respond appropriately typically appears as entrepreneurial ability. Entrepreneurship relates to the assembly of both private capital, labor, and technology and public capital, labor, and technology. This private-public distinction is crucial for community economic development (the private dimension will be reviewed in greater detail later). The public dimension is the ability of local government and community organizations to anticipate and influence change, to make intelligent decisions about policy, to develop programs, to implement policy, to attract and absorb resources, to manage resources, and to evaluate current activities to guide future actions (Honadale 1982) (see Chapter 9 for more detailed discussion). In essence, the institutional capacity question becomes: Can communities appropriately define problems and use available internal and external resources to guide their own economic development?

INSTITUTIONS AFFECTING COMMUNITY ECONOMIC DEVELOPMENT. The discussion of institutions and community economic development leads to a series of questions about the incentives and aspirations of individuals; orderly change through time; entrepreneurship; capital accumulation; technological change; labor supply; geographic and occupational mobility of labor; the resolution of conflicts; the negotiation of debts; the specification of rights, duties, liberties, and immunities; property rights and contracts; and the organization of businesses. Some of these are examined here.

Institutions influencing resource availability are as diverse as property rights, taxation of capital gains and dividends, general and vocational education, the presence of discrimination, and the distribution of job vacancy information. Attitudes about resource use also affect economic development. For example, attitudes about resource conservation or exploitation in Western society are quite different from those in Buddhist society, which explains, in part, differences in their choices of development alternatives.

An institutional change affecting labor supply is female labor force participation. Through the early 1950s, few women pursued permanent careers outside the home. However, since the mid-1960s working women have become a common phenomenon, and now more than half of all women aged 16–60 participate in the formal work force. As a result of this change, the labor supply and the economy's productive capacity increased dramatically. Societal standards on retirement age also affect labor supply and the availability of valuable human capital and experience.

Institutions also affect economic markets as they set the framework for the bargaining process and the resolution of inevitable conflicts. Institutions on enforcement of agreements such as contracts affect the functioning of markets, especially over great distances and among unfamiliar actors. Likewise, institutions related to methods of settling transactions (barter, cash, credit cards) influence markets.

Institutions affect income distribution directly by defining rates of reimbursement (e.g., minimum wages), by whom and how resources are owned, and how the returns from the use of resources are to be distributed. The distribution of income (e.g., highly skewed or nearly equal) directly affects development through its impact on incentives, the willingness to save, the willingness to invest, and the aggregate demand of society.

Institutions related to the ownership of resources and capital accumulation affect community economic development by defining the mechanisms for acquiring and controlling capital (e.g., corporation, limited partnership, money market account). Other institutions influencing capital accumulation are income and inheritance taxes. Income tax rules affect consumption and investment decisions as well as work incentives. Decisions as to which forms of income are taxable (wages and salaries) or nontaxable (fringe benefits) affect the economy. The tax system encourages various forms of capital accumulation. Tax-free interest on municipal bonds encourages public capital formation, while depreciation rules and tax credits encourage investment in new buildings or the rehabilitation of existing buildings.

As seen in this brief review, institutions can stimulate or restrict the shape and speed of community economic development in many ways. If the institutional structure fails to support community economic development, change is mandated.

INSTITUTIONAL CHANGE. Institutional change means changes in how individuals and organizations interact among themselves and with their economic-social-political environment. It may mean changes in rules or changes in relationships within a given set of rules. Changes in relative factor prices, in resource endowments, and in product prices coupled with socio-political strains on existing institutions due to ongoing change make institutional change necessary (North and Thomas 1970; Ruttan 1984). Economic development can occur within the existing institutional framework, but frequently institutional change must come first.

One or more of three strategies is usually used to effect institutional change. The first is to make a selective modification of customary social, economic, and political practices within the existing framework, the purpose being to strengthen those practices beneficial to economic development. For example, the Community Reinvestment Act requires federally chartered financial institutions to meet not only the deposit needs but also the credit needs of their community, so they must make a serious attempt to support local projects.

The second strategy for institutional change is to borrow institutions from a different cultural or economic context and superimpose them on an existing relationship. Examples are the use of "quality circles" in U.S. businesses or the idea of co-determination, giving a business's work force a formal role in policymaking.

The third strategy is to substitute completely new institutional arrangements for the existing ones. Recent examples include Employee Stock Ownership Plans (ESOPs) and Community Development Corporations (CDCs), which are alternative business ownership mechanisms designed to return control to community residents and those individuals most affected by the employment decisions of the firm.

Institutional change, typically, is gradual and subtle rather than sudden and dramatic. Economic decisions (investment, pricing, employment) are made with some awareness of the existing institutional framework. A change in that framework yields both gainers and losers (Davis and North 1971). Who the gainers and the losers are, and where they are located, varies and is often difficult to anticipate. Institutions generate around them economic, political, and social power which reinforces the existing structure. These forces will resist change and must be contended with when it is proposed or actually occurs. The deregulation of the trucking industry provides an example of institutional change and its ramifications. In some locales service increased and price declined; in other locales the opposite took place. The gainers from deregulation — those who can now enter the trucking business or can alter services more easily — will support it, while the losers — those who lose economic power (existing firms and their employees) — will, at best, be indifferent.

ENTREPRENEURSHIP. A key institutional ingredient in community economic development is entrepreneurship. When examining a community from the perspective of business expansions, start-ups, and in-migrations, the key actor becomes the entrepreneur. Entrepreneurs bring together resources, take necessary risks, have ideas, provide the ingenuity and energy to create new products and services, and search out markets. Al Shapero (1981, p. 28) defines entrepreneurs as "company formers and venturers or enterprisers [who] bring together resources to organize and manage a new company; and [they] are not necessarily the individuals who conceive the idea for the company, invent the product or service manufactured and sold or provide the capital." Wilbur Thompson (1965, p. 44) suggests a slightly different interpretation. He associates entrepreneurship with "inventiveness, promotional artistry, organizational genius and venturesomeness." This interpretation of entrepreneurship incorporates characteristics associated with public as well as private entrepreneurship.

While entrepreneurs are created, not born, they share certain specific personal characteristics (Pryde 1981, p. 525): (1) a disposition to accept new ideas and try new methods — they have a minimal commitment to existing norms and institutional arrangements, making it easier for them to perceive alternative ways of doing things, and are comfortable with uncertainty and risk and inclined to behave in an innovative way; (2) a need to achieve — they have some internal drive to succeed that permits them to accommodate risk and seek out new ways to reach their goals; (3) a tendency to set moderately difficult goals—entrepreneurs are very result-oriented but do not set goals for themselves that are either unachievable or unchallenging; (4) an ability to accept feedback and act accordingly—they use it to make adjustments to accommodate the difference between where they are and where they expect to be in the future; and (5) an interest in excellence—while monetary gain is important to most of them, excelling, in and of itself, is important, and money becomes just one measure of it.

Entrepreneurship requires particular skills as well as personality traits (Pryde 1981, pp. 525–26): (1) accurate perception of market opportunities and devising of effective strategies for exploiting them; (2) capacity to identify and meet resource needs (determination of resources in short supply and location of substitutes or alternative sources); (3) ability to manage political relationships effectively (e.g., working with people in the community, especially local government officials, to bring them around to an idea); and (4) ability to mange interpersonal relationships—the successful entrepreneur did not go it alone but built the business organization through effective teamwork.

Shapero (1981) suggests a constellation of elements present in many company formations: displacement, disposition to act, credibility to act, and availability of resources. *Displacement* refers to the phenomenon that many company formations are associated with some kind of personal displacement or dislodgement from a comfortable or otherwise acceptable state of being, resulting in either positive or negative pressures on the individual. A positive pressure would be a business idea and the belief that forming a new business is the only way to fulfill that idea. Examples of negative pressures are becoming unemployed or finding oneself a refugee. However, individuals finding themselves displaced need not form a new company. The individual must feel that he has some control of his life (a *disposition to act*), a feeling manifested in an independent and self-reliant attitude, rather than an attitude that life is controlled by external and random forces such as luck, fate, and nameless powerful people. *Credibility to act* means that initiating a new business is a reasonable and logical activity for an individual. Personal observation of other individuals successfully initiating a business reinforces this belief. *Availability of resources* means that the individual either has the capital, materials, equipment, and facilities required to initiate the business, or knows how how to acquire those resources.

Writers like Roger Vaughan (1985), Wilbur Thompson (1965), and Joseph Schumpeter (1961) have recognized the importance of innovative strength and entrepreneurial skills in economic development. The entrepreneur makes the economic, social, and political system come together to cause change. A community needs to build a cultural environment that encourages such activity. How can a community create conditions that foster an attitude that opportunities exist, and that attempts to generate new jobs, income, and products can be successful?

Several community features seem to encourage entrepreneurial innovation: (1) an atmosphere of "immunity" or "indifference" rather than one which highly esteems tradition; (2) highly diverse social institutions; (3) power relatively diffused throughout the community, so that vested interests are less in control; (4) an elite whose economic power comes from diversified sources rather than an elite whose wealth is based on a single source, such as mining, or forestry, or specialized farming; and (5) widely available and visible opportunities for social mobility.

SUMMARY. Economic institutions are the procedures, rights, rules, and sanctions that affect decisions about the production, exchange, and distribution of rewards. Institutions influence who can use resources, how they are used, and who receives the income generated from them. Traditionalism hampers economic development, while the willingness to accept change and technological innovation facilitates it. Economic institutions provide rules for adjusting and accommodating conflicting demands among the different interest groups within the society. Economic theory typically assumes that the necessary institutions either exist or will develop. However, the creation of an institutional framework supportive of community economic development is not automatic and may be critical to its development efforts.

The capacity of the community and its public and private decision-makers to perceive opportunities and to respond in an appropriate fashion is a crucial institutional strength in community economic development. Another critical element, and one lending itself to extensive manipulation by the community, is entrepreneurial skill. Stimulating, encouraging, and supporting entrepreneurs is not easy because of the difficulty in identifying them, matching them with appropriate opportunities, or training them prior to their involvement in starting a business. A high level of entrepreneurial events, or the process of business formation and expansion, characterizes a developed economy (Pryde 1981, p. 523). Undeveloped economies do not have a comparably high rate. Thus an important development strategy for a community would be removing barriers to entrepreneurial activity.

A community supporting new business formations must question their feasibility (what kinds of new ventures will succeed?). In many communities, reluctance to support entrepreneurial ventures derives from their high probability of failure. While failure is a definite possibility, the reluctance to risk failure may be misdirected. There is a mistaken notion that a developed or successful economy does not have failures. Failures are less-than-successful experiments which provide insight into what might work. Roger

Vaughan (1985) suggests that failure is a result of healthy experimentation. Growing economies differ from stable and declining economies in the rate of business formations, not the rate of business failures. As Al Shapero (1981, p. 30) puts it:

Empirical studies of company formations have shown that many successful entrepreneurs have failed at least once before their current success. Henry Ford failed in business twice before he finally succeeded. Individuals who previously owned a business have a much lower failure rate than those who have never been in business. If a community retained those who were part of a failed enterprise, there may be little loss from the viewpoint of a community for the experience, skills and capital remain available for other efforts.

A Synthesis

A careful analysis of the distinction between supply- and demand-oriented theories of community economic development reveals that the differences represent a pedagogical distinction rather than a clear conceptual difference. There still remains no general theory explaining community economic development. The existing theories, for the most part, do an excellent job in explaining specific phases and instances of economic development in a community (Anderson 1976; Edwards 1967a; Engle 1974; Nelson 1984; Richardson 1973; Richardson 1978). In this final section the theories discussed above are put into a general framework.

The basic questions to be answered by a general theory are these:

- What causes the growth and development of a community's economy? Do these causes vary over time in the same community? How do they vary among communities?
- How important are institutional dimensions, such as the capacity to perceive problems and solutions, to any local development effort?
- What role does the availability of local resources (natural, human, and man-made) have on current and potential development?
- How important is external trade to the development of a community? How does this importance vary over time and among types of communities?
- What is the significance of internal trade to community economic development and to the well-being of local residents?
- Can local efforts, both private and public, to alter economic development actually offset adverse national or regional forces?
- Does the economic structure (i.e., the types of businesses and owners) affect current and potential economic development prospects of the community?

- What socioeconomic groups are migrating into and out of the community? What influences their decision to migrate? How do they alter the stock of labor in the community?
- What is the level of private investment in the community? How is it changing? What forces influence its size and location? In what sectors is that investment being made?
- What influence does distance or space have on the movement of resources, information, products, and people?

The general theory of community development must not only explain what *is* (comparative statics) but *how* the community's economy arrived at this or that condition (dynamics). Any general theory must start with external forces (Anderson 1976; Edwards 1976a). National demand and national economic conditions are critical because they provide a market for locally produced goods and services, which is the initial stimulus for development. Nonmanufacturing must be recognized as a potential source of community exports. Nonlocal governmental expenditures and exogenous private investments are significant elements of community growth. Yet it is important to remember that local consumption, or the lack of it, is critical in translating exports into local economic change, including import substitution, by which the community captures dollars that previously escaped by producing and selling the product locally. Thus a general theory cannot be an either/or strategy because both nonlocal and local activities are equally significant.

For a community to respond to external demand, there must be existing businesses which are now selling or are capable of selling to the external market. These businesses should have strong linkages to the rest of the community.

The availability of resources must be considered simultaneously with external demand. This is the supply side of the development question. A community must have natural and man-made resources plus the public and human capital needed to produce the goods or services demanded either locally or nonlocally. The mobility of these resources must also be considered: our theory must explain why labor and capital migrate to or from the community and how that movement affects the community's economy.

The theory must explain investment in the community's resource base. This investment must either expand the total resource base of the community or implement new technological processes. The theory should explain the rate of investment, the economic sectors in which it occurs, and its location. It must explain the diffusion and adoption of new technology.

Typically, a community's resource base is given, as is demand for its goods and services. The development question really becomes how the community interprets demand and allocates its resources to produce the desired output. (By "interpretation" we mean its capacity to identify problems and perceive solutions so that many demand- and supply-related obstacles can be overcome.)

Demand appears to be the dominant short-run growth force and supply the dominant long-run growth force. However, the community is constantly in a long-run environment complicated by innumerable short-run situations. Yet both short- and long-run situations are conditioned by the community's capacity to perceive opportunities and respond to them.

CRITICAL ELEMENTS OF THE MODEL. Any effort to create a comprehensive theory of community economic development requires, first, that the model utilize economic theory to explain the behavioral patterns of economic units within the community and identify the various decision-makers (households, businesses, or governmental officials) and their roles in the community; second, that the model recognize the linkages that occur among economic units both within and outside the community; and third, that the model consider the policy variables available that allow either external or local political units[5] to intervene in the economy (Engle 1974). To be of much use, the model should contain both short-run and long-run policy tools to cope with the question of what the community can do next month and over the next decade to improve its situation. The presence of short- and long-run policy tools means that the model needs to be cognizant of both short- and long-run relationships within the economy.

The model must incorporate the community's current stock of durable capital, which is essentially fixed in the short run. Further, it must be cognizant of the types of durable capital (by levels of productivity, age, and specificity for particular businesses) that will make the community more or less attractive to particular economic activities.

In addition, the model must explain the change in man-made capital and associated technology and the changes in human capital. It must consider what skills are possessed, how investments in new skills occur, how worker productivity changes over time, and what causes the migration of labor into or out of the community.

The model must identify the community's exports and must describe their variations over time. What causes these shifts? An examination of the export sector should consider the influence of changes in export demand on local income, local population, and the price of the community's exports relative to its competitors. How can the community's comparative advantage in producing the exported good or service be maintained or improved?

Discussion of a community's production must consider the aggregate demand and the demand for specific goods and services as well as the spatial context of this demand. The demand generated by nearby regions will be more important and significant to the community than demand from an amorphous national market.

Communities are open economies, and any dynamic and comprehensive theory must include the migration of factors of production (capital and labor) into and out of the economy as well as within the community. The direction and magnitude of these flows determines changes in income, factor prices, and factor supply in the community in response to changes in production and demand.

In conclusion, a community is typically concerned about increasing or maintaining its output. This output translates into jobs and income for community residents, thus the concern about the level, growth, and distribution of jobs and income for residents. Both long-run and short-run changes in the community have to be evaluated in this light. Likewise, our general theory of economic development must address the institutional framework in which decisions are made and the way in which these decisions affect the job and income situation within a community.

Study Question

1. What are the three general categories of community economic development theories? What in general do they say? Do they represent independent ideas about how community economic development occurs? If not, explain.

2. The supply-oriented approach to community economic development is based on a continuous relationship between community output and factors of production. What is that relationship? What factors of production are included?

3. The supply-oriented approach contends that the economic development of a community is a result of four types of economic behavior or adjustment. What are they?

4. Several elemental assumptions are made in supply-oriented development theory about the condition of markets, availability of factors of production, interest rates, and prices. What are these assumptions, and why are they important?

5. If a policymaker is using the productivity approach, what does it say causes the lack of community economic development? How is this cause determined? What are the elemental assumptions required?

6. When the resource endowment theory was discussed, the terms "good" and "bad" resources were used. What do these words mean? What are the characteristics of each resource? What is their significance for community economic development?

7. In the review of market failure, the concepts of structural and performance failure were used. What are they? What is their significance to community economic development and supply-oriented development theory?

8. The supply-oriented approach to community economic development assumes that technology is instantaneously transmitted spatially. The discussion of technological adoption suggested that such a transfer was not likely to occur. What are some obstacles to the instantaneous/rapid transmission of technology?

9. The concepts of invention and innovation were used in relation to technological adoption. How are they similar or different? What influences the presence of either or both?

10. What distinguishes demand-oriented from supply-oriented development theory?

11. What is the significance of the export sector, and how does it affect community economic development?

12. How is an export transaction defined for community economic analysis? What forms does it take?

13. What are some of the assumptions made when using export base theory?

14. What might cause a change (either an increase or a decrease) in the export base over time?

15. What are the strengths and weaknesses of export base as a community development theory?

16. What are institutions? Why are they important to community economic development? Give some examples of how they work.

17. Why is entrepreneurship so important to community economic development?

18. Is entrepreneurship strictly a private phenomenon? Explain your answer.

Location Theory and Community Economic Development

SINCE MOST DEFINITIONS OF COMMUNITY have spatial or geographic dimensions, and community economics examines economic activity among spatially separated communities, this chapter will review the basic elements of location theory. Location theory focuses on the attributes of space, such as the location of resources, production, and markets, and the transportation system. These attributes explain where economic activity occurs.

Classical location theory can be divided into three schools of thought: the least cost school, the demand maximization or locational interdependence school, and the profit maximization school. An emerging theoretical approach to location is the behavioral approach to decision-making. Each of these approaches will be reviewed for its contribution to community economic analysis. The final section of the chapter synthesizes studies of location factors and location decision-making.

Significance of Location Theory
Community Economic Analys

Location theory explains how spatially separated economic units interact among themselves, their markets, and their sources of supply. While the traditional focus has been on firms, the reader need remember only that communities represent sites of a market, labor, and other resources in order to recognize the transferability of the concepts of spatial interaction.

The contribution to community economic development from the use of a resource depends upon where that use occurs. Likewise, the shifts in demand for products affect specific geographic locations of production (e.g., communities). A community represents the operating environment for economic units interacting in space (e.g., businesses and households buying and selling output, labor, raw materials, and capital). Location theory provides insight into how location decisions are made and why economic activities occur where they do; with this knowledge communities can consciously try to affect those decisions.

The narrow perception of location theory is that it explains decisions to relocate a business. But businesses face numerous other location decisions. Since every economic transaction has a spatial dimension, each represents a location decision, for example: Where to start a business? Where to expand as growth occurs? Where to relocate? Where to sub-contract surges in production? Where to merge to acquire capital or achieve market penetration or acquire sources of supply? Where to buy inputs? Where to market production? Each of these questions has a spatial connotation, and different location factors will influence the decision. In some cases, familiarity and personal contacts dominate. In others, markets, resources, labor, or transportation predominate. Thus the phrase "location decision" refers to any economic transaction with a spatial dimension, not just the traditional relocation decision.

Least Cost Approach

The least cost school of location theory, which parallels the neoclassical model of economic development (Greenhut 1956, pp. 5–22, 254–57; Moses 1958; Smith 1971, pp. 112–58), states that firms seek to minimize their total cost of production and transportation. The decision sequence in the least cost approach is as follows: first minimize transport costs to a site and then add other costs (labor and agglomeration) to determine whether adding the other costs alters the choice of site. The firm could minimize either labor or agglomeration costs first, but since location theory focuses on the spatial distribution of economic activity, the initial emphasis on transport costs has great appeal.

The least cost school makes six basic assumptions: first, that a firm exists in a purely competitive world with no monopolistic gains achievable from a specific location choice; second, that it can sell all it produces because its demand is perfectly elastic and unaffected by location; third, that its market consists of separate points with a given location and size; fourth, that the geographic distribution of materials is given, and some raw materials are found only in specific locations, where their supply is perfectly elastic; fifth, that there are several fixed locations where an unlimited labor supply at any given wage exists; and sixth, that there are no site-specific institutional factors such as tax rebates, political systems, or culture to affect the location choice (this assumption means that location incentives do not enter into the decision process because they do not exist).

TRANSPORT COSTS. Transport costs enter the least cost decision model not as dollars but as the weight to be hauled and the distance to be covered (Smith 1971, pp. 113–16). The location decision uses ton-miles rather than dollars because the model assumes no institutional (rate) differences for inputs vs. outputs, or short vs. long hauls, or for product characteristics (e.g., perishability and fragility).

The optimum location can be selected with a locational triangle, which is a simple geometric technique to demonstrate the influence of transport, labor, and agglomeration costs on a firm's location decision (see Figure 3.1).[1] The firm's objective is to minimize the ton-miles of hauling. Assuming no differences in rate schedules, ton-miles of hauling translates directly into transport costs for inputs and outputs.

In Figure 3.1, point C is the market; M_1 and M_2 are the locations of raw materials; P_1 is the business location being sought; a, b, and c represent the distances inputs and outputs must be hauled in miles; and X, Y, and Z represent the weight of inputs and outputs that must be hauled.

The locational triangle works on the premise that the consumption point (C) and the raw material sources (M_1 and M_2) exert a pull on the

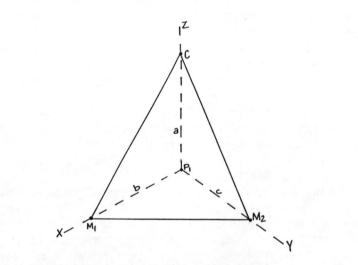

Fig. 3.1. Locational triangle. (After David M. Smith, *Industrial Location: An Economic Geographical Analysis* [New York: John Wiley and Sons, 1971], Fig. 8.1, p. 115; copyright © 1971 by John Wiley and Sons, Inc.; reprinted by permission of John Wiley and Sons, Inc.)

business's location, as measured by ton-miles from those points to the business's location. If the firm seeks to minimize ton-miles of inputs and outputs, the firm essentially seeks to minimize the equation: ton-miles $= bX + cY + aZ$. The location where this equation is minimized determines the production site (P_1).

LABOR COSTS. The business's location decision attempts to minimize total cost (i.e., the sum of transport, labor, and agglomeration costs), not just transport cost. Once the plant selects its minimum transport cost site, there may be another site with labor available at a sufficiently lower cost to overcome the higher transport costs associated with that alternate site (Smith 1971, pp. 116–17).

In Figure 3.2, P_1 is the least cost transportation point determined earlier, and labor is available at L_1 and L_2 at \$3 per ton of output cheaper than at P_1. The location question becomes: is labor sufficiently cheaper at L_1 or L_2 to cause the firm to move from the minimum transport cost site?

To determine whether labor costs affect the location site, draw isodapanes around the minimum cost transport site. (Isodapanes connect points of equal additional transport cost from the minimum transport cost site.) In Figure 3.2, the isodapanes are labeled \$1, \$2, \$3, \$4, and \$5. The business attempting to minimize total costs could incur up to \$3 of additional transportation costs to reduce labor costs by \$3. Site L_1 lies between the \$2

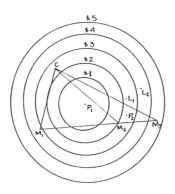

Fig. 3.2.   Effect of labor costs on least cost transportation site. (After David M. Smith, *Industrial Location: An Economic Geographical Analysis* [New York: John Wiley and Sons, 1971], Fig. 8.2, p. 117; copyright © 1971 by John Wiley and Sons, Inc.; reprinted by permission of John Wiley and Sons, Inc.)

and $3 isodapane curve. The business could lower total costs by moving from point P_1 to site L_1, where the $3 saving in labor costs more than offsets the increased transport costs (less than $3). Thus the business lowers its total cost by moving to a higher transport cost site. If the plant moves to L_2, labor costs will be $3 less, but transport cost will be $3 to $4 more, than the original choice, P_1. Thus the choice site L_2 does not reduce total cost. The $3 isodapane line which represents the labor cost savings from P_1 to L_1 or L_2 is the critical isodapane. It represents increased transport cost from the minimum transport cost site equal to the labor cost saving at alternate sites.

The firm must now repeat the process of minimizing transport cost, around point L_1, and then see whether there are cheaper raw material sources available that reduce total costs. In Figure 3.2, raw material source M_3, which has the same raw material as found at M_1, may now be cheaper for the firm.

AGGLOMERATION COSTS. Agglomeration and deglomeration forces, defined in the next paragraph, can also affect the site selection of a firm (Meyer 1977; Smith 1971, pp. 117–19). Agglomeration and deglomeration enter the decision in much the same manner as cheaper labor. First a business chooses the minimum transport cost site; then it evaluates the effect of labor; and finally it analyzes the effect of agglomeration and deglomeration costs on that site.

While agglomeration economies are treated separately, they are closely related to labor and transport costs. They arise from the presence of a skilled labor pool, well-developed transportation and utility systems, and the intensity and variety of information and personal contacts available at a particular location (Britton 1974, p. 368). They can be divided into four categories: transfer economies, economies of scale internal to a plant or firm, economies of scale external to a plant but internal to an industry, and economies of scale external to an industry but present in a large multi-industry and/or population concentration (Conroy 1975b, p. 27). Deglomeration forces represent cost increases rather than cost decreases, for the preceding reasons.

Transfer economies are the firm's transport cost savings from locating adjacent to other firms that purchase its products or sell it inputs. They can occur when the firm locates close to other firms for the benefit of the customer (e.g., shopping centers). *Economies of scale internal to a plant or firm* are those typically associated with level of production (i.e., economies of scale) and accrue to the firm even if it locates at an isolated site. *Economies of scale external to a plant but internal to an industry* occur if two or more plants in the same industry locate at the same place and reduce their cost per unit of output. This phenomenon encourages the development of specialized services (e.g., finance, communications), a skilled labor pool, transportation networks, etc. *Economies of scale external to a plant or industry* are called urbanization economies. They include the availability of improved transportation services such as terminal facilities; a larger, more flexible labor force; and commercial and financial services. The distinction between the last two forms of economies is that commercial and financial services are not industry-specific.

Figure 3.3 presents an example of incorporating agglomeration economies into the location decision. Assume that each of five firms (*A, B, D, E,* and *F*) selects its own least cost site (i.e., minimizes the sum of transport and labor costs). If at least three firms locate at the same site, agglomeration economies permit each firm to reduce total costs by $20 per unit weight

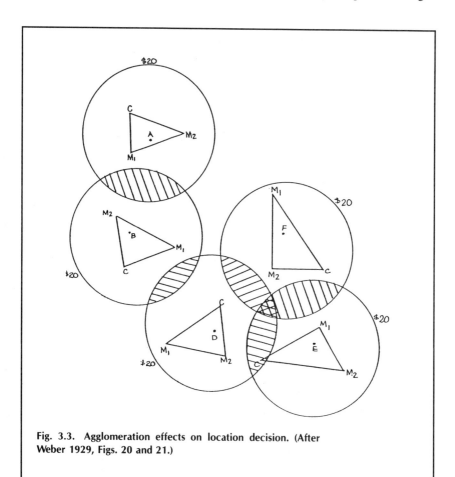

Fig. 3.3. Agglomeration effects on location decision. (After Weber 1929, Figs. 20 and 21.)

(ton) of output. Drawing a $20 critical isodapane around each of the present least cost sites permits determining whether agglomeration economies are possible. For sites *A* and *B* or sites *B* and *D*, the $20 isodapanes intersect, but three plants must locate together for the agglomeration economies to occur, and three critical isodapanes do not intersect. However, the critical isodapanes for sites *D*, *E*, and *F* do intersect. If all three firms move to this point of intersection, each lowers its total cost by $20 per ton of output.

The least cost approach to location decisions means that the firm makes its decisions by minimizing total costs (transportation plus labor plus agglomeration costs). Demand does not enter the decision directly, since the volume of sales is unaffected by location.

TRANSPORT VS. NONTRANSPORT COSTS. The least cost approach essentially substitutes transport for nontransport costs until total costs are minimized (Greenhut 1956, pp. 12–15). This substitution process can be depicted with an isosale curve connecting points at which equal amounts of output can be produced and sold, assuming a competitive market.

In Figure 3.4 the isosale curves (*FG, F′G′, F″G″*) represent different sales levels. The further the isosale curve is from the origin, the greater the amount sold.[2] Nontransport costs (labor and agglomeration) are not related to distance and weight; transport costs are affected by both distance and weight.

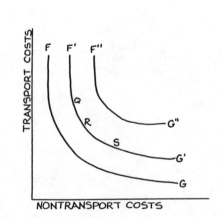

Fig. 3.4. Trade-off between transport and nontransport costs.
(After Greenhut 1956, Fig. 23, p. 163.)

The elasticity of substitution of transport and nontransport costs determines the optimum location. The elasticity of substitution is the percentage change in nontransport costs divided by the percentage change in transport costs. If the elasticity is greater than -1, it means that the firm will move from point S toward point R (in the figure) because the percentage increase in transport costs is less than the percentage decrease in nontransport costs. If the elasticity is less than -1, the business will move from point Q toward point R. In this case, the percentage decrease in transport costs is greater than the percentage increase in nontransport costs. Only at point R does the percentage change in nontransport costs equal the percentage change in transport costs (i.e., the elasticity of cost substitution equals -1). If the firm moves away from point R, it increases total cost for a given level of sales represented by the isosale curve.

The firm minimizes total costs by selecting a site from which movement away will increase either transport or nontransport costs more than such movement will reduce the other costs. This site becomes the optimal location for the firm to produce and sell its output.

SPACE COST CURVES. Smith (1971, pp. 181–206) extends the interpretation of isodapanes to generate space cost curves. They are a vertical cross-section of the total-cost isodapanes (transportation, labor, and agglomeration). They represent variations in total costs and profitability over space, given fixed demand. The upward-sloping portions of the space cost curve represent the spatial margins to profitability. A location where total costs exceed total revenues is not a viable long-term location. The steepness of this curve and the breadth of the "dip" indicates the sensitivity of total costs to location.

Figure 3.5 presents four possible space cost curves. In panel A, total costs are largely insensitive to different sites. In panels B and C, total costs are relatively sensitive to the site selected, with the raw materials site favored in B and the market site in C. In panel D, the firm selects a site between market and materials, possibly due to agglomeration or physical or institutional factors. Panel D also demonstrates the effect of a drop in output prices (e.g., at P_1 there are no profitable locations).

Figure 3.5 demonstrates that a community's selection as a location depends upon costs and product prices. Several communities offer equally low-cost sites in panel A, but only one community minimizes costs in panels B, C, and D (at price P_0). No community offers a profitable location at P_1 in panel D.

INSTITUTIONAL AND PHYSICAL FACTORS. The discussion up to this point has assumed that physical and institutional features have no effect on the selection of the minimum cost site. This invariably leads to a location

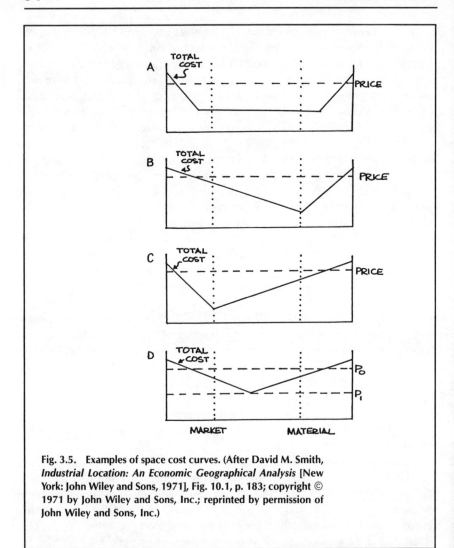

Fig. 3.5. Examples of space cost curves. (After David M. Smith, *Industrial Location: An Economic Geographical Analysis* [New York: John Wiley and Sons, 1971], Fig. 10.1, p. 183; copyright © 1971 by John Wiley and Sons, Inc.; reprinted by permission of John Wiley and Sons, Inc.)

choice either at the market or material or labor site, but seldom at an intermediate site. However, if institutional or physical features of the possible sites are allowed to enter the calculation (e.g., a change in the mode of transportation of the product, the presence or absence of terminals where loading and unloading of materials and product occurs, introduction of public incentives at one site or another, or the presence of physical obstacles such as rivers, mountains, or oceans), the choice of the market, materials, or labor site is no longer inevitable (Smith 1971, pp. 128–29).

This point is demonstrated in Figure 3.6, where Y represents the market, X the location of materials, and T a community where there is a change in transportation mode (e.g., ship to truck), an institutional change (e.g., an international border), or some physical barrier (e.g., a range of mountains with a limited number of passes). The firm may locate anywhere between X and Y. If the firm starts at the materials site (X), its production costs are Xx and the cost of transporting the output to the market (Y) is Xx'. The total cost of locating at site X is Xx''. As the firm moves toward the market site (Y), the cost of transporting materials increases (xy) and the cost of transporting output declines ($x'y'$), to produce a total cost curve of $x''y''$. The total cost curve $y''x''$ for an intermediate location is everywhere greater than at either site X or Y except site T. Institutional or physical features at community T offer the firm a cost break, making T competitive with site X or Y. The total costs at T are equal to the total costs at either X or Y. Thus communities can be viable least cost sites even though they are not market or raw materials sites.

SUMMARY. The least cost approach to location decisions assumes that a business faces a demand not affected by its location choice—that it sells to a

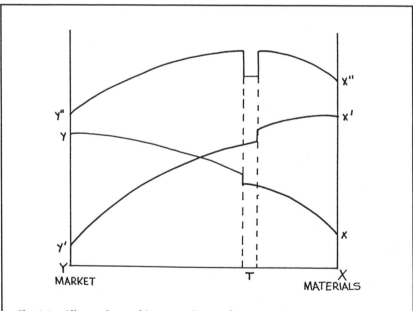

Fig. 3.6. Effects of transshipment points on least cost sites. (After Hoover 1948, Fig. 3.8, p. 39.)

point market. Costs can vary among production sites. The location decision substitutes nontransport and transport costs among different sites until the business has minimized total costs. Since demand is constant, the least cost site yields maximum profits. The weakness of this approach is that if demand varies with the site chosen, the least cost site may not be a site of maximum profit but only one of minimum production cost.

This approach to location decisions indicates that communities must be sensitive to the total cost of production in one community compared with other communities. Communities will seek to keep transportation rates low or to offset higher transport costs by reducing nontransport costs (e.g., through low wages, inexpensive land, or tax concessions). Communities may also attempt to create some agglomeration economies through creation of a fully serviced industrial park.

Demand Maximization Approa

The least cost approach to location selects the site by assuming that the firm sells its total output to a given point market (effectively eliminating demand from the location decision). The demand maximization approach, however, reaches the location decision by explicitly incorporating demand into the decision (Greenhut 1956, pp. 25–41, 257–63).

This approach contends that each seller will select a site to control as large a market area as possible. The seller exercises some monopoly control over whatever portion of the market area he can supply at a lower price than his rivals (see Figure 3.7). Consumer behavior and the location decisions of competitors determine the size of the market the firm controls. Concern about the location of competitors gives rise to the alternate description of this approach as the locational interdependence approach.

Among the basic assumptions (Greenhut 1956, pp. 25–57) of this approach are: (1) that the firm sells to a spatially distributed market, not to a point, as was the case with the least cost approach; (2) that customers and resources are uniformly distributed over a homogeneous plane; (3) that customers make their decisions on the basis of minimizing the delivered price of a good; (4) that there are uniform transport rates in all directions from any site that can vary among sites but are the same in every direction from any given site; (5) that abnormal profits can exist and will attract competitors; and (6) that there are no barriers to entry.

Since the delivered price determines a firm's ability to exert monopoly control, the pricing strategy pursued is of interest. Figure 3.8 demonstrates two basic pricing strategies the firm can pursue. In the first strategy, the firm's selling price includes the transportation cost, i.e., the firm receives a net mill price. Net mill price means that the firm has a uniform price for every customer in an area.[3] In this case, the firm pays the transportation

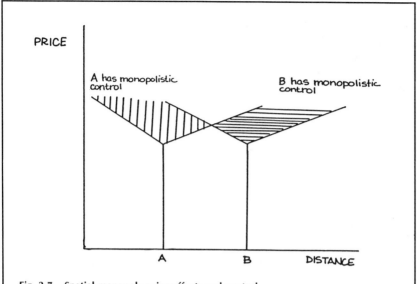

Fig. 3.7. Spatial monopoly price effects and control.

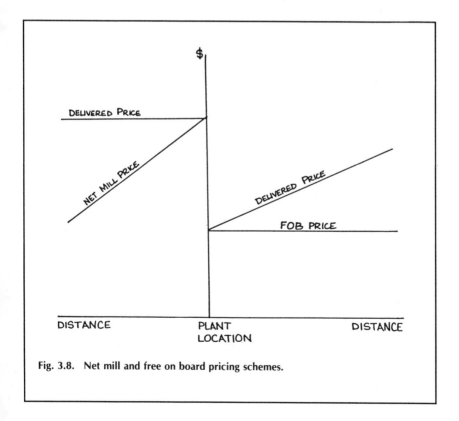

Fig. 3.8. Net mill and free on board pricing schemes.

costs. Customers closer to the plant yield a higher profit and subsidize the movement of product to more distant customers. In the second strategy, the firm sells its product free on board (FOB), which means that the customer pays the transportation cost from the point of production to the point of consumption. Both schemes can, but need not, yield identical returns to the firm.

BASIC MARKET AREAS. Assuming identical cost and revenue functions for all firms, the markets for firms become a series of identical hexagonal areas that completely cover the surface of the homogeneous plane (Smith 1971, pp. 130–37). This occurs in the following fashion. In Figure 3.9, *Stage 1* represents the market area of single firm. The single producer faces a demand curve labeled *QE*. The demand curve is symmetrical around production point *K* because there is no variation in the distribution of consumers over the homogeneous plane. *KQ* measures the quantity the firm could sell at zero transport cost. *KE* represents the maximum distance over which the firm can sell its product before the transport cost becomes prohibitive either to the firm or to the customer.[4] The volume under *QKE* represents the total quantity demanded within the market area. *Stage 2* replicates the single-firm analysis for a group of firms on the surface of the homogeneous plane. Each firm has a circular market area that touches the market of its competitors at just one point. Since all firms have identical revenue and cost functions, all the market circles are identical, but none of the firms can supply the entire market area, some portions of it are not supplied, and excess profits exist.[5] The excess profits, coupled with the unserved market areas, attract new businesses. As new firms fill the gaps, the market area for existing firms declines (*Stage 3*), excess profits disappear, and the average revenue or demand curve for existing businesses shifts to the left. New firms will enter the market until the excess profits have been competed away and the demand curve is just tangent to the average cost curve for all firms (see *AR₃*, Figure 3.10). When this occurs, the total market will be covered by a hexagonal-shaped market pattern, *Stage 4,* a shape that represents the most efficient covering of the surface (minimizes the distance from the center to all points) and does not allow for excess profits or unserved market areas.

The firm's average cost and revenue curves influence the formation of hexagonal market areas (see Figure 3.10). If the firm starts with an average revenue curve of *AR₁* and produces and sells *Q₁*, it has excess profits amounting to the difference between the average cost and average revenue at point *Q₁* for all units of output (*Stage 2,* Figure 3.9). This will attract competitors and cause the average revenue curve to shift to the left because the same total market now is divided among more sellers. At point *Q₂* much of the excess profits are competed away, but they still exist because average

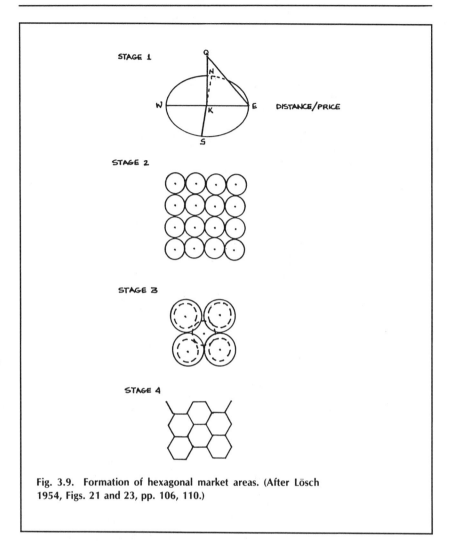

Fig. 3.9. Formation of hexagonal market areas. (After Lösch 1954, Figs. 21 and 23, pp. 106, 110.)

revenues exceed average cost. Finally, demand shifts to AR_3 and becomes tangent to the average cost curve at Q_3 (i.e., average costs and average revenues are just equal). Thus, there are no excess profits to attract other firms[6] (*Stage 4*, Figure 3.9). For AR_3, or demand curve 3, the firm faces a hexagonal-shaped market and Q_3 is the threshold demand or the minimum demand required for a firm to operate with a normal profit (the average cost curve includes a normal profit for the firm). If demand fell to AR_4, there would be an insufficient market to support the firm's profitable operation, and it would cease doing business.

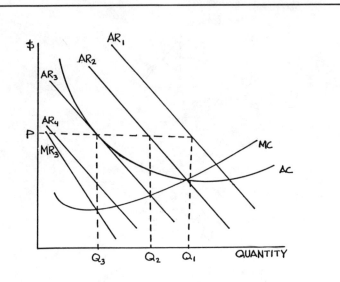

Fig. 3.10. Relationship of average cost and average revenue curves to market area.

DELINEATION OF MARKET BOUNDARIES. The least cost approach is appropriate when markets, materials, and labor are not uniformly distributed but found at discrete locations. The demand maximization approach assumes markets, raw materials, and labor to be uniformly distributed. The location question now becomes how does the delivered price affect the size of the area over which the producer can sell output? This is depicted graphically in Figure 3.11 (Smith 1971, pp. 119–30, 137–43). The firm sells its product free on board (FOB). The two firms in the system produce and sell the same product. Production costs and transport rates can be the same or not. Consumers are uniformly distributed over the market area and will purchase only from the lower-priced seller.

In panel *A* Figure 3.11, firms *A* and *B* have identical production costs and face an identical transport rate structure. In this situation the firms could locate in the middle of the market and divide the market area, or they could divide the market into thirds. Firm *A* would control the third that is to its left in the figure and half of the third that is to its right; firm *B* would control that portion of the market area to its right and half of the area to its left.

Panel *B* displays the influence of production costs on the size of the firm's market area. Both firms face the same transport rate structure; how-

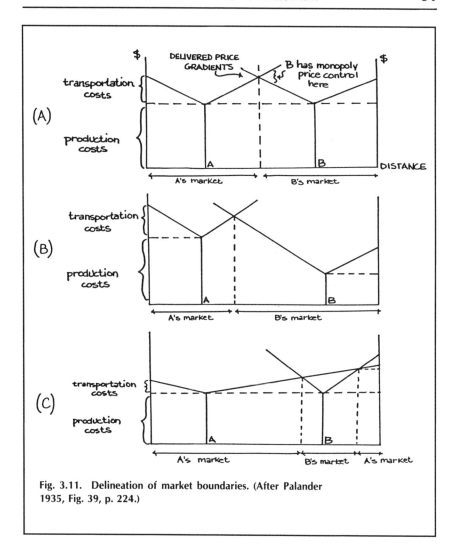

Fig. 3.11. Delineation of market boundaries. (After Palander 1935, Fig. 39, p. 224.)

ever, firm *A*'s production costs are higher than firm *B*'s. Therefore, firm *B* is able to capture, through a lower delivered price, a larger market area than firm *A*.

Panel *C* demonstrates the effects of different freight rate structures on the firm's market area. Firms *A* and *B* have identical production costs, but firm *A* faces a much lower transport rate structure than firm *B*. In this situation, an anomaly can occur; firm *A* is able to supply a market on the far side of firm *B* at a lower price than firm *B* can. Panel *C* clearly depicts the importance of freight rates.

The preceding discussion assumes production costs to be unaffected by volume. This assumption can be relaxed, permitting examination of the effect of volume on production costs and the market boundary (Smith 1971, pp. 125–27). In Figure 3.12, firms located at *X* and *Y* divided the market between them. The margin lines, *mm* and *m'm'*, trace out the possible division (boundary) of the market between firms located at *X* and *Y*, as transport costs and production costs increase over distance from the points *X* and *Y*. *Aa'*, *Bb'*, *Cc'*, and *Dd'* are the delivered prices from selling point *X* to the market boundary represented by *XA*, *XB*, *XC*, and *XD*. The increase in price reflects an increase in the production costs associated with producing *A*, *B*, *C*, and *D* levels of output plus the cost of transportation.[7] The market boundary for firms located at *X* and *Y* is the point at which their margin lines intersect and the price is *Dd'*. Firm *X* cannot sell beyond point *D* because its price exceeds that of firm *Y*.

This analysis suggests that the number of firms in the market will depend upon the slope of the margin line. If the margin line rises steeply, new firms will locate between *X* and *Y* to undersell firms located at *X* and *Y* and increase the number of firms in the market. If the margin lines are

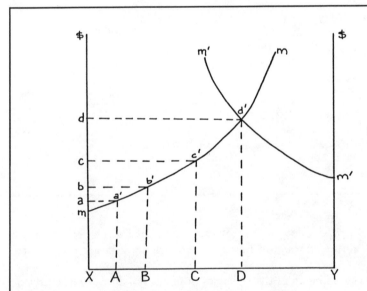

Fig. 3.12. Effect of varying production costs on market boundaries. (After Hoover 1937, Fig. 7, p. 17; used by permission of Harvard University Press.)

fairly flat, then existing firms can supply relatively large market areas from points X and Y, and relatively few new firms will be found in the market.

DISTORTIONS IN HEXAGONAL MARKET AREAS. The analysis thus far has produced hexagonal-shaped market areas. However, the efficient hexagonal shape may not occur, for several reasons. First, barriers to entry may prevent the entry of new firms to compete away excess profits (*Stage 2,* Figure 3.9). Second, hexagonal market areas may not occur because there may be discontinuous variation in market size, causing the demand curve to be either above or below but not tangent to the average cost curve (e.g., only AR_1 and AR_4 in Figure 3.10 may exist).

There are other causes of distortions in hexagonal trading areas. Political boundaries, international or state, can cause some distortion. Nonuniform transport rates in every direction can do so. The influence of backhauls, deadheading, transport cost absorption, and continuous or discontinuous rate changes can do so. There may be transportation rate differentials among major and minor transportation routes. Physical factors such as rivers, mountains, and lakes have a role. An unequal distribution of population can also influence the shape of the market area.

SUMMARY. The demand maximization approach to location theory assumes that the firm sells to dispersed customers rather than to a point market. Firms attempt to locate and exert some monopolistic control over their customers through a delivered price lower than that of their competitors. The location of labor and resources is insignificant. Disregard of the spatial variation in production costs constitutes the major weakness of the approach.

The demand maximization approach helps delineate the size and shape of the retail trade area of a community. This application is more obvious when the term "locational interdependence" rather than "demand maximization" is used. The community economic analysis questions become the location of retail and service businesses and their minimal market needs for profitable operations, and how this market is affected by the location of rivals. (Chapter 6 examines this issue in detail.)

Profit Maximization Approach

The *profit maximization approach* to location decisions declares that businesses select the site from which the number of buyers whose purchases are required for maximum sales can be served at the least possible total cost (Greenhut 1956, p. 267). This site need not be lowest in total cost but rather a site from which monopolistic control over buyers makes it more profitable than a lower-cost site. This approach recognizes the interaction between demand (locational interdependence) and the cost of production in site selection.

The profit maximization approach examines both the total revenues and total costs portion of the profit equation:

profits = total revenues − total costs.

While the least cost approach examines only the total cost portion, the demand maximization approach examines only the total revenue portion. Both approaches yield a profit-maximizing site by assuming that the other term in the equation is constant. The profit maximization approach permits analysis of both demand and cost factors and their influence on the location decision. This approach is more general than the least cost or demand maximization approaches which are special cases.

The profit maximization approach incorporates revenue and cost factors into its analysis (Greenhut 1956, pp. 279–83). Revenue factors are demand factors of location, revenue-increasing factors, and purely personal considerations. Cost factors are cost factors of location, cost-reducing factors, and personal cost-reducing factors. Typically, the location decision-maker believes that one of these factors is more important than the others, and that factor is either maximized or minimized first, with other factors entering the decision only after that initial choice is made. The decision process is much the same as with the least cost approach (i.e., the firm will minimize transportation costs initially and then see whether labor cost savings and agglomeration economies alter the calculation of least cost site).

Revenue factors either increase revenues (demand) or ensure that they remain at the previous level. *Demand factors of location* include socioeconomic characteristics of the market such as income, family composition, and population growth. *Revenue-increasing factors* arise from the gains the business experiences because of an increase in demand from either agglomeration or deglomeration forces. Agglomeration sales gains are produced by the location of the business close to similar businesses or supporting businesses (e.g., shopping malls). Deglomeration sales gains come from avoiding a site too close to competitors or being the first business in a new geographic market and selling at a lower delivered price than more distant competitors. *Purely personal considerations* become demand factors when they indicate new and expanding markets (e.g., access to trout streams, ski slopes, camping sites, and the like).

The *cost factors* include transport and processing costs. While transport costs are significant in a business location decision, their importance varies with the nature of the business, their contribution to total costs, and the ability to change them. If they are a major part of total costs or if the business can affect them significantly by choice of site, they will be a prime location factor. If there are only minimal differences in these costs among sites, they will have little influence on the location decision. Processing costs include labor, capital, taxation, and insurance related to production. They become important in the location decision when transportation costs and demand factors vary little among sites.

Cost-reducing factors accrue to the business from agglomerating or deglomerating locations. A pool of skilled labor and other infrastructure needed by business provides an agglomerating location. A deglomerating location avoids congestion and competition for scarce labor skills and other resources.

Personal cost-reducing factors are the gains to the business via gains to employees, such as personal contact with individuals in other organizations (clients or supporting businesses), reduced commuting time for workers in smaller communities, or willingness to substitute a pleasant environment for monetary rewards.

The profit maximization approach yields models with relatively low predictive powers, thus preventing its ready adoption. There are several reasons for this low predictive ability. It does not take into account personal preferences and psychic incomes or costs related to location decisions. These personal considerations cause the decision-maker to maximize total (money and psychic) satisfaction rather than just monetary profit. Second, it assumes that the individual making a location decision has perfect knowledge about the future, which is, of course, not so. Differences in opinion about risk and profit potential associated with various locations lead to different location decisions. A risk-averse owner or firm with limited financial resources may choose a site with less potential profit but less risk of loss. Third, location decisions are typically made infrequently during the career of a business owner/manager. This infrequency, coupled with imperfect knowledge, often yields site selection criteria such as long-run sales growth with reasonable profits or space for expansion. The cost of acquiring additional information about alternative sites deters the business from further inquiry; the result is the selection of a satisficing rather than a profit-maximizing site.

The profit maximization approach is the usual construct used in community efforts to attract or keep economic activity. The community economic development programs reported in Chapter 9 include efforts to reduce costs, improve access to markets, and alert the decision-maker to the subjective dimensions of the community. This approach is much more flexible than the least cost or demand maximization approaches. While the assumptions are less restrictive, the approach still does not represent a general theory of location decisions because of the shortcomings noted.

Behavioral Approac

The profit maximization approach represents the culmination of the rational economic man as a location decision-maker, with the associated assumptions that he desires to maximize profits, has information available on current and future events and conditions, and reviews and comprehends all necessary information.

The behavioral approach proposes a significant relaxation of these assumptions (Massey 1975; Miller 1977, pp. 51–54; North 1974; Shepard 1980; Smith 1971, pp. 105–9; Tornquist 1977). It allows for personal goals other than profit maximization; inadequate and inappropriately used information; and uncertainty about current and future conditions of markets, rivals, and inputs. It uses game theory and the concept of bounded rationality to analyze location decisions.

OBJECTIVE FUNCTIONS. The behavioral approach explicitly permits the decision-maker to seek some objective other than profit maximization in making location decisions. Alternative objectives could be market penetration/share, some minimal return, or expansion within some geographically bounded area to maintain management control. A satisfactory, rather than maximum, level of some monetary or nonmonetary goal is sought: the firm no longer necessarily seeks the location yielding maximum profits but the location meeting some minimal profit standard. This reduces the burden on the decision-maker. The inclusion of nonmonetary goals means that the site need not be the highest-profit site, but it must still meet or exceed some minimally acceptable profit standard and allow the decision-maker to increase welfare through other channels.

Including nonmonetary elements in the firm's location choice makes the analysis both more realistic and more complex. It is more realistic because it reduces the range of possible locations. Most sites fail to provide the noneconomic characteristics desired (e.g., they are not the owner's home town). The decision-maker calculates costs and rival's responses for a limited number of sites, not for all possible sites. The more complex dimension occurs with optimizing objective functions that may or may not include noneconomic criteria. Yet the behavioral approach to location decision-making, by allowing a broader interpretation of the objective function, offers great potential in explaining some "irrational" location choices. Figure 3.13 depicts the selection of unprofitable sites when good information was available but used improperly.

UNCERTAINTY. Relaxing the assumption of complete geographic and temporal knowledge by the decision-maker permits uncertainty in the location

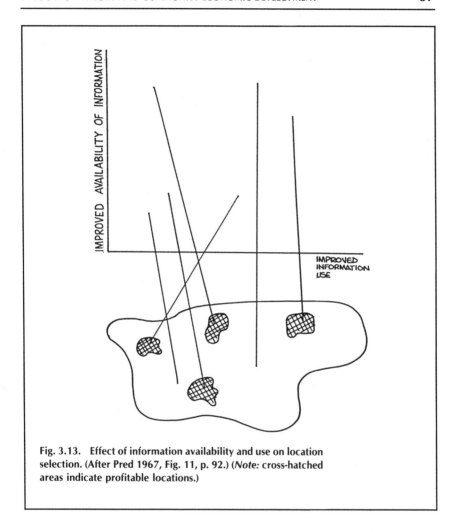

Fig. 3.13. Effect of information availability and use on location selection. (After Pred 1967, Fig. 11, p. 92.) (*Note:* cross-hatched areas indicate profitable locations.)

decision. Locational uncertainty occurs in many forms. National uncertainty appears as uncertainty about future general price changes, economic growth, interest rates, and federal monetary and fiscal policies. Regional uncertainty includes population shifts and regional response to national economic changes. Examples of local uncertainty might be strained labor-management relations, unstable water supply, or vacillating local governmental actions. Firm uncertainty includes the type of production processes, the location of competition, and the continued availability of inputs. Despite the allusion, the world facing the decision-maker is not completely chaotic. His intelligence and experience filters much of the apparent chaos and gives a pattern to events. There even may be relatively precise estimates of the probability of occurrence of some events (e.g., the point at which uncertainty becomes a risk). Uncertainty causes the decision-maker to produce a continuum of conditional decisions rather than a single location decision.

INFORMATION. The behavioral approach argues that the location decision-maker does not have full and complete information even without uncertainty (Lloyd and Dicken 1977, pp. 411–12), that human limitations prevent absorbing all the information available.[8] Furthermore, decision-makers are more sensitive to some sources of information than others—business associates, friends, family, and, occasionally, newspapers and television. The flow of information is further filtered by the decision-maker's own receptiveness, experiences, and perspectives (see discussion of information used in Chapter 2, "Technological Adoption").

Because the location decision-maker does not make such a decision frequently (note that the location decision is implicitly limited to the more narrow relocation decision), the amount of information actually incorporated into the decision may be far less than commonly presumed (Townroe 1974, p. 287). As an example, the small manufacturer seeking space for expansion or relocation reduces the information burden of the decision substantially by limiting, consciously or unconsciously, the choices of possible sites to the neighborhood or nearby communities. In the process, however, he forecloses other critical questions such as should the business move to another region to improve its access to markets or inputs and profits?

Pred's (1967) behavioral matrix displays the implications of the availability of information and the ability to use information in the location decision (see Figure 3.13). Movement from left to right in the matrix indicates improved use of information in the location decision for any level of information availability. Movement from bottom to top measures improved availability of information. The lower left-hand portion of Pred's matrix (1967) indicates poor information used in a poor fashion. The upper right-hand portion indicates good information used wisely. This matrix can be projected onto the existing/proposed locations of firms. Some locations are profitable; many are not. Firms may be in an unprofitable location because they have poor information or because they have used information poorly (they may have made a bad initial location choice, or there have been changes through time which made initially good choices no longer profitable) (Townroe 1974, p. 290). In either case, the firm either failed to use information properly or did not have good information to use. Figure 3.13 displays the possibility of a firm's locating in a profitable site despite having bad information or using information poorly.

SUMMARY. The behavioral approach to location theory postulates that firms seek a location maximizing profits but that they have limited ability to determine this optimal location. At least three factors can be identified as limiting this ability: the volume of information required, the quality of information available, and uncertainty surrounding future economic conditions and actions taken by rivals. These factors, coupled with differences in personal motivations, make it impossible to state unequivocally what location decision a particular firm will make, given a set of location information.

The behavioral approach to location decisions considers goals of the decision-maker, information sources, how information is used, and how new information is sought. The approach focuses community economic development on the information and objective functions. There is little the community can do about uncertainty beyond providing a stable public-private environment and helping the decision-maker acquire and use information through management counseling and assistance. The community affects the objective function by recognizing the importance of noneconomic factors in the location decision.

Critique of Classical Location Theory

Classical location theory conceives the location decision being made by a single-product, single-plant firm with a relatively simple organizational structure. This firm seeks to achieve a profit maximization objective (Hamilton 1974, pp. 4–5, 20). However, our current economy is characterized by large-scale, mass production operations that are part of complexly organized, multi-product and multi-establishment businesses. With a multi-product, multi-location, multi-divisional firm, the questions of optimality are complicated. Are they optimality for the total firm or a particular division, total product line or a particular product, internal flows of inputs or markets being served, or the interest of management or the owners? The firm's multiple objectives include those other than profit maximization which arise partially from the interaction between the firm and the communities (society). Noneconomic concerns, excluded from the classical location decision-making framework, are considered.

Summary of Location Theory

Location theory provides insight into location decisions made by business owners that indicate the probability that a given community will become the site for a specific type of economic activity. When the business sells to a given point (concentrated buyers), such as manufacturers do, the firm will seek the least cost location relative to the consumption center, and the location of the competition is generally ignored. The location of competitors becomes important when the firm sells to dispersed buyers (e.g., retail businesses). Then it will seek a site that allows the optimum sales output at a cost unmatched elsewhere. Thus the business has a sales goal and chooses a site that minimizes the cost of making those sales.

The behavioral approach to location decisions explicitly recognizes that business owners may not seek to maximize profits, may not have perfect information, or may not use available information wisely. Relaxing these three key assumptions of classical location theory increases the realism of the analysis and permits communities to become active participants in the location decision. No longer are they just collections of raw materials, workers, and markets but become actors in the decision-making process, providing information and having a multitude of economic and noneconomic influences on the location decision.

The Location Decision Proc

Figure 3.14 summarizes the process that firms follow in making location decisions.[9] The major features of the diagram relevant for communities are long- and short-term goals, reason for location decision, response alternatives by the firm, geographic scale of decisions, and learning.

The long- and short-term goals of the firm can be investment strategies, management control, new product development, new market penetration, or linkage with suppliers (Dean, 1972). Each of these goals alters the range of choices the firm perceives.

Businesses make a location decision for a variety of reasons typically associated with management stress (Hamilton 1974, p. 15): some include geographic movement of markets, depletion of existing resources, limited space at the present site preventing expansion, introduction of a new product, obsolete technology at the present site, environmental considerations, and positive or negative personal considerations. The stresses on the firm cause location decisions with different implications for a community seeking to encourage economic activity. Muller and Morgan (1962) found that costs appeared more important in relocation decisions and demand more important in expansions, while personal factors dominated start-up decisions.

The location decision is not instantaneous but occurs in a sequence of steps. Figure 3.14 displays three major steps in the location decision sequence (Blair and Premus 1987, pp. 74–75; Massey 1975, pp. 90–91; Nishioka and Krumme 1973, p. 201; Rees 1974, p. 191; Schmenner 1982; Stafford 1974, p. 173; Wallace and Ruttan 1961). The first step is to determine the major geographic region or target area, a selection dependent

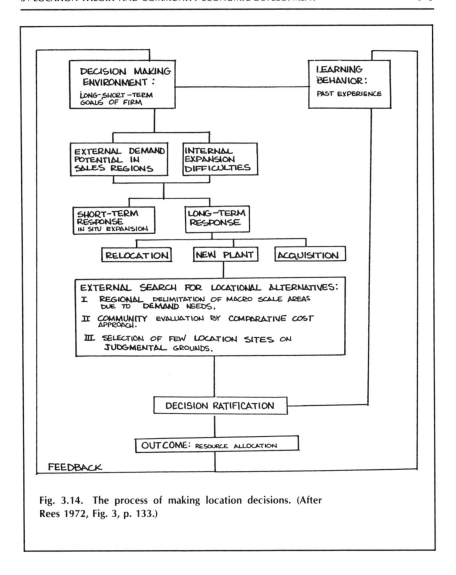

Fig. 3.14. The process of making location decisions. (After Rees 1972, Fig. 3, p. 133.)

upon the firm's marketing or management strategy. It could focus on market penetration, or the need to supply existing and growing markets better, or an opportunity to use new resources. At this stage the community has minimal, if any, input in the decision.

At the second stage, the firm compares numerous communities within the region to see whether they meet certain critical requirements. At this stage, a community is either in or out of further consideration on this basis.

These tend to be objective factors, such as the presence of an interstate highway, a railroad, or an adequate supply of water. Again, the community has little influence here beyond information dissemination.

At the third stage, the selection of a specific site, the community makes a significant contribution to the decision. If it has met the requirements noted above, subjective factors become important (Massey 1975, p. 87; Schmenner 1979).

The selection of a new site, with its associated start-up and relocation burdens, generally is a decision of last resort after numerous other alternatives have been exhausted (Hamilton 1974, p. 15; Rees 1974, p. 194).[10] For example, a growing business may first try to rearrange its production schedule at the existing plant by adding a second and third shift. It may try to subcontract the extra production required, perhaps even acquiring or merging with another operating business. It may expand physical production capacity at its present site. Each of these is a less costly, more flexible alternative than the construction of a new plant elsewhere. (This discussion will focus on growth and expansion, but the alternative of contraction/closure is also a location decision.)

The feedback and learning loop in the location decision depicted in Figure 3.14 is probably accurate for firms making numerous such decisions. However, most business owners make a new location decision only once or twice in their careers, and the feedback loop is largely nonexistent (Townroe 1974, p. 287). Small businesses spend less time on, and are less sophisticated in, their decision-making process than large ones (Dean 1972). Often the search process includes just a few nearby locations or communities about which the owner has some personal knowledge. In small firms, personal factors are likely to be much more important and enter into the decision-making process at a much earlier stage than they do in the more systematic approach of a large corporation (Muller and Morgan 1962). If this is accurate, the community can be quite influential in helping business owners, especially smaller business owners, make the location decision.

Location Fact

The discussion of the theory of location choice, of why firms wish to move, and of how they make their location decisions leads to a review of the factors influencing choices. The location factors for a retail business differ from those of a manufacturing firm. The importance of location factors to community economic development arises, as noted above, from the community's ability to manipulate some of them to achieve the type of economic development it desires (Deaton and Gunther 1974; Goeken and Dobbs 1982; Schmenner 1979).

The vast majority of location factor studies examine manufacturing locations; very few have examined the factors affecting nonmanufacturing firms. The most likely reason for this is the presumption that nonmanufacturing firms either are linked to manufacturing (export firms) or are population/market oriented. This view is changing, but there are only a limited number of studies of location decisions by nonmanufacturing firms (Clapp 1980; Smith and Pulver 1981). Thus the following review will of necessity emphasize factors influencing manufacturing location decisions.

Several typologies classify businesses according to their location characteristics. The firm's orientation becomes the element in the location decision that must be satisfied first. The simplest scheme classifies businesses as input-oriented, market-oriented, or no specific orientation (see also Figure 3.5). Input-oriented firms are concerned about raw materials (e.g., land, water, mineral deposits); intermediate inputs (e.g., petroleum distillates, semi-finished manufactured goods); or market inputs (e.g., information). Market-oriented firms consider the following markets: consumers, producers/businesses, and resources. Each of these markets exerts a different influence on a specific firm. There are numerous other typologies.

Typologies help a community understand what might be important to a business making a location decision. The community with limited markets (as measured by population size and income) but with an ore deposit will focus on firms with material, not market, orientations.

Virtually any study of location factors results in a fairly standard list of important factors (Blair and Premus 1987). The general categories of factors influencing location decisions are transportation, raw materials, labor, markets, specialized support services, and personal considerations.[11] This is not a particularly surprising list, given the theories reviewed earlier. Table 3.1 summarizes twenty-four studies over a fifteen-year span. Note that markets, labor, and raw materials are the most important location

Table 3.1. Significance of Location Factors according to Business Opinion, as Revealed by 17 Questionnaire and 7 Interview Survey Studies, 1945–1960

Factor	Number of Studies		
	Primary significance	Some significance	Little significance
Markets	22	2	—
Labor	13	11	—
Raw materials	13	10	—
Transportation	7	16	1
Taxes	1	3	20
Financial inducements	—	—	20

Source: Tweeten and Brinkman 1976, p. 247.

factors. Taxes and financial inducements had little significance in location decisions, an especially relevant fact for public bodies attempting to alter location decisions.

The factors in Table 3.1 are aggregations of several dimensions of location factors. For example, the labor factor includes availability of labor, skills possessed, trainability of labor force, location of labor force, wages by occupation, and degree of unionism. The importance of specific dimensions varies among firms; the purpose here is to review the importance of the general location factors for different types of location decisions.[12]

Table 3.2 gives the ranking (1 indicates the first in importance) by businesses in making their Wisconsin location decision. The first column of the table ranks markets, labor, materials, etc., for all firms, column 2 for new start-ups only. The shift to "personal/home area" as the factor of primary importance in picking a current site among new firms should not be surprising, but communities often forget to encourage the local entrepreneur in their economic development efforts.

Markets/linkages are the most important location factor for out-of-state firms, suggesting that they are trying to enter a new market or improve their linkage with a supplier. The selection of branch sites for in-state firms is influenced more by labor, which is also a major influence in the decision to relocate a firm from out of state. Yet, for the relocation of in-state firms, labor is relatively unimportant, and market/linkages along with personal reasons/home area dominate because the firm is attempting to enter new markets or improve linkages with suppliers; it may be owned by a former resident returning home with his/her business.

To firms selecting a specific community within the state, labor and land/buildings are dominant factors, with personal reasons/home area ranking somewhat lower; so a community should emphasize the availability of labor and land/buildings in its efforts to encourage the location of a nonlocal firm in the community. To firms selecting a specific site, land/buildings along with access to transportation facilities and room for expansion are important.

In Table 3.2, because of the aggregation of numerous more specific factors, the ranking of a given location factor is less important than noting that the importance of location factors varies with the level of geographic selection and the type of location change being made. Thus the community should not approach every business prospect with the idea that the same set of location factors will be critical (see the discussion of Figure 3.14 above).

The significance of this review is to point out that the importance of factors entering the decision-making process varies with the geographic area being considered and the type of location decision being made.

Table 3.2. Business Ranking of Factors for Specific Types of Location Decision, Wisconsin, 1967

Factor	All Firms	New Firms Only	Branches of Out-of-State Firms	Branches of In-State Firms	Relocating Out-of-State Firms	Relocating In-State Firms	Selecting a specific Community	Site
Markets/linkages	1	2	1	2		1	3	
Labor	2	5	2	1	1	5	1	
Land/buildings	3	4	4	3	2	3	2	
Raw materials	5	3	3	3	2	4	8	1
Personal reasons/home area	4	1				2	4	
Community attitude	6						5	
Local financial aid	7	7				6	6	
Transportation	2							2
Expansion room								3

Source: After Wisconsin, State of, Department of Development 1967.

Table 3.1 presented a summary of general location factors found in numerous surveys. No particular location possesses all the characteristics a firm desires in the appropriate amount and quality. Therefore, the firm must trade off among factors in making its location decision among specific sites. For firms locating in southeastern Kansas, for example, business facilities, community attitudes, and financial assistance overcame transportation inefficiencies and inadequacies, a lack of markets, and the availability of shipped-in and local inputs (see Table 3.3).

Table 3.4 sorts categories of location factors by the community's ability to exert influence. As shown there, four of the six most critical community location factors are under its direct control. This indicates that community economic development assistance efforts can influence location decisions.

Community factors enter the location decision in a subjective manner. For example: What is the community's attitude toward business? To be specific, What is its attitude toward business taxation, planning, zoning, public service provision? What type of civic leadership and organizations exist in the community? What is the quality of public services? What cultural amenities are available locally or within easy reach?

Site factors are less subjective than community factors and tend to enter the location decision almost simultaneously with community factors. Community factors are often the subjective forces distinguishing two or more equally acceptable sites. Some factors associated with sites are cost of land, site preparation costs, installed public services, transportation access, room for expansion, deed or zoning restrictions, and presence of a building.

Table 3.3. Location Factors Used to Overcome Deficiencies in Other Factors, Industrial Firms, Southeastern Kansas, 1960–1971

Location Factor	No. of Times Chosen despite Deficiencies	No. of Times Sacrificed
Business facilities (land, buildings, utilities, etc.)	11	1
Community attitude	9	2
Financial assistance	8	4
Labor	8	5
Community characteristics	2	0
Manager's preference	2	1
State and local legislation	0	3
Taxes	0	3
Availability of local inputs	0	3
Availability of shipped-in inputs	1	4
Markets	1	7
Transportation	0	12

Source: Tweeten and Brinkman 1976, p. 249.

Table 3.4.   Community Control of Important Community Choice Location Factors

Factor and Degree of Community Control	Critical Factor	Critical or Significant Factor
	(*percent*)	(*percent*)
No Community Control		
Natural gas service	32	83
Pool of unskilled workers	17	80
Raw industrial water supply	16	60
Soil-bearing capacity	14	72
Water transportation	3	17
Indirect Community Control		
Major highway within 30 minutes	37	94
Scheduled rail service[a]	23	62
Pool of trained workers	17	86
Scheduled air freight service	12	68
Scheduled air passenger service	12	63
Vocational training facilities	2	65
Higher educational facilities	2	57
Direct Community Control		
Fire protection	43	93
Contract trucking	30	79
Police protection	28	91
Processed industrial water supply[b]	23	74
Industrial sewage processing	20	78
Solid waste disposal	17	77
Tax incentives or holiday	8	78
Lenient industrial zoning	5	77
Local industrial development group	3	60
Local industrial bonds	3	40
Public warehousing	1	24

Source: Adapted from Deaton and Gunther 1974.
[a]A major rail line within a "reasonable" distance (no more than 10 miles from the site). The community *can* plan for construction of a rail spur.
[b]Availability of a raw supply of water for industrial use.

Summary

The four schools of location theory reviewed in this chapter are least cost, demand maximization (locational interdependence), profit maximization, and behavioral. The least cost school assumes that demand is fixed and thus cost minimization leads to maximum profits. The demand maximization approach allows costs to vary among areas, but not within an area. The firm's demand is variable, and the market captured by the firm is influenced by the location of the firm's competitors. The profit maximization approach allows both total revenues and total costs to vary as the firm changes locations and output. The behavioral approach permits uncertainty, objective functions other than profit maximization, and nonrational choices.

Uncertainty is a major force preventing profit maximizing location.

Decision-makers try to reduce the uncertainties and simplify the irregularities in the economy so that the location decision process can be comprehended. Generally, demand becomes a prime factor in the initial decision to move. At this point, costs at alternative sites are typically ignored. As the search process narrows, specific cost estimates are made for the remaining sites. This need not yield a profit-maximizing or least cost or demand-maximizing site, but invariably leads to a site that yields an adequate profit. This decision process reflects a mixture of objective and subjective weights for the various factors in the decision. As the firm's location decision moves from the general region to the more specific community level, the subjectivity of the decision-making increases.

Location factor studies enumerate critical influences in the location decision. These critical factors vary by level of selection (regional vs. site), type of business (manufacturing vs. nonmanufacturing), and type of location change contemplated (new start, branch, or relocation). Firms can be categorized as input-oriented or market-oriented or somewhat indifferent. Orientation means that certain characteristics become extremely important in the location decision and are prerequisites to the plant's profitable existence. Failure to meet prerequisites means that the firm will not locate at a particular site.

Some recent trends in location factors significantly affect communities. First is the declining importance of the linkage between an industry and its source of raw materials or markets and the cost of transportation of heavy and bulky goods. Of increased importance is high-speed flexible transportation of higher-valued goods and the transmission of information and intangible services. Second is the access to markets, which for most industries has increased in importance relative to their access to raw materials. Third is the access to energy, increasingly important and, in some cases, the most important criterion (e.g., the availability of natural gas). Amenities such as climate, housing, community facilities, and cultural and recreational opportunities are influencing decisions to a much greater degree than they once did. Finally, there is an increasing dependence on services supplied by other industries, or divisions of the same firm, or public bodies.

While location theory fails to provide the comprehensive explanation of how economic units interact in space, it does provide sufficient insight to assist communities in their economic development efforts.

Study Questi

1. Four schools of thought about location theory are discussed in the chapter. What are they, and, in general, what do they emphasize in location decisions? Are the approaches linked, and, if so, how?

2. The least cost approach seeks to minimize total costs. There are three types

of costs. What are they? How do they relate to each other? How are they incorporated in the location decision?

3. The profit maximization approach suggests that revenue and cost factors should be incorporated in the decision. What are revenue and cost factors?

4. Uncertainty, satisficing, and information are important elements of the behavioral approach to location decisions. What is their significance? How are they handled by the profit maximization and behavioral approaches?

5. When faced with meeting increased demand, a firm has several options that have locational dimensions. What are they, and why might each be chosen?

6. What are some of the economic or management reasons (stresses) that may cause a firm to make a location decision?

7. Why is the orientation of a business (labor, markets, etc.) important in location analysis?

8. Different levels of geographic selection are involved in a relocation or movement decision. What are they, and how do they influence the importance of location factors?

9. Do different types of location decisions (start-ups, expansions, etc.) rely on different location factors? If so, how do they differ?

10. A community can influence some location decisions. Which are they, and how might the community exert that influence?

Community Economic Development Policies, Goals, and Objectives

4

COMMUNITY ACTIVITY IMPLIES GROUP ACTION. For successful group action, even more so than for individual action, it is important to have a strategy of where, how, and what the group desires to do. This chapter will focus on formulating community economic development policy, including awareness of the community's goals and objectives and the relationship among various goals and objectives. The emphasis is not on the group or political processes in policy formulation but rather on an analytical framework of the economic purposes of policy. The policy model described shows the crucial elements a community must consider. Then the influence of different philosophical perspectives of decision-makers on the selection of community economic development policies is examined. Five generic community economic development strategies and several approaches to policy evaluation are reviewed before examining the question: Is community economic development zero sum? Before we proceed with these matters, however, some basic but often unasked questions concerning community economic development policy will be considered.

Basic Policy Questio

Whenever a community attempts to alter its economic development situation, it is setting public policy. However, before the public or private sector embarks on any community economic development policy, it should ask these basic questions: (1) Are the policy goals being sought of a national, regional, state, or local nature? (2) Who are the people setting the goals—the powerful or the powerless? Are they agency or clientele goals? (3) How are goals being set, by decree, or through a political process of voting for candidates or specific referenda, or through an analysis of socioeconomic conditions within the community, or through surveys of citizens of the community? (4) What is the relationship among community goals? Some goals are complementary, while others may conflict (more on this later). (5) Will community intervention have any effect, positive or negative, on current conditions and anticipated changes? This inquiry recognizes that some community actions have no effect and some may worsen the situation. The community cannot expend its energies in a quixotic quest for goals beyond its ability to reach. (6) When will intervention be necessary, and when will it actually take place? This question recognizes the time lag between problem realization, reaction, or response and policy implementation.

These questions should always be carefully considered before a community embarks upon any form of collective action to alter its economic situation.

Creating a Strategy

A community consciously attempting to alter its economic situation can pursue a comprehensive strategy, or it can simply implement a collection of programs that may not be cumulative or even effective in achieving the stated objectives. A collection of programs does not a policy or strategy make. Vaughan and Bearse (1981, p. 308) suggest:

strategic choices bear a positive integral and consistent relationship to the attainment of some objective. The set of actions must possess synergy: that is, have positive, cumulative, and mutually reinforcing effects on the attainment of objectives. Thus, if two actions are both chosen as part of a strategic set, each will reinforce, or at least not diminish, the effects of the other. Timing and phasing of actions are also important. Strategy is not merely the choice of actions but the ordering of each action to best achieve one's aim.

Any strategy must be based on a theory or model about how a given entity functions and will respond to stimulus. A community economic development strategy must be based on a theory of community economic development; see Chapter 2 and Leven (1985). Vaughan and Bearse go on to define an economic development strategy as:

the set of programs whose individual design and interrelationship correspond to an appropriate dynamic model of the economic development process. The choice of development programs must be consistent with how the economy actually develops, otherwise the programs may fail. . . . There are important judgments to be made, not only with respect to the choice of objectives and instruments but with respect to the relative weights and timing to be assigned to those elements. All elements are not equally important, and their relative importance changes over time.

There are at least five reasons for a community to create an economic development strategy (Bramley et al. 1979, pp. 145–46). The first and most obvious reason is that it clarifies the direction of economic development in the community. A strategy statement includes the community's goals and objectives; the role of local and nonlocal actors/agencies, explicitly recognizing the trade-offs among community goals; and the sources and the uses of political and technical/professional input. Second, a strategy helps delineate priorities (i.e., identifies key issues and target groups). Third, it assists in the allocation of resources by eliminating conflicts and linking apparently unrelated efforts (e.g., female unemployment and day care centers) and should increase the effectiveness of the community's effort. Fourth, it yields an organizational structure and response system that ensures knowledge of who is doing what and when, and links the community with nonlocal public and private resources. Fifth, it provides a framework to guide the small, incremental events that accumulate into a major event or effort.

Community economic development strategy should facilitate those forces perceived as crucial in the functioning of a community's economy. It requires more than just a collection of actions; it should reflect appropriate sequencing. It links separate efforts within the context of a conceptual understanding of community economic development. It permits the community and other actors to organize actions and resources to achieve objectives more efficiently.

Goals or Objectiv

Any community economic development strategy begins with a discussion of community economic development goals and objectives. *Goals* are general, qualitative statements that describe some hoped-for achievement that is largely unmeasurable. Community economic development goals are often intangible and abstract, and are always value-laden. *Objectives* are more specific statements that typically can be quantified and measured. Goals and objectives are intimately related: objectives are derived from goals and are indicators that they have been achieved.

An "objective tree" (see Figure 4.1) helps distinguish the relationship among goals and objectives (Hunker 1974, 201–7). The goals and objectives that apply to the whole community are high on the tree. Lower-level goals and objectives may be created to apply to a specific aspect of the community (e.g., to a specific project within the community).

Goals and objectives should possess the following qualities:

- They should be consistent with respect to expectations (e.g., desires to reduce youth unemployment should be explicitly recognized).
- They should be comprehensive and include *all* major dimensions of the

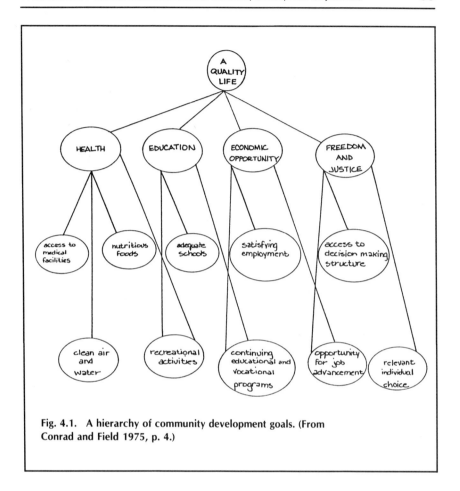

Fig. 4.1. A hierarchy of community development goals. (From Conrad and Field 1975, p. 4.)

problem(s) (e.g., job creation efforts should incorporate labor training components as well as encouraging increased business activity).

- They should be precise to assure effective action and response (e.g., attempts to reduce unemployment should specify the target group).
- They should be internally consistent and not redundant (e.g., attempts to reduce youth unemployment should not emphasize adult job creation).
- They should recognize resource constraints relative to any action program to be initiated (e.g., unavailability of land for industrial development certainly limits that particular type of activity).

These seemingly obvious qualities are often discounted because "everyone knows what we are all after and there is no real need to waste valuable time, energy, and enthusiasm belaboring the obvious." However, communities and groups skipping this important step frequently reduce their potential accomplishment because efforts are disjointed and nonsynergistic.

HIERARCHY OF GOALS. An objective tree appears because there is a hierarchy among community goals and objectives that affects the formulation of community economic development policy (Nelson 1984). The general goals at the top of the objective tree in Figure 4.1 are widely accepted and recognized, but difficulties often remain in accommodating individual views about how to achieve them, and this really becomes a problem when it comes to selecting specific objectives and lower-level goals—the point at which programs are being worked out (Reiner 1971).

The hierarchy of goals is not inflexible. Some dimensions of well-being appear more elemental than others, and the hierarchy varies among communities. Harvey (1971, p. 290) reports on a survey of St. Louis residents' opinions about air quality. Suburban residents, from areas with minimal air quality problems and sufficient jobs, are very conscious of air quality. Central city residents, where air quality is worse and job opportunities limited, value jobs, housing, and recreational facilities higher than air quality.

When viewed in the context of a hierarchy of goals/objectives, the importance of distinguishing between goals and objectives fades. Yet one characteristic of goals and objectives that cannot be ignored is that they need not reinforce each other. They can be independent, complementary, or conflicting.

RELATIONSHIP AMONG COMMUNITY GOALS AND OBJECTIVES. Figure 4.2 displays complementary, independent, or conflicting goals. Reading from left to right, in the first panel the community's pursuit of goal *A* leads to a simultaneous meeting, either partially or fully, of goal *B* (i.e., goals *A* and *B* are complementary). In the second panel, the effect of the efforts of the community seeking goal *A* has no impact on the level of achievement of community goal *B*. While the interrelationships in the community make this situation unlikely, it is possible that the influence of one goal on another is so small that the effect appears independent. The third panel displays the relationship between two community goals that conflict. Increased achievement of goal *A* leads to lower achievement of goal *B*. The first three panels of Figure 4.2 display rather simple, straightforward situations. In the fourth panel, at the extreme right, the two goals can be seen to be complementary, independent, and conflicting at different levels of achievement of either goal. This example is the most likely situation in setting community economic development policy. The extremely frustrating dimension of the display in this panel is the uncertainty about the nature of the relationship. The relationship may change at different levels of achieve-

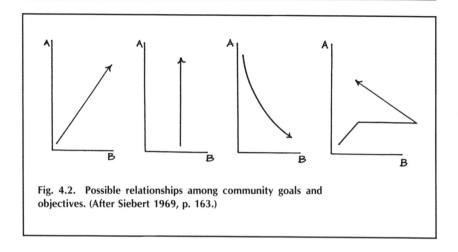

Fig. 4.2. Possible relationships among community goals and objectives. (After Siebert 1969, p. 163.)

ment, or variations in resource base, or variations in external (national) conditions, or over time.

The questions of complementarity and conflict can be studied in the context of preference functions and indifference curves (Hewings 1977, pp. 96–103; Hildreth and Schaller 1972). Another way to recognize preference functions and indifference curves is through the values people possess and their commitment to those values (Reiner 1971). In Figure 4.3 the axes on the diagram represent the amount of efficiency and equity the community desires. Equity and efficiency are the classic examples of public policy conflict in the market economy. (More detail can be found in the discussion of community economic development philosophy later in this chapter.) The community indifference curve (I_{co}) displays the trade-offs the community must make between equity and efficiency. Usually the choices exceed two, and they are seldom simple. At any point on the I_{co} curve the community is indifferent because any point on that curve yields the same community well-being.

In Figure 4.3 individuals' indifference curves are aggregated to create a community indifference curve (I_{co}). For simplicity, assume that just four people live in the community and their indifference curves lie in the four quadrants around point A. Although the community is at satisfaction level I_{co}, no individual is at that level (i.e., people are at satisfaction levels represented by the indifference curves (I_{10}, I_{20}, I_{30}, and I_{40}). Community well-being will not change by moving along curve I_{co}, but some individuals may experience a decline and others a gain in their well-being. The movement from point A to point B on the I_{co} curve can be accomplished when person 2 experiences a shift of his/her indifference curve down to I_{21} and person 4's indifference curve shifts to I_{41}. While the community maintains the same

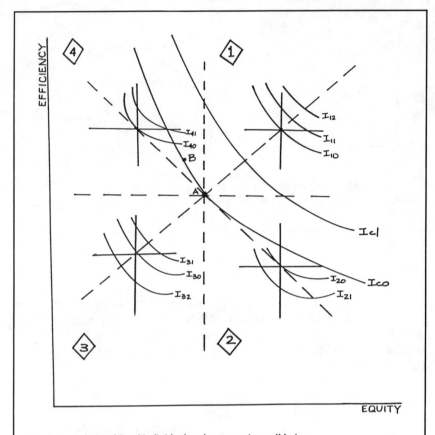

Fig. 4.3.   Relationship of individual and community well-being.
(After Hildreth and Schaller 1972, p. 767.)

aggregate well-being, an individual in the community loses absolute or relative well-being.

Even if the community pursues a policy of moving to higher indifference curves (i.e., I_{c1}, or improved welfare), that may be a mixed blessing. The community improvement may occur through person *3* moving out to I_{31}, or person *3* and person *1* moving out to I_{31} and I_{11}, or person *1* moving to I_{12} and person *3* staying at I_{30} or moving down to I_{32}. In three of the four alternatives presented, person *3*'s welfare does not change or declines, even though the community well-being increases.

The example can be complicated even further if unequal weighting of the individuals' preferences is permitted in estimating the community aggregate (McGuire and Garn 1969). A public policy emphasizing equity may place additional weight on person *3*'s well-being because he is below the community average. A program emphasizing efficiency may place extra weight on person *1* because he demonstrates an ability to produce.

The problem of efficiency vs. equity is clearly not as simple as Figure 4.3 suggests. First, the program choices a community makes will affect each goal in different degrees under different circumstances (see the discussion of community economic development goals earlier and of philosophy later in this chapter). Second, the relationship among program choices and goals may change over time because of new knowledge or changing conditions. Third, budget or resource limitations may preclude the selection of some viable program alternatives. Fourth, the selection of one option may foreclose other options in the future, even though goals or circumstances change. The fourth panel of Figure 4.2 represents the first and second situations. The third and fourth situations are discussed in Figure 4.4.

Given the inherent complications of choosing among equity and efficiency, the community can pursue five general decision modes (Hewings 1977, p. 102). These modes would also apply to other choices, and it should be recognized that the choices are seldom between just two alternatives. First, the community can ignore equity considerations and select projects/ programs on the basis of efficiency criteria alone. Second, the community

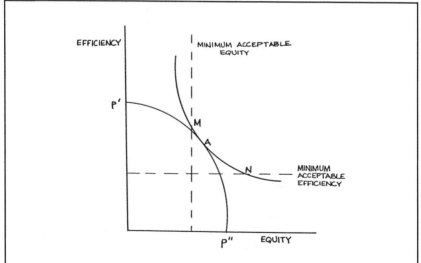

Fig. 4.4. Community preference functions and well-being. (After Hewings 1977, p. 103; © 1977 Geoffrey Hewings.)

can ignore efficiency criteria and select projects/programs solely on the basis of equity criteria. Third, the community can require all projects/programs to meet some minimal equity standard and then select according to efficiency. This choice would include all points to the right of point M on the community indifference curve in Figure 4.4. Fourth, the community can require all programs/projects to meet some minimal efficiency standard and then select according to equity. This choice would include all points to the left of point N on the community indifference curve in the figure. Fifth, the community can develop an explicit preference function to judge the various combinations of equity/efficiency embodied in each program/project. Hewings (1977, pp. 97–102) introduces the idea of using a preference function for the community to arrive at a decision. The shape of the preference function ($p'p''$) in Figure 4.4 represents the opinions of the community about more equity or efficiency. The shape of this preference function varies through time or among communities as community opinions change. The community will maximize well-being at the point of tangency between the highest indifference curve and the preference function, since it cannot trade preference for one community goal without lowering total well-being.

GOALS AND OBJECTIVES THROUGH TIME. Time influences community economic development goals and objectives through the uncertainty of future events. The community cannot be sure whether the present relationship among community goals and programs will continue into the future. Currently independent goals may become complementary or conflicting in the future (see the fourth panel in Figure 4.2). An example is the disassociation of environmental quality and economic growth prior to the late 1960s. Another form of uncertainty concerns the results of today's decisions about programs. For example, a community may have an opportunity for a sizable and immediate expansion in its employment base, with limited prospects of future expansion. The alternative it is offered may yield a smaller initial increase in employment but with the prospect of a much greater increase over time. Uncertainty about which of the two prospects will actually take place complicates the community decision. A further complication is that the two choices seldom occur simultaneously in the community, and that external forces may well adversely affect or eliminate both choices.

The hierarchy of goals and objectives (Figure 4.1) also has a time dimension. Time enters the relationship as short-run, intermediate-run, and long-run goals. Community economic developers hope that the goals build on each other over time (i.e., complement rather than negate each other). A long-run goal of improving the quality of life in the community is accomplished by providing well-paying, challenging, and satisfying jobs for workers (an intermediate goal). In the short run, however, the community may need to improve its sewer treatment plant or purchase land for an industrial park.

Policy Model

Once a community has examined its economic development goals and objectives, it must still determine the economic development policies to be pursued. A policy model (Tinbergen 1967) describing the context in which the community sets its economic development policy can be represented by:

$$W = f(P, X, E, Z).$$

W is the result of the policy chosen. Typically, W represents the social and economic welfare of community citizens. P represents the instrumental variables, or the controllable, independent policy tools the community uses to guide and encourage economic development activities. The equation suggests that the relationship between community welfare (W) and policy choices (P) is known. X represents exogenous forces, beyond the control of the community, which exert a definite influence on it. Exogenous forces could be interest rates, money supply, consumer prices, consumer tastes, or the price of energy. E represents the endogenous variables which describe the community and its economy, such as local employment, income sources, and types of businesses. Z represents the inadvertent and unanticipated side effects of the selection of a policy/program (P), i.e., the externalities of the community's economic development policies (Edwards 1976b). For example, the community might encourage the creation of a new business, which requires a set of skills that the local high school starts to emphasize. An unintended outcome is that these skills make local high school graduates very attractive to businesses in other locales. In the equation, f represents the structure of the community economy that the policymaker is trying to influence. It demonstrates how the endogenous, exogenous, and instrumental variables interact with each other; f is really a restatement of the community economic development theories reviewed in Chapters 2 and 3.

SOCIOECONOMIC WELFARE FUNCTION. Many community objectives are an intermediate step toward the achievement of improved well-being of community residents. This well-being can be represented by a community welfare function that the policymaker typically wishes to maximize as efficiently as possible.

Most definitions of community economic development assume that some identifiable socioeconomic welfare function exists. No doubt it does, but its empirical verification eludes our grasp. The conceptual components of a socioeconomic welfare function can be shown as: $W = f(I_1, I_2, G_1, G_2)$. Here W is the welfare of the residents in a community and can be measured on an individual or aggregate basis. I_1 and I_2 represent the socioeconomic effects significant to individuals. I_1 is the effect from goods and services with market prices or reasonable proxies for prices and thus represents the market effect of economic development on the individual. I_2 represents the development effects on the individual without market prices or reasonable proxies of market prices. It shows the extra-market effects of economic development on the individual. G_1 and G_2 represent the effects of economic development on groups within the community. G_1 is the distributional (equity) dimension of the market effects (I_1) among individuals and groups. G_2 is the distributional (equity) dimension of the extra-market effects (I_2) among groups and individuals within the community.

This rather simple formulation hides some critical caveats. The well-being function suggested in it focuses on economic development, which is just one dimension of a community's quality of life or well-being. The equation implies that well-being can be empirically estimated, which is not correct. How a change in employment or income affects the well-being of individuals is only partially understood. The tendency is to equate market-determined factors (I_1 and G_1) with well-being, so that the market value of an individual's assets (e.g., skills, house) will measure his or her well-being. While a close correlation exists between well-being and the value of an individual's assets, it is neither perfect nor complete (Stöhr and Todtling 1977, pp. 33–42). The difficulty in making well-being judgments for an individual seem minor in comparison to making the same judgment for a community (see the discussion of Figure 4.3). Another difficulty concerns aggregating the well-being of individuals into measures of community well-being. To make such comparisons implies a capacity to measure individuals' well-being, to determine what affects well-being, and to weigh the importance of each individual's desires so that an aggregate number can be computed (see the discussion of Figure 4.3). The weighing of individual preferences could be done by giving equal weights for all, or by annual income, or by number of family members, etc.[1]

Even though the total socioeconomic welfare function is undefinable, partial analysis of the components of the overall well-being can be accomplished by examining psychological well-being, or economic well-being, or only those components that change as a result of an economic development event.

Some partial measures of socioeconomic well-being include per capita income, income distribution, or real income (both monetary and nonmonetary). Jobs also measure well-being and include the skills the jobs require, opportunity for advancement, the satisfaction individuals receive from their jobs, and occupational health hazards. The health component of socioeconomic well-being can be measured by life expectancy and physical/mental health. The frequency and types of crime within the community affect well-being. Many consider the availability of and access to artistic and cultural events an important element of socioeconomic welfare. The quality and purpose of education and access to education measures part of community well-being. Opportunity for individuals and disadvantaged groups to participate in economic and social activities is another important dimension of a community's well-being. The physical-environmental aspects of the community have increasing importance in community decisions about well-being.

The output of community economic development policy is community well-being. Well-being includes the effect on individuals and among individuals as well as the monetary and nonmonetary effects. While the conceptual aspects of community well-being are known, the measures used are only partial and often are indirect.

SELECTION OF POLICY. Policies or instrumental variables are the tools available to the community to transform the existing situation. A partial list of policy instruments available to a community include forming merchants' associations, vocational education programs, pricing of public services, the placement of infrastructure, and zoning ordinances and variances.

Several factors restrain the selection of policy. First, some policies affecting local economic development are beyond the control of a community (e.g., control of money supply and interest rates). Second, political feasibility limits policy selection. Some activities simply cannot be achieved by individuals, groups, or governments (e.g., the municipality purchasing a nonlocal firm and moving it to the community). Third, the chosen policy's effect on the target population influences policy selection. If a community desires to increase youth employment opportunities, it could choose to increase manufacturing jobs, anticipating that some of the new employment opportunities will go to youth, or the community could encourage specific types of economic development which directly affect youth employment (e.g., fast-food restaurants). Fourth, other goals pursued affect the selection of policy. If a policy increases employment opportunities while adversely affecting air quality, that policy may not be a viable choice.

Implicit in the discussion of community economic development goals and objectives is the belief that once the goals and objectives are identified and the relationships among goals are understood, there will be agreement on how to achieve them. However, that is not the case. The very range of policy choices available to achieve the goals a community sets for itself almost assures that unanimity on means will not occur. A brief listing of policies to increase employment will illustrate the differences that can arise when considering specific options. One choice would be to take no action by either public or private actors to achieve the desired goal. This choice is always available to a community, yet frequently is not explicitly considered. Another choice would be to let the private sector be responsible for achieving the community's employment goals, with no intervention by the public sector. A third choice would be for the community to generate incentives to encourage private decisionmakers to alter their decisions and actions to achieve community goals. A final choice would be to opt for heavy public involvement in the decisions affecting employment in the community, which could take the form of a full partnership between the public and private sectors or a completely public sector project. This list of alternative policy choices is presented on a scale ranging from least to most public involvement. Other scales are possible.

PHILOSOPHY OF COMMUNITY ECONOMIC DEVELOPMENT POLICY. Decisions about community economic development policies depend upon value judgments of the policymaker and the individuals involved (Richardson 1969a, pp. 358–428; Richardson 1978b, pp. 221–43). There are at least four particular values or philosophies of interest. The first is sometimes referred to as "place vs. people programs." The second is equity vs. efficiency considerations. The third is the judgment of the urgency of the time factor; the fourth is that of the target for the effort.

The question of place vs. people programs is more a matter of degree than clear distinction. *Place* programs attempt to alter the geography of the economy in favor of some economically depressed area (e.g., the upper Great Lakes and Appalachia; or rural vs. urban; or central city vs. suburbs) (Cumberland 1971, pp. 10–12). Examples are water and sewer systems and industrial parks. Place programs or place prosperity is really a means to an end—people prosperity. *People* programs attempt to alter the economic circumstances of particular categories of people (e.g., the disabled, the unemployed, the elderly). Examples of people programs include sheltered employment, training, dissemination of job information, and Medicaid. Place programs, which usually offer a quick and visible payoff, are often chosen over people programs because the immediate value exceeds the present value of future returns from a people program. The premise of place programs is that using geographically immobile factors of production (e.g., land, buildings) contributes to economic development. Labor can be an immobile factor, but this immobility depends upon the length of time involved and the characteristics of the population base (see Chapter 8). Unemployed labor usually does not benefit from a place program to the extent that owners of other immobile resources do (see Chapter 10). Place programs are a clumsy tool to redistribute economic activity to population subgroups.

Another philosophy affecting the choice of community economic development policy is that of *equity vs. efficiency* (Cumberland 1971, p. 14; Ledebur 1977, pp. 14–15; Richardson 1969a, pp. 365–76; Stöhr and Todtling 1977). Creating the greatest return (e.g., jobs, income) from the resources used characterizes a priority of economic *efficiency*. The philosophy can also be: Should public or private resources be used to achieve a given goal? Limited resources available to support community economic development efforts, at both the local and national levels, require maximum efficiency. A public policy focusing on economic *equity* emphasizes the distribution of the rewards and burdens of economic development among individuals and groups inside and outside the community. This type of policy emphasizes the need to include deliberately those segments of the community excluded from the mainstream of the economy. An equity program might also compensate groups who bear a disproportionate share of the burden of change. It is important to remember that equity is not synonymous with equality. Equality means dividing economic output evenly among all people in the community. Equity means distributing access to opportunity or avoidance of arbitrary and external constraints to opportunity. An equity policy objective requires giving priority to areas of greatest distress (i.e., a worst-first policy) to reduce their economic disparities from the norm (Ledebur 1977, p. 14). Compare this equity objective with an efficiency objective, where priority would be given to areas with greatest potential for high productivity. The policy dilemma is that areas with potentially high productivity typically are not the areas of greatest distress.

Some believe that equity and efficiency are the major economic development trade-offs confronting communities and policymakers (see "Are Community Economic Development Programs Zero Sum?" later in this chapter for more detail). However, this may not be so (Vaughan and Bearse 1981, pp. 312–13). The major trade-off occurs when equity, defined as a static redistribution of economic output, income, and resources, conflicts with activities to improve efficiency. However, development is a dynamic process concerned with creating new products, mobilizing new resources, improving the quality of existing resources, and altering structural and institutional arrangements which impede the effective utilization of resources. Thus the pursuit of dynamic efficiency may also yield the equity results desired. Yet the need for trade-offs may remain. Short-run decisions can create some efficiency/equity trade-off problems and, more important, may conflict with the long-run dynamic efficiency concept.

An often-overlooked dimension of community economic development policy choices is *time* (Robock 1966, p. 132). The politics of the problem places a premium on solutions achieved quickly (by the next election in two to four years). However, development is a long-run concept, and a community did not become economically depressed during a single electoral term. The lack of development reflects a long-term, cumulative process. Short-run attempts to reduce distress, if viewed as "single-shot, turn-the-corner attempts," are doomed to failure. Alleviating the causes of distress rather than the symptoms requires a long-run transformation of the economy. Time also affects policy choices among alternative forms of economic development. The choice is seldom recognized because the development opportunities (choices) often do not occur at the same time. For example, a community may have an opportunity to help industry A or industry B, but does not have the resources to help both. However, the chance to help either A or B seldom occurs simultaneously, so the time factor often precludes the necessity of making such choices, and inadvertently closes future options.

While the selection of an economic development policy ends up being a political choice, several aspects of the decision still yield to economic theory. Since the resources available for economic development policy are limited, the issue of *targeting* those efforts becomes crucial. There are three basic targeting questions (Vaughan and Bearse 1981, p. 322). The first is what sectors should be the target of the economic development effort? Should declining sectors or emerging growth sectors be emphasized (equity vs. efficiency)? The second question is should development efforts focus on small or large businesses to generate jobs and income? The third question is should there be a geographic basis for targeting (people vs. places)? There are no definitive answers to these questions, but they will be discussed in greater detail in Chapter 5.

In summary, the philosophical beliefs of the policymaker affect the choices perceived and made and the options created. The basic differences appear to be the weighting of equity vs. efficiency and people vs. place emphasis, the importance given to the time required to improve community well-being, and the choice of priorities in targeting efforts.

Community Economic Development Strategie

There are numerous strategies a community can pursue to accomplish its goals for the economic future. The standard strategy is to attract a manufacturing plant, with its associated secondary development.[2] A second common approach is to encourage the expansion of existing businesses. These are valid strategies, but a community that limits its job and income development efforts to them needlessly restricts its opportunities. Pulver (1979, pp. 105–18) offers a much broader range of options as possibilities for virtually every community. The five general strategies are: (1) attract new basic employers, (2) improve efficiency of existing firms, (3) improve ability to capture dollars, (4) encourage new business formation, and (5) increase aids/transfers received from broader governmental levels or units. These strategies are now discussed, with examples of specific community actions.

ATTRACT NEW BASIC EMPLOYERS. The addition of new basic employers to a community will add employment and income directly. Basic employers include (a) manufacturing; (b) nonmanufacturing, such as tourist attractions, insurance headquarters, computer services, and wholesale warehouses; and (c) nonlocal government. Examples of community actions to attract new basic employers are:

1. development of local industrial sites and public services, and dissemination of labor information to potential employers;
2. development of community and regional facilities necessary to attract new employers:
   a. transportation (e.g., airports, railways, highways)
   b. recreational facilities (e.g., parks, hunting grounds, restaurants, hotels, convention centers)
   c. communications (e.g., newspaper, telephone)
   d. services (e.g., banking, computers, legal assistance, accounting);
3. encouragement of collective action through formation of organizations such as industrial development corporations;
4. identification and organization of community capital resources to assist in attracting new business (e.g., industrial revenue bonding, bank loans);
5. identification through research of basic employer(s) with greatest potential; and
6. identification of specific public programs, projects, offices, and/or services that could be located in the community and taking political action to secure them.

IMPROVE EFFICIENCY OF EXISTING FIRMS. The more efficient existing firms are, the more competitive they can be in regional, state, and national markets in the long run and the more net income they can return to the community (especially locally owned firms). Examples of community actions to improve efficiency are:

1. strengthening management capacities of existing firms through educational programs (e.g., personnel, finance, organization);
2. encouragement of business growth through identification of equity and loan capital sources;
3. increasing knowledge of new technology through educational programs in science and engineering;
4. aid to employers in improving work force quality through educational programs, employment counseling, and social services (e.g., day care, health services); and
5. development of community and regional facilities that improve local business efficiency and access to nonlocal markets (e.g., transportation, services, communications).

IMPROVE ABILITY TO CAPTURE DOLLARS. Every dollar spent in the community for consumer goods and services and commercial/industrial inputs adds to employment and income. Examples of community actions to capture dollars are:

1. identification of market potential of retail outlets through surveys of consumer needs and buying habits;
2. improvement of share of retail market captured through downtown analysis and renewal through:
   a. use of consumer and merchant surveys
   b. provision of convenient parking or public transit
   c. review of store hours and merchandising;
3. aid to businesses in developing employee training programs to improve quality of service;
4. expansion of purchases by nonlocal people (e.g., tourists, neighboring citizens) through appropriate advertising;
5. information programs to encourage local citizens and businesses to buy locally; and
6. encouragement of collective action through formation of organizations such as chamber of commerce, merchants association.

ENCOURAGE NEW BUSINESS FORMATION. There is a continuing need for new businesses to meet changing community needs (e.g., from growth and/or different demand). A new business can meet these needs and can mean new income and employment. Examples of community actions to encourage new business are:

1. organization of community capital resources to assist new business formation:
   a. encouragement of investment of private funds locally through formation of capital groups
   b. encouragement of the use of secondary capital markets and public financing programs;
2. identification of market potential for new retail, wholesale, and input-providing businesses;
3. provision of individual counsel and intensive education for those interested in forming a new business; and
4. provision of the same services to start-up businesses as provided to businesses sought from outside the community.

INCREASE AIDS/TRANSFERS RECEIVED. A community may strive to reacquire dollars taxed away by broader governmental units and, if possible, to acquire tax dollars from wealthier communities. Examples of community actions to increase aids include:

1. ensuring correct use of public assistance programs for the elderly, handicapped, and others who cannot work;
2. utilization of aids from broader governmental units whenever possible (e.g., for streets, parks, lake improvements, emergency employment) through active monitoring and support of activities of local officials;
3. support of political activities to ensure fair treatment of community concerns by broader governmental units; and
4. recognition of the important role of flow-of-funds transfers into the community (e.g., retirement benefits, unemployment compensation).

These strategies are all capable of creating jobs and income in the community over time. No single strategy is adequate for a community, nor should any community accept unquestioningly a strategy that was successful elsewhere.

Policy Evaluation

When a community pursues an economic development policy, it must also evaluate the types of actions taken, to confirm their effectiveness. Community economic development programs must be judged by their efficiency in achieving stated objectives. The evaluation should attempt to isolate a given program from other programs and their effects (Ashcroft 1982; Bartels et al. 1982; Nicol 1982), in recognition that no single program affects an objective but that several programs affect it directly and indirectly. If possible, the evaluation should also project outcomes of unused alternatives to see whether the initial choice was correct (Ashcroft 1979).

Evaluation can occur at two levels of economic-political aggregation, national and local. The evaluations can yield conflicting results (e.g., positive on a national level, negative on a local level, or vice versa). While local-national level evaluation methodologies can be the same, they often are appropriate at only one level.

COMPONENTS. An evaluation of community economic development policies requires: (1) a statement of policy goals; (2) identification of program inputs and costs; (3) a statement of the policy's effect on community goals (output); and (4) identification of the distributional effects of the policy.

Any evaluation must begin with a statement of what the program seeks to accomplish (*objectives*). The complexity of the evaluation increases geometrically with the number of objectives sought.

Easily identifiable *program inputs and costs* facilitate evaluation. Preferably these inputs and outputs (e.g., dollars used, jobs created) are directly measurable and not clouded by the use of proxies. Most programs seek to improve regional/community welfare, which is difficult to measure (see the earlier discussion of the socioeconomic welfare function). The costs of the program largely depend on the prior use of the resources devoted to it. The costs will be minimal for unemployed resources. If the resources are employed or the economy is fully employed, the program must represent a better use of those resources because the foregone output is a cost.[3] The source of these inputs, inside or outside the community, is not the crucial question unless the analysis addresses local impacts only.

The next step in the evaluation framework is to see a particular policy's *effect on community goals*. Does the program have a positive, negative, or mixed effect? What conditions cause such effects to occur? The effects may not be uniform among communities. This step attempts to measure the linkage between program inputs and outputs. Output or benefit measures of a local economic development program must be interpreted with care.[4] Take, for example, a program designed to reduce local unemployment. A decline in local unemployment could be caused by the program, out-migration of the unemployed, withdrawal of the unemployed from the labor force, or improved national economic activity. The last three causes do not result from the local program. On the other hand, an increase in local unemployment could be caused by the fact that the program kept unemployed potential out-migrants in the community or attracted unemployed persons to the community to seek jobs (for further discussion of impacts and program output, see Chapter 10).

The final evaluation question is that of the *distribution of impacts* among communities and within the community. What are the effects on targeted and nontargeted groups? Which communities bear the costs? Which communities reap the benefits? Are they target communities? Why do they receive program benefits? Within the community the same questions apply to specific subgroups. One of the critical questions concerning distribution among communities or within the community is whether the community benefits are truly benefits and not just transfers of benefits among communities or segments of a community. The presence of immobilities, unemployment, and increasing returns to scale are necessary for true benefits to occur (Haveman 1976).

One possible further criterion for program evaluation not mentioned above is *target efficiency*. Target efficiency is "the degree to which the actual redistribution [of economic activity, e.g., income] coincides with the desired redistribution" (Weisbrod 1977, p. 114). This concept has two aspects. First is the extent to which the program benefits the target group in relation to nontarget groups (vertical efficiency), measured by the proportion of total program benefits received by the target group. Second is the degree to which program benefits reach all members of the target group (horizontal efficiency), measured by the ratio of target beneficiaries to total members in the target group or by the ratio of benefits received by the target group to the total benefits needed by that group.

METHODS. Richardson (1978b, pp. 30–32) suggests four different evaluation methods: (1) ad hoc assessment; (2) comparison of actual vs. expected performance; (3) measurement in terms of meeting predetermined goals; and (4) benefit/cost assessment.

Ad hoc assessment, the most common evaluation approach, uses indicators such as the number and types of firms receiving assistance. This approach considers new jobs created in the depressed area; the fiscal cost of the policy; and changes in industrial structure, unemployment, and migration rates. This fairly unsystematic approach emphasizes evaluation based on data availability and subjective judgments about the changes occurring in measurable data.

The second evaluation approach, *actual vs. expected performance,* compares community economic development changes with and without the economic development policy, and attributes whatever difference there is to the policy (Ashcroft 1982; Nicol 1982; Isserman and Merrifield 1982). (Note that care must be exercised here—measurement *with and without* is not the same as measurement *before and after.*) Difficulties with this approach include accurately predicting trends that might have occurred without the program and anticipating the types of impacts from the policy, which are often more varied than those chosen for examination (e.g., unintended consequences).

The third method of evaluating community economic development policy examines the extent to which the policy *meets predetermined goals.* This approach essentially assesses the achievement of policy objectives. In limiting the assessment to predetermined criteria, this approach fails to measure the unintended side effects of a policy. Furthermore, fixed targeting creates an incentive to underestimate the target to ensure program success.

The final approach to evaluating community economic development policy is the *benefit/cost approach* (Haveman and Weisbrod 1975), in which the community quantifies the impacts from the economic development policy. The approach places a heavy emphasis on measurable economic factors or the conversion of noneconomic factors into economic measuring units. Community benefit/cost studies measure the jobs, wages, output, etc., created by the program and compare their value with program costs. Indirect program benefits include effects on private investment and consumption, population and labor supply response, and nonmarket impacts. Direct program costs include program and administrative expenditures. Secondary costs are lost production elsewhere and environmental costs. Cost/benefit studies must indicate how, if at all, the program affected the location decision, size of investment made, or number of workers hired. The analysis should include the secondary effects on the target community as well as other communities and the effect of the policy on ancillary location decisions, investment, and labor supply.

Haveman (1976, p. 460) offers his "counsel of perfection" for program evaluation:

Several of the important welfare impacts of a policy decision have not been captured in any of the existing regional impact models. These include:

The discontinuous or strategic dynamic investment impacts of policies or programs (so often emphasized in discussions of regional development programs) and the income generation efforts of these investments.

The effects of policies and programs on regional and national socio-demographic behavior, labor supply, migration, human investment — which may also alter the expected pattern of regional and national growth.

The impact of policies or programs on broader social and political variables, such as regional environmental quality, public service provision, or the public provision of infrastructure and the values of these.

The impact of policies or programs on regional income distribution.

The preceding discussion offers one approach to the economic evaluation of community economic development programs. An approach explicitly incorporating other community considerations offers six general criteria to evaluate community economic development policies (Cornia et al. 1978, p. 18). The criteria are equity, revenue producing potential, administration and compliance, target efficiency, neutrality, and indirect effects (see Table 4.1).

The *equity* criterion asks several questions. Will the program benefit some at the expense of others? Will it increase the value of resources held by some (e.g., land, specific skills) without affecting others? Are all firms eligible, or only nonlocal firms or new firms or firms with specific types of production? Are all communities eligible, or just those in certain geographic areas or those meeting certain socioeconomic conditions?

Public economic development programs entail governmental costs that must be paid either by general taxpayers or by future taxes from the new economic activity. Will the *public revenue produced* (property taxes, income taxes, reduced public assistance payments) offset the costs incurred to create the economic activity?

An implicit cost to any incentive program is *administration* (e.g., determining eligibility, confirming compliance, making offers). Administrative costs are not all public. Business firms incur some costs in becoming

Table 7.1. Evaluation Matrix for Community Economic Development Programs (Note that each program should be evaluated in terms of the criteria shown in the column headings.)

Sample Programs		Criterion				
	Equity	Revenue-Producing Potential	Administration and Compliance	Target Efficiency	Neutrality	Indirect Effects
Incentives						
Capital:						
Grants						
Loans						
Public facilities						
Labor:						
Employers' tax						
Start-up training						
Vocational training						
Price:						
Transportation subsidies						
Disincentives/Regulations						
Zoning regulation						
Effluent controls						
Joint Ownership						
Government Purchases						
Investment:						
New office buildings						
Operation:						
Social Security						
Regionalized employment						
Capacity-Building						
Private:						
Locational guidance						
Management counseling						
Public:						
Regional planning						

aware of the program, making an application, and adjusting their internal decisions and recordkeeping to meet any continuing compliance requirements. These private costs vary dramatically from program to program.

Target efficiency refers to the ability of the program actually to affect the firms, the workers, and the communities of public concern. The criterion includes determination of what proportion of the target population is affected and what proportion of program recipients are part of that population.

The *neutrality* criterion addresses the question of how an economic development program specifically influences location decisions. Does this influence reduce overall national and community economic efficiency by distorting both the place where economic production occurs and the mix of factors used in production?

The *indirect effects* of an economic development program are its effects on the environment, population concentrations, social issues, political consciousness, and community stability. Does the program affect these and other dimensions of the community, and, if so, how?

Figure 4.5 displays an application of the simplified evaluation system to various local economic development programs. This approach provides a concise statement of the range of economic development programs a community is operating and permits checks for duplication or deficiencies in the strategy. It also permits checking the complementary or conflicting elements among various programs. A similar table should be created for each major community economic development objective.

Any community economic development program should be evaluated for effectiveness in achieving its stated objectives and for any indirect or unanticipated outcomes. Imprecise measures of program outputs and inputs hamper evaluation efforts. Furthermore, there remains a continuing problem of distinguishing changes attributable to this program from those brought about by some other program or some exogenous uncontrolled economic force (e.g., national economic growth). Given these limitations, the results of program evaluation must be viewed with skepticism.

Are Community Economic Developme
Programs Zero Su

Community economic development programs are often accused of being nothing more than a zero sum exercise because of the apparent shifting of economic activity from one location to another or from one group to another. Here we will examine that claim. To do so, the forms of zero sum, the conditions necessary for zero sum to appear, and the community economic development activities leading to zero sum are reviewed.

Zero sum is defined as an increase of economic activity in one locality or population subgroup that occurs only at the expense of another locale or group. It is important to distinguish the macro/micro perspective of zero sum. The micro perspective is that of the community and is less likely to display the conditions of zero sum since the community is gaining jobs, income, and wealth from its economic development activities. Yet, even at the micro level, shifts of economic activity among segments of the community can yield a zero sum change for the community as a whole. The macro perspective is that of the state or nation, and zero sum is more likely to result from conscious efforts to encourage economic development in specific locales or specific groups. Even here, however, zero sum is not a foregone conclusion if the national or state economy is growing, if there are differences in efficiencies among sectors or areas, or if public policy uses nonuniform welfare weights for the jobs, income, or other results generated in different locales or among different segments of the population (see the discussion of Figure 4.3).

FORMS OF ZERO SUM. Zero sum outcomes from local economic development activities appear in several forms and can be discussed under several headings, among them equity/efficiency, spatial, socioeconomic groups, and public/private. Each of these will now be discussed in greater detail.

The classic statement concerning the zero sum nature of community economic development activity is that it must represent a loss of *efficiency* or the market would have made that decision of its own volition (Cameron 1970, pp. 25–26). If society in its wisdom chooses to counteract market judgments, it must do so at the risk of lost efficiency. The major shortcoming of the efficiency/equity trade-off is that it is a static concept (Vaughan and Bearse 1981, pp. 312–14). A dynamic economy reduces the prospects of an efficiency/equity trade-off but need not eliminate it entirely. Dynamic efficiency in an economic development context means that the economy is creating new products, mobilizing new or unemployed resources, improving the quality of existing resources, and altering structural and institutional arrangements that impede the efficient use of resources. Thus in a dynamic context there need not be a trade-off between efficiency and equity.

The second major form of the zero sum game is *spatial,* when economic activity is diverted or relocated from one locale to another. The gain by one is loss to the other. For this to be an accurate statement the relocations must not yield different output/employment levels. Yet several empirical studies suggest that is not the case (Miller 1980), particularly if the firms relocate to gain access to resources, labor, markets, or space to expand (see the discussion of the location decision process in Chapter 3). Furthermore, from a macro perspective, some resources, labor in particular, are not completely mobile, and conscious steering of economic activity from one locale to another improves total economic activity by using unemployed resources (Haveman 1976).

The belief that there is just so much economic activity to be shared stimulates the concern about whether community economic development activities yield a zero sum outcome within the community—whether gains by one *socioeconomic group* in the community come only at the expense of others in the same community. Reaching a conclusion about the zero sum nature of the outcome requires comparing the welfare weights of the affected groups in the community (Haveman 1976). Such a comparison represents a static analysis, yet the prospects of zero sum are affected by whether or not the entire economy is growing. If it is, then the prospects of zero sum are reduced (Chisholm 1976). What is likely to happen in a growing economy is not that people are thrown out of work elsewhere as a result of community economic development efforts but rather that the rate of increase in that other locale is reduced. In a stagnant economy the prospects of zero sum increase, but again require comparing the welfare weights among losers and gainers.

The final major form of zero sum is the *public/private* dimension. Zero sum outcomes need not appear only from public decisions. Private decisions to alter production levels or composition of output or to change technology or locations are seldom viewed in a zero sum context. Yet decisions to change the composition of output mean that some consumers will no longer be able to purchase the product, while other consumers will reap the rewards of the output of the reallocated capital and labor resources.

Zero sum outcomes from community economic development activities mean that there are no differences in efficiency or welfare among areas or people. The prospects of a zero sum outcome are heightened when a simple static analysis is used. Zero sum outcomes are not foregone conclusions if the above conditions are absent.

CONDITIONS FOR ZERO SUM. In a general sense, zero sum is a foregone conclusion in a perfectly competitive market, but need not be so in an imperfectly competitive market. If the market is perfectly competitive or behaving in that fashion, public intervention cannot improve the outcomes derived from private decisions, an observation which leads to the frequent assertion that community economic development activities are zero sum. Yet even if perfectly competitive market conditions exist, this argument ignores the equity issues and the dynamics of economic development. The equity perspective recognizes that all workers are not intrinsically the same, that all forms of capital do not yield equally profitable returns, and that all communities are not equally blessed with the same sets of endowments, such as location or mineral deposits. Society can seek equity goals that offset the loss of efficiency (see discussion of Figures 4.3 and 4.4). The argument against zero sum contends that all economic actors (e.g., workers, business people, communities) are not created equal and that public policy is justified in aiding those people, businesses, and places through difficult transitions.

If the economy is not functioning in a perfectly competitive fashion, the prospects for a zero sum outcome from community development efforts still exist, but appear much more unlikely. There are several reasons why a zero sum outcome will not result, and most are linked to a failure to meet the fundamental assumptions of a perfectly competitive market.

Capital and labor resources in the economy are not perfectly mobile among places and uses. Without the mobility implicit in the perfect market analysis, community actions promote the employment of underused resources. Even if the economy might yield a higher return if resources were used elsewhere, any positive return from immobile unemployed resources is a net addition to both the local and national economy.

One reason why capital and labor are immobile is the often very high transaction cost associated with mobility. It takes time and effort to learn a new skill or even to identify what new skills might be needed. Unemployed workers and workers with limited financial resources may not be able to make the expenditures of either time or funds. Likewise, investors must commit time and funds to acquire information about new businesses, production technologies, or investment locations. For small firms or more isolated communities, these transaction costs discourage change and lock resources into their present use or unemployment. Community economic development activities that reduce transaction costs increase the mobility of resources among uses and places, and lead to increased local and national output.

Information is not perfect through time and over space. Workers and investors do not have good information about future trends or may even make different choices given the same information. Many community economic development activities disseminate information on job opportunities, advertise community attributes to nonlocal investors, or announce interest subsidies to attract capital to depressed areas. Activities that improve information flow do not yield a zero sum outcome.

The perfectly competitive model assumes constant returns to scale, yet many activities exhibit increasing returns to scale. For example, more trainees mean lower costs for training each person and maybe even a wider variety of training choices. Likewise, there is little difference in the skills and time required to process a loan request for $100,000 and a request for $10,000,000; in fact, there is a tendency for the smaller request to cost more, thus discouraging applicants. Community intervention in the labor and capital markets can overcome some of the cost disadvantages associated with size/scale and improve access for smaller or more isolated activities. Community economic development activities that permit or create increasing returns to scale reduce the probability of zero sum outcomes.

Externalities are not present in the perfectly competitive model, but in reality they are a significant component of any investment in either physical or human capital. In this situation, even if the direct returns from economic development activities among communities appear equal (indicating zero sum), if the spinoffs in one locale exceed those in another, a zero sum outcome is less likely to result.

The existence of perfect market conditions in all input and output markets is implicit in the perfectly competitive model. However, nonoptimal market conditions in one market can yield suboptimal conditions in another. For example, a failure to generate or allocate sufficient risk capital leads to inadequate future employment opportunities. Community economic development efforts that facilitate the movement of risk capital to new enterprises or depressed locales yield long-run employment growth that might not otherwise have occurred. Community economic development activities that help markets approach a perfectly competitive mode of operation do not yield a zero sum outcome.

Public intervention can also distort market signals, causing a need to counteract the original signal. A prime example is banking regulation by FDIC, as administered by bank examiners. While the regulations legitimately ask banks to protect our money, examiners' insistence on "safe" loans may mean that new business ideas are not financed, thus reducing future output and employment. Community initiatives can supplement the bank as a source of funding, yielding long-term development for the local economy.

Community economic development efforts need not yield a zero sum outcome when conditions allow economic actors sufficient power to influence the market. Community actions may be required to alter a noncompetitive market suffering from low incentives for product and process innovation. The resultant new activity in the locale can reduce overdependence on current sectors. Communities also can act to stimulate competition among existing firms for local labor or consumer spending. Communities that encourage alternative retail development contribute to lower product prices and improved selection for consumers. Activities that stimulate competition within the community do not yield zero sum outcomes if prices decline, product selection improves, or wages increase.

While it appears that the idea of market failure becomes the major justification for community economic development activities, that conclusion is insufficient. Market failure is a quasi-static concept that ignores the dynamic functioning associated with community economic development.

Summary

The overall purpose of community economic development policy is to reduce and/or abolish the barriers in product and factor markets that prevent the positive culmination of economic development processes. Such policy must be viewed in the long-run dynamic context of those markets and the surrounding socio-politico-physical environment.

It is important to remember that development is an inherently uneven process in terms of sectoral distribution, timing, and geographic distribution. However, disruption (disequilibrium) is a necessity in a dynamic economy and is part of the dynamic process associated with development (Vaughan and Bearse 1981, p. 310). Joseph Schumpeter referred to this dynamic process as "creative destruction," in which old resources become less valuable, new resources become more valuable, and gaps and spillovers of externalities are generated among markets as some institutions, industries, or resources lead and some lag the development process. The economy does not adjust instantaneously and painlessly to the disruptions caused by development. There are inherent structural barriers, inconsistencies in the market, that make this process less than smooth. One goal of development strategy is to smooth the development path. The goal of development policy should not be to avoid disruption and adjustments, but to facilitate the adjustment process (Vaughan and Bearse 1981, pp. 309–10).

Four basic tenets underlie any attempt to set community economic development policy and to generate action programs. First, a community is a logical economic unit that can exert some control over its economic future. Second, intervention in the form of conscious group decisions and actions will affect local economic welfare more than the sum of individual actions. Third, the action or policy must be comprehensive: it cannot focus only on economic activity but must also include noneconomic dimensions. Fourth, the resources needed will be available to implement the policy.

The preconditions in the community affect the wisest choice of policy, and policy effects differ among communities. Care must be exercised in transferring a policy/program from one locale to another. Apart from the need to distinguish among types of community economic development situations, policymakers must distinguish between forces that initiate and those that perpetuate the adverse economic conditions in the community. While the two phenomena are interrelated, they are usually different forces requiring different policy responses.

The general categories of issues/problems that community economic development policies must address are: where development should occur, what kind of development should occur, for whom should development occur, and what preconditions are needed for development to occur.

Setting community economic development goals can be a frustrating experience. Goals can be simple or complex, complementary or conflicting. Setting a community's goals and objectives for economic development is a very critical but difficult component of any development effort. It is important to specify the objectives clearly so that the community can effectively set a policy and strategy. Without this, the inevitable result is a disjointed nonstrategy, an eclectic collection of efforts. A community may not be able to satisfy all of the goals and objectives that it sets for itself because of one or more of the following factors: (1) inadequate political support, (2) inadequate resources, (3) conflict with other goals and objectives, (4) the need to conform with higher-level goals and objectives, and (5) inability to control the means by which the goals and objectives can be reached.

There may be continuing tension in the community caused by differences of opinion about goals and objectives. Opinions vary about the nature of the problem and its priority; about the capacity of suggested programs to achieve the desired goal; and about the consequences of the actions proposed to correct the perceived problem. Even if all parties agree on these matters, differences of opinion about the proper political, economic, or social solution may continue to cause tension and fragmentation in the community.

Zero sum outcomes are not inherent to community economic development efforts. They are more likely to occur when a static analysis is used in a perfectly competitive market at the macro level and when issues of equity are ignored. If these conditions are not present, then the prospects of a zero sum outcome from community economic development activity are unlikely.

Study Questic

1. What are some basic elements of a community economic development strategy? Why create such a strategy?

2. What are some of the possible relationships among different goals and objectives, and how might they affect community economic development policy?

3. Are goals and objectives identical concepts? If not, what is the difference?

4. The choice of specific community economic development policies is affected by numerous factors. What are they, and why are they important?

5. What is the relationship between community well-being and the well-being of individuals or groups in the community? Do they always respond in the same fashion to policies? Why is an understanding of this relationship important for community economic development policy?

6. What are the elements of the community economic development policy model, and how does each element relate to creating community economic development policies?

7. Is it necessary to incorporate time in the selection of goals and objectives or in the implementation of policy? Why?

8. In a general sense, what are the elements of community well-being? What is the significance of distinguishing between group and individual well-being?

9. What are the six generic strategies of community economic development that were discussed? Are they mutually exclusive?

10. The following basic issues were raised regarding the evaluation of community economic development policy: level of political-economic aggregation, objectives/output of policy, inputs/resources used to implement policy, relationship between policy output and community goals, costs of policy. Why are they important?

11. Five general evaluation strategies were mentioned. What are they, and what are the strengths and weaknesses of each?

12. What are the four tenets underlying community economic development policy? Why is each important?

13. Is it possible to achieve all worthy community economic development goals? If not, why not?

14. What is the elemental purpose of community economic development policy?

15. What are the major forms in which zero sum outcomes can appear?

16. What is the significance of the statement: Zero sum often appears in static analysis, but is far less likely in a dynamic analysis?

17. Why is a perfectly competitive market almost a necessary condition before a zero sum outcome can occur?

Implementing Community Economic Development Programs

5

THIS CHAPTER EXAMINES HOW TO INITIATE an economic development program and some methods for targeting economic development. Attracting a new manufacturing plant, for example, is only one of the many avenues available to create local economic development (see "Strategies" in Chapter 4). Expansion of existing businesses and formation of new businesses are two other routes through which the community can pursue economic development. While the following discussion may appear to emphasize the attraction avenue, the steps outlined apply equally to the formation of new businesses, the expansion of existing businesses, and the development of the community's nonmanufacturing sector, e.g., the services/trade sector and resource-based businesses such as agriculture, forestry, and mining.

Starting an Economic Development Program

There are three basic questions involved in starting an economic development program. The first question, *Where are we now?* examines the community's existing economic activities and resources and determines the potentials for and restrictions on economic development. Economic development objectives are identified, the residents' attitudes are determined, and support is built in the community. The second question, *Where do we want to be?* identifies potential economic development prospects for the community, builds consensus about the type of development desired, and evaluates the desirability of any given business prospect. A targeting model or other less sophisticated tools can be used. The final question, *How are we going to get there?* translates the analysis into an action program, deciding what specific actions will be undertaken, and by whom.

The first question is addressed in greater detail in Chapters 4 and 11. The third question is examined in Chapters 2 and 4. The balance of this chapter will focus on the second and third questions.

PREPARING. Figure 5.1 displays one approach to preparing an economic development program. While there are numerous ways to outline systematic community economic development, the basic steps remain those of the familiar scientific method, in which the investigator defines the current situation, states a goal, lists the steps that must be taken to reach the goal, then evaluates the project to determine its effectiveness. In community economic development, the process boils down to four basic questions; the three listed above and a fourth, *Did we make it?*

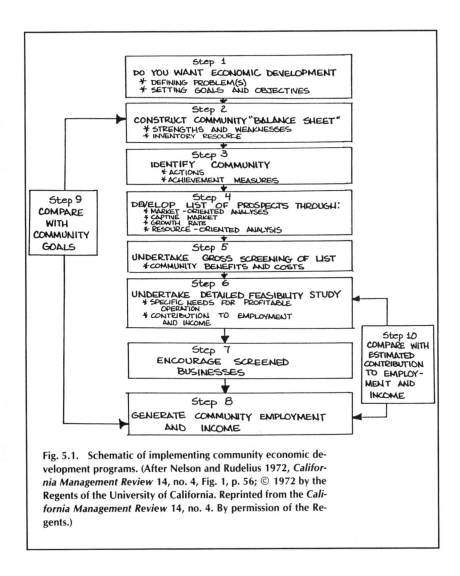

Fig. 5.1. Schematic of implementing community economic development programs. (After Nelson and Rudelius 1972, *California Management Review* 14, no. 4, Fig. 1, p. 56; © 1972 by the Regents of the University of California. Reprinted from the *California Management Review* 14, no. 4. By permission of the Regents.)

In *Step 1* of the figure, determining the opinions and problem(s) of the community is part of the first of our questions, *Where are we now?* At least two sources of community opinion regarding community economic development should be examined.[1] A general attitude survey is needed to identify what type and degree of economic development citizens desire. This survey can help the community crystallize its economic development goals and objectives and can get a broad spectrum of residents involved. Second, a business survey is needed, asking managers of existing businesses about the community's strengths and weaknesses. It is especially important to check new firms in the community, as well as firms that have just expanded or closed or reduced their size, to find the causes for these changes. Along with this survey, the community may also check on past inquiries from firms thinking of locating there to see what similarities there might be in the types of firms making these inquiries or in the reasons why they decided not to locate there. In marketing the community, the strengths identified by this business survey become part of the marketing program; the weaknesses and obstacles identified become targets for corrective action.

Before deciding to pursue economic development actively, the community must define the problem. The presence of low per capita income and unemployment are just symptoms of the problem(s). Low per capita income and high unemployment occur for many different reasons, such as the depletion of a natural resource, like an iron ore deposit; changes in technology, like those affecting the steel industry since the early 1960s; the migration of industry, like the movement out of urban to suburban locations; the out-migration of people, in particular younger, better-trained individuals, making the community less attractive to new or existing industry; and over-dependence on a single industry for economic activity. Each of these potential causes of low income or high unemployment requires a different policy response. In most cases the problem is not as obvious as is suggested in the examples given here, but nevertheless the community must address the problem, whatever it is, not symptoms or unrelated problems, to achieve success.

Next, the community must articulate specific goals about what is desired. Goals must be specific enough to guide programs and actions. Furthermore, in setting goals the community must recognize *the relationship among goals, the hierarchy of goals,* and *the time context* (see Chapter 4). The goals the community sets for itself should ideally be complementary or, at least, the conflicts should be recognized and resolution attempted. Identifying the hierarchy of goals permits the community to maintain a central focus for seemingly disparate efforts. Recognition of the time context allows the community to set short-term goals that build toward a long-term goal. Setting and achieving a succession of short-term goals allows the community to maintain enthusiasm and involvement in economic development efforts over the long run. For example, the community might set a long-run goal of improving the quality of life for community residents. An intermediate goal might be attracting a rapid-growth, high-wage industry. A short-run goal might be creating jobs using existing labor force skills. An even more immediate goal might be preparation of a parcel of land for industrial development by purchase of the land and extension of municipal services to the property.

The goals and objectives set should represent broad economic interests within the community (Leven 1985). They should incorporate the views of different segments of the community to encourage and maintain support for the economic development effort. In reality, the community must make trade-offs between what is desired and what is possible. These trade-offs cannot, however, be made systematically and logically unless the community examines what it wishes to accomplish.

In *Step 2* of the figure, the local development group inventories community resources. (For smaller communities a regional perspective may be necessary.) It should appraise its strengths, weaknesses, and underutilized resources, focusing on recent conditions, not historical facts with little current relevance. The "balance sheet" should include natural, human, institutional, and economic resources (see the discussion of social accounts in Table 11.1 for more detail). Table 5.1 provides one detailed version of a community inventory (Fernstrom 1974, pp. 103–6; Moriarty 1980, pp. 310–29; Weitzell 1969). For individual communities some of the items in the table may be inappropriate.

In *Step 3* of Figure 5.1, after community goals and objectives are identified, an action strategy is formulated. A typical community goal is to increase community income or output. Two possible action strategies are fuller utilization of local resources and creating additional value added locally. To use local resources means that the community possesses a currently underutilized resource; an example would be mining a mineral deposit. Creating additional value added locally means that the community adds labor associated with the additional local processing of products. In the example, if the ore mined is refined in the area, additional local jobs (value added) are created. Another example would be the additional processing of agricultural products. The multitude of cheese factories in Wisconsin represents an attempt to create additional local value added. The cheese factories purchase raw milk from local farmers and employ local people to make processed milk products.

Another typical economic development goal is to alter the structure of the local economy. For example, the community may experience employment instability through business cycles and seasonal cycles. The community can create alternate employment opportunities for slack periods of existing industries.[2] Cambridge, Wisconsin, diversifies its employment

Table 5.1. Community Inventory

A. *Location*
1. Geography
2. Access to major markets
3. Climate

B. *Government*
1. Form
2. Assessment policies
3. Types of taxes
4. Tax rates and trends, last 5 years
5. Zoning ordinances, land use policy
6. Building codes
7. Regulations

C. *Local Services*
1. Fire protection
   a. fire insurance rates
   b. special equipment
   c. station location
   d. water availability
2. Police protection
3. Solid waste disposed
4. Snow removal

D. *Population Characteristics*
1. Demographic profile
   a. age/sex
2. Population trends
   a. migration
3. Income characteristics
4. Cost of living
5. Home and durable goods ownership

E. *Housing*
1. New home construction and cost
2. Adequacy of sale or rental
3. Rental costs
4. Condition of residential neighbor-hoods

J. *Postal Services*
1. Type and frequency of service

K. *News Media*
1. Newspapers
2. TV and radio
3. Degree of local coverage

L. *Local Industries*
1. Cooperation of business leaders
2. Supply and service firms
3. Types of industries

M. *Utilities*
1. Electrical power: availability and rates
2. Gas service: availability and rates
3. Telephone service: type and rates
4. Water service: availability, source, usage, rates
5. Sewer service: adequacy, regulations, charges

N. *Financial Services*
1. Banking services
   a. loan policies
   b. asset steructures
   c. interest in financing new ventures
2. Local investors
3. State, federal, or local sources of financing

O. *Education*
1. Elementary and secondary schools
   a. number
   b. pupil-teacher ratio
   c. accreditation
   d. student enrollment
   e. programs for students with special learning needs

2. Availability of labor
   a. types
   b. location
   c. seasonal
3. Unions
4. Transportation for commuters
5. Wage scales
6. Employee turnover rate-absenteeism
7. Unemployed
   a. skills
   b. sex
8. Labor relations history
9. Labor practices
   a. vacations
   b. holidays
10. Labor legislation
11. State and local taxes applied to labor

Q. *Transportation (rail, truck, water, air, pipe-lines)*
1. Types available: freight and passenger
2. Adequacy of facilities
3. Record of performance
4. Cost and rates
5. Regulations or tariffs
6. Transit privileges

R. *Income*
1. Per capita
2. Purchasing power
3. Percent of poverty level
4. Percent receiving public assistance
5. Sources of income

S. *Economic Development Program*
1. Industrial – commercial facilities
   a. sites
   b. buildings
   c. services

114

F. *Medical Facilities*
1. Availability of doctors, dentists, and hospital beds
2. Availability of lab facilities
3. Cost of medical and dental care

G. *Religious Facilities*
1. Number and denominations of area churches

H. *Accommodations*
1. Availability for corporate traffic
2. Availability for group meetings

I. *Cultural and Recreational Facilities*
1. Civil and professional organizations
2. Libraries
3. Recreation facilities

2. Vocational schools
a. number
b. types of training
c. number of graduates
3. Higher education
a. availability of universities
b. research facilities
4. Other
a. adult education
b. testing services

P. *Labor*
1. Labor profile
a. education
b. age
c. skills

3. Incentives

T. *Recreation*
1. Public
a. parks and playgrounds
b. organized programs
1. crafts
2. soccer
3. swimming
c. Youth clubs
2. Private
a. golf, tennis
b. boating
c. bowling
d. theaters
e. restaurants

through a series of part-time jobs. From spring through early fall the jobs are in the tobacco fields. In the fall and early winter, workers move to jobs at a candy manufacturing plant as its production peaks for the holiday season. During the late winter and early spring months, the workers sort, grade, and pack animal furs for a wholesale distributor. Another strategy is to improve and strengthen linkages within the local economy. This strategy may be in conflict with an attempt to diversify the local economy, but its purpose is to create support businesses for local producers.[3]

If the community chooses to become an *active* participant in economic development (a passive participant takes no overt action to encourage development), it cannot afford to support every business or entrepreneur that hints even a passing interest in the community. Thus it is critical for the community to focus its economic development efforts. In *Step 4* of Figure 5.1, the community creates a list of prospects who meet community criteria for factors such as jobs, wages, and environmental impacts (see "Targeting" below for details). The list of prospects can be created in at least two ways, through a resource requirement/availability analysis and through a market analysis.

The *resource requirement/availability analysis* identifies businesses using resources available in the community. These businesses become the target of community efforts. An example would be encouragement of businesses based on the number of workers required compared with the potential number of workers available or skills required compared with existing skills.

The *market analysis* examines existing and potential markets in the community to see whether a business could feasibly operate in a given market area: If the community is a net importer of a specific good or service (capital market), might there be sufficient local market (people, income) to support the local production of that product? This is an import substitution strategy, important in commercial development and in development of businesses that market their product as inputs to other local industries (see Chapter 6, "Introducing New Goods and Services," for details). Another form of market analysis is growth rate analysis to identify businesses with recent and potential rapid growth compatible with local resources. These businesses become the target of community efforts.

In *Step 5* of the figure, a gross screening of the prospect list occurs. At this point, the community addresses questions of how each business fits into the community. Do the benefits significantly exceed the costs that would be incurred by the community from the location or expansion or start-up of this particular business? Are there actions the community should take to mitigate adverse impacts and reinforce positive outcomes? (See Chapter 10 for more detail.)

In *Step 6,* a detailed feasibility study is undertaken. What are the specific needs of the business (e.g., transportation facilities, labor)? What is its economic viability? How strong is the management? How financially sound is it? How stable is its market, and is it growing? Does the business have a strong credit rating? What is its history of community citizenship? Table 5.2 shows an example of a screening device.

In *Step 7,* the firms surviving the feasibility study in *Step 6* are actually encouraged. Here actions such as prospecting trips, downtown redevelopment efforts, and new business support programs are appropriate. In *Step 8,* the actual change in community income and employment occurs. This change is compared with community goals and objectives (*Step 9*) and anticipated changes (*Step 10*) to determine the degree of achievement and/or needed adjustment in goals or actions.

ORGANIZING. Community economic development is a function of ecological, social action, and initiative factors (Davis et al. 1975). The *ecological*

Table 5.2. Outline for Evaluating Various Business Prospects

I. Type of Industry
  A. Relationships to Local Economy
    1. Use of local raw materials
    2. Complementary to existing industry
    3. Completely new addition
    4. Dependence on related industries and services
  B. Basic Requirements
    1. Capital intensity
    2. Labor intensity
    3. Water
    4. Fuel and power
    5. Raw materials
    6. Other special requirements
 	
II. Historical Characteristics
  A. New products or processes
  B. Expansion of established firms
  C. Relative stability in terms of tendency to change locations
  D. Growth history, past years
  E. Dependence on short-term military and research contracts
 	
III. Overall Probability of Success
  A. Financial experience past 10 years
  B. Marginality of operations and growth
    1. Size and volume of operating growth
    2. Financial backing of individual firm or units
    3. Demand for product as a necessity or luxury
    4. New or obsolescent equipment and methods
	IV. Employment Characteristics
	  A. Primary employment
	    1. Skilled, unskilled, and professional
	    2. Full- and part-time
	    3. Men and women
	  B. Wage levels, by classes (union/nonunion)
	
	V. Financial Requirements
	  A. Entirely self-financing
	  B. Financing and other types of assistance expected from the community, and on what basis
	
	VI. Environmental Feasibilty
	  A. Air, water, and soil pollution possibilities
	  B. Relative freedom from offensive odors
	  C. Conformity with zoning and other requirements of local government
	
	VII. Summary, Contributions to the Local Economy
	  A. Probable level of economic benefits
	  B. Intangible benefits
	  C. Negative factors
	
	VIII. Conclusions and Recommendations
	  A. Most desirable industries in terms of varying local needs and local resources
	  B. Contributions to the economy

Source: After Weitzell 1969, Exhibit A, pp. 16–17.

factors are significant locational factors external to the community over which the community has little control, at least in the short run. They could be access to markets or raw materials or the size of the local labor force. *Social action and initiative factors* are the local efforts involving planning, broad-based community participation, and community efforts to stimulate particular types of economic development. Research indicates that communities organized for economic development are not guaranteed success, but that organized communities seem to be more successful then nonorganized ones (Summers and Hirschl 1986; Smith et al. 1980; Williams et al. 1977).

To conduct its economic development efforts, the community must create some form of organization, either formal or informal. Community economic development is a time-consuming process that will simply exhaust the energies of one person. Furthermore, "community economic development" suggests a community rather than an individual effort. Some suggest that the overriding problem in most community-based development efforts is a lack of managerial and technical capacity to pursue development (Daniels et al. 1981, p. 184). This is addressed in the discussion of decision-making capacity in Chapter 2, "Institutions and Community Economic Development."

Economic development organizations serve two roles. The first is to create a community institution to mobilize local resources, including public support, to initiate change. The second is to respond to requests from business prospects. It is unlikely that any one individual possesses the entire range of information necessary when talking to a prospect. An economic development organization with specialized committees is one alternative, so that individuals with particular knowledge about the community can be consulted quickly, and the prospect can be given current and accurate answers to specific and unusual questions. While the committee structure can take numerous forms, Fernstrom (1974, pp. 166–68) suggests creating a number of two- to three-person committees based on specific location factors. Each committee has two or three members to permit more input and wider interpretation of data. Fernstrom suggests that such committees focus on labor and training, public and private financing, facilities (sites and buildings), public services (including taxes), transportation, and living conditions (housing and amenities).

While local development groups tend to emphasize attraction efforts, it is critical not to forget the businesses already in the community as well as local residents wishing to start a business. Existing and prospective businesses also have needs, and the local development group can assist in resolving difficulties with local government, financing, or other issues. A fundamental question that local development groups should always ask is:

Are we offering anything to attract a business that we would not offer an existing or new business in the community?

PROSPECTING. Prospecting is part of the implementation phase of attracting new basic employers. It is also appropriate for an import substitution strategy (i.e., capturing existing markets in Chapter 4; see also Chapter 6, "Introducing New Goods and Services"). A prospecting strategy requires developing a prospect list, making an initial contact, following up with potential prospects, and qualifying a prospect's intent (Bessire 1970; Fernstrom 1974, pp. 139–54; Howard 1972; Moriarty 1980, pp. 338–47).

A community can compile a prospect list through the files of the state department of development, the utilities, the state chamber of commerce, and trade associations; through manufacturing directories; through talking with local merchants about their suppliers and markets or visiting with community residents who travel and soliciting hints from them about firms considering a move. Prospecting also includes the targeting ideas mentioned later, as well as the market and growth analysis in *Step 4* of Figure 5.1.

The initial prospecting contact with a nonlocal business can occur in one of four ways. The first, and probably most effective, is through some type of personal contact because of a business relationship. The second is through an advertisement in trade magazines or business newspapers (e.g., *Wall Street Journal*). The third is through a direct mailing of information about the community to the corporate headquarters of selected businesses.[4] This tends to be an ineffective approach because corporate headquarters are inundated with this type of mailing; unless the community's brochure hits the appropriate desk when a decision is being contemplated, it is likely to be discarded. A variant of the broadcast mailing is a "cold call," where a personal visit is made to the firm without prior contact.

A prospecting program is a sales effort. This means that the community must determine who wants to buy, what they want to buy, and why they are buying (see Chapter 3, "The Location Decision Process"). Other key elements in any prospecting effort are preparation, persistence, and patience. The community must identify the needs of the prospect and see how the community can respond to those needs. It must be persistent in contacting and following up potential prospects. Finally, the community must be patient because it may take months or even years after the initial contact before a firm locates or successfully starts. In many cases, it will not be selected by this prospect in spite of all of the community's work.[5]

TARGETING. The community can pursue two widely different prospecting strategies. Using the first, commonly referred to as the "shotgun" approach, the community seeks and accepts any firm indicating some interest in the community. While this is a relatively inexpensive approach, it is not very effective. The second strategy, the "rifle" or "targeting" approach, requires extensive analysis by the community to match community goals and resources with industry impacts and requirements, but it is also more cost-efficient. The targeting strategy is a conscious attempt to reduce all of the possibilities to some very definite prospects (Hansen and Munsinger 1972; Klaasen 1967; Minshall 1979; Moriarty 1980, pp. 329–40; Sweet 1970). There are two general philosophies regarding targeting. The first contends that communities and public bodies should actively seek desired types of economic activity. The second contends that the community and public body should not engage in picking "winners" or desired types of economic activity, but rather should create conditions conducive to entrepreneurial activity and managing public goods (Vaughan 1985). The latter philosophy presumes that the collective well-being is maximized by summing unfettered individual decisions. This section, however, reviews ways of implementing the first perspective.

Targeting the businesses the community wishes to encourage (attract, expand, and start up) can be a fairly simple or a complex matter. The items in Table 5.3 embody a simplified industrial targeting model and revolve around what the industrial prospect contributes to the community's economy relative to employment, income, and environmental changes. Note that the questions to be asked of a prospect go beyond a simple count of jobs and change in payroll, and include types of jobs, type of wage scale, type of demands are being made on the environment, and the need for public services.

A screening matrix system, more sophisticated than the checklist in Table 5.3, can be used to identify the types of businesses that most appropriately meet community goals and use existing community resources (Hunker 1974, pp. 247–52; Moriarty 1980, p. 255). This nonoptimizing locational approach attempts to satisfy locational needs. It requires a tremendous amount of data on both the specific business sectors and the community. The screening approach identifies those sectors with the greatest potential for location or expansion in the community. There are two components in the screening system, a desirability matrix and a feasibility matrix.

Table 5.4 displays a screening matrix. In this example, the specific four-digit industries are compared for recent and future growth, intensity of labor use, wages, extent of blue-collar labor requirements, size of plant, and proportion of plants locating in urban areas. A community can use any set of criteria it wishes in judging desirability. Furthermore, the community can place any importance it wishes on the various desirability components. In Table 5.4, the criteria weights suggest that this community believes recent growth is important, but only half as important as future growth of that

Table 5.3. Industrial Evaluation Checklist

I. Economic
  1. Number of employees at a new plant
     a. men
     b. women
     c. part-time
     d. seasonal
  2. Number of employees expected to reside in community
  3. Number of new jobs created
  4. Number of management-level employees
  5. Types of skills required of plant's employees
  6. Yearly payroll/average employee salary
  7. Projected appraised/assessed value of plant's real and personal property in community
  8. Number of years prospective tenant has been in business
  9. Number of plant relocations since 1970

II. Environmental
  1. Size of plant (sq. ft.)
  2. Amount of land required (acres)
  3. Proximity to area zoned residential
  4. Pollution
     a. water/type of effluent
     b. air/toxic substances
     c. odor
     d. glare
     e. noise
  5. Use of pollution control devices
  6. Physical appearance and landscaping
  7. Projected number of vehicles entering plant area per day
  8. Drainage/storm sewer requirements

III. Community Services
  1. Ability of the streets to carry additional traffic load
     a. access to plant
     b. safety
  2. Utility requirements
     a. gallons of water used per day
     b. water and line requirements needed for fire protection
     c. sewerage requirements
        1. amount
        2. type/BOD level
     d. projected electrical and gas usage
     e. need for water main and sewerage line extensions
  3. Ability of schools to accommodate enrollment increases

IV. Civil Awareness
  1. Evidence of the industry's past civic activity
  2. Responsiveness of the industry to community requests

Source: After International City Managers Association, "How Should Your City Grow: Governing Industrial Growth in Liberty, MO," *Management Information Services* 9 (1977): 5, Fig. 2.

particular business sector and half as important as the intensity of labor use. The values assigned to the various sectors are relative. In other words, they compare the magnitude of that particular criterion against the average for the total economy. Summing the weighted values for the various criteria gives a score of the desirability of the particular sector. This permits the community to array "objectively" the multitude of possibilities and create

Table 5.4. Screening Matrix

	Desirability									Feasibility				
	Growth, recent	Growth, future	Labor intensity	Wages	% Blue-collar	Small size (low mean)	Small size (high mean)	% Urban	Desirability sub-total	Forward linkage	Backward linkage	Demand in region	Feasibility sub-total	Total score
Criteria Weight	5	10	10	5	10	5	5	5		5	5	10		
2011 Meat packing	1	2	3	3	3	4	4	4	165	3	2	1	35	200
2031 Sausage & prepared meats	3	2	2	4	3	5	5	1	160	2	2	5	70	230
2015 Poultry & small game	4	2	5	1	5	4	4	5	210	3	2	1	35	245
2292 Lace goods	3	4	5	3	5	5	5	3	235	0	0	5	50	285
2297 Wool scouring & worsted	3	4	4	3	4	5	4	5	220	0	0	5	50	270
2298 Cordage & twine	3	4	5	3	3	5	4	5	220	0	0	5	50	270
2311 Men's Suits, coats, & overcoats	2	2	5	2	5	4	3	3	190	2	2	1	30	220
2321 Men's shirts, collars	4	2	5	1	5	4	3	5	195	2	2	5	70	265
2323 Men's underwear	4	2	5	1	3	2	3	5	195	2	2	5	70	265
2327 Men's neckwear	4	2	5	1	3	5	5	1	180	1	1	5	60	240
Men's trousers	4	2	5	1	5	4	3	5	205	2	2	4	60	265
2328 Men's work clothing	1	2	5	1	5	2	3	5	180	2	2	2	40	220
2329 Men's clothing NEC	4	2	5	1	5	3	4	5	205	2	2	1	30	235

Source: After Hunker 1974, Fig. 9-3, p. 250.

an ordinal ranking of the relatively more desirable sectors.

The second portion of the screening matrix process is the feasibility matrix, which identifies sectors with definite supply and market linkages in the community or region. Businesses in these sectors possess short-run location potential. The locational needs can be much more specific than displayed in Table 5.4 and could be expanded to include the availability of various labor skills, transportation needs, raw material needs, linkages with other businesses in the area, and water requirements. This type of matrix asks the question: What is the probability of attracting a business in a given SIC code? The answer to this question requires incorporating the locational factors reviewed in Chapter 3. Remember, however, that Chapter 3 indicates that there is no deterministic approach to location decisions.

The ability to alter the criteria and weights assigned in the screening matrices permits flexibility with this procedure. A major limitation of this approach, however, is the enormous amount of data required on linkages, growth rates, etc.

A targeting approach refining the screening matrix identifies the pool of workers seeking employment by worker characteristics (Gillis and Shaffer 1985). Since the community seeks to create jobs for specific categories of workers, the community targeting efforts need to consider firm characteristics — capital intensity, wage levels, occupational structure, and the like. Variation in these and other characteristics influence hiring choices.

DIVERSIFYING. If a community seeks to minimize fluctuations in income and employment subject to existing resource restrictions, it can approach this objective through a diversification strategy that utilizes the concepts of portfolio analysis (Barth et al. 1975; Conroy 1975b; Cho and Schuermann 1980).

To use portfolio analysis, the community starts with its existing economic structure and resource base and asks what types of changes need to be made to reduce the fluctuation in total income and total employment. Fluctuations occur over time as secular changes or cyclical or seasonal variations in income and employment. The community reduces total fluctuations in its local economy by reducing either the absolute or relative size of the unstable sectors. This may mean reducing a major sector that is unstable or supporting alternative sectors that offset the instability in the major sector.

The important concept in a diversification strategy is that adverse impacts and fluctuations in the community depend not only upon an individual sector but also upon linkages with other sectors (i.e., covariance). If other firms change in a counter-fashion, the community can absorb and reduce fluctuations and improve community economic stability. If other sectors in the local economy change in a sympathetic fashion with the stimulus, this amplifies the fluctuations.

Summai

The economic development conditions of a community are a function of the social-political-economic environment surrounding the community and group actions. Implementing community economic development programs requires action by a group rather than an individual. An individual may be the initiator, but the effort will require more energy and time than any one person can devote to it. The three basic questions to be asked before starting a community economic development effort are, Where is the community now? Where does the community want to go? How will the community get there? In the end, the community must prepare for economic development, it must persist in its economic development efforts because success may be elusive, and it must be patient and maintain its commitment to its long-term goal of improving the well-being of community residents.

Any community economic development program must consider the following points: (1) What do we need to accomplish our income and employment goals? (2) How will we determine the desirability of particular types of development? (3) What do we need to increase the prospects of success for our development efforts?

Study Questio▮

1. When initiating an economic development program, there are at least three fundamental questions that should be asked. What are they, and why are they important?

2. One of the preliminary steps in initiating a local economic development program is constructing a "balance sheet" of current conditions and resources. Briefly explain how such a balance sheet might look and why it is important to construct one.

3. Two forms of screening were recognized in the discussion of a local economic development program, "gross screening" and "detailed feasibility study." Are these different? If so, how?

4. Why might a community seek to create a formal organization to manage its economic development program? What are the advantages and disadvantages of such an organization?

5. The terms "shotgun" and "rifle" approach to economic development were used in the chapter. What do they mean? Are there advantages to selecting one over the other?

6. Why might a community seek to diversify its economy?

7. If a community were preparing a "comprehensive" economic development program, what are some of the general elements that you would suggest be included?

Central Place Theory and Market Analysis

6

THE PROVISION OF GOODS AND SERVICES by community merchants affects the well-being of community residents and is of particular interest for community economic analysis, for two reasons. First is the interdependence among merchants in various communities. Second is the merchant's interpretation of the market's socioeconomic characteristics and how they influence decisions to provide particular goods and services. Central place theory is the conceptual framework that addresses these two facets of economic activity. It does not provide all the detail needed to determine the feasibility of a particular investment in a particular market, but it does help to collect the details necessary for community analysis.

Central Place Theory

Central place theory offers insight into why specific goods and services are or are not present in a particular community. It specifically recognizes that no community's trade sector can be viewed in isolation. The theory initially assumes that the surface of the earth is a homogenous plane completely and uniformly covered with self-sufficient farming units (Berry 1967, pp. 59–73; Kivell and Shaw 1980, pp. 107–13; Parr 1973; Parr and Denike 1970, pp. 568–69; Potter 1982, pp. 23–56). Some farmers become more efficient in the production of some goods and services and sell that excess production to their neighbors. Economies of size and the cost of moving a good or service to the customer limit the amount these farmers can sell. Transportation cost advantages give each farmer/trader a spatial monopoly over nearby consumers (see Figure 3.7). The individual trader can increase sales through a lower delivered price, which generates more demand per person or increases the geographic area included in a trader's market. A circular market surrounds each trader (see Figure 3.9). Transportation costs, consumers' willingness to pay the delivered price, and competition from other locales determine the limits of each market. This system of circular markets leaves some areas unserved. Freedom of entry permits competitors to enter the market, serve presently unserved areas, and compete away the excess profits of current merchants. Thus entry of competitors creates a series of regular, hexagonal market areas. In central place theory the formation of these market areas parallels the locational interdependence or demand maximization approach to location theory (see Figures 3.9 and 3.10 in particular). Two critical behavioral assumptions of central place theory are that businesses will attempt to maximize the area served and that consumers will attempt to minimize the distance traveled.

TERMINOLOGY. Some integral concepts of central place theory are central places, tributary areas, central functions, functional units, thresholds, and range of a good or service (Foust and de Souza 1978). A *central place* is the physical location (place) from which goods and services are made available to the market. Central places are a cluster of retail and service functions at a geographic point; they provide a convenient focus for consumers to visit and purchase the goods and services they desire. Central places or service centers exist by trading with their tributary areas and are settlements exclusively supported by their role as market centers.

A *tributary area* is the countryside surrounding a central place and contains farms and the smaller central places that relate to a major central place.

A *central function* is any type of wholesale, retail, or service business or institution that serves a population. Some examples are an auto dealership, a bank, a grocery store, or a restaurant. The number and type of central functions vary with market size (the central place plus its tributary area).

Functional units are the separate types of goods and services provided by a central function or business. For example, a drugstore is a central function which provides the functional units of drugs and prescriptions, a lunch counter, magazines and newspapers, and sundries.

The terms *thresholds* and *range of a good or service* will be defined later.

CENTRAL PLACE HIERARCHY. When we recognize that central places and their tributary areas cover the entire market surface, the elements of a system of central places emerges (Berry and Garrison 1958b). Figure 6.1 shows central places (cities) arranged in tiers with each member of the tier, except those on the highest tier, subordinate to at least one other central place on a higher tier (i.e., hierarchy).[1] The lower levels of the hierarchy contain more central places serving smaller tributary areas and populations than the upper levels. Moving up the hierarchy, there are fewer central places, but each serves an increasingly larger geographic area and population than the communities (central places) at lower levels (see Figures 6.1, 6.2, and 6.3). At higher levels of the hierarchy, the number of central functions increases, and they become increasingly specialized (see Figure 6.4)[2]

A mutual dependence exists between the central place and its tributary or complementary area. The central place provides higher-order goods and services and the tributary area provides a market. The tributary area contains lower-order central places for all but the lowest-order center, which contains only farms or scattered-site residences.

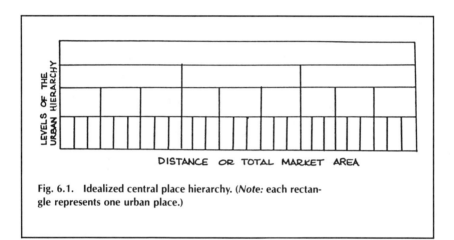

Fig. 6.1. Idealized central place hierarchy. (*Note:* each rectangle represents one urban place.)

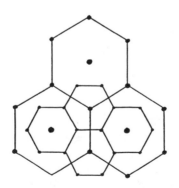

Fig. 6.2. Overlapping market areas in a central place system.

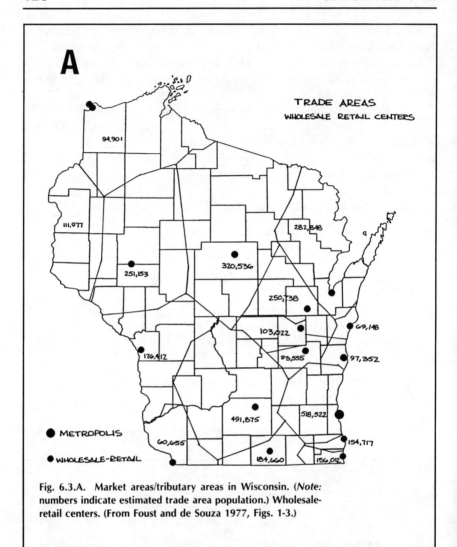

Fig. 6.3.A. Market areas/tributary areas in Wisconsin. (*Note:* numbers indicate estimated trade area population.) Wholesale-retail centers. (From Foust and de Souza 1977, Figs. 1-3.)

The tributary areas for different central places in a central place system become a collage of overlapping boundaries. The larger cities provide more specialized activities to a larger tributary area. These cities also provide the same general services found in the smaller cities. The smaller cities offer more generalized goods and services to geographically restricted trade areas. Each level of the central place hierarchy has its own system of hexagonal markets. A result of minimizing consumer travel and maximizing firms' markets is that many hexagonal market areas at different hierarchical

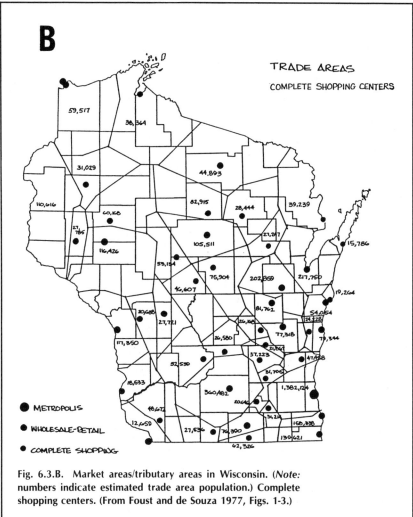

Fig. 6.3.B.   Market areas/tributary areas in Wisconsin. (*Note:* numbers indicate estimated trade area population.) Complete shopping centers. (From Foust and de Souza 1977, Figs. 1-3.)

levels will center at the same point (see Figure 6.2). This offering of several goods and services from one location prevents a totally random settlement pattern and increases the efficiency of providing each good or service.

The number of different economic (central) functions available differentiates city (central place) hierarchies (Berry and Garrison 1958b; Brush 1953; Parr 1973; Parr and Denike 1970). The number of central functions performed depends directly upon the population of the city and its tributary area (i.e., market size). This statement recognizes the economies of size

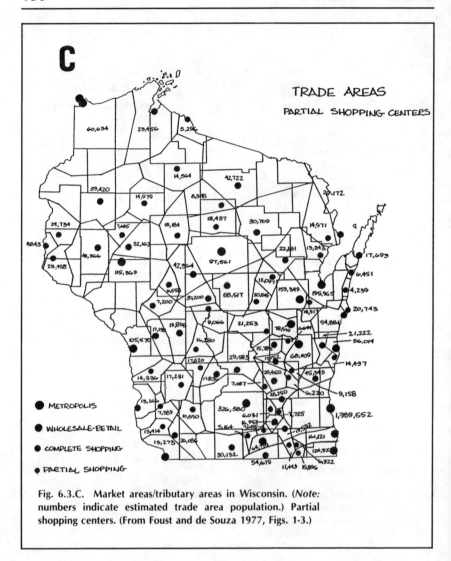

Fig. 6.3.C. Market areas/tributary areas in Wisconsin. (*Note:*
numbers indicate estimated trade area population.) Partial
shopping centers. (From Foust and de Souza 1977, Figs. 1-3.)

associated with providing various goods and services. Since economies vary
among types of goods or services (i.e., central functions), some are available only in the larger markets, while others are available in even the smallest markets. Likewise, economies of size vary with each community's social
and economic characteristics.[3] While the goods and services (central functions) provided determine where a place should be located within the central place hierarchy, population typically serves as a proxy for differentiating cities within the hierarchy. The logic for substituting population for an

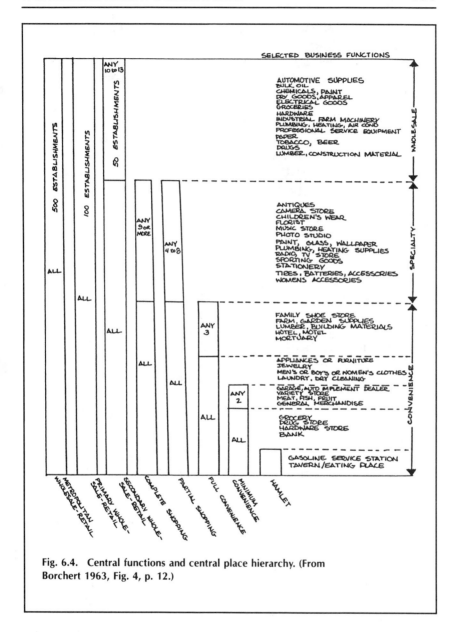

Fig. 6.4. Central functions and central place hierarchy. (From Borchert 1963, Fig. 4, p. 12.)

actual tabulation of central functions is that the market required to achieve economies of size and to make certain goods and services available is linked to population (see the discussion of Figures 3.10 and 6.5).

Figure 6.3 demonstrates the similarities of market size within a given hierarchical level and the differences between hierarchical levels (Foust and de Souza 1978). Figure 6.4 demonstrates how places come to be described as central. Every hamlet has a gasoline service station and a tavern/eating place. Every minimum convenience place has all the central functions found in a hamlet plus a grocery, drug store, hardware store, and bank. In addition, a minimum convenience place should have any two or more of these central functions: a garage/auto implement dealer, a variety store, a meat/fish/fruit market, and a general merchandise store. Different writers use different labels for the various levels of the central place hierarchy, but the labels, per se, are less important than the recognition that different levels of the hierarchy provide a different mix of goods and services.

The hierarchy of central places arises for several reasons (Parr 1973, pp. 185–87; Parr and Denike 1970, p. 568). From the point of view of business, one reason for the hierarchy is conditions of entry. With free entry[4] and the minimum market required (threshold) to support the business available, the business will exist. It cannot exist without the minimum required market. Another reason why this hierarchy arises is economies of scale. How much output must be produced for the business to reduce its average costs to some minimal amount? Both minimum market and economies of scale are linked to the number of customers or volume of sales in the community and available to the business (i.e., not already served by competitors).

Consumers play a part in creating the hierarchy of central places as well. First, they wish to minimize the distance traveled to purchase any good or service. Therefore, frequently purchased items should be available nearby; less frequently purchased items need not be located nearby (Curry 1967). Consumers' desire to minimize total travel means that they go to higher-order centers only for the goods and services not available in lower-order centers. (Even people who live in higher-order centers will purchase lower-order goods and services in their neighborhood stores; see Figure 6.4.) Consumers make only single-purpose shopping trips to the higher-order centers. Second, the type of shopping also influences the hierarchy of goods and services. Goods and services that are everyday convenience items (milk, bread) will be available in smaller central places, but if an item is subject to comparative shopping (furniture, automobiles), it is likely to be available only in larger centers. Third, the type of transportation system available affects the hierarchy through the frequency of shopping and the spatial dimension of the market area. An important element here is whether individual (automobile) or mass transit is the source of transportation. Consumers dependent upon public transportation may find geographic as well as time limits placed on shopping. Both factors limit the market available to businesses in a central place.

The business and consumer forces described above are woven into the concept of the *threshold* of a good or service and of the *range* of a good or service used to delineate the central place hierarchy.

RANGE OF A GOOD OR SERVICE. The *range of a good or service* is the maximum distance that people will travel to purchase that good or service at a particular location (Berry and Garrison 1958a, p. 304; Olsson 1966; Parr and Denike 1970). The range of a good or service is the outer limit of the geographic market for this good or service from a particular location.[5]

The geographic limit of a market is measured in terms of physical separation, time, and travel costs. Other determinants are the ease of access to competitive markets, transportation facilities, and technology (Shepard and Thomas 1980, pp. 44–55). Ease of access to competitive markets affects the geographic limits of the market area. Physical features (mountains, rivers, lakes) influence access. Transportation facilities and technology are important because better facilities and faster movement permit greater spatial movement by consumers.

Individual characteristics (age, income, education, movement imagery, and behavior space) influence the distance people are willing to travel (Shepard and Thomas 1980, pp. 44–55). Young, well-educated, high-income people are likely to travel farther and more frequently than others. The distribution of income affects the number of people able to pay the transportation costs of greater movement. Movement imagery involves the consumer's perceived options about movement from one place to another in the quest of a desired good or service (see the discussion of Table 6.4 below). The mode of travel, travel time, the cost of overcoming distance, and communication flows affect movement imagery. Behavior space is that part of the total central place system which the individual perceives as a potential source for satisfying his demand for goods or services. It is influenced by previous shopping experiences in the various central places and by the individual's sources of information (e.g., advertising).

The range of a good or service is the distance people will travel to purchase it. It is influenced by frequency of purchase, transportation modes and facilities, and communication flows as well as by the socioeconomic characteristics of the consumer.

DEMAND THRESHOLD. *Demand threshold* is the minimum market required to support a particular good or service and still yield a normal profit for the merchant (Berry and Garrison 1958b; Berry and Garrison 1958a, p. 306; Olsson 1966; Parr and Denike, 1970, pp. 570–72).[6] The concept is based on the internal economies of the firm and the characteristics of consumer demand. Demand thresholds are not absolute, but vary with the type of good or service. In estimating whether the local market is sufficient to yield a market threshold for a good or service, the market contained within the real, not the ideal, range of a good or service should be used. Demand thresholds are usually measured in terms of population, rather than quantity sold, on the assumption that consumers are homogenous in their buying power (income) and tastes.

The internal economies of the firm affect the thresholds (Parr and Denike 1970, pp. 569–71; Olsson 1966). Without any shift in demand, an increase in costs requires a greater market area to break even. In Figure 6.5, both firms face the same demand curve, AR. Firm 1, with cost structure AC_1 exhibiting earlier economies of size, operates at a profit even at output Q_1, while firm 2 experiences a loss at that output. Firm 1 could experience a leftward shift in its demand curve to AR' and still maintain profitability at Q_1 sales (firm 1's threshold). Firm 2 requires at least Q_2 output to be profitable (firm 2's threshold). If firm 1 and firm 2 sell the same product, the reason for the different thresholds is internal costs. Labor costs, along with other production and selling costs plus different technologies, shift the average cost curve up or down and have an effect analogous to a shift in the demand curve. Higher cost structures require a higher threshold ($Q_2 > Q_1$) for profitable operations by the firm.

Economies of size imply that a firm can increase production, lower

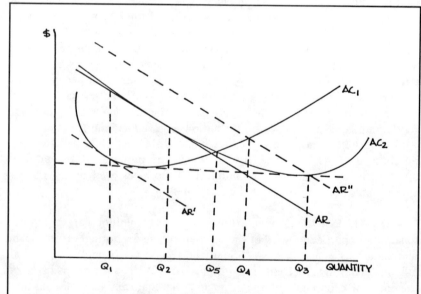

Fig. 6.5. Effect of cost structure on demand threshold.

unit costs, and compete in delivered price for the customers of other producers (with higher production costs) even if it is located farther away from the customers. In Figure 6.5 the economies of size for firm 1 are achieved at a sales volume of Q_2, but firm 2 requires sales of Q_3 to have a comparable unit cost. Beyond output Q_s, firm 2 produces at a sufficiently lower price to overcome the delivered price advantage firm 1 currently enjoys; in this situation, firm 2 can underprice firm 1 and capture some of firm 1's market, providing the demand curve is tangent or lies to the right of the cost curve (i.e., AR $\geq$ AC).

Shifts in demand have effects on thresholds analogous to a shift in average costs. According to Figure 6.5, if demand shifted to AR'', firm 1's cost structure would cause it to operate at a loss at sales of more than Q_4.

Figure 6.5 demonstrates why demand thresholds vary among goods or services. Average cost curves AC_1 and AC_2 could represent the cost of producing and selling two separate items. The product represented by AC_1 achieves its economies in a smaller market and therefore can be found in smaller central places. AC_2 requires a larger market or central place to be feasible. The differences in either demand, or costs, or both, affect thresholds.

Changes in the central functions offered by a given central place occur because of population changes, income changes, and changes in production and marketing techniques (i.e., changes in either markets or firm economies) (Johansen and Fuguitt 1984; Johnson 1982; Parr and Denike 1970, pp. 574–77).

Income and population changes affect the market threshold. An increase in income usually increases the volume of purchases by the same number of people (assuming a normal or superior good). In Figure 6.6 the original income level is represented by AR_1 and the demand threshold by Q_1. If income increases, demand shifts rightward to AR_2, exceeding the merchant's demand threshold, and the merchant experiences excess profits. This attracts competitors into the market and eventually forces the merchant's demand back down to AR_1 (i.e., the merchant will sell only Q_1 output). A decline in income shifts the demand curve to AR_3, and the merchant will stop providing that good or service because he cannot cover his average costs.[7] A demand curve of AR_3 means that the good or service will be offered only from a higher-order central place with a sufficient market to generate threshold sales.

Changes in marketing and production technology that require either larger or smaller markets to achieve economies of size (see Figure 6.5) affect thresholds. If the new technology requires a larger market, the number of firms offering that good or service will be reduced, and pressure for it to be offered only from higher-order places will be generated. If the new technology lowers average costs (i.e., permits a smaller market), then higher-order

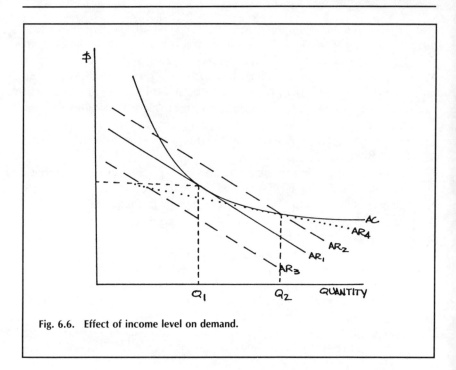

Fig. 6.6.   Effect of income level on demand.

goods or services appear in lower-order places (Parr and Denike 1970, pp. 575–77). A shift in the average cost curve from AC_2 to AC_1 in Figure 6.5 represents this situation.

Forces that shift the demand curve for a community also affect demand thresholds. The rate of population change within the market area, including the change in the social or ethnic or rural-urban mix, is one force altering the slope of the demand curve from AR_1 to AR_4 in Figure 6.6.

ESTIMATES OF DEMAND THRESHOLDS. The thresholds for different goods or services vary by type of good or service, location within the country, number of competitors in the community, and over time. Reasons for these variations have been articulated previously; some empirical evidence of the variation will now be offered.

Table 6.1 provides estimates of the average number of people associated with the presence of a given the good or service. The threshold varies with the good or service. Only 77 people were required to support a tavern in Wisconsin in 1974, while a shoe store required almost ten times that many people (712). Part of the difference, of course, is differing frequency of purchase. It is important to remember that demand thresholds represent the average number of people associated with a specific number of firms

Table 6.1. Population Required To Support One or More Establishments of Selected Functions, Wisconsin, 1974

Function	Number of Establishments			
	1	2	3	4
Tavern	77	244	478	711
Food store	92	1,104	4,697	29,119
Fuel oil dealer	164	685	1,577	2,850
Gas station	186	459	799	1,135
Feed store	247	4,895	28,106	97,124
Beautician	268	851	1,673	2,702
Insurance agency	293	666	1,077	1,514
Farm implement store	309	3,426	14,004	38,025
Restaurant	316	754	1,253	1,797
Hardware store	372	1,925	5,032	9,949
Auto repair shop	375	1,148	2,209	3,517
Motel	384	2,072	5,557	11,189
Real estate agency	418	1,226	2,301	3,597
Auto dealer	420	1,307	2,937	4,063
Plumber	468	2,717	7,604	15,780
Physician	493	1,352	2,436	3,702
Lawyer	497	1,169	1,927	2,748
Radio-TV sales	521	1,815	3,765	6,316
Drive-in eating place	537	4,851	17,572	43,799
Dentist	563	1,744	3,379	5,402
Supermarket	587	2,968	7,610	14,881
Appliance store	607	3,709	10,691	22,659
Liquor store	613	4,738	15,669	36,509
Barbershop	632	5,297	18,372	44,404
Drugstore	638	4,285	13,053	28,771
Auto parts dealer	642	5,496	19,284	46,991
Laundromat	649	5,665	20,114	49,264
Women's clothing store	678	5,471	18,544	44,133
Department store	691	5,408	18,012	42,295
Drycleaner	692	4,131	11,746	24,655
Shoe store	712	7,650	30,670	82,146

Source: Foust and Pickett 1974, Table 1.

offering a particular good or service—there is no guarantee that 77 people will yield sufficient sales and profits for a tavern to succeed. Differences in costs and profit expectations also play a role.

Table 6.1 also provides information on the demand thresholds for multiple stores (functional units) providing the same central function. Not only do different goods and services have different initial demand thresholds, but the additional population required to support the second, third, and fourth store also differs. It requires 167 more people to support a second tavern in Wisconsin, and 234 more people to support a third; this compares with 6,938 more people to support a second shoe store. The differences in the average population required to support one more firm offering a particular good or service reflects the average population needed to support a single firm. There is no reason why one firm cannot serve more people (it takes a total of 244 people to justify the second tavern because many of them will also go to the first tavern). A second reason is that the indivisibility of the investment in a tavern prevents marginal adjustments until some critical market mass is reached and the second firm appears.

Figure 6.7 displays information about the number of stores and population. Each additional functional unit (store) of the same central function requires an increasing number of people. The curves in the figure are of the form:

$$P = aB^n \qquad\qquad (6.1)$$

where P is population size, n is number of stores, B is a measure of the economies of size for this particular good or service, and a is an empirically estimated parameter (Parr and Denike 1970, p. 578).

Table 6.2 compares the population required to support similar businesses in three distinctly different locales. While the threshold populations are generally of comparable magnitudes, they are not the same; compare the figures for dentists and florists in New Zealand with those in the other

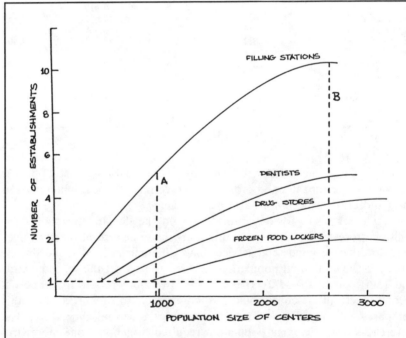

Fig. 6.7. Rates of change of selected central functions and population size. (After Berry and Garrison 1958a, p. 308.)

Table 6.2.   Thresholds for Selected Functions in Three Different Locales

Function	Washington	New Zealand	Wisconsin
		Threshold Size	
Tavern	282	–	77
Gas station	196	261	186
Physician	380	491	493
Barbershop	386	668	632
Dentist	426	1,019	563
Hardware store	431	414	372
Auto repair shop	435	293	375
Lawyer	582	830	497
Clothing store	590	388	678
Bank	610	759	643
Farm implement dealer	650	431	309
Florist	729	1,280	726
Drycleaner	754	781	692
Jewelry store	827	926	722
Undertaker	1,214	1,137	–

Source: Foust and de Souza 1978, p. 92.

two locales, for example. Factors such as tastes and preferences, access, income, and cost of operation in different locales prevent a simplistic head count from being a uniform measure of market sufficiency in different communities.

Table 6.3 displays the temporal change in average number of people required for the appearance of the specific central function. There is no consistency in the pattern. Of the 41 functions, 17 required a larger supporting population and 24 required a smaller supporting population ten years later. In some cases the population increase is a factor of five (appliance stores) and the decrease is an factor of three (veterinarians).

Thresholds vary among goods and services, over time, among areas, and by the size market required for multiple occurrences. The size and characteristics of the market, along with internal economies of size, also influence thresholds.

IRREGULARITIES IN CENTRAL PLACES. The hexagonal markets of central place theory presume a homogenous plane with a uniformly settled population. However, many distortions affect the size and shape of these hexagonal markets (Goldstucker et al. 1978, pp. 6–15; Simmons 1973/74). The transportation network (roads, railroads) influences the size and shape of markets. An unequal distribution of natural resources and physical barriers, such as rivers and mountains, affects the shape of the market area. Economies of size and different population densities alter market area size but not shape.

LIMITATIONS OF CENTRAL PLACE THEORY. While central place theory offers considerable insight into the spatial allocation of consumer functions, its

Table 6.3.   Population Threshold Sizes and Ranks for Selected Central Functions, Central Iowa, 1960 and 1970

Function	1960 Population Threshold	Rank	1970 Population Threshold	Rank
Grocery store	528	1	428	1
Automobile dealer	605	2	752	5
Gas station	811	3	558	2
Hardware store	852	4	1,392	16
Bank	872	5	850	9
Restaurant	887	6	763	6
Physician	935	7	751	4
Animal husbandry service	1,030	8	1,234	14
Lumberyard	1,037	9	1,121	13
Furniture store	1,060	10	1,631	19
Fuel oil dealer	1,273	11	690	3
Appliance store	1,452	12	7,389	35
Drygoods and general merchandise	1,614	13	2,505	26
Radio-TV repair	1,641	14	1,902	23
Frozen food locker	1,656	15	4,334	33
Insurance agency	1,668	16	1,073	12
Church	1,709	17	1,053	11
Beautician	1,775	18	938	10
Tavern	1,889	19	830	8
Drugstore	1,906	20	1,502	18
Railroad terminal	1,907	21	2,671	27
Dentist	1,938	22	1,860	22
Auto repair shop	2,038	23	1,716	20
Veterinarian	2,196	24	768	7
Real estate agency	2,436	25	1,390	15
Hay, feed, and grain store	2,740	26	2,047	25
Electrical supply shop	2,770	27	1,489	17
Laundromat	2,813	28	2,779	28
Lawyer	2,825	29	1,971	24
Drycleaner	3,239	30	1,746	21
Sporting goods shop	3,416	31	10,721	37
Women's clothing store	3,793	32	3,121	29
Electrical repair shop	3,971	33	3,803	32
Farm implement dealer	3,975	34	3,259	30
Radio-TV sales	4,221	35	7,031	34
Assembly hall	4,309	36	3,320	31
Intercity bus terminal	6,295	37	12,157	38
Hospital	7,596	38	10,229	36
Stockyard	11,829	39	13,293	39
Movie	11,897	40	16,434	40
Men's clothing store	21,291	41	18,068	41

Source: Bell 1973, pp. 122–23.

limitations must be recognized (Blomnestein et al. 1980, p. 160; Cohen and Lewis 1967; Henderson 1972, pp. 436–37; Parr 1973; Parr and Denike 1970; Shepard and Thomas 1980, pp. 21–23; Turner and Cole 1980). It emphasizes the demand elements of the market almost to the exclusion of supply factors by assuming that suppliers of a given good or service have similar cost structures. It assumes that the physical dimension of space is the dominant element; the consumer's perception of space is not even considered. New transportation technology that reduces travel time, or costs, or both, and alters consumers' perceptions of access to a given place is not seen as altering market size because physical distance is unchanged. The theory does not consider qualitative variations among alternative shopping locations (central places), such as product selection, parking availability, store hours, and clerks' attitudes.[8]

The theory implicitly assumes that an equilibrium between demand and supply will be maintained, ignoring the process of adjustment to disturbances. Since the spatial distribution of shoppers is given, the potential effects of changing residential patterns are not considered, though fluctuating residential settlement patterns make it difficult to determine whether a market threshold exists in a given area.

The exclusion of multipurpose shopping trips distorts the results of the analysis (Parr 1973, p. 191). If the consumer makes multipurpose trips, the total cost (purchase price plus transportation) for any item will be lowered because transportation costs are shared among more than one good or service and thus the real range of all goods and services is increased.[9] This phenomenon is particularly significant for stores offering lower-order goods and services in higher-order central places; such stores can acquire excess profits because their market is larger than it would be if that good or service had to bear the full cost of consumer travel.[10] This, of course, assumes that the bidding for labor or land in the central place does not shift the average cost curve. The spreading of travel costs over several goods and services purchased on a multipurpose shopping trip reduces the price advantage of firms locating near the consumer (i.e., reduces the effective market where the local firm has some monopoly price control). The assumption that consumers have complete knowledge of their spatial options in purchasing a given good or service eliminates the consumer risk reduction strategy of bypassing a nearer intermediate center, which may or may not have the item, and making the purchases in a higher center (Shepard and Thomas 1980, p. 22; Stabler and Williams 1973, pp. 457–58).

A final criticism of central place theory is that it fails to explain the evolution of places among different levels of the hierarchy (Parr 1981). The theory is not dynamic but uses comparative statics to explain conditions, not changes.

SUMMARY. Central place theory is appropriate when considering trade and services rather than resource-oriented production, such as mining or manufacturing. The major elements of this city-centered organization of economic activities include the following important concepts: (1) the system of cities can be arranged in a hierarchy according to the functions performed by each city; (2) lower-order centers provide generalized goods and services and depend upon higher-order centers for more specialized services; (3)

areas of economic influence emanate from each central place (Carroll 1955); and (4) the size of a central place, the complexity and number of central functions, and the magnitude of its geographic influence are directly proportional.

The significance of central place theory to community economic analysis is its recognition that the community is part of a system. No community, especially a smaller one, can provide all the goods and services necessary and desired. Residents in smaller communities and their surrounding tributary areas must rely on larger communities for many goods and services.

The community economic analyst must recognize the relationship between the range of a good or service and the demand threshold for it. The range of a good or service indicates the geographic limits of the market area for that central function. The threshold of a good or service indicates whether there are sufficient sales within that market area to justify offering that particular central function from a certain central place.

The geographic limit of a good or service depends upon its delivered price compared with the delivered price from a supplier at an alternative location. Economies of size (production costs), the density of demand (settlement), and transportation costs influence the geographic limit. The greater the production required to achieve economies of size, the greater the market area required. The density of demand is the number of consumers per acre or square mile within the market area, and includes their income level. An increase in the density of demand implies, *ceteris paribus,* that the geographic area needed to provide a sufficient market decreases. Increases in transportation costs reduce the geographic limit of a market, and declines in transportation costs increase the geographic limit of the market.

Market Area Analy

The community economist's concern with market area analysis derives from the influence of the availability of goods and services on the quality of life and the role that trade and service activities play in the community's economy. Some of the basic questions addressed in a community's market analysis are: (1) What goods and services are being offered? (2) What is the sales potential? (3) How much of the potential sales is actually being captured? (4) How can sales be increased?

The first question can be answered through a relatively simple survey of merchants or consumers. This survey could use secondary data such as the Census of Business, the Yellow Pages of the telephone directory, Chamber of Commerce membership, and, in smaller communities, just familiarity. Questions 2, 3, and 4 require delineating the community's trade area and examining the market characteristics within it. In addition, these questions require some awareness of the concepts embodied in central place hierarchies.

TRADE AREA. A *trade area* is a geographically delineated area containing potential customers for goods and services offered for sale by a particular firm or group of firms (Davies 1977, pp. 146–48; Huff 1964, p. 34). This geographically delineated area corresponds to the central place theory concept of range of a good or service. The trade area for a given functional unit (e.g., drugstore) depends upon the highest-order good or service (central function) it provides. Thus, the drugstore's trade area will depend upon how far people will travel for prescriptions, magazines, toiletries, or sundries or to eat at its lunch counter. The trade area of a community depends upon the highest-order good or service offered by the community because consumers will make multipurpose trips. Once they have traveled to the community to purchase that item, consumers are quite likely to purchase other items for which, alone, they would not have traveled as far.

Trade area analysis enables the merchant to understand the market better—its geographic size and shape, the number of potential customers, and potential sales. The analysis also helps to focus promotion and gives the merchant some idea of whose tastes and preferences should be considered in marketing decisions. For the community, the same questions are relevant.

DELINEATING TRADE AREAS. Any community market analysis must start with a delineation of the geographic area from which the community draws its retail customers. This delineation can be accomplished through several techniques (Goldstucker et al. 1978, pp. 19–51; Turner and Cole 1980; Wagner 1974, p. 31), all of which attempt to measure the range of the highest-order good or service the community offers. One approach assumes that the trade area of the community matches the circulation area of the local newspaper. Since much of the advertising by businesses in smaller communities is newspaper-oriented, this approach has some merit. (For smaller neighborhood businesses in an urban area, a local shopping guide or neighborhood paper might be used, rather than the metro area paper.) The key is to determine from what geographic area the merchant expects to draw clientele. There is no reason to presume that newspaper circulation areas correspond to the trade area for most of the goods and services offered by a community.

A second approach uses post office routes. Again, the presumption is that a communications link (mail) is the major determinant of retail trade information and the range of a good or service.

A third approach is to find the geographic location of existing customers by tracing the addresses on checks and charge accounts.

A less subtle mechanism of determining customer location is for the community to do a formal customer survey asking customers in the community where they live, about information sources used before shopping, about other businesses visited, why they are shopping here rather than elsewhere, etc. Two types of surveys can be done. The first is at the "shop door," in which actual shoppers are asked for their opinions. The second is a random survey of area households. The first approach does not give an indication of market penetration but provides relatively good insight into who customers are, where they live, and why they shop locally. The second approach yields information on market penetration, but tells little about the geographic size of the market area or the specifics about customers.

A final approach relying solely on secondary data is called Reilly's Law of Retail Gravitation, which derives from gravity models of spatial behavior. It is discussed a bit later in detail.

GRAVITY MODELS. Any discussion of retail market analysis requires an understanding of the spatial distribution of consumers and of how they make spatial decisions (i.e., where they live and where they shop relative to where they live). The gravity model predicts these decisions. It relates the rates at which users will make use of an activity or commodity provided at a given location by considering the effect of the distance separating the user from the activity. It thus incorporates the influence of mass and distance on interaction, and is sometimes referred to as social-physics because it is analogous to the physical laws of gravity (Carrothers 1956; Colwell 1982; Isard 1975; Niedercorn and Beckdolt 1969). The logic is that the larger a place is, the greater the attraction, and the farther away it is, the less the attraction. The specific measures of mass and distance vary with the analytical questions raised. Some measures of mass are population, employment, income, total sales, and retail space. Some measures of distance are miles, time, and travel cost.

The gravity model postulates that the interaction between two population centers will vary directly with some function of the population size of each center, and inversely with some function of the distance between the centers (Bucklin 1971; Goldstucker et al. 1978, pp. 24–27; Kivell and Shaw 1980, pp. 113–18; Olsson 1966; Richardson 1969a, pp. 97–102; Shepard and Thomas 1980, pp. 23–28). Equation (6.2) is a generalized version of the model:

$$I_{ij} = K \frac{A_i^a A_j^b}{D_{ij}^c} \tag{6.2}$$

where I is the expected interaction between places i and j or the influence of place j on place i, A_i and A_j represent the size (mass) of places i and j, D_{ij}

represents the distance between places i and j, and K is a constant. Exponents a, b, and c are estimated parameters for the gravity model and vary with the type of economic activity being considered. For example, c is a measure of the disutility of distance to perform the economic activity. The general value of c is 2, but it will vary depending upon the specific activity (Bucklin 1967, p. 11; Bucklin 1971; Goldstucker et al. 1978, pp. 27, 67–72; Mottershaw 1968). Exponents a and b are generally assumed equal to 1, but need not be. Equation (6.2) is an unconstrained gravity model because the interaction (the number of trips between two centers) increases with population size and decreases with an increase in distance.

A slight modification of the model in (6.2) yields a measure of the interaction between a given place j and all other places i:

$$I_{ij} = Z \sum_{i \neq j} \frac{P_i}{D_{ji}} \qquad (6.3)$$

where I is interaction, Z is an empirically estimated constant, P_i is population in city i, D_{ji} is distance between city j and city i. This interaction can be mapped to show equal levels of interaction, i.e., isopotential contours, as shown in Figure 6.8. Any point on the B, C, or D contour of the figure has the same interaction with city A as any other point on that respective line. Note that city B is sufficiently large to overcome the disadvantage of distance and still has the same level of interaction as the much nearer, but smaller, city D.

The unconstrained gravity model presumes that interaction (sales) increases with increased attractiveness of the community. However, exoge-

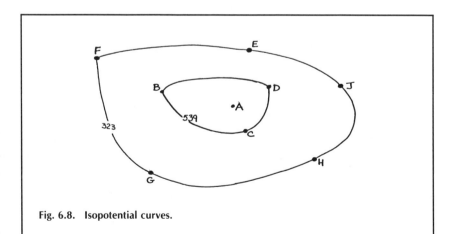

Fig. 6.8. Isopotential curves.

nous factors (e.g., family size and income) limit the total volume of sales from any given location despite increases in retail facilities or decreases in distance. In this situation a constrained gravity model estimates the proportion of the fixed total that site i receives. This proportion is sometimes referred to as market share (Krueckeberg and Silvers 1978, pp. 300–302):

$$P_{ij} = S_j / D_{ij}^\lambda \sum_{j=1}^{n} \frac{S_j}{D_{ij}^\lambda} \qquad (6.4)$$

The constrained gravity model expresses the probability of the consumer at i going to j when there are n possible alternative shopping sites and only a fixed number of trips from i is possible (Huff 1964, pp. 36–37). In (6.4), P_{ij} is the probability of a consumer at place i going to place j to shop when he/she has n possible alternative shopping areas, S_j represents the size of the shopping area and proxies the variety of goods and services available D_{ij} is the distance/travel time from point i to point j, and λ is a parameter measuring the effect of distance or travel time on different goods. A nonlinear size effect (e.g., multipurpose trips, congestion) can be incorporated with a nonunitary exponent on S_j; it seldom is, however (Shepard and Thomas 1980, p. 26).

Once the probability of a consumer at place i shopping at place j is estimated (P_{ij}), Equation (6.5) yields the expected number of customers (E_{ij}) at i going to j, given the number of potential customers (C_i) at i (Huff 1964, p. 36):

$$E_{ij} = P_{ij}C_i \qquad (6.5)$$

The gravity model estimates the expected flow from one economic center to another. Gravity models move away from the simplistic notion of central place theory in which people go to the nearest available place; rather, customers trade off between attraction (size) and disadvantage (distance). Gravity models deal with customers' reactions to size and accessibility of shopping locations rather than with customer perceptions and characteristics (Blomnestein et al. 1980, p. 160; Huff 1961). When used in market area analyses, gravity models suffer from an inability to incorporate the effects of multipurpose trips, which distort actual and expected interaction. They are not deterministic or optimization models but give a probable interaction between two economic units. They are more appropriate for existing shopping locations than new ones because a new location requires customers to change existing spatial shopping patterns. The model does not provide insight into what causes customers to change spatial shopping patterns; it collapses spatial behavior responses into just distance and size (Shepard and Thomas 1980, p. 27).

REILLY'S LAW OF RETAIL GRAVITATION. Reilly's Law of Retail Gravitation derives from the gravity model and is used to identify market boundaries (Batty 1978, pp. 185–91; Reilly 1931). It states that shoppers living at any point between two towns (*A* and *B*) will be attracted to one town or another in accordance with the relative population of the two towns (P_A/P_B), and inversely with the square of the relative distance of the shopper's point from the two towns (D_B/D_A)^2 (Krueckeburg and Silvers 1974, p. 292). This presumes that people will shop only in the town with the greatest attraction and that customers will not cross market boundaries.

To identify a market boundary requires only setting the formula as follows:

$$\left(\frac{P_A}{P_B}\right) \times \left(\frac{D_B}{D_A}\right)^2 = 1 \qquad (6.6)$$

At the point where the formula is equal to one, the customer is indifferent about where to shop. In other words, if the market boundary is impenetrable, the customer must be sitting on the market boundary. The boundary of a community's trade area is the point in space where the potential customers flow equally in opposite directions (i.e., the trade area breaking point). Population measures the city's attractiveness and ability to influence its surrounding countryside or tributary area. Alternative measures of attractiveness are advertising expenditures, sales volume, and retail floor space (Wagner 1974, p. 31). Distance impedes the flow of customers to the community and acts in a negative fashion on retail sales. All this says is that a community will draw a higher proportion of the residents closer to it than of residents farther away. Some measures of distance are miles, time, and costs.

Converse (1949) adapted Reilly's Law to estimate the breaking point or maximum distance from point *A* that customers will travel to shop at place *A* rather than go to place *B*:[11]

$$D_A = \frac{D_{AB}}{1 + \sqrt{P_B/P_A}} \qquad (6.7)$$

Figure 6.3 uses Reilly's Law to delineate market areas/tributary areas for different levels of the Wisconsin central place hierarchy.

The ease of application of Reilly's Law requires some simplifying assumptions that the analyst must acknowledge (Batty 1978, pp. 185–91; Wagner 1974, pp. 31–32). First, it assumes that the population in the two places is homogenous except for size, that there are no demand differences caused by cultural, economic, or social factors (e.g., income, education). Second, the law should be used to compare communities of similar size.

For example, it cannot be used to delineate the trade area boundary between a community of 180,000 people and one of 5,000 people. The analyst should compare boundaries only between places at the same level of the central place hierarchy. More explicitly, to use Reilly's Law to calculate market boundaries requires assuming that each of the cities involved offers the same package of goods and services and that this package does not change dramatically over time. Third, Reilly's Law is not very useful in delineating the trade area of urban shopping centers or neighborhood shopping centers in metropolitan areas. It is most useful when applied to trading centers surrounded by rural areas where the number of alternative shopping areas is relatively limited (Huff 1964, p. 36). Fourth, the law's use of population to measure both origin and destination assumes that the number of people has a symmetrical influence on both, yet population is not a symmetrical measure and has no correlation with shoppers' perceptions of a shopping area (Batty 1978, pp. 188–91). Fifth, the use of distance to measure spatial relationships does not capture consumers' perceptions of distance. The model does not permit adjustments by businesses in an attempt to respond to or alter consumer shopping patterns (Blomnestein et al. 1980).

Reilly's Law tends to overestimate the number of potential customers in an area because it assumes that the consumers inside the trade area boundary shop only in the community. This generates a discontinuous trade area because all shoppers within a trade area are assumed to shop only at the nearest shopping area (Figure 6.9, A). However, market boundaries are not impenetrable, and trade areas are not discontinuous. Rather, most consumers at A generally shop at A, but some will generally shop at B, and frequently those who generally shop at A sometimes shop at B, or vice

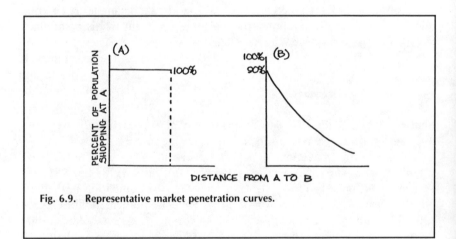

Fig. 6.9. Representative market penetration curves.

versa. It is thus true that distance affects frequency of the shopping visit (*B* in the figure), but it is not an absolute measure, as seen in *A* in the figure. Reilly's Law is more appropriate for identifying the trade area for shopping goods (nonstandardized goods and services such as furniture, automobiles, and health care) than for convenience or intermediate goods. The purchaser buys shopping goods only after comparing price, quality, and type among stores and places. The purchaser buys convenience goods and services (groceries, gasoline) with a minimal amount of effort and usually at the most convenient and accessible store. Convenience goods or services typically have a small unit value; purchases are frequent; they are made soon after the idea of the purchase enters the buyer's mind. Intermediate goods (drugs, hardware items, banking and drycleaning services) possess characteristics of both shopping and convenience goods; the purchaser will spend some time shopping, although the time is minimal, and typically the purchase is made close to home.

Reilly's Law has a considerable amount of appeal in its logic and relative simplicity, and it has some economic justification, but it cannot be used by itself to identify trade area boundaries. It is also necessary to consider other community linkages (e.g., school district boundaries) and physical features.

OTHER DETERMINANTS OF TRADE AREA BOUNDARIES. Up to this point, a community's market area has been assumed to be a function of population and distance. However, other physical and nonphysical features affect the market area (see the discussion of irregularities in central places earlier in this chapter) (Cohen and Lewis 1967; Goldstucker et al. 1978, pp. 6–15; Turner and Cole 1980). The trade area of a community can be influenced through distribution of information by newspaper, television, or radio coverage. Proximity to larger trade centers alters the shape and size of a community's trade area. The shopping atmosphere present in the community (variety of goods and services offered, customer credit policies, reputation of the businesses, and customer service) also influences its market area. If the community's businesses are progressive and dynamic in their leadership and marketing techniques, they will capture more customers than would be expected on the basis of population and distance alone. Since shopping is more than just buying goods and services, social and recreational attractions bring shoppers to the community.

Such considerations become the elements of the *behavioral approach to consumer shopping decisions* (Cadwallader 1975; Potter 1982, pp. 132–80; Shepard and Thomas 1980, pp. 29–55). Behavioral approaches move away from spatial choice based solely on population and distance, as embodied in central place and gravity models. Huff (1961) suggests three forces that interact to affect the spatial shopping decision. They are: (1)

geographic location and social differentiation, (2) nature of available stores, and (3) influence of personal mobility. Table 6.4 displays the forces influencing the shopping decision made by the consumer. The purpose here is not to review the socio-psychological forces affecting retail markets, but to recognize their importance to the question at hand and to illustrate the limitations of using just size and distance as a guide.

Table 6.4.   Elements of the Shopper's Location Decision

Geographic and Social Differentation (Elements of Value System)
   Geographic location
   Ethical and moral code
   Ethnic affiliation
   Income
   Personality
   Sex
   Occupation
   Age
   Education
   Mental synthesizing abilities

Nature of Available Stores (Elements of Behavior Space Perception)
   Reputation of source
   Personal amenities
   Services rendered
   Product price

Influence of Personal Mobility (Elements of Movement Imagery)
   Transport mode
   Travel time
   Travel cost
   Parking cost

Source: After Huff 1961.

TRADE ENVIRONMENT. An *ecological approach to retail trade analysis* focuses on how different businesses relate to each other to form a complete or incomplete trade sector and considers those business relationships, the location of the population, work, and transportation (Davies 1977; Goldstucker et al. 1978, pp. 35–40; Kivell and Shaw 1980, pp. 118–20; Shepard and Thomas 1980, pp. 61–71; Turner and Cole 1980). The dynamics of change affect both the causes for spatial shopping decisions and the range of choices available to both consumer and merchant. In some cases these forces are external to either party (e.g., new retailing technology, transportation costs, national advertising campaigns, and national monetary policies). In other cases the stimulus for change is internal (e.g., shifts in marketing strategies, store hours, reallocation of spending through family life cycle).

Blomnestein et al. (1980) argue that consumer and retail market analyses must consider the dynamics of the interrelationship between consumers and merchants. Profits, market share, shifts in marketing strategies, and marketing priorities affect the merchant. At the same time, changes in income, social status, and opinions about and satisfaction derived from the use of specific goods or services affect the consumer. The dynamics of the system means that a change by either merchant or consumer affects the other, which in turn feeds back information and causes further response.

Blomnestein et al. (1980) suggest a need to integrate the quantifiable and nonquantifiable aspects of the merchant, the consumer and their interaction. The major aspects they select are personal attributes of consumer, and merchant, consumer and merchant perceptions of shopping facilities, and shop attributes.

The personal attributes of the consumer they believe to be important are age, income, residential location, average expenditures for daily and nondaily commodities, and frequency of shopping. These attributes create a typology of shoppers that permits the aggregation of data on individuals into trends and general market characteristics and permits the merchant to determine what merchandise, merchandising techniques, advertising, and pricing strategies might be most appropriate.

The second component of the analysis is the merchants' and consumers' perception of the shopping area (community) and its facilities. Some measures include floor space, average prices, accessibility, and physical attractiveness of the shops and neighborhood.

Individual merchants and shops are put into homogenous groups on the basis of type of shop, floor space, average profits, annual sales, growth prospects, liquidity position, and competitive power. These characteristics give some indication of the merchant's ability to bring about change in the market environment.

A comparison of merchant and consumer rankings of perceptions of the shopping area (community) characteristics gives an indication of how well the shopping area meets consumer needs. The difference in perceptions among merchants and consumers becomes the starting point for a community strategy to change the community's shopping image and facilities and the type of goods and services available.

SALES POTENTIAL AND RETENTION. Once the trade area is delineated and described, the next question becomes what proportion of potential sales are actually captured (Goldstucker et al. 1978, pp. 53–60). *Sales retention* is an indirect measure of locally available goods and services, assuming that people buy locally if possible. Sales retention is appropriate only for consumer goods and services such as clothing, appliances, and groceries, not such things as construction or business services or tourist-related activities.

While measurement of actual sales is relatively easy, measurement of the *sales potential* presents some difficulty. Equation (6.8) assumes that local potential sales can be estimated by statewide average sales per capita adjusted by the ratio of local to state per capita income (Hustedde et al. 1984; Stone and McConnon 1983):

potential sales = municipal population × state sales per capital

$$\times \frac{\text{local per capita income}}{\text{state per capita income}} \qquad (6.8)$$

Care must be used in accepting the estimate from (6.8). It ignores all of the shopping area and consumer characteristics enumerated in the ecological approach to trade area analysis. The potential sales estimated assumes no differences in local consumption patterns except adjusting the level by relative local income. It assumes that all of the population in the municipality (trade area population can be substituted) do all their shopping locally. Yet, (6.8) does provide readily calculated estimates that represent a logical first guess. To estimate sales retention, divide actual sales by sales potential:

$$\text{percent sales retained} = \frac{\text{actual sales}}{\text{sales potential}} \times 100 \qquad (6.9)$$

TRADE AREA CAPTURE. Another approach to sales potential estimates the number of people buying from local merchants (Hustedde et al. 1984; Stone and McConnon 1983). Trade area capture an estimate of customer equivalents, used in conjunction with the pull factor, permits the community to measure the extent to which it attracts nonresidents (tourists and nonlocal shoppers) and differences in local demand patterns.

Trade area capture estimates the number of customers a community's retailers sell to (i.e., if one person buys food for a family of four, all four are counted). Most trade area models consider market area as a function of population and distance. Trade area capture incorporates income and expenditure factors but excludes distance. The underlying assumption is that local tastes and preferences are similar to the tastes and preferences statewide. Thus the trade area capture estimate suffers from the same caveats enumerated for potential sales estimated via (6.8).

$$TAC_{ij} = \frac{AS_{ij}}{(AS_{sj}/P_s)\,(Y_c/Y_s)} \qquad (6.10)$$

where TAC_{ij} represents trade area capture for retail category j in community i measured by number of customer equivalents, AS_{ij} represents annual retail sales in category j in community i, AS_{sj} represents annual retail sales in category j in the state, P_s is state population, Y_c is county per capita income, and Y_s is state per capita income. The number calculated from (6.10) is the number of people purchased for, not the people sold to or actual customers in the store.

If trade area capture exceeds the trade area population estimated by Reilly's Law, either the community is capturing outside trade or local residents have higher spending patterns than the state average. If the trade area capture is less than the estimate from Reilly's Law, either the community is losing potential trade or local residents have a lower spending pattern than the statewide average. Further analysis is required to determine which cause is more important. Comparison of the trade area capture estimates for specific retail or service categories with the total permits insight into which local trade sectors are attracting customers to the community. It is important to make trade area capture comparisons over time to identify trends.

Trade area capture measures purchases by both residents and nonresidents. The *pull factor* is the ratio of trade area capture to municipal population and measures the community's drawing power. It makes explicit the proportion of consumers that a community (the primary market) draws from outside its boundaries (the secondary market, e.g., residents in neighboring areas or tourists). Over time, this ratio removes the influence of changes in municipal population when determining changes in drawing power:

$$\text{pull factor} = \frac{\text{trade area capture}}{\text{municipal population}} \tag{6.11}$$

The first of two major limitations in using trade area capture and pull factor analysis is the difficulty of obtaining up-to-date data. Typically, data are limited to the U.S. Census of Retail Trade and Services, which is available only every five years, to the categories of businesses enumerated in that census, and by disclosure problems for smaller places. A second major limitation is the assumption of uniform consumer buying throughout the state, adjusted only for income. The strength of the approach is ease of computation and of understanding.

INTRODUCING NEW GOODS AND SERVICES. The preceding discussion presumes that the assortment of goods and services offered by the community remains fixed and only their quantity varies. Community market analysis provides guidance about what different goods and services might be offered, depending on costs to the firm, access to alternative sources, and consumer demand. Temporarily ignoring cost differences among merchants, the question becomes, what good or service currently purchased elsewhere (imported) by residents can be provided locally (*import substitution*)?

The most obvious method for identifying the potential for import substitution is to compare the goods and services offered by other communities on the same level of the central place hierarchy and to identify the differences. The display of thresholds and multiple functional units in Figures 6.5, 6.6, and 6.7 and Table 6.1 and the presentation of the mix of goods and services present at a given level of the central place hierarchy in Figure 6.4 indicates how this is done. Any import substitution analysis must examine nearby and accessible alternative sources of supply because there may not be sufficient market to support multiple firms (see the discussion related to Figure 6.4 and Table 6.1).

Location quotients (*LQ*) and population-employment (*PE*) ratios identify import substitution potential (Isserman 1980a, pp. 52–53; Murray and Harris 1978, pp. 13–16). The location quotient is the ratio of the share of local employment in a particular sector to the share of national employment in that sector:[12]

$$LQ = \frac{\% \text{ local employment sector } i}{\% \text{ national employment sector } i} \qquad (6.12)$$

The key location quotients in an import substitution analysis are those with a value less than 1, which signifies that the community has less employment in that particular trade sector than the national average. One interpretation of location quotients is that a value of 1 measures self-sufficiency. If the community location quotient is less than 1 when it is at least 1 for similar communities, there is a potential local market for that trade function.

Murray and Harris (1978) supplement location quotient analysis with the population-employment ratio. This ratio is population divided by employment in a particular retail or service sector. Municipal population is used rather than trade area population.[13] Since there is no critical value such as a location quotient of less than 1, population-employment ratios require intercommunity comparisons to determine whether a community's employment in a certain activity is unusually high or low. A relatively high population-employment ratio indicates that each worker in this sector serves more people than the average, implying a potential for expanding employment. The population-employment ratio circumvents reliance on national averages that may not be appropriate for the local situation. It also avoids the computational bias of location quotients that arises from the requirement that both the numerator and denominator must sum to 100 percent. This creates a subtle bias, especially in smaller communities, because a dominant sector distorts all the sector shares. Furthermore, the population-employment ratio incorporates the total population, not just those who are employed. Counting just employed people produces distorted results if the community has a high proportion of younger and/or older residents.

A simple example will show how import substitution potential can be identified. Let's compare five cities of similar population size, each a freestanding community (i.e., not closely linked to a major urban center), each a county seat, and none with a sizeable state or federal employer. The information to determine the import substitution potential for furniture retailing (SIC 57) is summarized in Table 6.5.

Table 6.5. Estimating Import Substitution Potential, Furniture Retailing (SIC 57)

	City				
	A	B	C	D	E
Population	6,000	6,972	7,920	9,071	6,039
Employment in SIC 57	24	28	24	47	11
Percent of local employment in SIC 57	1.18	3.61	2.10	3.24	0.84
Location quotient for SIC 57	0.98	3.01	1.75	2.70	0.70
Population-employment ratio for SIC 57	250	249	330	193	549

Location quotients of less than 1 indicate some possibility for import substitution. This is the case for cities A and E. Dividing the municipal population by employment in furniture retailing in each city produces the population-employment ratios. The average ratio for the five cities is 314. The *PE* ratio for cities A, B, and D is less than the average *PE* ratio, while the opposite is true for cities C and E. An above-average *PE* ratio indicates a potential to increase retail furniture sales and employment in cities C and E.

The simple average is not a rigorous enough standard to make this judgment. A *t* test can be used to establish a confidence interval (e.g., 95 percent) to show that the true average *PE* ratio for furniture retailing in all similar cities is between 159 and 469. Only city E, therefore, has an "abnormally" high *PE* ratio.

The *LQ* and *PE* provide two somewhat independent insights into import substitution potential. An *LQ* of less than 1 coupled with a high *PE* ratio indicates good import substitution potential (city E). An *LQ* of less than 1 and a low *PE* ratio is a mixed signal requiring further analysis (city A). An *LQ* greater than 1 and a low *PE* ratio indicates minimal import substitution possibilities (cities B, C, and D).

Location quotients and population-employment ratios are only the first step in import substitution analysis. The community must also examine local conditions. What are unique local demands? What are the productivity factors affecting the number of workers in this particular service or trade sector? What are the alternative sources of supply in the area?

Communities and business people are interested in whether a given type of business will be successful in a specific location. *Threshold analysis* is one method of estimating business viability when pursuing an import substitution strategy. The basic method of estimating thresholds is to examine the relationship between the number and types of businesses and population levels in several communities. If a single community has fewer establishments than the average for its population size, there is a possibility for adding business (see Table 6.1). To use the threshold technique requires several assumptions of homogeneity among the communities in question, especially in terms of (1) income, tastes, and preferences; (2) extent of nearby competition; and (3) similar-sized businesses in all the communities.

While a community is justifiably concerned about the aggregate package of goods and services offered, it is often a single good or service that is the initial lure that attracts customers. All the merchants in the community benefit from that key good or service. In shopping centers, that key merchant is referred to as the shopping center "anchor." When a community examines its retail trade sector, there are three types of businesses to consider (Kivell and Shaw 1980, p. 122). The first type is the *generative business,* which produces sales by itself or attracts customers to the community, such as the shopping center anchor. The second type is the *shared business,* which secures sales from the generative power of nearby businesses; an example is a small specialty shop located near a large general merchandise store. The third type is the business whose sales are a *coincidental* occurrence to other activities; such businesses do not generate sales themselves nor from association with nearby shops. Examples are small ice cream shop and cafés in shopping malls. For the community to realize its retail trade potential, a balance among the different categories of retail shops must be struck.

SUMMARY. Some empirical regularities appear in trade area surveys: (1) the proportion of the population patronizing a community varies inversely with the distance from that community; (2) the proportion of the population patronizing a community varies directly with the variety of merchandise offered; (3) the distance that customers are willing to travel to purchase a good or service varies with the type of good or service; and (4) the pull toward any given shopping area is influenced by the proximity of competing communities.

The size of a community's market area depends upon two factors, the size of the community itself, because larger communities offer more goods and services and can attract consumers over greater distances, and the nearness and direction of competing communities. Competing communities determine both the size and shape of a market area. A market area may extend a short distance in one direction where there is competition, and a greater distance in another direction where there is no competition.

Communities compete for customers in a multitude of ways including prices, access to stores, variety of goods or services, store hours, clerks' attitudes, credit policies, delivery policies, and personal knowledge of the customer.

An often-overlooked dimension of retail market analysis in small communities is that the presence of a competitor can increase rather than reduce sales for both merchants. This is especially true for comparison-shopping goods and for goods and services with definite submarkets, such as clothing.

Community market analysis provides three sets of data that must be known in order to capture existing markets. First, each community should know the size, shape, and composition of its market area in order to function efficiently, especially in terms of merchandising and advertising. Second, each community should have some idea of the kinds of goods and services similar communities support in order to determine potential gaps in the local trade-service sector. Third, each community should know what proportion of its total business comes from local residents and what proportion from the surrounding market areas. This will assist in identifying key markets and perhaps redirect local marketing strategies.

Study Questions

1. Some central place terminology used in the chapter included central functions, central places, range of a good/service, demand threshold, and tributary area. What do these terms mean, and how are they linked to community economic analysis?

2. What are the implications of central place hierarchies for community economic analysis, especially for the provision of goods and services? What behavioral assumptions for firms and households are required?

3. Why might demand thresholds vary among places, over time, and among different goods/services?

4. What is meant by a central place system?

5. Several reasons were given for the presence of a central place hierarchy. What are they?

6. What is a trade area?

7. What is Reilly's Law of Retail Gravitation? What are some of its assumptions? What economic model is it derived from? What are the implications of those assumptions?

8. Describe and explain the ecological approach to trade area analysis.

9. What is trade area capture? What information does it provide? How is it used with the pull factor?

10. Can the tools of location quotients, population-employment ratios, and demand thresholds be used for import substitution analysis? If so, how?

Capital Markets and Community Economic Development

7

A KEY ELEMENT in community economic development activities is the availability and use of capital—in particular, financial capital. Financial capital is the mechanism that permits the community to purchase or develop the labor and physical capital base critical for community economic development.

The importance to economic development of the structure and functioning of an economy's financial institutions and its capital markets has been pointed out by Baumol (1965, pp. 1–2):

The allocation of its capital resources is among the most important decisions which must be made by any economy. In the long run, an appropriate allocation of real capital is absolutely indispensable to the implementation of consumer sovereignty, or of the more appropriate concept—public sovereignty, which takes into account all of the relevant desires of the individuals who constitute the economy. For unless the flow of capital goods is responsive to the goals of the members of the public, the community will only be able to exercise a very short run and temporary control over the composition of output and its activities. After all, capital is the economy's link with the future, and unless our desires can influence the apportionment of capital inputs, our wishes can at most, effectively control only today's events.

Baumol goes on to describe how the critical relationship between financial markets and real capital formation occurs (p. 2):

The selection of the physical forms which constitute the embodiment of our capital resources is largely controlled through the funds market—the market in which money capital is provided. Thus, the allocation process is heavily influenced by the decisions of the nation's financial institutions, its banks, its insurance companies, and a variety of other bodies. In addition, the government's monetary and fiscal policy obviously play a highly important role in a variety of ways.

This chapter reviews the elements of the community's capital market, the role played by the various actors, and the implications of various imperfections and activities for the movement of capital in the community.

Capital Markets

Kieschnick and Daniels (1979, p. 13) define *capital markets* as: "a web of institutions and mechanisms by which resources are saved, investment opportunities are identified, and savings channeled to enterprises for their productive and possible use. These markets are operating efficiently if the way funds are channeled meets every opportunity for improving the overall welfare of consumers." The basic theoretical model of financial markets contends that capital is allocated among uses, regardless of place or type of use, in such a fashion that the return in all uses and places is equal. This also maximizes returns to the lender.

In its most simplistic form, the community's capital market can be represented by Figure 7.1. The suppliers of capital are households and businesses with more income/capital than they currently need (i.e., savers). The demanders of capital are households and businesses with less income/capital than they currently need (i.e., investors). These two parties meet, negotiate a transaction, and thus improve welfare. The capital market moves funds from the suppliers to the demanders of capital. The exchange of financial resources can be a relatively simple or fairly complex exchange. It may involve a transaction between an individual demander of financial resources and an individual supplier of financial resources; it might involve a single demander/supplier facing a multiple supplier/demander or a multiple supplier/multiple demander exchange.

Because individuals who supply and demand capital have difficulty matching exactly the time, place, amount, or judgment about the soundness (risk) of capital market transactions, financial institutions have developed to facilitate the flow of capital among the parties in the market. Such institutions include commercial banks, savings and loan associations (thrifts), consumer credit companies, stock exchanges, insurance companies, and investment bankers. They offer suppliers of financial capital a place to put their excess funds until some time in the future when they need them. Financial institutions accumulate funds from numerous savers/investors to meet the needs of those requiring funds in excess of their current income flow. Thus, a commercial bank collects deposits from numerous households and compensates them with interest or services such as checking accounts. In turn, the commercial bank becomes the single place where a borrower can acquire necessary funds without approaching each saver individually.

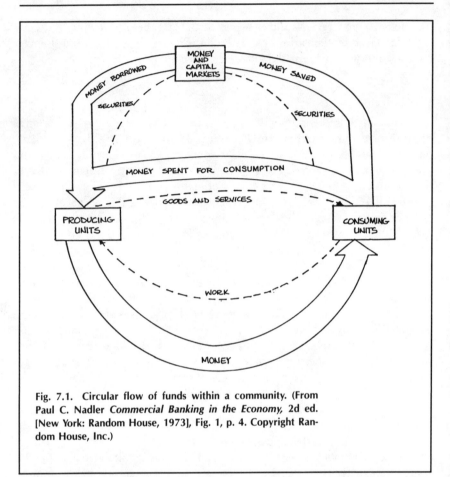

Fig. 7.1. Circular flow of funds within a community. (From
Paul C. Nadler *Commercial Banking in the Economy,* 2d ed.
[New York: Random House, 1973], Fig. 1, p. 4. Copyright Ran-
dom House, Inc.)

The organization and structure of the capital market will determine its
efficiency in clearing its surpluses and deficits as well as its flexibility in
making pricing adjustments. Under ideal conditions, if there are demand/
supply inequities, financial markets, at any given point in time or space,
create a set of interacting forces to bring the market into balance. The
equilibrating force is interest rates (Cebula and Zaharoff 1975; Romans
1965). Ideal performance occurs when the capital market adjusts smoothly
and quickly and with minimal economic costs to the host community
(Dominguez 1976, p. 5). Straszhiem (1971, p. 219) indicates that "a perfect
financial (capital) market exists when financial assets (loans and equities) of
comparable maturity and risk, yield the same return in all communities, not
including a premium for location rent to cover the cost of transmitting
information and funds to and from borrowers and lenders." This last re-

striction means that if transportation costs are significant, borrowers located some distance away from the lender will pay more. This cost is associated more with the movement (acquiring) of information than with the actual physical movement of capital.

NONHOMOGENEITY OF CAPITAL MARKETS. It is important to recognize that capital markets are not homogeneous but segment into numerous submarkets (Straszheim 1971, pp. 219–26). Some of these submarkets are defined by type of capital, such as short-term, long-term, operating, real estate, commercial/industrial, or farm. Debt or equity capital represents another category of submarket. Geography whether local, regional, or national, also segments capital markets. There are also both public and private capital markets.[1] The capital market can be characterized by the form capital takes, e.g., financial, physical, human, or natural.

Both the type of capital traded in the market and the providers of capital can be diverse; they can be households, businesses, government, young families, retired workers, pension funds, or insurance companies. (Straszheim 1971, pp. 223–32). Likewise, the demanders of capital are diverse; they can be young households, schools, farmers, retailers, or speculators. Most financial institutions serve only a subset of the various components of the financial markets.

The products exchanged in financial markets can be highly differentiated in terms of risk, length of time of exchange, size, price and nonprice component of the transaction, pledged assets or collateral, location, type of business, and type of borrower (Mikesell and Davidson 1982, pp. 167–69; Straszheim 1971, p. 221). The price and nonprice components of the transaction include interest, collateral required, and maturity. Size of transaction refers to the fact that small borrowers are usually limited to local commercial banks or local investors for capital sources, while large national corporations can approach national capital markets.

Traditionally there are three reasons why financial institutions are active in only a few segments of the capital market. These reasons are: information costs, types of liabilities carried, and regulation. Because of recent changes in federal legislation, regulation and types of liabilities are becoming less important as limitations but still exert some influence. Information costs refer to the cost of developing the capacity to evaluate the feasibility of various kinds of investments. For example, banks located in agricultural communities have developed a capacity to make relatively good judgments about credit requests by farmers. However, since such banks may service only a few commercial-industrial loans each year, their evaluations of those requests often are based less on insight and experience and more on formula. This shortcoming can limit their support of new development opportunities in the community. The types of liabilities category refers to the fact that financial institutions must return cash to depositors when they ask for it. Thus savings and loans, with the majority of their liabilities (deposits) composed of less volatile savings accounts, are able to make long-term housing loans. Money market funds, while yielding higher returns, must also be liquid and ready for the customer who calls for his money back today. They are typically invested in highly liquid government securities and high-grade corporate paper. Regulation can be a limitation on financial institutions because some regulations prevent some financial institutions from becoming involved in certain types of activities. For example, the Glass-Steagall Act restricts commercial banks' involvement in investment and brokerage banking.

Community Capital Mark

Figure 7.2 displays the community's capital markets in a supply/demand/institutional context (Borts 1971, pp. 189–93; Moore and Hill 1982). The supply of capital funds for a community comes from the demand, time, and savings deposits made by households, businesses, and government. Capital also comes from the purchase of federal funds, the sale of loans and guarantees and securities to external sources, the participation in loans among local financial institutions, and the sale of overlines (loans) to correspondents. The use or demand for community capital arises from households that need real estate, installment, and personal loans and from businesses that need capital for real estate, or to start up, operate, or expand. It takes the form of short-, medium-, and long-term loans. Governments also use community capital through either short- or long-term

Supply	Financial institutions	Demand
Deposits	Banks	Households
Households	S and L's	Real estate loans
Business	Credit unions	Installment loans
Government	Insurance companies	Personal loans
Federal funds bought	Brokerage firms	Business
Guarantees sold		Real estate
Securities sold		Operating
Participations		Government
Overlines		Federal funds sold
		Guarantees bought
		Securities bought
		Participations
		Overlines

Fig. 7.2. Community capital markets.

borrowing. The institutional dimension of a community's capital market can be characterized as those sectors in a local economy actively involved in the processing and exchanging of financial capital. Community financial institutions include commercial banks, credit unions, savings and loans, insurance companies, brokerage companies, and pension funds.

A slightly different perspective of a community's financial markets appears in Figure 7.3, which shows (1) the significance of community boundaries and the flow of capital among various users across those boundaries and within the community and (2) the variety of mechanisms that a community has available to support either household or business borrowing.

The three major components in Figure 7.3 are households, financial institutions, and businesses (Mikesell and Davidson 1982, pp. 160–62; Straszheim 1971, pp. 223–32). They represent providers, facilitators, and users of capital, respectively. As providers of capital, households have several options. They can hoard idle cash in the backyard, or they can deposit their financial assets in some local or nonlocal financial institution. They can use a commercial bank, a savings and loan, or an insurance company. They can buy stocks and bonds. They can provide capital directly

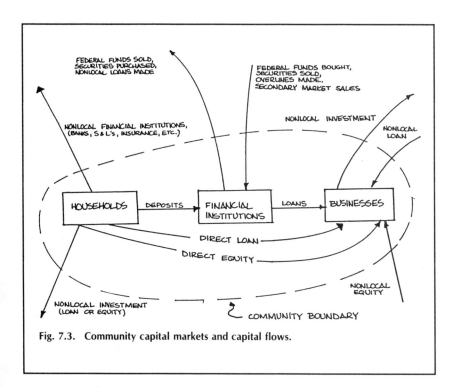

Fig. 7.3. Community capital markets and capital flows.

to the business sector of the community through an equity investment as an owner of a business or through some form of loan made to that business. They can also export capital from the community by making direct loans or equity investments in nonlocal businesses.

Local financial institutions can choose between using community capital for local or nonlocal activity (Borts 1971; Cebula and Zaharoff 1975; Romans 1965). They can hold idle cash balances and/or reserve balances; they can make local loans; or they can export funds through the sale of federal funds, purchase of securities, or participation in nonlocal loans. They obtain most of their capital from deposits by local households. These institutions also purchase federal funds, sell previously purchased securities, participate with outside financial institutions in locally generated loans, use overlines from correspondent banks, and sell local loans in secondary markets.

The local business sector is the major user of community capital. Local businesses acquire their local capital through direct loans or equity investments from households or through loans from local financial institutions (Kieschnick 1981b). They acquire nonlocal capital through loans from nonlocal financial institutions and equity investments by nonlocal households.

It is important to recognize that a community's economy operates within a regional, national, and international financial capital market that is relatively expeditious in facilitating the movement of capital among regions and communities. Two important elements of the local/nonlocal capital market linkage and capital movement are secondary markets and correspondence banking.

SECONDARY MARKETS. Secondary financial markets are a very important and often little-understood mechanism by which capital moves about the economy. A simple example will demonstrate their importance. Joe's Bar and Grill obtains a $10,000 loan from a local bank. The bank can sell $9,000 of the loan in the secondary market, then use the $9,000 received to make another local loan (i.e., import capital). The $9,000 sold in the secondary market carries with it a variety of assurances and guarantees that the loan is good.[2] The guarantee on loans sold in the secondary market can take several forms; most common is for a government agency such as the Small Business Administration, the Farmer's Home Administration, the Economic Development Administration, or the Department of Housing and Urban Development to guarantee it. Such agencies have a relatively long tradition of guaranteeing loan risk. (All loans sold in the secondary market do not have guarantees; in these cases the loan evaluation capacity of the initiating bank is crucial.)

An example will show how a loan guarantee works. Because the Small Business Administration will guarantee 90 percent of a loan up to $500,000, a commercial bank can make a $550,000 loan of which $500,000 is guaranteed. Let this hypothetical loan be for ten years at 17 percent interest. The bank sells the guaranteed portion of the loan in the secondary market. The originating commercial bank charges a service fee for servicing the loan (e.g., accounting, collection). In this example, let the bank collect a 2.5 percent service fee on the $500,000 sold. Since the borrower pays 17 percent, the bank can pay the owner of the secondary portion an interest payment of 14.5 percent. The bank can sell the guaranteed portion at a lower interest rate because it is literally a risk-free investment.

Using the secondary market can be very beneficial for our bank. First, it has received the $500,000 from the sale in the secondary market, which it can reinvest for additional returns. Second, it receives a return on its investment in the original loan far exceeding the apparent 17 percent. The originating commercial bank will collect, in the first year, $12,500 from the 2.5 percent service fee on the $500,000 sold in the secondary market. The commercial bank will also collect $8,990 in interest on the $55,000 of the bank's money still in the loan. The originating commercial bank thus collects $21,490 during the first year of the loan, or 39 percent ($21,490 divided by $55,000). We can see that the use of secondary markets and guarantees become very attractive mechanisms by which commercial banks can move funds into the community while also providing themselves a substantial return. The implicit assumption in the preceding discussion is that the bank can find opportunities to reinvest the funds imported.

CORRESPONDENT BANKING. Banks also can acquire funds through their correspondent bank (Mikesell and Davidson 1982, pp. 175–77). A correspondent bank provides funds by participating in loans made by the smaller bank (i.e., overlines), by trading securities on behalf of the smaller bank, by facilitating the trading of federal funds, and by borrowing on behalf of the smaller bank from the Federal Reserve Bank's discount window. In return, the correspondent bank charges a fee, which may be a couple of points or compensating balances (compensating balances are funds that the smaller bank leaves in interest-free accounts at the correspondent bank, providing some free funds for the larger bank to invest).

An example may clarify the correspondent relationship. Assume that the local (initiating) bank has a lending limit of $100,000[3] but has a loan request for $300,000. In this situation, the local bank can either turn down the loan or make it, using a $200,000 overline from its correspondent. The initiating bank charges an interest rate of 14 percent on the loan. The correspondent bank charges an additional 2 percent. The borrower now can get his $300,000 loan but will be paying either an interest rate of 16 percent or some blended interest rate reflecting both local and correspondent bank interest charges. The 2 percent charge for servicing the overline does not represent the correspondent bank's total return from the transaction. It also will require the local bank to maintain anywhere from 10 to 20 percent of the overline loan balance in a noninterest-bearing account at the correspondent bank, which the correspondent bank can use for its own investment purposes. One can easily see why local banks might be reluctant to initiate overline arrangements. However, in our example, the local bank's desire to maintain a valuable deposit relationship with this particular borrower may justify the cost of the overline.

Correspondent banks may not respond to community credit needs for several reasons, including lack of sensitivity to local borrower needs, higher cost of funds, or different documentation and evaluation standards.

Capital Market Failure

The discussion up to this point has implicitly assumed that the actors in the capital market and the signals given lead to market clearing performance, and that capital is used in its most productive manner. Yet capital markets often appear not to allocate capital to its most productive use. Litvak and Daniels (1979, p. 26) indicate that *capital market failure* occurs when "specific enterprises cannot get the funds they need, even though either private or social returns justify it. Sometimes a failure manifests itself in a firm having to pay an unnecessary high price. . . . Other times it shows up in the complete rationing away of credit at any price. In either case, capital is effectively unavailable."

There are three major types of capital market failure affecting community economic development (Bearse 1979, p. 83; Michelson 1981, pp. 539–40). *Type 1 failure* occurs when the capital market does not put funds where they yield the greatest private return, thus violating the profit maximization rule of the market. This failure occurs because of a lack of information about profitable uses and/or the cost of information so high that returns are reduced below the level available in other areas and investments. In Type 1 failure, individual investors are not able to find all their good investment possibilities. Some mechanisms to overcome this are credit reporting services, feasibility studies, and secondary markets.

Type 2 failure occurs when the capital market places funds where they yield the highest private return, but not the highest social return. A lack of information is not the cause here because there are no more good investments to uncover. If society is not satisfied with the distribution of capital uses, it must encourage providers of capital to move it into those investments deemed desirable. An example of this sort of failure is "redlining," where a financial institution deliberately outlines a geographic area within which it will not invest regardless of the quality of the individual loan requests. Here the question really becomes what form of public intervention (subsidies/regulation) should take place (see Chapter 9 for more detail).

Type 3 failure occurs when capital fails to maximize its returns because of legal/social or size constraints even though the market is able to identify opportunities and wishes to act on them. Examples of Type 3 failure are the inability of private individuals to assemble land for downtown redevelopment or the inability to finance a project because it is either too large or too small, or because countervailing forces (e.g., environmental concerns) block the placement of capital.

Some causes of capital market failure are mobility, information, risk, and regulation; they will be discussed below.

MOBILITY. Capital typically is perceived as the most mobile resource in the economy, but to a large extent it does not possess the perfect mobility it is presumed to have. The failure to be perfectly mobile prevents capital from moving among uses and sites in response to minor changes in interest rates and rates of return.

In a purely competitive market, capital flows freely among production processes in a community or among communities until it yields an equal marginal product in each use and place (Richardson 1969b, pp. 304–10; Roberts and Fishkind 1979, pp. 17–22). In other words, the marginal product of capital in each use in every community is equal to the interest rate or profit rate after adjusting for the transportation cost of capital: $MP^1_{ki} = MP^1_{kj} = MP^2_{ki} = MP^2_{kj} \ldots = r$, where i and j are different communities, 1 and 2 are different uses (commodities), and r is the interest rate determined by the national capital market.

Capital, in its financial form, comes as close as any factor of production to being a truly mobile resource, but its mobility is still far from perfect. Capital movement among communities in response to local interest rate differentials may or may not be sufficient to eliminate those differentials, for a variety of reasons (Moore and Hill 1982, pp. 506–7; Richardson 1973, pp. 105–13).

First, the vast majority of community capital is not in monetary form but in some physical form, such as housing, factories, office buildings, stores, trucks, inventories, and machinery, that defies quick adjustment to minor changes in interest rates and rates of return. These forms of capital do not or cannot move in response to minor market signals or within a short period of time. Changes occur only at the margin as replacement occurs.

Second, a community's capital base and investments are indivisible and lumpy (i.e., you purchase a complete machine, not just a portion of it). This prevents marginal shifts in response to minor or even major interest rate differentials.

Third, communities may have differences in taxing structures which either encourage or impede the movement of capital between communities. Tax structure differences are more likely to occur between states than within a state, but they can occur within a state if communities hold different operational philosophies about property taxes. Common examples of such differences in taxing structure are the state system of taxing capital gains and inheritances or the local assessor's valuation of property.

Fourth, investors may be ignorant or may have imperfect information about investment opportunities and potential returns in different communities. For capital to move to alternative uses and places requires that its owner have and comprehend information about alternative uses and places that can yield higher returns. An important dimension of capital market information is *inertia* (failure to change investment patterns because of the cost and effort involved) and *bias* (belief that community X is economically depressed and does not offer any investment opportunities) about alternative uses and sites. Economically depressed communities must convey information about local investment possibilities to local and nonlocal owners of capital to overcome inertia and bias.

Fifth, differences in the private and social effects of investments may affect the movement of capital. Often the private investor makes a decision equating private return with private cost. The decision to cease investment is consistent for the individual but inconsistent with the community's desire for social benefits. For example, the private investor cannot capture the returns derived from investments in most forms of social overhead capital, such as education and waste disposal equipment, and will not invest.

Sixth, uncertainty and differences of opinion about investment risk involved in various communities will cause investors to require rates of return based upon perceived risk.

Seventh, if investors make decisions based on average returns, and average returns exceed marginal returns, the resulting overinvestment creates a continuing interest rate differential. (The converse is also true.)

Dynamic mobility also creates continuing interest rate differentials among communities. Investment in the community is a function of one community's investment opportunities and returns relative to those in other communities. A community will attract capital as long as its demand for capital equals or exceeds the demand in other communities. This demand will take the form of higher interest rates or higher return on investment; it is measured by the marginal product of capital times the price of the output produced (MP_kP_o). This means that as long as a community produces a higher-priced product or uses its capital to produce more units of the product at the same price, it will demand more capital than another community.

In a dynamic setting, shifts in community demand for capital can cause interest rate differentials. Community demand for capital shifts for a variety of reasons. Technological change resulting in new products or new production processes causes a community to demand different amounts and types of capital. A shift in the demand for community output will affect the investment demand associated with the production of that output through the capital-output ratio. Changes in expectations may shift a community's capital demand curve in or out, as occurs when speculators build residential housing in boom towns created by the energy industry. Finally, changes in factor prices may make capital either more or less expensive relative to labor and may cause a shift in the demand for capital. These shifts in the demand curve for capital do not occur uniformly over time or space and generate continuing interest rate differentials among communities.

In summary, capital is often not sufficiently mobile to eliminate interest rate differentials between communities. This situation occurs because of the form the capital takes, uncertainty, indivisibilities of investments, ignorance, and shifts in demand and technology over time. In most cases these forces can be counteracted by community actions.

INFORMATION. The high cost of information and transactions can obstruct the smooth functioning of capital markets (Kieschnick and Daniels 1979, pp. 16–17; Litvak and Daniels 1979, pp. 20–21; Mikesell and Davidson 1982, p. 173; Moore and Hill 1982, p. 506; Roberts and Fishkind 1979, p. 17). It takes time and skill to arrange a financial transaction, and the greater the transaction and information costs, the higher the rate of return on the investment must be before it will be funded.

The evaluation of a project is a costly and time-consuming process that need not be proportional to the size of the loan. Activities such as record inspections, site inspections, and discussions with decisionmakers can discriminate against smaller borrows or borrowers in more distant locations (Mikesell and Davidson 1982, p. 173). The high cost of information encourages lenders to develop a conservative, skeptical attitude toward new or unfamiliar products, technologies, processes, locations, and firms.

Some of the transaction costs incurred when putting together a financial package are governmentally imposed for public protection (e.g., a prospectus, accounting standards, auditing). Transaction costs also include the time required for the entrepreneur, financers, lawyers, and accountants to write business plans, prepare financial statements, negotiate the terms, and complete the investment agreement. These business costs do not necessarily represent a market failure, but they can be disproportionately high for some investments. Information costs increase for firms that are smaller, newer, involved in new technology or unusual markets, or located in an isolated place. For these reasons investors tend to continue to invest in known firms, known markets, and known technologies even though their expected return may be lower (Kieschnick and Daniels 1979, p. 16).

RISK. One key element frequently overlooked by a community attempting to capitalize a project is the risk that must be borne either by the community or by individuals. For investors making an equity contribution, risk is part of the return. For individuals and financial institutions making a debt contribution and expecting to be repaid in full, risk takes on a different dimension. Obligations to third parties (e.g., depositors) often cause financial institutions to be reluctant or to demand risk premiums that appear exorbitant before they will participate in the activity.

Four major types of risk are default, liquidity, inflation, and interest rate (Haggard 1982). *Default risk* reflects the possibility that a borrower will fail to repay the loan completely. Lenders face greater default risk in communities experiencing economic decline than in communities experiencing economic growth, for two reasons: declining sales imply reduced cash flow to pay off the loan, and declining asset values reduce the collateral pledged against the loan. The availability of fire or property insurance for a business may be a very subtle but key element in a lender's willingness to make loans.

Liquidity risk occurs when the lender experiences an unanticipated cash outflow. Depository financial institutions must always have on hand, or be able to acquire quickly, sufficient cash to meet sudden outflows caused by depositor withdrawals. These surges of cash outflow can occur for a variety of unanticipated reasons. The financial institution must meet these cash outflows from the cash inflow from new deposits, loan repayments, the sale of liquid assets such as government securities, the purchase of federal funds, repurchase agreements, or discount windows. This is a major reason why the kind of liabilities a financial institution acquires (e.g., demand deposits, time and savings deposits, insurance benefits) become a major determinant of the kind of loans it can make. If its deposits are all short-term, then it will be vulnerable to a liquidity risk problem if it makes too many long-term loans.

Inflation risk refers to the changes in the purchasing power of funds when loans are made for long periods of time. The lender's perception of this risk may also reflect a preference for money now vs. money at a future date.

Interest rate risk, which has become more prominent since the mid-1970s, is the risk that interest rates will increase dramatically after the financial institution has made fixed rate loans. The lender incurs an opportunity cost equal to the difference between the increased market interest rate and the interest rate on the loan. He avoids this risk by making variable-rate loans or shorter-term loans, permitting a periodic change in rates.

Perceptions of unduly high risk levels can cause some suppliers of capital to withhold their funds altogether or to require very high returns. Financial institutions can deal with risk through four general strategies.[4]

First, they can diversify the type of investments made. Diversification can take place on the basis of type of activity (e.g., farming vs. manufacturing vs. retail establishment loans); type of loan (e.g., installment loans, real estate mortgages); geographic area (e.g., some local loans, some nonlocal loans); or type of risk. Diversification by type of risk means that the lender uses portfolio analysis and attempts to bring new loans into the loan portfolio that have a negative default risk correlation when compared with loans currently in the portfolio. Thus diversification reduces the default risk of the total portfolio even though the risk on any given loan has not been altered. Financial institutions' second major mechanism for dealing with risk is "pooling" (Kieschnick and Daniels 1979, pp. 15–16). Pooling does not reduce risk per se, but it spreads it out among other financial institutions so that no single lender is overly exposed when a given loan defaults. A third risk-reducing mechanism is to guarantee (insure) against default. In this case, someone (usually the government or a co-signer on a loan) stands behind the borrower and will repay all or part of the lender's loss in case of default. A fourth risk-reducing mechanism is better information. The lender's ability to improve his evaluation of the loan request reduces the level of risk associated with lending judgments.

REGULATION. Many forms of government regulation affect the flow of capital among uses and places (Daniels 1978, pp. 11–12; Litvak and Daniels 1979, pp. 3, 22–24, 61–67; Mikesell and Davidson 1982). These include bank examiners, Regulation Q,[5] prevention of interstate banking, and the Community Reinvestment Act. Some suggest that one capital market problem is that financial institutions in the United States are over-regulated, and that many of these regulations, despite their obvious intention of protecting depositors, have an adverse affect on small- and medium-sized businesses (Guenther 1981; Hansen 1981b, pp. 218–20; Hansen 1981a, pp. 55–71; Mikesell and Davidson 1982, p. 166). The emphasis on protecting depositors' monies leads banks to try to reduce the risk of loss and therefore to avoid newer, smaller, more innovative, more dynamic, and riskier businesses in favor of larger, better-established businesses with less growth potential. Banks, which are highly leveraged (a debt-to-equity ratio averaging 16:1), assume almost a zero-risk position in their lending because of these tremendous regulatory pressures (Hansen, 1981b, p. 219). As a consequence, they tend to favor real estate, consumer products, low-risk business, and government lending, and the new small business so critical to community economic development becomes unacceptable at the neighborhood bank.

Government regulation of capital markets is usually initiated to correct some type of market failure. However, it can have some very perverse effects. For example, many regulations regarding the assets of banks, savings and loan associations, life insurance companies, and pension funds are designed to control the financial intermediary's level of risk and thus protect the depositor or policyholder, preventing these institutions from actively supporting risky enterprises which may yield very high employment growth. Regulations preventing price competition for deposits among financial intermediaries may cause funds to flow out of the regulated market into unregulated markets; an example is the movement of funds out of savings and loan associations into money market accounts in the late 1970s. Another unintended regulatory side effect is the fact that the cost of meeting security regulations and information requirements designed to protect the investor from fraud may effectively close off these capital sources to the smaller firm (Litvak and Daniels 1979, pp. 22–24).

An unanticipated outcome of regulation itself or of overly cautious responses to it is that lending by financial institutions does not yield the new productive capacity required for community economic development.

The Role of Bank
Community Economic Developm

Depository financial institutions can be the core of community economic development (Grzywinski and Marino 1981, pp. 247–50). Neither banks nor other financial institutions should be expected to finance all the investment needs of the community singlehandedly. They must maintain some investment diversity (local vs. nonlocal; agricultural vs. commercial vs. personal) as a hedge against a major economic disaster in one place or sector. Bank deposits are short- to medium-term (monthly in duration), preventing the commitment of funds to long-term loans. Furthermore, the credit needs of some businesses may exceed the limit a bank can loan to one business or individual. Also, the banker may not feel sufficiently well informed about the potential of a particular business line to make a loan. Finally, many new small business ventures lack market potential or management abilities, defects an infusion of capital cannot overcome. Despite these caveats, however, financial institutions, especially banks, are critical actors in community economic development.

There are at least four ways in which bank practices can be examined against community goals and objectives. First, where is the commercial bank using the dollars generated in the community? Are community funds being used in local or nonlocal investments? If the local bank is using a relatively large share of its available funds for nonlocal investments, it may be hampering the long-run economic health of its home community.

Second, how are local banks using community funds? Are bank loans being used for commercial and industrial, agricultural, personal, or real estate purposes? Each of these local investments carries direct implications for future economic activities in the community. Real estate loans are typically very safe, but often fail to generate jobs and income for the vast majority of people within the community. Many rural community economies are dominated by agriculture, and it cannot be ignored. However, agriculture has provided fewer and fewer employment opportunities over the years as consolidation and mechanization have occurred. Housing loans can help a community in two ways: construction of a new house generates employment and also provides housing for another family. Commercial and industrial loans to Main Street merchants and manufacturers are likely to be the source of continued employment opportunities for the community. What type of commercial and industrial loans are being made? Are loans being made for inventory and working capital, or for real estate? Are long-term loans available? Are the loan terms practical for smaller firms struggling through growth pressures? Is the bank, through its loan policies, actively involved in promoting the growth of existing local businesses, the formation of new local businesses, or the attraction of new businesses to the community?

Third, what types of services does the local bank offer which may facilitate economic activities within the community? Does it provide financial counseling to businesses within the community? How does it gain information and/or improve its capacity to judge unique loan requests? Does it provide advice on taxes and accounting? Does it provide credit card service to merchants and customers? Is it willing to purchase industrial revenue bonds and water and sewer bonds in the municipality? Has it formed a "development finance" subsidiary that permits it to make equity investments?

Fourth, what type of relations does the local bank have with other financial institutions? Often a single local bank cannot meet the credit needs of some of its customers. Has it actively sought to participate with other local financial institutions on major community projects? Has it used Farmer's Home Administration or Federal Housing Authority or Small Business Administration lending assistance to help finance a major local project?

Commercial banks can affect local income in two ways, through returns paid on deposits and through its lending and investment policies. While the deposit interest rate approach is not as dramatic as bank lending policy, it may affect more people because of the greater number of savers. Small savers traditionally have not participated in long-term, high-return investments such as certificates of deposit. The relaxation of Regulation Q and the advent of money market accounts means that individuals with small savings accounts can now get relatively higher returns on their savings.

The investment decisions the bank makes affect local income because a simultaneous relationship exists among bank lending policies, local income, and local bank inputs (time and savings deposits and demand deposits). An analysis of commercial banks in Wisconsin found that if banks increased their average loans outstanding by 1 percent over a four-year period, the rate of change in county per capita income over that period would increase by 4 percent (Ho 1978). An example will indicate the significance of this relationship. Let banks in a county have an average loan balance of $1,000,000 over 1969–1973, and let the county's per capita income increase by $100 over that same period. If the average volume of loans increases 10 percent to $1,100,000, then the change in per capita income will increase to $104. For a county with 1,000 people, the bank's additional $100,000 of loans will yield additional personal income of $4,000.

As noted above, commercial banks cannot solve community economic problems alone; they must work in concert with other components of the community, yet if they are not supportive of community economic development activities, they can negate the best efforts of others. If the local bank is active and positive in its actions, it should be supported by community citizens. If it is ambivalent or even reluctant, citizens should encourage it to take a more active role. Both the community and the commercial bank must focus on the long-run objective: today's investments will yield income and employment in the future, which translates into more deposits for the bank.

Policy Responses to Capital Market Failu

In general there are two approaches to solving capital market problems (Bearse 1979; Kieschnick and Daniels 1979, pp. 23): (1) the behavior of private investors can be influenced by giving subsidies that lower the cost of capital, by imposing taxes that raise capital costs, by guaranteeing investments, thereby reducing the risk, or by improving the flow of information; and (2) new public financial institutions can be introduced to act in ways consistent with the public interest. Either approach can be used to address both efficiency and equity problems.

Since the rate of return on a loan is the criterion lending institutions will use, for the community to cause capital to flow to underfinanced viable firms, it must either enable the firm it wishes to support to pay those additional interest premiums (through some type of interest subsidy) or it must assume some type of guarantee or co-lending position to reduce the lending institution's risk exposure and reduce interest premiums. It may be that community sources could provide additional information that would reduce the risk to the lender (Litvak and Daniels 1979, p. 66).

It is important to recognize that there is no such thing as a perfect market, and governmental intervention into the capital market can only improve its workings: it cannot perfect it (Bearse 1979, p. 363). The dynamic character of the economy creates shifting patterns of opportunity, technological innovation, and investment decisions that change market conditions. The public sector should therefore address long-term market trends and conditions, rather than trying to respond to short-term symptoms.

Summary

Capital by itself is not sufficient for community economic development, although it is a necessary component of it. It is important to realize that markets, management, and labor are equally, if not more, important to community economic development. Capital, however, is an important ingredient once the other factors are available. Furthermore, all forms of financial capital are not equally useful. For newer, smaller firms, with wide fluctuations in earnings, debt capital is less useful than patient or equity capital.

A review of the failures within the capital market identifies supply, demand, and institutional gaps. A community's capital market may not be able to attract sufficient funds to support local investment (capital gap). In this case, local financial institutions are not attracting deposits or using regional money markets to support local investment. A capital gap can also occur when a community is unable to generate sufficient equity capital. A demand gap exists when an area lacks the management and entrepreneurs capable of transforming existing financial capital into the physical capital required for production (e.g., buildings and equipment). In this case, the community needs to assist entrepreneurs and managers in the preparation of financial applications. An institutional gap exists when the area does not have the institutions to bring together providers and users of capital. Possibly as important as any shortage of capital is the shortage of talent to mobilize and utilize capital in a fashion both publicly and privately rewarding while protecting all parties against loss. This is particularly important in the public sector (Bearse 1979, p. 366). An area may lack a bank, a credit union, a small business investment corporation, or a community development corporation. Supply, demand, and institutional gaps are not mutually exclusive.

The basic question in using financial markets to promote community economic development is whether capital is being allocated to those enterprises that use it most productively. As there is a limited amount of capital available to be allocated, the question becomes, to whom is it allocated, and on what basis (Litvak and Daniels 1979, p. 17)?

It would appear that firms at the front of the capital allocation queue can present evidence of both relatively higher probable returns and lower risks to those who control the supply of capital. Languishing at the end of the line are enterprises with both low returns and high risk. Funds are likely to be exhausted before these firms make it to the lending window.

All this would seem to make good economic sense if there were no failures in the capital market. The first major failure involves projects that offer a competitive private return yet frequently fail to get the capital needed because: (1) there may not be mechanisms to reduce the risk to potential capital suppliers; (2) financial intermediaries may not have accurate or sufficient information about certain types of firms and their potential, placing them at a disadvantage when seeking funds; (3) there may be high transaction costs in making and administering loans to some types of business enterprises; (4) some financial intermediaries have a monopoly position and therefore raise the cost of funding above what it would be under conditions of open competition; (5) savers of capital and/or financial intermediaries may discriminate against credit applications for such reasons as race, sex, or politics; and (6) government regulation and intervention in the market place may have unintended side effects, distorting the allocation of credit among equally worthy applicants.

It is the availability rather than the cost which is critical when capital becomes an important location determinant. Capital cannot make a bad deal good, but the wrong type of capital can nullify a good deal or stop an otherwise promising enterprise from being born or growing (Daniels 1979, pp. 27–29). The right kind of capital on the right kind of terms can help a good venture start or expand and thus create vital economic activity in the community.

Capital is obviously crucial to the process of economic development. It is important in changing the productivity of labor because of its contribution to the quantity/quality of capital goods available to work with. But it must be recognized that while capital is necessary, it is not sufficient in itself for economic development (Daniels 1979, p. 8).

Study Questic

1. When capital markets were defined, the statement was made that capital is allocated among uses in such a way that "the return in all uses and places is equal." What is the significance of this statement to community economic analysis?

2. What role do financial institutions play in an economy? In particular, what role do they play between demanders and suppliers of capital?

3. How would you respond to the claim that capital markets are homogeneous?

4. Why might a financial institution not be involved in all types of capital markets?

5. What are some of the reasons for capital market failure? What is the significance of each to community economic development?

6. Why might capital not be mobile enough to cause the rates of return to equalize over all uses and places?

7. What is the significance of information costs in the functioning of capital markets?

8. Four forms of risk and four general strategies to accommodate risk were discussed. What are they? What do they mean for community economic development?

9. Four questions were suggested as a way of examining commercial bank practices in terms of community goals and objectives. What are they, and why are they important to community economic development?

Labor Markets and Community Economic Development

8

LABOR ECONOMICS TRADITIONALLY EXAMINES the interaction between the worker or group of workers and the firm or group of firms. This approach will be followed initially here, but then we shall examine the implications of such an analysis in the context of community economic development. In a community where land and capital are fixed, economic output and growth are a function of the size and quality of the labor force and how it is utilized.

Society places great emphasis on jobs. The possession of a job in the American economy provides an income that determines, to a large extent, the capacity to pursue a particular lifestyle. Because jobs are central to society and personal perception of worth, preparing for a job, getting a job, keeping a job, leaving a job, and finding another job are critical.[1] Thus a job represents a very valuable piece of property, with many economic, social, and psychological benefits attached to it (Kruger 1983, p. 70).

We shall examine some of the major theories concerning the role of labor in the economy and its utilization, with specific emphasis on employment and unemployment and corrective actions and on the emerging concern about job quality. The components of a labor market, the demand for labor, and the supply of labor will be reviewed and the institutional forces affecting them discussed. The major economic theories of labor markets will be outlined. Finally, unemployment and imperfections in the equitable and efficient allocation of labor resources will be examined.

Labor Marke

The exchange of labor services between worker and employer occurs in the context of demand for and supply of labor, within an overarching institutional framework that affects the interchange.

The market for labor displays many of the same characteristics as the market for capital or any other commodity (Clark 1983, pp. 166–68). At the same time, labor is not a commodity but is embodied in people, and therefore requires particular attention not necessary in other markets (Kreps et al. 1974, p. 24). In theory, a *labor market* is an institution within which labor services are bought and sold and thus allocated to various occupations, industries, and geographic areas to yield the greatest output to society. The market sets the price of labor, and the price allocates labor to its most productive use (Kreps et al. 1974, p. 23). The labor market need not be a physically contiguous area, although it generally is, but can be widely separated spatially and linked only by information flows.

Employers perceive their labor market as being the geographic area containing people who are either in the labor force or are willing to enter the labor force if offered an appropriate job (Lever 1980, p. 37). A job's appropriateness can be judged in many ways, including skills required, wages, fringe benefits, opportunity for advancement, working conditions, and commuting distance to work.

The *supply of labor* is a function of the existing population base of the community and nearby area. It reflects the age, sex, skills possessed, and lifestyle of that population (Kreps et al. 1974, p. 62). Workers generally view the labor market as the range of employment opportunities open to them without changing their residence (Lever 1980, p. 37).

In a perfectly competitive labor market, workers move among jobs, occupations, firms, and locations to eliminate differentials in wages and yield an efficient allocation of labor (Kreps et al. 1974, pp. 4–5). Shortages of workers cause wages to be bid up, while a surplus of workers depresses wages. The wage rate becomes the market clearing signal.[2] However, the wage paid to the worker depends upon the firm's return from that worker's service.

The perfectly competitive labor market assumes a nondifferentiated market with similar jobs and substitutable workers. Labor markets, however, are segmented, and the boundaries between them are often impenetrable. Segmented labor markets occur in a variety of ways, the most important of which are spatial, occupational, and institutional (Chesire 1979, pp. 29–31; Clark 1983, pp. 168–71; Kreps et al. 1974, p. 24). Labor markets in California or southern Illinois are different from labor markets in Alabama or northern Illinois; *spatial segmentation* occurs when distance prevents the exchange of information about job opportunities and worker availability. *Occupational segmentation* occurs when workers possess different skills, jobs require different skills, and workers are not totally substitutable. The proverbial ditchdigger may not be substitutable for the store clerk or the chief executive officer. Substitution can occur, but it requires time. *Institutional segmentation* of labor markets can be very explicit or very subtle.

When accreditation or membership in an union is required, segmentation is explicit. Many occupations predominantly filled by either males or females display a subtle labor market segmentation. Internal or external labor markets are another subtle form of segmentation. An internal labor market is the labor market that exists within a firm, usually a large firm; the external labor market is the relationship among individuals seeking employment but not currently attached to the firm.

However arbitrary, some boundaries must be drawn to define a labor market. For individuals with comparable skills and productivity, the boundaries typically include the area where information is available about employment opportunities and potential workers.

The boundaries of a labor market are not fixed, but vary according to the worker's occupation and mobility. The unskilled worker's labor market boundary probably extends for a relatively short commuting distance (Clark and Whiteman 1983, pp. 85–86), while for professionals the boundary is regional or even international. The geographic boundary depends also upon the information transfer mechanism about job opportunities and potential workers (Kreps et al. 1974, pp. 25–27). An added dimension to defining labor market boundaries is a tendency for firms and workers to be only partially integrated into the external labor market. Workers are best informed about job availability, job requirements, and the associated working conditions in the internal labor market. Likewise, firms know most about existing workers and their potential to fill new job openings. Thus, the tendency is for the labor market boundary to extend no further than the business premises.

Some important points about labor markets should be emphasized. First, labor market or labor shed boundaries depend upon people's ability and willingness to travel from their place of residence to their place of employment.[3] Second, there is an emphasis on the matching of skills with job requirements (i.e., nonhomogeneous components). Finally, the flow of information about job opportunities and availability of workers is an important determinant of the labor market boundary.

A well-functioning labor market is critical to community economic development. A labor market that transfers workers from jobs that yield lower-valued output to jobs that yield higher-valued output increases community output and worker per capita income. Furthermore, properly functioning labor markets improve the distribution of income by facilitating the transfer of workers from lower- to higher-paid jobs, so that the worker who moves up now receives a higher wage and the pay in his former job increases as a result of the movement of labor out of that activity.

Demand for Labor

The *demand for labor* consists of existing employment opportunities, filled and unfilled, both local and nonlocal. There is no single demand for labor but numerous demands, varying among occupations/skills, places, and sectors and over time. This nonhomogeneity of demand must be recognized in any effort to analyze and manipulate the labor market.

The demand for labor is a *derived demand*. Employers do not desire workers because of their intrinsic value but because of labor's productivity and the price of the product labor produces. The demand for labor is really determined by several economic forces. First is the demand for the output labor actually produces, expressed in terms of the price and elasticity of that output. Second is the productivity of labor, implicitly embodying the capital and technology used and the capacity of individuals to use that capital and technology. Third is the price of other resources used with labor. Thus, if the price of a substitute (complementary) resource falls, there will be a decline (increase) in the demand for labor. A fourth shifter of the demand for labor is a change in the firm's goals, such as dropping profit maximization for product/market development, or maximizing owner's leisure time (Fleisher and Kneisner 1984, p. 174).

The *demand for labor* represents the wage the firm is willing to pay for a given number of workers or quantity of labor time. This can be represented by the equation:

$$W = MPP_L \times P_O = VMP_L \qquad (8.1)$$

The firm is willing to pay a worker wages (W) based on that worker's marginal physical product (MPP_L) and the price of the output (P_o) produced. The statement that labor has a derived demand becomes explicitly clear in (8.1). First, the marginal physical product of any given worker depends upon the worker's inherent productivity (i.e., human capital). Second, the marginal physical product of any worker depends upon the amount of physical capital and other fixed resources used by the worker along with the technology embodied in the capital. Third, the wage the firm would be willing to pay the worker depends upon the price of output produced.

Equation (8.1) assumes that the firm and the worker are both in competitive markets. Thus the workers in a community are willing to provide all the labor needed at any given wage rate (i.e., the supply of labor is perfectly elastic). At the same time, the product demand the firm faces is also perfectly elastic, and therefore the firm is willing to demand all the workers it can acquire as long as their productivity justifies it.

In Figure 8.1 the value marginal product of labor (VMP_L) curve repre-

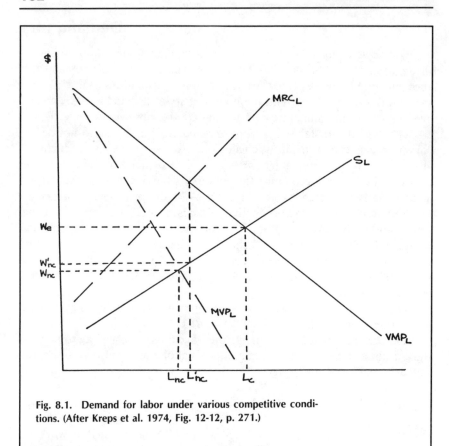

Fig. 8.1. Demand for labor under various competitive conditions. (After Kreps et al. 1974, Fig. 12-12, p. 271.)

sents the firm's short-run demand for labor. The position of the VMP_L curve is governed by the MPP_L and the P_o, or the productivity of labor and the price of the output produced. The MPP_L is governed by the amount of fixed physical capital used with labor and the specific type of technology embodied in the it.[4] The P_o is governed by the competitive conditions in the product market and consumer preferences. In a competitive labor market the firm's marginal cost of labor is the supply of labor curve (S_L). The firm will hire L_c labor and pay W_c if it faces competitive product and factor markets.

When the firm faces a less than perfectly competitive product market its demand for labor will be altered because it can no longer sell all of its output at P_o but must lower product prices to sell more. Thus the D_L' or MVP_L curve will lie below and to the left of the D_L curve for a firm in a competitive product market. The result is fewer workers hired and lower wages.

If a community has a less than perfectly competitive labor market, the equilibrium will differ from the competitive equilibrium (Kreps et al. 1974, pp. 270–72). This occurs when a firm is the only purchaser or one of a few purchasers of labor in the community (e.g., the firm must raise wage rates to hire additional workers).[5] Noncompetitive labor supply can also occur as a consequence of unions, certification of qualified workers, and restrictions on in-migration or in-commuting of workers. In Figure 8.1 the marginal cost of labor, MRC_L, in the less competitive labor market, lies above and to the left of the average cost of labor curve, S_L. In this market environment the firm maximizes its profits when $MRC_L = VMP_L$ (assuming a competitive product market). The amount of labor used is L'_{nc} and wages paid are W'_{nc}, both less than the equilibrium values in a competitive product and labor market.[6] The less than competitive conditions in the labor market could be caused by a geographically isolated market or by specific occupational demands with little substitutability among jobs and workers (Madden 1977).[7] Imperfections in either the product or factor market reduces both the number of workers hired and the wages paid relative to the conditions present in a perfectly competitive market.

Beyond the competitiveness of local labor markets, the level of community demand for labor is a function of industrial mix, technology used, community priorities, and level of national economic activity. The composition of the local economy (industrial mix) affects the level of labor demand (expanding/declining sectors) and the composition of the demand for labor (skilled/semiskilled/unskilled).

The question of technology extends the discussion of industrial mix one more step. Obviously, different sectors use different technology, but firms in the same sector of the economy may also use different technology to produce their output. In the most general sense, technology is either labor-intensive or capital-intensive. In a more specific sense, different technologies require different types of worker skills. For example, the change in the delivery of health care from hospitals to clinics alters the types of health care skills required.

Community or social priorities cover the level and type of public and private sector production. The level of public sector production refers to the type and quality of public goods desired (e.g., fire protection, police, social service agencies) and whether the public sector or the private sector is perceived as an employer of last resort. An example of the type of output that has experienced a recent dramatic increase is the demand for health care. The advent of medical insurance, particularly as part of the standard wage package, increases the demand for medical care and for health professionals.

Another, and very obvious, determinant of labor demand is the level of external demand for local products. The openness of a community's economy (i.e., a high level of in erchange between local and nonlocal economies) is a factor here, since the local economy can easily be influenced by the regional, state, or national economies.

The demand for labor varies over time because of changes in technology, consumer tastes and preferences, income levels, and the price or amount of other available factors of production. These changes affect communities and groups of workers differently. The dynamic nature of the demand for labor means that workers must change jobs or residence or acquire different skills. The ability of labor to respond depends upon its mobility. The demand for labor in a community is influenced by the inherent skills and productivity of the resident labor force (human capital); competitive conditions in both product and input markets; and the type of technology and capital used, as represented by the types of sectors present in the community, community priorities, and nonlocal economic activity.

Supply of Labo

The *supply of labor* refers to the various combinations of wage rates and quantities of labor offered. For the individual, the wage rates and quantities of labor offered represent a trade-off between time spent in the formal and informal labor markets. The *formal labor market* includes working in a factory, farm, or office (e.g., work for which the individual receives a monetary wage). The *informal labor market* (sometimes labeled leisure or nonwork) represents activities carried on to meet the personal and psychic needs of individuals, such as home maintenance, child care, food preparation, sleep, and vacation (Becker 1965). Since individuals are constrained by the twenty-four hours in a day, they allocate those hours between work and nonwork daily, weekly, annually, and over a lifetime.

The *community labor supply* is made up of the local population base, in-commuters, and in-migrants. The composition of the labor force in any given community derives from many factors, including the participation rates of various components of the population (influenced by age, sex, race), attitudes toward work for pay, attitudes toward work after certain ages (retirement), acceptability of teenagers joining the labor force, labor legislation (e.g., hours of work restrictions, antidiscrimination provisions, minimum wage laws), and rules governing retirement and welfare benefits (Beck and Goode, 1981; Kreps et al. 1974, p. 62; Scott et al. 1977).[8]

The total supply of community labor offered to employers depends upon the number of hours each worker is willing to work and the number of workers available. What is relevant here is not the supply of labor to the economy as a whole, but the supply of a particular kind of labor to a well-defined group of employers requiring specific skills at a particular location. This specificity means that the supply of labor depends upon the length of time involved and the skills required.

The time required to acquire skills, the worker's need to have non-monetary aspects of life satisfied, the time required to move among occupations and places, and the division of total available hours in the family among work and nonwork activities lead to the various shapes of the labor supply curve (Kreps et al. 1974, p. 268). The labor supply curve could be vertical, backward-bending, or even sloping upward to the right. To suggest that it could actually slope upward to the left (i.e., backward-bending) appears to defy economic logic, but it does recognize the noncommodity aspects of labor.

Figure 8.2 demonstrates one possible explanation of the backward-bending labor supply curve. In the figure the individual has OH hours in the day, of which HH_w are used for work and OH_w for nonwork activities. The family of indifference curves (U_i) represents the trade-off that this individual makes between work and nonwork activities. The budget line ($W_0 W_0'$) represents the income individuals earn if they use all their time (24 hours daily) for work, leisure, or combinations of work and leisure. The slope of budget line $W_0 W_0'$ represents the ratio between work income and nonwork income ("nonwork" is used here to represent the informal labor market, for simplicity). Nonwork income consists of psychic income and other income sources such as welfare, dividends, or interest. In the figure, total income (OY_t) is the sum of nonwork income (OY_{nw}) and work income ($Y_{nw}Y_t$). An increase in wage rates to W_1 (change slope to $W_0 W_1$) increases hours worked from HH_w to HH_w', and the worker achieves a higher indifference curve (U_2). If nonwork income increases to W_3, with no difference in wage rates (e.g., a parallel shift in the budget line to $W_3 W_3'$), then the worker achieves U_2 with only HH_w'' hours offered for work.

The movement from U_1 to U_2 is an income effect due to an increase in either work or nonwork income. The movement along U_2 because of the new ratio of work-nonwork income is a substitution effect. When a worker receives a wage increase, his/her observed response is the sum of the income and substitution effects (Kreps et al. 1974, pp. 263–64). The *income effect* occurs when the individual increases his/her demand for nonwork activities as wages increase. It means that the worker can maintain current income while reducing hours worked. The *substitution effect* means that leisure hours now have a higher opportunity cost, thus creating an incentive to work more hours. The net effect on hours offered for work depends upon the indifference curves of the individual and upon whether the income or substitution effect dominates (Ehrenberg and Smith 1985, pp. 156–59).[9] When the substitution effect dominates the income effect, increases in wages increase the amount of time supplied for work (a labor supply curve

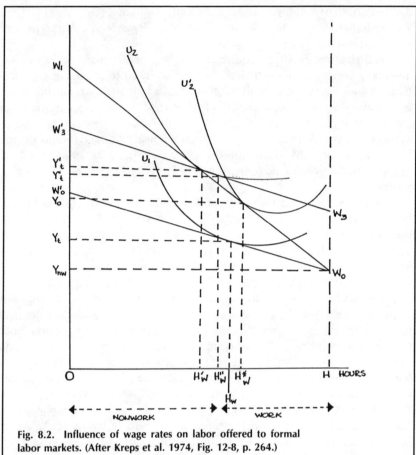

Fig. 8.2. Influence of wage rates on labor offered to formal
labor markets. (After Kreps et al. 1974, Fig. 12-8, p. 264.)

slopping upward to the right). If the income effect dominates, the labor
supply curve becomes negatively sloped (upward to the left). In Figure 8.2,
if the worker's utility curves are U_1 and U_2', the increase in wages from W_0
to W_1 actually increases the worker's utility by reducing the time spent in
the formal labor market (e.g., HH_w^*). The implication of Figure 8.2 is that
the labor supply curve is backward-bending above some wage.

Another dimension of the labor supply curve is elasticity (Madden
1977). The long-run supply curve of labor is naturally more elastic than the
short-run curve because time permits greater changes in human capital and
fixed capital and greater mobility among occupations and locations. Long-
run cultural changes, such as attitudes about the age of retirement, child
labor, or the participation of women in the formal labor force, alter the

supply of labor. Elasticity of the labor supply varies among skill levels also (Kreps et al. 1974, p. 220). The less specialized the skill, the more elastic the supply of labor function. The geographic scope being analyzed also affects the elasticity of labor supply. The elasticity of labor supply for the entire economy is more limited than the labor supply in a particular locale because of the potential to transfer workers from one locale to another. Changes in wage rates affect labor force participation and the elasticity of labor supply. An increase in wages or in number of job openings attracts individuals only marginally attached to the labor force (e.g., youth, discouraged workers). These individuals essentially substitute formal for informal work. The marginal workers buffer dramatic changes in official unemployment over the business cycle (Kreps et al. 1974, pp. 55, 302–3).

It is important to distinguish between the supply of labor and the labor force as officially defined. The *labor force* is officially the sum of employed and unemployed workers (unemployed are those actively seeking work but unable to find it). The major difficulty with this definition is *hidden unemployment,* which takes two distinct forms. The first is *underemployment,* where individuals work in jobs that do not fully utilize their skills. These workers count as employed. By the same token, people may be overemployed (e.g., their job requirements exceed their skills). Overemployment can be explained by the famous Peter Principle. The second form of hidden unemployment is represented by the group of *discouraged individuals* who are no longer actively seeking work because they perceive that their chance of locating a job is minimal. Since they are not looking for work, they are not unemployed or even members of the labor force, as officially defined. These people enter the labor force when they perceive employment opportunities. The employed worker represents an often overlooked source of community labor because employed individuals are presumed to be satisfied with their current jobs and not willing to change. However, such individuals may hold jobs for which they are either over- or under-qualified, may be dissatisfied with working conditions, or may desire higher wages. Regardless of their willingness to pursue new employment opportunities, currently employed persons typically represent the major portion of the local labor force.

New entrants and returnees to the labor force represent a hidden supply of potential labor. *New entrants* are individuals entering the labor force for the first time. They may be recent graduates of high schools, vocational schools, or universities or individuals leaving the informal labor market (e.g., housewives) to enter the formal labor market. *Returnees,* on the other hand, previously worked in the formal labor force and left because of unemployment or discouragement about employment opportunities, family responsibilities, or changes in life style; they now choose to re-enter the formal labor force. In many communities, new entrants and returnees represent a large reservoir of individuals available for employment if they perceive an opportunity.

Two additional sources of local labor, in-commuters and in-migrants, explicitly recognize the spatial dimension of local labor markets. *In-commuters* reside in nearby areas and commute to the community on a regular basis to fill local employment opportunities. *In-migrants* are new residents who move to the community for a variety of reasons, including employment opportunities, noneconomic reasons such as retirement, or a desire to escape their current residence.

The supply of labor by an individual or group depends upon several factors that determine behavioral response (i.e., hours of labor supplied) to changes in wage rates. Shifters of the supply of labor include changes in nonlabor income (e.g., Social Security payments, investment income), changes in wages or earnings of other family members, changes in household productivity, changes in the desire for market vs. nonmarket work, and changes from the goal of income maximization to a different goal. For the community, these forces are joined to those associated with changes in the number of workers and their families.

The local labor supply can shift because of in-commuters, in-migration, new entrants, or changes in investment in human capital. The human capital change is a long-run phenomenon and will be discussed later. The short-run phenomenon of in-commuters, in-migrants, and new entrants represent more obvious sources of shifts in supply. A less obvious source is labor mobility among jobs and occupations.

Age, family responsibilities, and current skills influence labor mobility. Job mobility of younger workers is reinforced by lack of family responsibilities, lack of inertia, lack of job security, and lower wages.[10] Very specific and small segments of the labor force account for much of the labor mobility in the economy (Kreps et al. 1974, pp. 33–34).

The labor supply depends upon the time allowed for adjustment to occur, the level of wages offered, the skills required, the preferences for work/nonwork activities and the composition of the local population, and the extent to which people will either commute or move to the community.

Institution

Institutions affect both the efficiency and equity outcomes of labor supply and demand. *Labor market institutions* provide the rules that govern the mobility of workers among jobs, the acquisition of skills and training, and the distribution of wages and other rewards obtained from working (Clark and Gertler 1981, p. 11; Kalleberg and Sorensen 1979, p. 351). Since labor is not a commodity, it responds to market signals in a slightly different fashion than commodities would. Rather than a single characteristic, jobs possess a bundle of qualities such as working conditions, location, climate, company prestige, chances of promotion, seniority rules, and friendliness of co-workers that alter their character. These qualities combine to affect the worker's choice of where and at what wage to work (Clark and Whiteman 1983, p. 89; Lester 1966, pp. 24, 41).[11] At the same time, firms do not perceive workers as homogeneous in skills, attitudes, motivation, stability, and health (Kreps et al. 1974, p. 24).

Wages are the job's most obvious characteristic—who has not asked about the wage rate or annual salary associated with a particular occupation or job? Yet fringe benefits are increasingly important. What type of health insurance, life insurance, vacation plan, and sick leave are linked with the job?

Working conditions are also important. Is the work environment inside or outside, relatively clean or dirty, noisy or quiet, safe or dangerous? What is the nature of labor-management relations? Individuals often find co-workers instrumental in helping to form positive or negative perceptions of a job. Opportunity for advancement, either perceived or real, also shapes one's judgment of the job. Some jobs offer no opportunity for advancement, while others represent stepping stones toward something better. A final important dimension of a job is stability. How sensitive is the job to seasonal variation (as in construction work, farm work), to cyclical variation (as in the auto industry, construction work, heavy manufacturing), or to secular trends (e.g., replacement of many low-skilled jobs with jobs requiring different or higher skills because of changes in technology)?

In essence, all that has been mentioned here can be summarized as characterizing jobs as good or bad. This judgment is typically made on the basis of wages, fringe benefits, stability of employment, working conditions, job security, and opportunity for promotion (Gordon 1972). Most would agree that a *good job* provides adequate wages and fringe benefits, job security, decent working conditions, and an opportunity for advancement and for control of one's work environment. Beyond this, however, perceptions of good and bad differ. Workers place different values on prestige, income and fringe benefits, authority and power, career opportunities, ability for self-direction, need to think about what they are doing, and interpersonal relationships associated with a job (Kalleberg and Sorensen 1974, p. 8). A community seeking to attract jobs must therefore recognize the diversity of characteristics that can make a job attractive or unattractive to workers.

Labor Market Theories

This section, which draws on the work of Gillis (1983), reviews the major labor market theories, which can be categorized as either supply- or demand-oriented. Both schools offer some insight for community economic analysis.

SUPPLY-ORIENTED THEORIES. Human capital theory dominates theories emphasizing the supply side of the labor market. *Human capital theory* builds on the neoclassical model of perfectly competitive labor markets and argues that human capital investments influence future monetary and psychic income by increasing the productive capacity of individuals (Becker 1985, pp. 12–44; Clark 1983, pp. 166–68). Examples of human capital investments include schooling, on-the-job training, and medical care. Such investments make a worker more productive by augmenting his/her skills, knowledge, health, or other productive attributes.

According to this theory, workers bring to the job skills and knowledge acquired through schooling, training, and work experience. No worker will be paid more than the value of his/her marginal product because a replacement worker is willing to work at a wage rate equaling marginal productivity. Likewise, an employee paid less than the value of his/her marginal product will seek another job with a wage rate reflecting his/her productivity. A worker's productivity is a function of the skills and knowledge he/she acquires through schooling, training, or work experiences and health status and mobility. Workers increase their future earnings by investing in productivity-augmenting activities. Human capital theory describes how an individual chooses the "correct" amount and type of human capital investment.

Investment in schooling or training activities provides a worker with the skills and knowledge to perform more complex job tasks and therefore to command a higher wage because he/she is more productive. Each worker weighs the discounted benefits of increased earnings against the cost of obtaining additional schooling or training. If the discounted value of the future benefits from a productivity-augmenting activity exceeds its cost, the investment will be undertaken.

Differences in the amounts of human capital among individuals can be accounted for in at least four ways: different expected annual returns, different costs, different expectations of time to be spent in the labor force, and different discount rates. According to human capital theory, people receive different returns from investment in schooling or other training because of variations in talent or ability (Becker 1985, p. 94), thus leading to variations in human capital investments. Expectations of time remaining in the labor force influences individuals considering additional schooling, training, or other productivity-augmenting investments. Women often spend a substantial amount of time out of the labor force or work reduced hours in order to care for children, causing them to invest less in human capital because they have less time to recover their investment (Kahne and Kohen 1975, p. 1,273). Finally, people differ in their time preference for income (i.e., different discount rate), which influences the amount of investment they will make in school or training. This discount rate also varies because of uncertainty about future returns.

To accumulate a productive labor force requires a substantial investment by the community or the worker. From the community's perspective, the investment takes the form of providing elementary, secondary, vocational, or university education. The community also bears a burden in the form of foregone output or poor quality output during the training process. From the individual's perspective, the investment takes the form of foregone income during training, the cost of tuition, and other costs such as transportation back and forth to class. However, both the community and the individual perceive that future returns from these investments, both in wages and increased output, will more than offset the cost. Investment in human capital appears to conform to the law of diminishing returns. Unlimited investment in human capital need not yield continuing increases in income and output both nationally and locally (Dresch 1977, p. 112; Levitan 1983, p. 15). The rational worker/community invests only to the point where the future benefits from the investment equal its cost.

The important insights from human capital theory can be summarized as follows:

- The amount an individual invests in human capital depends upon the expected annual return from the investment, the cost of the investment, the expected time in the labor force to recoup the investment, and the discount rate.
- Persons who expect to spend a significant amount of time out of the labor force to raise children will invest less in human capital than workers planning to be in the labor force for several years.
- Compared with other members of the labor pool, youths possess less human capital because they have not completed their formal education and lack work experience.
- Compared with individuals in the middle of their life cycle, individuals at the end of their labor force careers possess less human capital because some skills have become obsolete. Because their remaining time in the labor force is short, they are less likely to invest in updating old skills or learning new skills. In addition, they are more likely to have health problems.

Neoclassical human capital theory provides a foundation for understanding how local labor markets function. This approach emphasizes efficiency in allocating labor resources among competing uses. Yet the major problem in local labor markets is access by some individuals to full participation. The neoclassical model does not provide very good insight into these equity questions.

Another limitation of the neoclassical approach as a basis for policy is that the worker carries the implicit burden for all the adjustments. The theory is silent on how adjusting labor demand (i.e., quantity and skill requirements) influences the use of labor and employment/unemployment levels.

While the neoclassical model provides an excellent starting point, it relies too much on the assumption that the rational person understands his/her investment return options and has control over his/her life and equal access to job opportunities. People are subject to family and psychic ties as well as institutional constraints (e.g., discrimination) that prevent equal access. These shortcomings of the neoclassical model have stimulated the creation of alternative explanations.

DEMAND-ORIENTED THEORIES. According to neoclassical theory, the production skills and other worker characteristics demanded by a given employer depend upon the firm's technology. Specifically, the occupational requirements and the type of physical capital employed determine an employer's choice of workers from alternative groups in the labor pool because these factors define the type of production skills workers need to perform a job (Griliches 1969, pp. 465–68; Hammermesh and Grant 1979, pp. 525–29; Welch 1970, pp. 764–71). In the neoclassical model, the match between workers and jobs is relatively uncomplicated: Workers with production skills most closely matching those required for a given job are hired.

The refined version of human capital theory outlined above diverges substantially from the neoclassical theory of labor markets. First, the assumption of homogeneous workers and job requirements is relaxed. Second, restrictions on occupational mobility are recognized through the need to acquire additional training. Third, the uncertainty about educational investments is implicitly recognized in the variation of discount rates among individuals.

Critics argue that human capital theory masks the importance of behavioral parameters on the demand side of the labor market. Alternative labor market theories focus on the role played by the hiring rules used to match workers with jobs (Cain 1976). Hiring rules are established by companies when they set up their personnel policies, by trade unions, and by governmental actions (Kerr 1982, p. 51). These rules state which workers are preferred by employers. Three major theories emphasizing the role of hiring rules are signaling/screening theory, job competition theory, and segmented labor market theory.

Signaling/Screening or Credentialing Theory. The roots of signaling/screening theory lie in organizational behavior theory under conditions of uncertainty and imperfect knowledge (Arrow 1973, pp. 193–216; Spence 1974, pp.

355–79; Walpin 1975, pp. 949–58). Advocates of signaling/screening theory argue that the majority of job skills are acquired on the job, either by specific training or through "learning while doing" (Piore 1973, pp. 337–78; Spence 1974, p. 356). Consequently, employers search for workers efficient in learning new job tasks who will be dependable once trained. The firm needs quick and cheap techniques that can improve its prospects for hiring dependable workers efficient in learning new skills. Signaling/screening theory suggests that hiring standards are not prerequisites for satisfactory job performance but rather are proxies for personality characteristics such as ability, motivation, dependability, and willingness to learn (Spence 1974, pp. 355–57).

The limited number of points of entry to the firm reinforce the employer's interest in hiring standards to screen potential employees. Many firms possess distinct families of jobs (i.e., career ladders) (Reich et al. 1973, p. 362). Within each family of jobs is a skill or responsibility hierarchy. Jobs at the bottom of each hierarchy require the least skills and are associated with the least responsibilities. Many firms customarily hire from outside the firm only to fill jobs at the bottom level of the hierarchy. Intermediate and upper-level positions are filled by promoting workers from a lower level (Doeringer and Piore 1971, p. 79). Lower-echelon hiring thus determines the future labor pool for higher-echelon positions. The group of unskilled workers hired is frequently the pool from which key semiskilled workers and foremen will later be selected—in hiring this year's salesperson, an employer may be selecting a future sales manager. Minimum educational and experience standards may be set higher than required for the entry job (Kalachek 1973, p. 73) because of the desire to hire workers capable of ascending the skill and responsibility ladder.

Job Competition Theory. Job competition theory explicitly incorporates the concept of labor market screening into the model of firm profit maximization (Thurow 1975, pp. 77–97). Like screening theory, job competition theory assumes that most job skills are acquired either formally or informally on the job after the worker finds an entry-level position and a foot on the associated promotion ladder. Firms profit by minimizing the training cost associated with bringing the worker up to the standard level of job performance.

A bundle of personal characteristics (age, race, sex, work experience, and education) differentiates workers. From the employer's perspective, these personal characteristics indicate the cost of training a worker for new job tasks. Based on past experiences in training workers, employers rank workers with different bundles of personal characteristics according to their perceived cost of training. Workers perceived by employers as the least costly to train occupy the front of the "labor queue." Workers judged to be more expensive to train for new job tasks occupy positions further down the labor queue.

There is also a queue of vacant jobs. Jobs paying the highest salary, with the greatest opportunities for promotion and nonmonetary benefits such as status and desirability, occupy the front of the queue. Jobs further down the queue possess less desirable monetary and nonmonetary benefits. The hiring process, then, matches the queue of job seekers to the queue of vacant jobs. The highest-placed person in the labor queue gets the job with the highest monetary and nonmonetary rewards in the job queue.

Dual Labor Market Theory. The dual labor market theory divides the economy into core and peripheral economies (Doeringer and Piore 1971, pp. 67–97; Reich et al. 1973, pp. 359–60; Vietorisz and Harrison 1973). High productivity, high profits, intensive utilization of capital, high incidence of monopoly elements, and a high degree of unionization characterize firms in the core economy. In contrast, small firm size, high labor intensity, low profits, low productivity, intense product market competition, and a lack of unionization characterize firms in the peripheral economy (Bluestone et al. 1973, pp. 18–34).

The economic advantages enjoyed by large core economy firms include: (1) extensive assets, allowing core firms to outspend smaller peripheral firms; (2) better geographic and product diversification; (3) vertical integration, permitting core firms to become their own suppliers and distributors, thus ensuring low-cost inputs and a distribution network; (4) favored access to finance when credit is scarce or restricted; (5) political advantages such as favorable laws and administrative rulings on tariffs, taxes, and subsidies, achieved through information preparation, public relations, and political lobbying; and (6) extensive resources allowing core firms to spend greater amounts on research and development and have early access to new technology (Averitt 1968, p. 24).

Along with this dualism in the industrial structure is a corresponding dualism of working environments, wages, and mobility patterns (Doeringer and Piore 1971, p. 76; Reich et al. 1973, pp. 363–64). Firms in the core economy, with more stable production and sales, offer jobs reflecting that stability. Peripheral firms, with unstable product demand, offer jobs characterized by instability. Core firms are larger and more diverse than peripheral firms, thereby providing more promotional opportunities. Firms in the core economy are more capital-intensive and earn higher profits than peripheral firms. Because of their economic advantage, core firms generally provide jobs with more monetary and nonmonetary benefits.

According to dual labor market theory, dualism in the economy leads to segmentation of the labor force (i.e., different subgroups of the labor pool fill different job slots) (Gordon 1972, pp. 43–52). In particular, minority workers, women, the less educated, and youths tend to be concentrated in low-wage, unstable employment with few promotional opportunities (i.e., peripheral jobs).

The reason for labor market segmentation, according to this theory, is less initial differences in human capital than hiring standards established by employers and unions, as well as custom and tradition. As in job competition theory, dual labor market theory holds that employers rank workers according to their preferences for personal characteristics such as education, training, work experience, sex, age, and race. Because of their economic advantage, firms in the core economy pay a wage higher than the market clearing price, thus permitting them to follow selective employment practices.

Dual labor market theory focuses on the roles of workers' attitudes, motivations, and work habits and suggests that employers believe that some segments of the labor force are less dependable, less disciplined, and less motivated than other worker subgroups[12] (Reich et al. 1973, p. 360). Employers in the core economy, because they are able to pay relatively high wages, are less likely to draw from these subgroups of the labor force.

SUMMARY. The preceding theories were originally formulated to explain the actions of an individual worker or firm, yet they have implications for communities as well. All four theories contend that workers and jobs are not homogeneous nor completely substitutable. Human capital theory recognizes the need for training investments that may require significant community involvement (e.g., provision of facilities and support for travel and living expenses). Another form of community involvement would be reducing the risk of future unemployability and the workers' qualitative differences among jobs that the community must realize and take into account in its job development efforts.

Community Labor Market Issues

While labor markets typically are viewed as an interchange among workers and employers, the community performs a crucial role in facilitating the functioning of the labor market. This role most frequently appears as helping match workers to jobs, developing policies to alleviate unemployment, and aiding information followup and worker mobility.

JOB/WORKER MATCHING. The community's interest in its labor market arises from the need to facilitate the exchange between the providers of jobs and the suppliers of labor. Each party in this exchange attempts to maximize his/her objectives. Workers seek employment that meets their goals for self-fulfilment and skill application. Firms seek workers who best fill employment requirements.

In examining the exchange or matching process between workers and firms, it is critical to examine the workers, the job, and the characteristics of the matching process itself because the creation of a labor force and the creation of jobs in a modern society are almost independent processes (Sorensen and Kalleberg 1974, pp. 9, 38). Job/worker mismatches lead to reduced output, negative job attitudes, and low job satisfaction. There are three types of mismatches that can occur in this exchange (Sorenson and Kalleberg 1974, p. 5). The first is a discrepancy between the skills possessed and the skills required. The second is a discrepancy between the actual earnings and status of the job and the jobholder's aspirations. The third is the presence of both these discrepancies in a given job situation. Gleave and Palmer (1980, p. 61) would add spatial mismatch between jobs and workers.

There are two forms of skill discrepancies (Kalleberg and Sorensen 1974, p. 18). The first, labeled quality underemployment or overtraining, occurs when an individual works in a job not requiring the full use of his/her skills or occupational capacity. The second, labeled undertraining, occurs when a person is in a job for which he/she does not have the necessary skills or occupational capacity. This situation can occur in firms experiencing rapid occupational and technological change. Neither the firm nor the worker may be fully aware of the job skills required in this period of transition. Either the worker acquires the skills required or the components of the job are altered to match the skills the worker possesses. The prospect of a mismatch increases with inadequate information exchange, rigidity in the composition of the job, or difficulty in acquiring new skills.

At least two factors influence the potential for a job requirements/skills mismatch. First is the type of skills the worker possesses. Are they broad-based or highly specialized? Workers with highly specialized skills not easily transferable to other tasks are more likely to be the victims of a skills mismatch (Grossman and Shapiro 1982; Sorensen and Kalleberg 1974, p. 12). The second factor influencing the potential for a skills mismatch is the composition of the job. Does it require specialized skills? If so, can it be subdivided into different skills components? To the extent that the job can be subdivided or requires generalized skills, a skills mismatch will be less likely (Sorensen and Kalleberg 1974, pp. 19, 39–40).

The presumption that the worker is the only party in the exchange who adjusts to meet job requirements ignores the employer's option of adjusting the skill requirements of jobs (Sorensen and Kalleberg 1974, p. 19). It is usually possible to restructure the skills requirements of a particular job (i.e., to reduce skills mismatch through flexibility in designing the tasks performed). The type of technology used and the willingness of management to tailor skills requirements to workers will determine the potential of this option (Appelbaum 1983, p. 35).

Another type of mismatch occurs between job quality and individual aspirations (Sorensen and Kalleberg 1974, p. 16). Individuals have aspirations about job status, income level, fringe benefits, and self-actualization. To a large extent these job qualities are noneconomic but nonetheless very important. This mismatch tends to be corrected over time as the worker's perceptions of the job and the aspirations converge.

The matching of the supply of jobs, differentiated by wages, skills, and working conditions, to the demand for particular types of jobs by workers represents a major concern in community labor markets. This concern heightens with the level of unemployment.

UNEMPLOYMENT. There are some very important and traditional assumptions associated with the functioning of the labor market: (1) that workers and employers have complete and adequate knowledge of job opportunities and wages; (2) that workers and employers are rational and will maximize either their satisfaction or their profits; (3) that workers and employers are sufficiently numerous that neither can influence the wage rate, or that there is no collusion among the parties concerning wage rates; (4) that labor is homogeneous and interchangeable within a particular market; (5) that there are no barriers to workers' occupational or geographic mobility; and (6) that unemployment arises only when these assumptions are relaxed.

Any community labor market analysis must address the question of unemployment. While the initial reaction to unemployment is adverse, some unemployment can be considered normal or even beneficial. As Edward Kalachek (1973, p. 77) puts it, "All unemployment is not socially disruptive or economically wasteful. Some unemployment is a natural concomitant of technical progress and free labor markets, and can be considered socially and economically beneficial. We need a framework for distinguishing the harmful from the beneficial or indifferent instances."

Unemployment is not a homogeneous phenomenon; its various components respond to different market forces. This differentiation helps focus public policy response. While labels vary, unemployment typically divides into demand-deficient unemployment, structural unemployment, and frictional unemployment (Ehrenberg and Smith 1985, pp. 496–508; Gleave and Palmer 1980, pp. 58–66).

Demand-deficient unemployment occurs because the total number of unemployed workers exceeds the total number of job vacancies across all occupations and places. It really measures the vitality and strength of the economy.

Structural unemployment appears as a mismatch of the job requirements and skills available in a particular locale. This category recognizes the nonhomogeneity of the labor force, which prevents any worker from filling any job. It also recognizes that differences in the location of jobs and workers cause unemployment.

Frictional unemployment measures that irreducible minimum at which unemployment and vacancies occur simultaneously in the same occupation because of imperfections in information both about job availability and about supplies of unemployed workers, because of the time required for workers to shift between jobs, or because of a spatial separation of vacancies and workers.[13]

Some causes of unemployment include a geographic mismatch between the worker and the job vacancy; a time mismatch between the skills the worker possesses and the skills the job requires; and information flow constraints (i.e., constraints on the transmission and reception of information) (Gleave and Palmer 1980, p. 61). Regardless of the cause, the burden of unemployment invariably falls on workers in a nonuniform fashion (i.e., on specific groups of workers defined by their geographic location, age, sex, and occupational skills) (Cecchette et al. 1981, p. 31; Smith 1981).

When examining local unemployment, it is important to look beyond the three categories listed above. Local unemployment differs from national unemployment for a variety of reasons. First, the economic sectors in the community may have cost structures and technologies different from the national average. Second, because of the dynamics of the economy, communities continually face situations in which demand has changed and supply is trying to adjust. The cost of information and labor immobility[14] prevent instantaneous and complete adjustment of local employment to these shifts. The capacity to adjust also varies among geographic areas. One hypothesis argues that market forces will not reduce the imbalance between labor demand and supply in a specific locale even over long periods of time regardless of growth in aggregate demand and shifts in the supply of labor because of labor market segmentation; the immobility of labor among uses and locations; and labor's nonmonetary attachment to an area and co-workers, which acts to resist monetary market forces.

INFORMATION. For a labor market to work well, information on the location of jobs and the skills required must be widely available to members of the labor force (Kreps et al. 1974, p. 23; Lester 1966, p. 34; Lever 1980; Shaeffer 1985). Likewise, information on worker availability, skills, and willingness to work or to move to a new job location is necessary.

One problem is that the market may not give the appropriate signals to allocate the labor force optimally (Lester 1966, p. 109). Workers and employers are hampered by their own ignorance or uncertainty not only about current but about future manpower needs. Institutional wage rigidity (e.g., union contracts) may be higher than the equilibrium wage, sending a market signal of labor shortage in certain occupations even though those occupations are actually shrinking.

Widespread dissemination of labor market information depends upon numerous forces (Lever 1980, pp. 51–52), some of which are geographic size of the labor market, number of workers and employers, and relative market power possessed by either workers or employers. The larger the labor market (in numbers of job opportunities, numbers of workers, and geography), the more difficult it is to dispense information to all parties. The greater the economic concentration (i.e., the more noncompetitive the market) and the greater the homogeneity of economic activity, the fewer the sources of information needed by labor market parties.

Job information can be disseminated both formally and informally. Information is disseminated formally through want ads, job service bureaus, and private employment agencies. Informal channels are friends or relatives. Often market signals about current and future job/occupation needs are particularly inadequate or ineffective in motivating some groups that are less sensitive or less responsive to market signals (e.g., racial minorities, youths). Sometimes even though the market signals are there, individuals are unable to comprehend their meaning and implications.

A well-functioning labor market requires that appropriate signals be sent and received by both employers and workers. When this fails to occur, the needed adjustments are less likely to occur.

LABOR MOBILITY AND WAGE DIFFERENTIALS. Traditional economic theory suggests that labor migrates from low-wage to high-wage communities to equalize real wages among communities. This presumes that wage differentials are the only cause of migration among jobs and/or communities (Krumm 1983; Lester 1966, p. 135; Moomaw 1983). Yet other forces also influence labor migration (Kalleberg and Sorenson 1974, p. 16). Wage differentials no doubt affect the migration of those workers most sensitive to financial incentives (i.e., the most mobile workers and those with the least social attachment to their residence) (Ehrenberg and Smith 1985, pp. 308–10). Such workers value the monetary portion of their income more than the psychic or nonmonetary portion. Yet even here nonwage factors can either accentuate or dampen this migration.

The number of job opportunities in a community receiving in-migrants also influences the mobility of labor among places (Krumm 1983). Numerous job opportunities in a community increase the probability that workers will migrate in regardless of wage differentials. National employment growth also affects labor mobility. If the national economy is stagnant (if workers perceive labor market conditions to be bad everywhere), there is little incentive for workers to incur the cost of moving. The question of the stability of the job in the other community vs. the current job and the loss of seniority caused by the move can reduce mobility stimulated by wage differentials.

The distance of the move affects labor mobility (Krumm 1983). Distance becomes an obstacle to the movement of labor or economic activity, and more than just a minor wage differential is needed to overcome it.

The amenities associated with a community, either the one sending or the one receiving the migrants, affects the extent to which wage-stimulated migration occurs. Some individuals will accept lower wages or seasonal unemployment because they substitute mountains, hunting, fishing, or access to the opera for money wages. The mobility of labor among communities sometimes depends upon the psychological attraction of family and friends. Age, race, or sex discrimination can prevent worker mobility from eliminating the wage differential (Krumm 1983; Madden 1977).

Even with a large movement of labor among communities, wage differentials can continue to exist (Krumm 1983). One reason for this is that the people moving are the unemployed, and therefore wages are neither reduced in the high-wage community nor driven up in the low-wage community. Likewise, differences in production technologies and economies of scale associated with similar industries in different communities can yield a continuing community wage differential. Institutional rigidity, such as caused by union contracts, maintains wage differentials in the face of extensive labor mobility. Wage differentials among communities may be caused by different occupational structures (different jobs pay different rates) or by the fact that labor is heterogeneous. The apparent wage differentials among communities continue to exist because the communities produce different products, thus altering the demand for labor.

In summary, while the general perception is that labor mobility will eliminate geographic and occupational wage differentials, differences among community economies, workers, and time will probably prevent full equalization of wages.

Community Actie

Public attempts to generate a more efficient and equitable labor market generally fall into three categories. The first attacks institutional imperfections, the second attacks supply imperfections, and the third attacks demand imperfections. Attempts to correct *institutional imperfections* in the labor market include such things as job information programs, affirmative action codes, and unemployment compensation systems. Here, the emphasis is on improving the equity dimension of labor market activity. Attempts to correct *supply imperfections* typically revolve around improving the quality of existing and potential workers by providing them with appropriate skills, good work habits, and improved geographic and occupational mobility. Attempts to correct *demand imperfections* generally either increase the aggregate demand for output, and therefore jobs, or reduce the costs of specific types of labor by subsidizing wages, providing training, or reducing institutional minimum wages.

Summary

Two subtle shifts in labor market analysis in recent years are a focus on *inclusion* and a focus on *job quality*. The first shift explicitly recognizes that some individuals, because of race, sex, age, or other factors, have been systematically excluded from full participation in the labor market and its associated rewards—that institutional barriers and heterogeneity in the labor force prevent certain segments of the population from earning a living. The second shift recognizes that a job is more than mere employment and that some jobs possess characteristics that workers appear to value more than others. Yet not everyone desires jobs having the characteristics so highly valued by many workers. For example, some people do not want a job that requires them to solve problems or to work fulltime. Thus it is important to maintain a mix of jobs in designing any community employment program.

One inherent difficulty of manipulating the supply of labor is that labor is only a necessary but not a sufficient condition for employment: its availability does not assure that people will be employed. However, the presence of capital, in the form of plant and equipment, suggests that jobs are also available. (Whether the available jobs are appropriate for the target population is another issue.)

To correct conditions of underemployment or unemployment requires emphasis on both the demand for and the supply of labor. To focus solely on either the demand or the supply dimensions of the labor market would be to assume, mistakenly, that only one force lends itself to policy manipulation or is the cause of the unemployment.

Often overlooked in community economic development planning is the fact that an operating business yields two economic outputs. The first, and most obvious, is the product or service the firm produces. The second, and less obvious, is a worker with a set of skills and an attachment to the labor force. This second dimension becomes an important interface between community economic development programs, the labor market, and business activities. If the community can structure a series of employment opportunities that match workers' differing skills and desires for working hours and conditions, then it has created a full range of employment opportunities that allow each worker to meet his or her individual needs.

Study Questio

1. What is a labor market, and what economic purpose does it serve?

2. Is a labor market homogeneous? If not, how are labor markets differentiated from both the employee and the employer side?

3. What is the significance of time to the demand for and supply of labor?

4. What is meant when the demand for labor is referred to as a derived demand?

5. What are some of the factors that shift the community demand for labor?

6. What are some of the socioeconomic characteristics influencing the supply of labor?

7. From a community perspective, what are some of the sources of labor?

8. When the influence of wage changes on the supply of labor is examined, why are the income and substitution effects important?

9. How do the official definition of the labor force and the description of the supply of labor in a community differ?

10. What are some of the characteristics associated with a job that distinguish jobs?

11. What are the similarities and differences between the human capital and dual labor market theories of labor markets?

12. What forms of labor market mismatches might occur?

13. What are the different types of unemployment and their causes?

14. Why might labor mobility not achieve wage equality among communities?

15. Why is the supply of labor not a sufficient condition for employment?

16. Why is it important for the community to create a range of employment opportunities?

Government Involvement in Community Economic Development

THIS CHAPTER ADDRESSES THE ROLE that local, state, and federal governments play in community economic development. The basic governmental approaches of incentives, regulations, joint ownership, market expansion, government spending, and capacity building for stimulating community economic development are reviewed, followed by an economic analysis of incentive programs.

To a large extent this chapter analyzes efforts by the public sector to compensate for performance and/or structural market failures (see Chapter 2, "Market Failure"). Public programs generally seek to overcome market failures (e.g., immobility of resources, economies of agglomeration, and incomplete information). Labor mobility assistance programs and secondary markets for government-guaranteed loans attempt to increase the mobility of labor and capital, respectively. The designation of smaller communities as targets for public investment in water, sewer, and transportation systems helps them capture some of the economies of size associated with larger units. Government guarantees of loans and employment services reduce market failures caused by imperfect information.

Public Sector Involvement

The government sector is necessary in a private economy or free market system for five reasons (Hewings 1977, pp. 97–98). First, there may be a distribution malfunction in which, even if the market is operating at a full employment level and allocating resources to their most efficient use, the distribution of income among groups of people or places is not equitable. Second, the private economy may fail to achieve or to sustain a high and stable level of output and employment. Third, there is no guarantee that the free market economy will allocate resources among alternative uses and places in an efficient manner to prevent either shortages or surpluses in

203

some activities. Fourth, the planning horizon in the marketplace is too short to comprehend fully the long-term effects of private decisions. Fifth, market prices associated with the migration of capital or labor do not incorporate social costs in either the sending or the receiving area.

Conscious government intervention in the market must yield a more desirable result than if the market were left to operate independently. This judgment typically revolves around questions of efficiency and equity. The *efficiency* question presumes that the free market economy will eventually allocate resources among uses and places to maximize output, income, and employment. If an area or economic sector is not as economically viable as other areas or sectors, then the market is signaling that continued use of resources (e.g., labor and capital) in that place or those activities will limit the development of the national economy (Cameron 1970, pp. 11–14; Chisholm 1976, pp. 209–10), and resources should be permitted to migrate away from those activities or that place into other uses and places.[1] The use of public resources to maintain the "nonviable" sector/area is seen to be wasteful and to entail a significant social cost in foregone opportunities. The justification for a governmental response to this efficiency question is that government has better insights into efficiency than does the market, for the five reasons listed above, or that government must act for equity reasons.

The *equity* question presumes that market forces alone will not yield a socially optimum distribution of economic activities among groups, uses, and places. Inequity occurs when the market fails to send the correct signals leading to the desired national output, income, or employment level, or when resources do not respond (i.e., are immobile) to them.

The equity/efficiency dilemma forces decisions about the allocation of scarce public resources (financial, managerial, and intellectual) to maximize national income, output, and employment or to aid those systematically excluded from full participation in the economic system. There may be a conflict between equity and efficiency, but this need not always be so (see "Philosophy of Community Economic Development Policy" in Chapter 4).

The efficiency perspective emphasizes facilitating the fastest and least-cost movement of resources among uses and places to minimize losses over time in national output, income, and employment. This emphasis on mobility is neutral in its focus on either capital or labor. The policy goal of facilitating mobility justifies the movement of capital into areas of immobile and unemployed labor, as well as the movement of labor into areas of fixed capital.

The equity perspective emphasizes generating returns for factors of production (capital or labor) presently not enjoying rewards comparable to the same factors in other locales or uses. This perspective supports programs such as income transfers or unemployment compensation aimed at specific groups of people or areas, as well as capital and labor mobility programs.

Public Response

Government stimulates community economic development in two general ways (Papi 1969, pp. 12–20; Peirce et al. 1979, pp. 11–15; Vaughan 1977, pp. 21–26). The first affects the level of goods and services demanded and can be implemented through monetary policy, fiscal policy, or direct government purchases of goods and services. The second affects the prices and availability of productive inputs and can be implemented through programs and policies affecting the availability, price, and skill of labor; the availability and price of capital and methods of production; and the general business climate. Since this text is concerned with the community, the following discussion focuses on local, rather than national, government activities.

DEMAND FOR GOODS AND SERVICES. Figure 9.1 indicates that the sources of local government influence on the demand for goods and services can be broken into three general categories, export base expansion, income transfers, and the purchase of goods and services (Vaughan 1977, pp. 23, 84–101).

Local government encourages the local export base through activities such as infrastructure investments, purchase of sites and buildings, or labor training. The activities to expand the export base are predicated on the assumption that the multiplier process hooks into the local economy to stimulate the demand for local goods and services (see the discussion of export base theory in Chapter 2). When considering the export sector, it is important to include nonmanufacturing as well as manufacturing (e.g., infrastructure investments in telecommunications that affect data processing operations).

Income transfer programs redistribute income and spending among socioeconomic classes and geographic areas (Bain 1984; Harmston 1979; Hirschl and Summers 1982). The Social Security system, for example, transfers current income from some areas of the United States to other areas with concentrations of retirees. This transfer of income shifts buying power from the "taxed" groups and areas to others. Local governments can help local residents eligible for income transfer programs participate in the programs by providing transportation assistance or distributing information about them.

Local government's purchases of goods and services influence the community through decisions about where and what type of goods and services

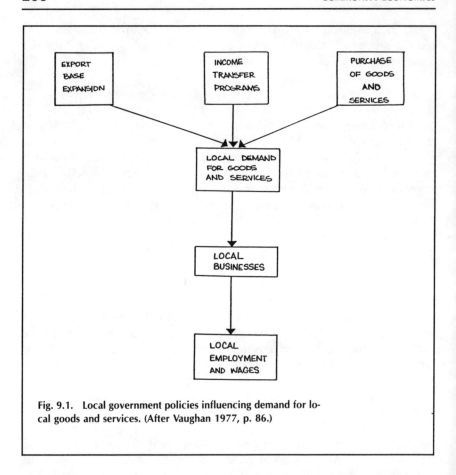

Fig. 9.1. Local government policies influencing demand for local goods and services. (After Vaughan 1977, p. 86.)

are required as well as through the volume needed (e.g., large purchases
discriminate against smaller businesses) (Smith 1978).

Each of the direct government actions described has indirect effects
(Bain 1984; Kubursi 1974; Stern 1975). Private jobs and income are created
indirectly by the spending of transfer payments, by government employees
spending wages, and by spending of wages earned in firms supplying gov-
ernment-purchased goods and services. The important consideration here is
that the same volume of government expenditures for transfer payments,
wages, or purchases of goods and services will not generate the same direct
and indirect income and employment effects in all sectors and places of the
economy (see "Multipliers" in Chapter 10 and "Input-Output Analysis" in
Chapter 11).

SUPPLY OF FACTORS OF PRODUCTION. The economic vitality of a community in part depends upon the prices of the factors of production (e.g., labor, capital, land, transportation). If these factors are priced too high relative to their productivity, the competitiveness of the community is reduced.

Two basic components of the supply of productive inputs in the community are the wages/prices paid and the availability or stock of the resource (see Figure 9.2) (Vaughan 1977, pp. 23, 102–20). If the community does not have an iron ore deposit or miners, it cannot supply iron ore. Inmigration can, however, provide the miners if the ore is present and wages

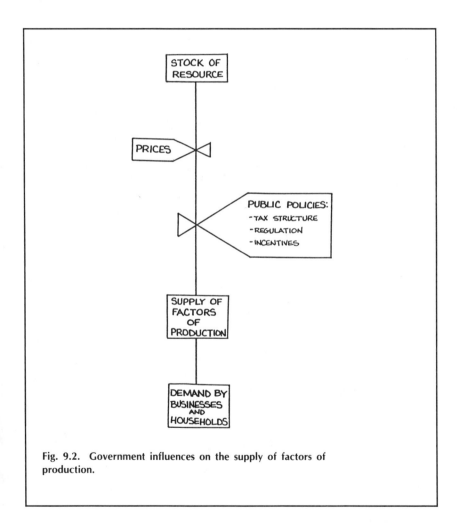

Fig. 9.2. Government influences on the supply of factors of production.

are high enough to attract them. To take a more realistic situation, a community may have capital and labor resources, but public policies inhibit their effective use. Public policies affecting factor markets are of three kinds: tax policies, regulations, and incentives (subsidies).

Tax policy creates market signals if special allowances are made for the use of specific factors of production. Giving firms a tax credit when they hire and train members of certain groups (e.g., veterans, youths) encourages hiring those workers. Depreciation schedules biased toward new capital investment encourage abandoning older facilities rather than remodeling. *Regulations* govern factor markets in an overt fashion by limiting which factors of production can be used or how they can be used. For example, child labor laws prevent hiring children in certain work situations. Likewise, migrant labor laws guide the employer-employee relationship. *Subsidies* affect the use of factors of production by altering the relative prices determined by the market. Local governments subsidize downtown revitalization by using their power of eminent domain to assemble small contiguous parcels of land that are sold to developers. The subsidy is the time and cost of assembling land from numerous owners.

Figure 9.3 shows how government actions affect the supply of one resource, labor. The interaction of the demand for and supply of labor determines its price. Extramarket institutional forces (regulations on minimum wages, union contracts, workplace safety laws, etc.) also influence the market. The labor supply comes from the existing population base (assuming no in-commuting or in-migration). Socioeconomic characteristics such as age, education, single-parent families, income, present occupation, and skills affect the size and type of the labor force. Transfer payments (e.g., general assistance benefit rates) affect individuals' willingness to begin or continue participation in the labor force. The education and training of the labor force bears directly upon its quality and its ability to produce. Laws on minimum wages, workplace safety, and equal opportunity all affect the demand for and supply of labor and the level and structure of wages.

Government influences local economic development by altering the forces of demand and supply. The ability of different levels of government (national, state, or local) to affect demand and supply varies. The macroeconomic fiscal and monetary policies pursued by the federal government affect the vigor and stability of the general economy and its associated income and employment change. This establishes the context for local government efforts. Thus each level of government exerts some influence, but no one level completely directs demand and supply in a decentralized market economy. The direct effects of government actions on the target area or population often are short-run in nature and tend to be visible. Some examples are industrial parks, water and sewer systems, and public assistance payments. The indirect effects tend to be long-run in nature and

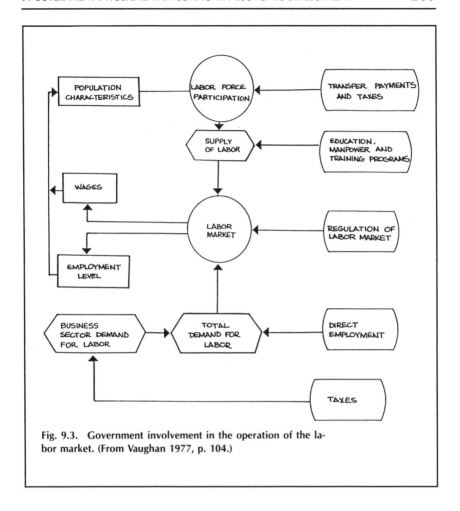

Fig. 9.3. Government involvement in the operation of the labor market. (From Vaughan 1977, p. 104.)

less visible. They change the circumstances of location and production choices. Some examples are education programs, highway construction, changes in freight rates, environmental controls, etc.

Basic Approaches

There are several basic approaches to public sector intervention in community economic development.[2] These approaches are not mutually exclusive, and some are more appropriate for national than for local governmental units. The most elemental national government policy for local economic development is the encouragement of the vitality and stability of the national economy. Beyond the general encouragement of national economic activity, there are six basic categories of government economic development programs. They are incentives, regulations, joint ownership, market expansion, government expenditures, and capacity-building.[3]

Incentives and regulations are closely related. *Incentives* or subsidies seek to direct economic activities covertly through market signals; *regulations* seek to direct economic activity overtly through extramarket limitations. Allen et al. (1979) enumerate five types of incentives: capital grants, soft loans, accelerated depreciation, tax concessions, and labor subsidies. The first three are capital incentives; the last is a labor incentive; the fourth could be both. Capital incentives influence both the public and private capital market. Loan guarantees, subsidized interest rates, favorable repayment schedules, and the creation of secondary credit markets are programs to influence the private capital market. Grants and loans for industrial parks, water systems, sewers, and roads related to economic development needs influence the amount and type of public capital. Labor market incentives take the form of employment information, mobility assistance programs, and low-cost training.[4] The end result of these efforts is either increased mobility of labor among places and uses or reduced real cost of labor.

Some local government *regulations* attempt to direct private economic development decisions through outright refusal to permit an activity or through cost increases (taxes, fees, delays). Regulations cause private decisionmakers to incorporate public dimensions into the private decision calculus (Nicol and Wittman 1979, pp. 157–64). Requiring social-economic-environmental impact statements and agency approval creates awareness of the nonmonetary dimensions and community implications of many investment projects. Banking regulations requiring federally chartered financial institutions to meet both the credit and deposit needs of their community encourage using local financial capital in the community rather than exporting it to other areas. Regulations can be used in isolation, but usually they increase the effectiveness of other programs in allocating economic resources by limiting the choices available. Their public costs are relatively low, just administrative, and are often paid by the private firms affected through licenses and fees.[5]

The *joint ownership* approach, while not common in the United States, sets up an explicit partnership between private investors and the government in selected economic activities. Typically, these activities pose great risk, require substantial capital, or involve a basic industry needed to support further economic development. In a joint ownership program, the government takes an equity position in the company and is represented on the management team. The purpose is to provide a broader public perspective in decisionmaking. In the United States, local governments achieve joint ownership through community development corporations (CDC) or local development groups. CDCs, quasi-public corporations that take an equity position in a business, often are initially financed with federal or local government dollars. The CDC invests in businesses that provide employment for low-income or minority families and build the business management skills of the local population.

Market expansion programs offer considerable opportunity for local government involvement in economic development. The setting aside of minimal amounts of government contracts for minority-owned businesses or small businesses is a form of market expansion for specified business segments. Likewise, local government attempts to buy locally are market expansion strategies. Conscious differentiation of freight rates for specific commodities, directions of travel, or locations are also forms of market expansion programs.[6] Market expansion for isolated communities can take the form of support for a business owner's attendance at trade fairs or conventions to make his/her product known to potential users who otherwise might not have been aware it. Some Wisconsin counties do this through their financial support of local hospitality, recreation, and tourism programs at the Milwaukee and Chicago sports shows.

The location of *government expenditures* and investments (e.g., roads, water and sewer lines, office buildings) is another mechanism to stimulate the geographic redistribution of economic activity (Buhr 1973). There are, however, other equally important mechanisms not as obvious. Income transfer programs to disabled, retired, or economically disadvantaged individuals and families direct the flow of spendable income to people located in economically depressed areas (Bain 1984; Harmston 1979; Hirschl and Summers 1982). Another mechanism is the purchase of a minimum proportion of government materials and supplies from specified categories of businesses (e.g., minority-owned firms, small firms, or firms located in a depressed area; see the discussion of Figure 9.1 above for an elaboration of these two points). A third economic stimulant is the spending of workers employed at government facilities and office buildings (Ashcroft and Swales 1982).

Government agencies and programs thus play a multifaceted role in local economic development. They are vital in introducing purposive sociocultural-technical change into a community. But the mere existence of government programs or a vibrant national economy does not ensure that opportunities will be utilized. *Capacity-building* is a conscious effort to increase the technical, financial, and managerial expertise of public and private decisionmakers and their range of options. Planning industrial parks, downtown renewal plans, and trade area surveys requires *technical expertise*. *Financial expertise* includes the art of grantsmanship and the ability to package development projects so as to maximize the leveraging of public funds. An understanding of how key business and political forces integrate and organize to achieve local economic development objectives is part of public *managerial expertise*. Counseling for small business managers on legal responsibilities, accounting methods, personnel management, or financial management is one way to create informed private decisionmakers.

While government involvement in a mixed economy can occur in various ways, the most obvious form it takes is that of incentives/subsidies.

Incentives/Subsidie

Incentives/subsidies are justified on two broad economic grounds: to lubricate market processes and to catalyze market processes (Kieschnick 1981b, pp. 21-32; Laird and Rinehart 1967). The *lubrication argument* contends that incentives speed eventual free market adjustments by reducing historical and institutional barriers, by reducing risk to the entrepreneur, by compensating for the lack of agglomeration economies (e.g., transportation facilities, a skilled labor pool), and by neutralizing resource misallocation caused by immobile labor, minimum wages, or other factors. The *catalytic argument* contends that incentives stimulate the development of specific skills in the labor force or stimulate investment in critical businesses or services that are precursors to other development efforts. Subsidies that operate at the margin (e.g., training workers in new skills not currently available in the community, or encouraging investment in new technology or new types of business) always alter the structure of the local economy, but there is no reason to believe that the changes they bring about will improve the long-term economic structure of the community (Buck and Atkins 1976, p. 216).

The lubrication/catalytic arguments are typically offered to justify the need for government incentives in community economic development (Leven 1985). An obvious example would be the self-interested group that visualizes community economic development as using resources they have to offer, ranging from an industrial building or site for a retail store with excess sales capacity to some form of labor skill. The concern about local economic activity voiced by such a group is a perfectly legitimate economic response: It wishes to maximize its returns from the use of its resource.

Government seeks to overcome the problem of capital immobility through public involvement in the capital markets. The attempt here is to improve external/internal investors' information about opportunities in the community, to reduce risk to a level that stimulates investment, or to overcome the "herd instinct" by which capital is invested in other projects and/ or other areas because that is the way it has always been (Cameron 1970, pp. 14–17; Kieschnick 1981b, pp. 27–30). A variation of this argument is that a community is depressed because its existing economic structure does not respond to changing economic conditions, because its products are income-inelastic or are subject to wide cyclical variation. Conscious public efforts (i.e., subsidies) can alter this economic structure, it is argued, and link the community to the growing elements of the national/regional economy.[7]

Government involvement may also be justified because human resources are often immobile among places and uses (Cameron 1970, pp. 25–26; Moes 1961, p. 187; Rinehart and Laird 1972). Inadequate market signals and/or personal characteristics hinder the movement of labor into productive activities, and society loses the potential output of these irreplaceable human resources. The small public subsidies to training, health, job information, or mobility assistance that facilitate labor force adjustment yield large returns to the community.

A final argument for subsidies parallels the infant industry argument in international trade (Alyea 1967, pp. 139–41). Subsidies allow a new local firm to begin operations under conditions of reduced competition (i.e., tariffs) or create cost savings, which established industries enjoy through economies of size and agglomeration. The new business will eventually grow and become sufficiently competitive to forego support. In the meantime, the community reaps the rewards of the employment and income generated.

The theoretical support for local subsidies derives from relaxing three basic assumptions of neoclassical growth theory, the most important of which is that wages are flexible both up and down as workers and management negotiate (Laird and Rinehart 1979; Moes 1962, pp. 3–18). In fact, union contracts, minimum wage legislation, associated labor costs (e.g., social security, health insurance), and labor market regulations prevent full flexibility of wages. The second assumption relaxed here is that labor is homogeneous among uses and places and is equally productive. The third assumption relaxed is that of complete mobility of labor and capital among uses and places.

Let us examine the case for subsidies in terms of inflexibility of wages. Assume that labor is wage-immobile, that it will not move among places or uses even though there is a wage differential (Gray 1964, pp. 168–70). This inelastic supply of labor appears to exist in many rural and urban communities because labor mobility is not solely a function of wage differentials among communities (see Chapter 8, "Labor Mobility and Wage Differentials," for details). In Figure 9.4 we see that the current demand for labor (D_L) is incapable of employing all the workers at the fixed wage (W_1). The wage may be fixed by minimum wage legislation or union contract. The amount of unemployment is $N_0 - N_1$. The demand for labor is inadequate to use all the existing labor because the cost of labor (W_1) exceeds the

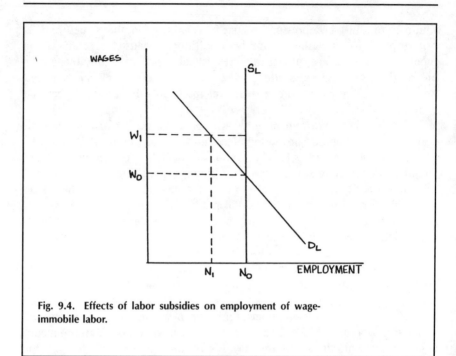

Fig. 9.4. Effects of labor subsidies on employment of wage-immobile labor.

VMP_L or $MPP_L \times P_0$. Labor can be fully employed if it is used in more productive processes (higher MPP_L)[8] or if it yields a higher-valued output (P_0) or if a community offers a subsidy of up to $W_1 - W_0$ to encourage hiring more labor. This subsidy lowers the real cost of labor to the firm to W_0.

Figure 9.5 displays the effects of less than complete capital and labor mobility among uses and places, even though the two remain complete substitutes. The demand and supply of labor curves are not perfectly elastic, and the question becomes one of what size subsidy will overcome the less than complete mobility of labor. Again, let W_1 be some externally determined wage (e.g., a national minimum wage or wage mandated by union contract). Movement along the S_L curve represents the movement of labor into or out of the community (i.e., migration and commuting). A wage of W_1 will cause the amount of labor offered to be equal to N_2, but the demand for labor is only N_1, resulting in unemployment of $N_2 - N_1$. Excess labor will move to the community in hopes of getting one of the jobs paying relatively higher wages, and labor will not be discouraged by the unemployment.

Again, a subsidy can bring about an equality of labor supply and demand. The subsidy becomes a mechanism to reduce the cost of labor

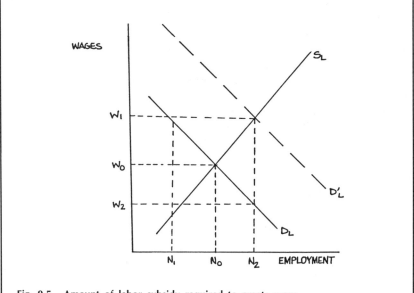

Fig. 9.5. Amount of labor subsidy required to create wage-mobile labor.

relative to capital and increases employment. But since labor will continue to migrate into the community in response to the higher wages (W_1), the unemployment problem will continue unless the demand for labor shifts to D_L'. The community's capacity to shift demand is limited. The only way to discourage continuing in-migration of labor is to lower the wage labor receives. Since the wage (W_1) is externally determined, the only recourse is to tax labor (i.e., wages) for the cost of the subsidy (Buchanan and Moes 1960). If labor pays the full cost of the subsidy, wages to employees will decline from W_1 to W_0 and N_0 employment will result. The economy will achieve full employment (i.e., the demand for labor will equal the supply), and continued in-migration will cease because labor will receive an effective wage of only W_0 and not the visible wage of W_1. If labor pays none of the subsidy cost, the effective wage required to hire N_2 workers will be W_2. In this case, a subsidy of $W_1 - W_2$ is required to equate labor demand and supply. This yields an inefficient use of labor. There are $N_1 - N_0$ redundant jobs in the community, and although everyone is working, many are under-employed. There is no wage incentive for underemployed workers to move because they receive a full wage of W_1.

While the preceding analysis provides some insights into how subsidies can work, it has some limitations that must be remembered (Cumberland and Van Beek 1967, pp. 256–57; Morss 1966). First, capital and labor are not completely and freely substitutable, thus preventing the marginal changes required in labor and capital use. Labor may have imperfect information about wage differentials and job opportunities elsewhere, reducing migration rates. More important, although the arguments for subsidies recognize imperfections in the labor market, they do not recognize that similar imperfections occur in the capital market and in the market for subsidies (Morss 1966, pp. 166–67). Imperfect information exists about what subsidies are available or about the amount of subsidy required to overcome the excess wage.[9] If the subsidy is not in the form of cash, but occurs as public infrastructure or industrial buildings, the subsidy market suffers from the same capital immobility problems mentioned in the section on capital market failures in Chapter 7. And finally, the equity question remains: Why should labor pay the full cost of the subsidy (Kieschnick 1981, pp. 29–30)?

TYPES OF SUBSIDIES. Economic development subsidy schemes take the form of labor, capital, or price subsidies. Labor subsidies generally reimburse the firm for some proportion of the hourly or annual wage payments made or reduce the cost of labor by lowering the cost of training. They are intended to increase the use of labor relative to capital.

Capital subsidies provide capital to firms at below market rates through an outright grant on some portion of the firm's investment, or favorable interest rates, or favorable repayment terms on loans. They are intended to increase the use of capital relative to labor, on the implicit assumption that labor is immobile and unemployed.

Price subsidies are factor-neutral, unlike labor or capital subsidies, since they do not overtly encourage the use of either labor or capital relative to the other. They take the form of raising the net mill price the firm receives for its product by providing some form of market information, transportation cost reduction, or artificially created agglomeration economies. Freight rate structures that permit firms producing specific products in certain locations to move their product at a cheaper rate per ton-mile represent a price subsidy. Public infrastructure investments (e.g., fully serviced industrial parks) that artificially create agglomeration economies are a form of price subsidy.

Haveman and Christiansen (1978) have identified two broad labor subsidy schemes, public service employment and wage subsidies. Public service employment programs offer the advantage of targeting jobs to specific categories of workers (e.g., minorities, youths, the unskilled, veterans, refugees). Public service employment programs hire workers for ongoing public services or public works (construction) projects or for training and sheltered employment. The training and sheltered employment programs create new human capital, with sheltered employment typically offering long-term permanent jobs.

In wage subsidy programs the government pays some portion of the worker's hourly wage rate or weekly, monthly, or annual wage income. The subsidy can be paid to the employing firm or to the worker directly; it can apply to all employees, to newly hired employees, to employees above some previous work force level, or to particular categories of employees (e.g., older workers, long-term unemployed workers, or youths).

One form of labor subsidy is an *employment tax credit,* through which the firm receives an income tax credit based on its total amount of labor time used or total payroll (Kesselman et al. 1977).[10] A marginal employment tax credit (METC) is based on a change from some prior employment level (e.g., last year's average). A METC generates greater employment change per dollar of tax expenditure than other forms of subsidy. Kesselman et al. (1977) contend that measuring total hours worked or total payroll is easier than distinguishing types of assets (new/replacement equipment) or payment methods (purchase, lease-purchase), as is done with capital subsidies. The use of a tax credit means that firms using the subsidy must have profits, thus encouraging continued viability of the firm but limiting their usefulness for firms with an erratic profit picture. One of the major drawbacks of a labor subsidy scheme is the implication that if the subsidy stops, workers will again become unemployed. Discontinuation of capital subsidy does not create these social pressures.

Capital subsidies occur in numerous forms; some of the more obvious are grants, soft loans, accelerated depreciation allowances, and some tax concessions (Allen et al. 1979). National, state, or community public agencies offer capital grants. Public agencies, depending upon their legislative authority, condition the rate of their awards by discriminating on the basis of size (e.g., total assets of less than or more than $5 million); of location (e.g., located inside or outside a SMSA); of type of economic activity (e.g., manufacturing vs. trade); and of project type (e.g., start-up, expansion, or relocation). A key element of the expected impact from capital grants is their effective rate. The *effective rate* is a function of the proportion of investment supported, the taxability of the award, and the payment schedule (e.g., at start-up, at fixed time intervals, or after completion). If the grant becomes taxable income, or if payment occurs after the firm has made the expenditure, the effective rate of the grant is reduced. The higher the effective rate of the grant, the more impact it has on capital investment.

When a loan carries a below-market interest rate, or has an extended repayment period, or has principal repayment and/or interest-free holidays, or has reduced collateral requirements, it is a *soft loan.* An extended repayment period, which allows delays before any repayment is due and/or a lengthened maturity date, aids the firm's cash flow. Reduced collateral requirements can take the form of guarantees on the unpaid principal and interest, higher collateralization rates on assets, or acceptance of a wider range of assets as collateral. Soft loans use the private financial market for screening applicants and administration, but the use of this intermediary reduces the discretion of the public agency in using funds for public purposes. The effective rate of soft loans is much lower than that of grants because the loan must be repaid and the reduced interest costs increase the firm's taxable income.

Accelerated depreciation, income tax forgiveness, and property tax relief are also forms of capital subsidies. The first two require that a firm make a taxable profit before they have much impact; the lag before taxes come due reduces the effective rate of the subsidy. Accelerated depreciation permits a firm to postpone tax liabilities and improve its cash flow. This subsidy can be linked to specific assets (e.g., new buildings, equipment) and areas (e.g., high unemployment areas). Income tax forgiveness programs are credits against income tax liabilities or exemption from tax of a proportion of taxable income if a firm locates in a selected area. The tax credit will not occur until a profit is made; the income exemption occurs with the first sale. The Norwegian Regional Tax Act permits a firm to deposit up to 50 percent of its taxable income in a tax-free account to be invested within five years in designated economic development areas. Property tax concessions granted by municipalities are of varying duration (some up to twenty years), do not require that the firm make a profit, and can apply to nondepreciable assets such as land.

The community can subsidize the use of either capital or labor in a variety of ways. The appropriate form of subsidization depends upon the specific firm involved. The effect of a particular subsidy on a firm depends upon the effective rate of the award.

WHICH TYPE OF SUBSIDY? The community using subsidies must choose the form that will be most effective in achieving its goals. If the general goal is to increase employment, a labor subsidy appears most appropriate. Price subsidies are factor neutral, but labor or capital subsidies, by definition, are not.

Although the usual argument is that a capital subsidy will not increase and may even reduce labor use, examination of Figure 9.6 indicates that this is not always the case (Buck and Atkins 1976, pp. 215–17). The amount of capital used appears on the horizontal axis, labor on the vertical axis. I and II are isoquant curves of different levels of output. The slope of the LK line is the initial ratio of factor prices, and the equilibrium use of capital and labor to produce output level I is at point A. A capital subsidy

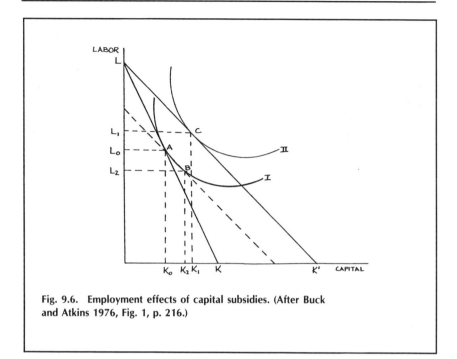

Fig. 9.6. Employment effects of capital subsidies. (After Buck and Atkins 1976, Fig. 1, p. 216.)

lowers the price of capital, and up to K' units of capital will be demanded as output increases to level *II*. There is a substitution effect as more capital is used per unit of labor (i.e., movement from A to B), if the level of output remains the same (i.e., level *I*) the use of labor declines from L_0 to L_2. There is also an output effect in the movement from B to C, or from output level *I* to *II*, which increases the use of labor from L_0 to L_1. Thus, a capital subsidy increases the use of both capital and labor.

The figure measures only the direct labor used to produce the good or service represented by the isoquants. It does not measure the labor used to produce the new capital used from K_0 to K_1, or the changes in employment in firms linked to the firms subsidized. The end result, if an output effect occurs, is that the amount of labor used increases through the use of capital subsidies. If the level of output does not change (i.e., if there is no output effect or if capital and labor are perfect substitutes), the capital subsidy reduces the level of labor used in the economy (movement from A to B). The most likely case, however, is that capital subsidies increase output; since capital and labor are not perfect substitutes but are complementary to some degree, the result is increased use of labor. This argument does not deny that the community may get more employment per dollar of subsidy if a labor rather than capital subsidy is used, nor does it address the spatial or occupational shift in the use of labor that occurs through the use of a capital subsidy.

The vast number of existing capital subsidies, in comparison to labor subsidies, suggests that they must offer significant advantages. The preceding analysis tends to support that position, but theoretical and empirical evidence is mixed. Richardson (1978b, pp. 26–28) offers two major reasons for the emphasis on capital subsidies. First, capital-intensive industries are perceived as dynamic and vigorous businesses that generate numerous spinoffs. Unfortunately, these spinoffs and linkages with other firms often do not take place in the same community, especially if it is economically depressed (see Chapter 10, "Local and Nonlocal Impacts"), and furthermore, recent studies suggest that service industries are the growth sectors of the future. Second, emerging or smaller businesses require capital subsidies to overcome the higher costs of start-up or the cost of obtaining capital in an economically depressed community. This argument is somewhat undermined by evidence that larger businesses (e.g., conglomerates, multinationals) are not only getting these subsidies but are getting proportionately more than their share relative to the number of new businesses (Connelly 1978; Gurwitz 1978; Harrison and Kanter 1978; Jacobs 1979; Peirce et al. 1979, pp. 37–43).

Despite the preference for capital subsidies, labor subsidies offer several advantages, most obvious of which is that they subsidize the underutilized resource of public concern. While the administrative structure of labor subsidy programs can be complex, it need not be. Eligibility requirements (e.g., new vs. old firms, skilled vs. unskilled laborers, previously employed vs. unemployed, net vs. gross additions to the work force) will determine whether they are cumbersome and unwieldy or not.

The important point to remember is that neither labor nor capital subsidy programs should be used in isolation but should be part of a coordinated effort to encourage the use of labor and capital (Peirce et al. 1979). This means a combination of labor, capital, and public infrastructure subsidies.

In summary, the effects of any community economic development incentive or subsidy program depend upon the type of subsidy offered, the importance of that inducement in the final location and/or production level decision, the alternative production lost by diverting resources into either the subsidy or the activity supported, the type of activity supported; and source of payment for the subsidy (e.g., will it be labor or capital, or local or nonlocal?).

Reservations about Subsidies

There are seven major reservations about subsidy programs (Bearse 1979, pp. 86–89; Cumberland and Van Beek 1967, p. 259; Harrison and Kanter 1978; Jacobs,1979; Kieschnick 1981b, pp. 35–87; Thompson 1962): (1) they have no self-regulating mechanisms like those operating in the market;[11] (2) there are imperfections in the capital, labor, and subsidy markets; (3) there is a tendency for subsidy programs to be duplicated and to become common to most communities rather than unique to a few communities; (4) the diversion of growth from one locale to another is believed to be zero sum; (5) subsidies are not critical in location decisions; (6) firms are more sensitive to demand factors than cost factors in their location decisions; and (7) subsidies are given to the wrong factors of production and the wrong firms.

The response to the first criticism, lack of a self-regulating mechanism, is that communities seek to acquire benefits or jobs, and each community must pay some price for those jobs (Moes 1962, p. 59). Some communities must pay more than others to overcome adverse community circumstances, while some need pay no explicit price because of positive community attributes — fortuitous natural circumstances such as a harbor, fertile soil, or mineral deposits; institutional arrangements (a community at a border or transport junction); or prior community investments in a school system, water supply, roads, and the like, none of which impose current costs. Viewed in this context, the offering of subsidies for new jobs is an economic transaction, although a somewhat unusual one, in which the new jobs go to the highest bidder (Morss 1966, p. 165). The question becomes one of what is to prevent communities from becoming caught up in an endless cycle of increasingly larger bids (i.e., subsidies)?[12]

Rinehart and Laird (1972, pp. 75–77) offer three reasons why subsidies will be self-limiting. First, some communities will not participate because they already have all the jobs they need (full employment). Furthermore, communities will lose interest if they must pay all or most of the cost of the subsidy. Second, communities with unemployment will only bid the value of the new jobs to the citizenry. As the communities with unemployed workers experience success in creating jobs, they reduce their subsidy efforts. Third, some communities with unemployed workers will not offer incentive programs because of lack of interest, community beliefs, or expected out-migration and out-commuting of unemployed workers. These responses prevent unfettered subsidies from draining the community treasuries.

The beneficial results from an incentive program are based on overcoming market imperfections in either the capital or the labor market. In theory, the decision to offer an incentive is made with full knowledge that the community must bear the full cost of the subsidy, that there are no state or federal programs lowering its cost to the community[13] (Morss 1966, pp. 162–66). Full knowledge means that the community knows what the benefits and costs of the incentive program are. Ideally, if some individuals in the community are made worse off by the subsidy program, then intracommunity compensation, a legitimate cost of the program, will be made. Scholars postulate that all communities freely bid for jobs, but only up to the point where benefits equal costs. Furthermore, it is assumed that the initial distribution of income among communities is acceptable; if it is not, the "richer" communities will continue to outbid the "poorer" communities for jobs (Goffman 1962; Morss 1966, pp. 164–65).

These assumptions seldom hold in reality. Subsidy programs are rarely completely financed by local resources, but depend heavily upon state and federal funding. Their full benefits and costs are not known and generally do not fall on the same individuals/community (Morss 1966, pp. 165–67). Not every person in the community has equal access to the decision to offer a subsidy (compare business owners with laborers or the unemployed). The distribution of income among communities is not acceptable, as evidenced by the numerous state and federal programs to equalize income, employment, and tax burdens. Furthermore, information about the minimal amount and type of subsidy required is not available to the community. Finally, the use of capital or labor or price subsidies need not lead to the most economical use of national and community resources.

Regarding the question of duplication of programs, Table 9.1 clearly indicates that many successful programs have been duplicated. There is nothing wrong with that, but if every community (depressed or not) is using a given program, how has the situation been changed from what it was before the program was first created?

It is commonly believed that local economic development efforts yield zero sum results. Chapter 4 addresses the question directly, but suffice it to say here that zero sum outcomes are not a foregone conclusion. In addition to the arguments advanced in Chapter 4, the net effect of subsidies also depends upon who receives them. If they go to firms entering markets with minimal barriers to entry and a growing demand, the market should signal the need for additional investment. Thus changes in employment stimulated by the subsidy must be the net of the jobs lost by existing firms forced to leave or reduce their growth (Stutzer 1985, pp. 3–4).

The importance of incentives to the location of economic activity continues as an empirical debate. Anecdotal evidence suggests that they have great significance. The almost universal response in surveys about location decisions is that incentives were not critical in the decision about place or size of investment (Advisory Commission on Intergovernmental Relations 1967, pp. 59–70; Aleya 1967, pp. 147–51; Due 1961; Harrison and Kanter

Table 9.1. Number of States Employing Various State-Local Incentives for Industry, 1966–1976

Incentive	1966	1967	1968	1969	1970	1971	1972	1973	1974	1975	1976
Tax exemption or moratorium on land, capital impr.	11	15	14	16	17	15	16	18	19	21	22
Tax exemption or moratorium on equip., machinery	15	20	22	21	21	22	24	25	25	27	28
Sales/use tax exemption on new equip.	16	23	26	29	26	25	26	28	31	33	32
Accelerated depr. on indus. equip.	9	12	14	15	14	17	19	20	20	21	21
State rev. bonds	8	13	13	15	16	16	17	18	17	18	21
City and/or county gen. oblig. bonds	14	17	15	15	14	14	14	17	20	21	21
City and/or county rev. bonds	28	39	39	42	42	43	43	42	43	43	45
State financing air for existing plant expansion	14	17	24	27	26	25	25	25	25	27	28
State incentive for establishing indus. plants in high-unem-ployment areas				10	8	9	9	10	12	13	15
City- and/or county-financed spec. bldg.		5	7	10	13	12	14	14	17	16	16
City- and/or county-owned indus. parks	28	36	38	39	42	45	48	48	48	47	47
State funds for city and/or county development-related pub. wks. projects				23	25	24	25	28	28	27	31
State retraining of indus. employees	38	44	47	45	45	46	46	47	48	48	48
State-supported training of "hardcore" unemployed	17	26	25	28	28	28	32	33	33	33	36

Source: Conway Research, Inc. 1966–76.

1978; Kieschnick 1981, pp. 46–58, 68–78; Stinson 1968; Thompson 1962, pp. 115–16; Vaughan 1979, pp. 19–31) (see the discussion of location factors in Chapter 3).

Arguments that incentives reduce total costs of operation cannot be denied (Bridges 1965, pp. 177–83; Due 1961). But the important question is whether firms are more sensitive to the total revenue or total cost portion of the profit equation (Harrison and Kanter 1978; Vaughan 1979, pp. 21–23). To argue that total costs are dominant presumes that a firm faces a competitive market and is unable to influence prices. If a firm is facing a competitive market, the dual labor market theory (see Chapter 8) suggests that the types of jobs created are marginal (i.e., low-wage, low-skilled jobs with no upward occupational mobility and limited fringe benefits), in contrast to jobs in the primary labor market, in which the firm has some monopoly power. If a firm has monopoly power, it can control prices and output.

There is no guarantee that the reduced costs from the incentive will be passed on to consumers as lower prices rather than adding to the firm's profits (Harrison and Kanter 1978, pp. 426–27). An increase in profits as a result of subsidy is a direct transfer of income from the general taxpayer to the business owner. Let us assume that the firm in Figure 9.7 is somewhat indifferent to its specific location within AB, since all sites in the area yield identical profits. A subsidy to the AB area will either increase the profits of firms or lead to lower product prices. If profits increase or if prices do not drop enough to eliminate the profit increase, there is a direct transfer from those who financed the subsidy to the firm to support an already profitable decision.

Figure 9.7 also displays the significance of the unequal amount of information held by the firm and the community and their unequal power in the incentive bargaining process (Bearse 1979, pp. 81–85; Morss 1966, pp. 166–67). If the firm implies that it needs the subsidy to make the location profitable, and the community responds, an already profitable site will yield a greater profit, a result that explains negative connotations associated with subsidy programs (Thompson 1962, pp. 116–17). However, a carefully structured subsidy program can expand the range of profitable locations as shown in Figure 9.7, where subsidies are limited to $A'A$ and $B'B$. If the additional profitable areas permit output to expand, national welfare probably will increase. If no increase in national output occurs, however, but firms relocate into $A'A$ or $B'B$, a transfer of activities occurs. This represents a zero sum outcome unless $A'A$ and $B'B$ are the targets of national concern and unequal welfare weights are used (see Chapter 4, "Are Community Economic Development Programs Zero Sum?").

The preponderance of capital subsidies creates a subtle bias toward

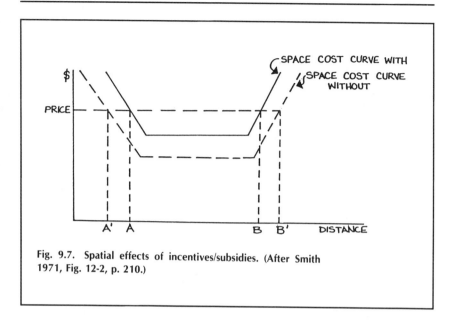

Fig. 9.7. Spatial effects of incentives/subsidies. (After Smith 1971, Fig. 12-2, p. 210.)

capital-intensive manufacturing enterprises and discriminates against the trade and service sectors. The end result is a tendency to promote economic activities with limited employment-generating prospects. The argument that capital subsidies promote the use of immobile unemployed labor has several implicit assumptions. The first is that unemployed workers will get the new jobs created—that the reason why they are unemployed is because their former employer closed or moved, not because they do not have appropriate skills. The second is that capital and labor are perfect substitutes, an assumption which ignores the realities of production processes, technologies, and labor-management agreements (see the discussion of Figure 9.6).

Incentive programs presume that new jobs come from the relocation of nonlocal firms. The implicit assumption here is that local economic development programs should attract plants changing locations. Unfortunately, incentives seldom apply to the start-up of a new firm, though new start-ups are a significant source of new job creation.[14] Furthermore, the need for keeping abreast of complex programs, coupled with business owners' attitudes toward accepting incentives, tend to self-select the larger firms for participation (Connelly 1978; Gurwitz 1978; Jacobs 1979; Kieschnick 1981, pp. 26–38, 73).

The use of tax concessions, tax expenditures, or fiscal incentives is a particularly insidious policy. The evidence is that these incentives have only a marginal impact on location and investment decisions. They have only a minimal effect on the number of people hired—their prime reason for being. This form of incentive either drains the public treasury and limits financing of other legitimate public needs or shifts the tax burden to other businesses and households. Finally, the question of discrimination and discretion in awarding incentives remains. Are awards made to firms that will contribute to the economic future of the community or merely to those who know about the program? How much discretion do communities have in award rates, so that they neither over-subsidize nor offer too little to affect decisions?

Summar

Government programs for economic development are designed to increase utilization of underemployed local resources. These resources are underemployed because they are immobile among uses and places. The causes of this immobility are imperfect information and noneconomic factors. The short-term objective of a public program is to ease the hardship of transition from past to future economic activity. The long-term objective is to restructure the local economy (firms and labor) into a more viable entity.

In a mixed private/public economy like that of the United States, the majority of decisions about what type of economic activity is to occur, and where, remain in the private sector. The public sector (local, state, and federal governments), however, influences the type of economic activities (e.g., federal support of alternative energy sources) and the location of those activities (e.g., efforts to retain businesses in the northeastern United States vs. the Sun Belt). These public efforts can be broadly classified as having either a demand focus (e.g., those aimed at general economic conditions or purchases from specific types of businesses based on location, size, or ownership) or a supply focus (e.g., provision of trained labor, reduction of capital costs).

An important element to keep in mind is that the economic development policy tools available to government are not uniformly appropriate. Subsidies and moving allowances are financial incentives that work at the margin to cause capital and labor to migrate. Yet they have little power to bring about structural changes in local institutions or to change attitudes about opportunities and perceptions of future courses of action.

An often-used phrase associated with local government and community economic development is *business climate*. It requires no clear definition, because everyone knows what it means. Its typical connotation is low taxes, yet to limit the meaning in this way is to ignore much of the involvement of government in community economic development. Business climate really refers to the quality of the relationship between the community's private and public sector in pursuing economic development. What is the nature of the partnership? Is it harmonious or turbulent? While there will never be complete agreement between business and government, in a high-quality business climate businesses accept their social responsibilities (for layoffs and closures, effluent discharges, etc.) and government supports legitimate business needs (responds quickly to permit applications, for example, or works with business to implement a cost-effective solution to a pollution problem). The complexity of this relationship is often collapsed into the simplistic issue of tax burden.

The differing responsibilities for economic development activities among levels of government often are not fully recognized in community development efforts. At the national level, efforts must be directed toward maintaining a vigorous, stable national economy; ensuring that resources flow among regions; and redistributing income among specific socioeconomic groups (e.g., minorities, the disabled). At the state level, efforts focus on making regional labor and capital markets function and facilitating the movement of capital and labor through information, reduction of risk, and uniform regulations. The task of local government is to generate an environment that facilitates the mobility of resources among uses and applications promising high returns in output, income, and employment. Rather than devoting time and effort to generating new programs, the local officials should apply existing federal and state programs to local needs in a creative manner. In contrast, state and federal programs must be sufficiently flexible in their guidelines so that they can meet unique local needs while still maintaining some integrity to their state/national purposes.

Study Questions

1. What are some economic reasons to justify community intervention in economic development activities?

2. Describe the efficiency-equity dilemma associated with public intervention.

3. It was suggested that local government affects economic development in three general ways. What are they? Describe the specific ways in which these general forces appear.

4. What are the six basic approaches of public sector involvement in community economic development?

5. What economic justifications can be made for the use of subsidies and incentives?

6. Under what conditions will a capital subsidy scheme increase the use of labor, and under what conditions is it doubtful?

7. What is the economic rationale for communities' refusal to offer ever-increasing subsidies to new firms?

8. What are some of the implications of subsidizing a firm in a competitive market and a firm in a monopolistic market, in terms of product price, profits, and job implications?

The Impacts of
Community Economic
Development

10

WHEN AN ECONOMIC DEVELOPMENT EVENT OCCURS in a community, change is inevitable.[1] However, there is a difference between change and impact. Impact reflects the interaction between the economic change and the host community. In particular, it represents concern about the effect of change on specific socioeconomic groups, sectors, or locations, or its effect over time.

An impact analysis of a community must first consider what types of change are occurring, whether physical, demographic, social, fiscal, or economic. *Physical impacts* are changes in environmental quality caused by a development event. *Demographic impacts* are changes in the size, location, and composition of the population in the local community and its environs. *Social impacts* are changes in the relationships among groups and individuals. *Fiscal impacts* are changes in local government revenues and expenditures. *Economic impacts* are the changes in the level and distribution of local employment, income, sales, and wealth. For convenience here the phrase "socioeconomic impacts" is used to refer to all forms of change, a generalization not uniformly accepted (Howell and Weber 1982, pp. 243–44).

In examining the socioeconomic impacts of an economic development event, three major elements must be recognized (Cortese 1979; Krannich 1979; Leistritz et al. 1984; Leistritz and Murdock 1981, pp. 43–50; Summers et al. 1976). First, socioeconomic impacts result from the interaction between the development event and the community. Demand, supply, and institutional forces interact to amplify, mitigate, or divert local socioeconomic changes. The size of the development event relative to the host community influences this interaction. A large project in a small community has different impacts than a small project in a large community, not only in magnitude, but also in the form of the impacts. For example, the expansion of a shopping mall affects labor, public services, and housing

228

differently than would construction of a boutique. Second, it is important to be sensitive to the community's economic development goals and objectives, for these represent the dimensions of particular importance to an impact analysis. Third, an economic development event is a dynamic phenomenon, and no single number can estimate its impact. It is important to use a range of estimates because changes in the project (e.g., types of output, changes in the size and timing), changes in the local economy (e.g., new workers, new shopping facilities, or new support services), and changes in the regional economy (e.g., in-migration, the appearance of regional shopping facilities, improved transportation facilities) all alter the impact of the event.

To conduct impact analysis requires understanding how the community's economy responds to the stimulus of the development event and thus represents an application of the community economic development theories discussed previously. Yet a great deal of uncertainty remains regarding how and when the community responds. This chapter provides only a review of the possible forms of impact and the forces affecting them, not a listing of all assured impacts.

ECONOMIC DEVELOPMENT IMPACTS. When an economic development event occurs, it affects population, employment, income, sales/output, property values/wealth, taxes, public services, and quality of life. An analysis of the socioeconomic impacts in a community arising from an economic development event must therefore address the following questions. What type of changes are occurring? How much change is occurring? To whom is it occurring? Where is it occurring? When will it occur?

Figure 10.1 graphically represents some of the linkages considered in impact analysis. It is critical to collect baseline data to establish the standard against which change is measured. In the figure the impact questions focus on the time associated with different phases of mining development (i.e., exploration, development and construction, actual mining, and the post-mining or closedown phase). The variations over time in the development of other types of activities proceed through similar phases. Figure 10.1 also indicates that impacts occur both on-site (local) and off-site (nonlocal). It highlights the interconnections among social, political, economic, and environmental-legal changes.

Figure 10.2 displays another method of conceptualizing the interrelations of the different impact dimensions within a community. The community is a socioeconomic entity stimulated by the development event. This leads to a multitude of potential changes in the community's social, demographic, fiscal, and economic dimensions. These changes are not independent but interact, either dampening or amplifying changes in other dimensions (Cortese 1979; Gotsch 1972; Leistritz et al. 1984; Murdock and

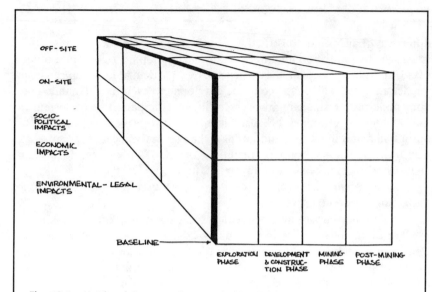

Fig. 10.1. Matrix of impacts of an economic development event—mining. (From Wisconsin, State of, Department of Revenue 1977, p. 12.)

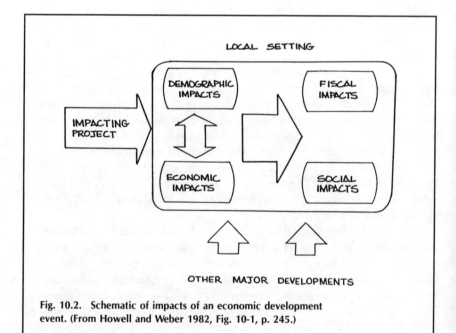

Fig. 10.2. Schematic of impacts of an economic development event. (From Howell and Weber 1982, Fig. 10-1, p. 245.)

Schriner 1978). For example, one form of economic impact is employment change. An increase in employment can lead to increased in-migration or reduced out-migration or demand for different labor force skills, thus changing the population base, which then may alter social relations within the community. Furthermore, other external developments influence the magnitude and form of local changes.

The type of economic development event that takes place influences the socioeconomic impacts occurring in a community. The two general types of development are manufacturing/nonmanufacturing and location/expansion/start-up. The socioeconomic impacts differ among manufacturing/nonmanufacturing development events because of differences in demand for material inputs, public services, and labor. For example, a manufacturing firm's interest in transportation is in the availability of long-haul trucking and access to major arterial highways, while a data processing firm's interest is in the availability of telephone service capable of handling high-speed data transmission.

Differences in the magnitude and timing of socioeconomic impacts depend upon whether the development event is a new location, the expansion of an existing firm, or the start of a new firm. A start-up typically requires a minimal amount of labor and other inputs initially. Expansions, on the other hand, reflect a situation where some factors (e.g., public services) are already in place and may have the capacity to accommodate the expansion. A new location often requires the construction of new buildings, new public facilities, and labor skills previously not available in the community.

The socioeconomic impact of a development event can fall into one of at least five different categories. These are not mutually exclusive, as will become obvious. For purposes of this discussion, they are: (1) local and nonlocal; (2) monetary and nonmonetary; (3) primary and secondary; (4) private and public; and (5) positive and negative. It is impossible to draw clear demarcations between the types of impacts mentioned, but it *is* necessary to review only one type at a time.

LOCAL AND NONLOCAL IMPACTS. Communities are open economic units, which means that there is an easy flow of economic activity into and out of them. Because of the porous nature of a community's economic boundary, many of the anticipated socioeconomic changes from an economic development event occur elsewhere. The smaller the community relative to the magnitude of the development event itself, the more likely that the socioeconomic changes it brings about will spill over into the rest of the region (Boehm and Pond 1976; Chalmers 1977; Guedry and Rosera 1979; Longbrake and Geyler 1979; Mellor and Ironsides 1978; Shaffer 1979; Temple 1979; Wadsworth and Conrad 1965). The local economy's ability to respond to the needs of the development event influences the local-nonlocal incidence of change.

It is important to recognize that leakage of economic activity out of the community occurs because the community does not provide some types of activities (see "Central Place Theory" in Chapter 6). These leakages into the rest of the economy are a legitimate economic activity (i.e., an economic linkage). Economic development event linkages occur with local businesses and households as well as with nonlocal households and businesses and other communities (see Figure 10.3). They are likely to change over time (Townroe 1974, p. 297).

Leakages are singled out here because of the concern about change in a community vs. total change. They keep some of the direct stimulus from the development event from entering the community and causing secondary change. For example, let community X have an income multiplier of 2, and let plant Y increase its payroll by $100,000. Is the community's total change in income $200,000? Possibly, but not likely. First, part of the new payroll is never received by the worker; it represents income tax withholding, social security taxes, employee contributions to retirement, health programs, etc. It is not unusual for 20 to 30 percent of gross payroll never to reach the worker's pocket. Second, some workers may live and/or spend their new wages elsewhere. Let this account for 10 percent of the new payroll. Thus, in this simple example, up to 40 percent of the new payroll never enters the community, leaving a total income change of $60,000 × 2, or $120,000.

The location of the residence of workers at the new economic development activity, the capacity of local businesses to respond to new demands for consumer shopping and business services, and the rate at which the change takes place all influence the degree of local private sector change caused by a development event. If the rate of change is rapid and the change is quite large relative to existing capacity, then impacts are more likely to occur elsewhere. These forces are addressed in greater detail under "Multipliers" below.

MONETARY AND NONMONETARY IMPACTS. Monetary impacts involve a price determined in the marketplace; they provide a common denominator which permits comparison. Thus, when examining monetary changes (e.g., dollar volume of sales to businesses) there is a common unit of measure. Nonmonetary impacts, on the other hand, do not have a common denominator by which to make comparisons or trade-offs. Our inability to predict monetary impacts precisely is surpassed only by our inability to predict nonmonetary impacts. Still, the nonmonetary dimensions of economic development events must be incorporated in community decisionmaking so that decisions are made on the basis of the most complete information possible. Furthermore, it is important to recognize that the nonmonetary impacts from an economic development event need not be negative. Nonmonetary impacts are of many types (Branch et al. 1984, pp. 29–34; Cortese and Jones 1977; Freudenburg 1982; Greider and Krannich 1985; Leistritz and Murdock 1981, pp. 155–84; Stöhr and Todtling 1977, pp. 39–42). There is no standard list of nonmonetary impacts, but a partial list would include distribution of benefits and burdens, employment related changes, population changes, housing changes, political changes, health changes, and changes in the quality of life.

The answer to the question of who shares in the benefits and burdens must be sought among economic sectors of the local economy, among socioeconomic groups within the community, and among communities. The benefits and burdens of an economic development event fall on different groups of people within the community (Beck et al. 1973; Bender et al. 1971; Deaton and Landes 1978; Gillis and Shaffer 1985; Kuehn et al. 1972; Mellor and Ironsides 1978; Nelson 1979; Pulver et al. 1984, pp. 71–84; Shaffer 1974; Summers et al. 1976, pp. 106–25; Vander Muellen and Paananen 1977). Thus, even though the community experiences an improvement in its socioeconomic welfare, some groups' positions may actually worsen (see the discussion of Figure 4.3).

When the distribution of benefits and burdens among socioeconomic groups is examined, the question becomes one of which individuals are able to respond to the economic development event by finding employment, selling a resource, or increasing the sales for a business they own. Individuals with inappropriate skills, or with no resources to sell, find themselves in a relatively worse position as a result of the event. An impact analysis must recognize the distribution of changes so that mitigation or reinforcing policies can be initiated.

Benefits and burdens are also distributed among economic sectors. For example, the building of a major industrial park at the edge of the community will have a negative impact on farming in that area. The development of a shopping center on the edge of the community will adversely affect retail merchants in the central business district. At the same time, development of the industrial park may keep a railroad open to service it and at the same time permit the continued bulk hauling of agricultural supplies such as fertilizer, creating nonfarm supplemental employment for the farm families on whom the park's initial effect was negative.

The phrase "employment-related nonmonetary impacts" appears almost contradictory, yet some of the nonmonetary dimensions of employment include job satisfaction, career opportunities, and the reduction of seasonal or cyclical variation in local employment (see Chapter 8 for more detail). These impacts are directly related to employment, but are not measurable simply in terms of job numbers or size of payroll. Changes in jobs also reflect what skills are required and whether existing workers, displaced workers, new entrants, or nonresident workers take those jobs. Each of these labor supply responses will alter the community impact of the development event.

Other forms of nonmonetary impacts also occur, but for our purposes here it is sufficient to recognize that a community impact analysis should identify and integrate both nonmonetary and monetary impacts.

PRIMARY AND SECONDARY IMPACTS. Primary impacts from an economic development event are changes closely associated with the event itself; secondary impacts are changes caused by the event. If the economic development event is the expansion of a commercial establishment, then the jobs, sales, and wages paid by that establishment are primary impacts. Secondary impacts are the changes in employment, output, and income resulting from the initial change. (For more detail see "Multipliers" below.) For the sake of the current discussion, a multiplier represents a summation of all the interactions of the development event with households and other businesses in the community. The absence of interaction means that here has been no multiplier effect. Interaction takes the form of workers hired at the business, payroll paid, and purchase of inputs and supplies from local merchants (see Figure 10.3). The key question for impact analysis is determining the extent to which this interaction occurs either in the community or elsewhere. It is not an either/or situation, but ranges along a continuum from nothing happening locally to almost everything happening locally.

Multiplier estimates tend to exceed actual experience, for a variety of reasons (Boehm and Pond 1976; Leistritz and Murdock 1981, pp. 19–43; Mellor and Ironsides 1978; Shaffer 1979; Shaffer et al. 1982; Silvers 1970, pp. 188–89; Summers et al. 1976, pp. 47–71; Wadsworth and Conrad 1965). Some reasons for the overestimates are these: (1) in-commuters spend most of their salaries in their home community; (2) local residents who previously commuted to jobs elsewhere now work at a local job and no longer bring in money from outside the area; (3) local residents have switched to new local jobs from old local jobs that are not refilled;[2] (4) local residents increase purchases outside the community as their income increases (i.e., there is a declining marginal propensity to consume locally); (5) increased savings by local residents reduces local spending if the savings are not used for local investments; and (7) old debts are retired faster than new debts are assumed.

All these explanations for the inaccuracy of multiplier estimates hold to some extent, but the two basic points at issue here are (1) the location of the interaction between local and nonlocal economic units (see also "Local and Nonlocal Impacts" and "Multipliers" below) and (2) the time required

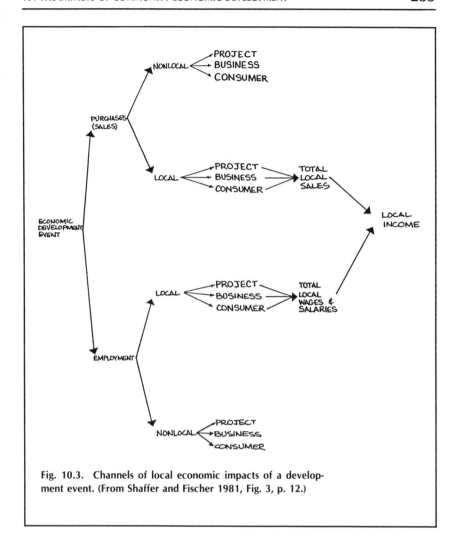

Fig. 10.3.   Channels of local economic impacts of a development event. (From Shaffer and Fischer 1981, Fig. 3, p. 12.)

for the multiplier effect to occur, i.e., for changes to spin off from the development event (time here does not refer to the changes in the development event over time mentioned earlier). If the interaction between the development event and the rest of the economy occurs within the community, the local impact (multiplier) will naturally be higher. However, nonlocal purchases of supplies, labor, and other support services, coupled with nonlocal spending of workers' earnings, reduces the local impact. For smaller communities these leakages can be substantial. To a large extent the degree of leakage depends upon the level of the community in the central place hierarchy. The "economic size" of the community is the degree to which it captures the indirect effects of a development event, i.e., its degree of self-sufficiency. Larger communities are capable of capturing and keeping a higher proportion of the spending connected with a development event than are smaller communities (i.e., they have a larger marginal propensity to consume locally; see the discussion of multipliers below).

Community preconditions influence the extent that secondary changes occur locally. A study of rural communities in the northern Great Plains area (Bender and Parcels 1981, p. 8) indicated that communities experiencing a decline in basic employment followed by a large increase in basic employment initially had a decline in the ratio of nonbasic to basic employment (i.e., a proxy for the multiplier). This suggests excess capacity in the nonbasic sector capable of absorbing the increase in basic activity without an associated increase in nonbasic activity.

The second factor that can make multiplier estimates inaccurate is the time required for change to occur (Longbrake and Geyler 1979; Mandelbaum and Chicoine 1985; Temple 1979). Multiplier estimates assume that the local supply of resources (labor and other inputs) is perfectly elastic and can expand instantly to meet demand. Yet it takes time for local businesses to make the changes to capture the secondary effects from the development event (Shaffer et al. 1982). Merchants must first recognize and then respond to market signals, make investments, adjust inventory, and hire and train new employees. This time lag also reflects merchants' uncertainty about the nature of the economic development event itself and about the response to it by other economic units.

Figure 10.4 demonstrates the importance of time as a factor in typical projections of changes in local population resulting from a major energy project. Note that the population in this example does not peak until five years after the start of construction. The population related to the project drops dramatically once construction is finished. If local workers and businesses fail to anticipate the magnitude of the eventual change, secondary changes are delayed.

The figure also demonstrates the implications of the permanence of jobs created by the economic development event. In this case, the construction work force is more than twice the size of the operating work force, and its transitory nature puts major but temporary burdens on the entire community. The much smaller operating work force does not appear until seven years after construction starts. While most communities will not have a 2,250-megawatt, coal-fired electric generating plant locating in their midst, other projects will show similar changing work force patterns.

PRIVATE AND PUBLIC IMPACTS. Any analysis of economic development impacts must distinguish the changes in the private and public sectors. The

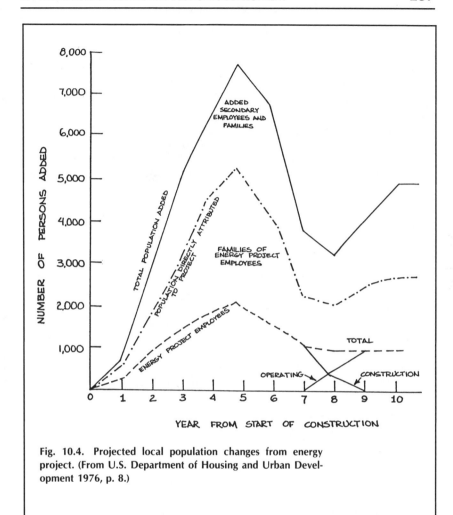

Fig. 10.4. Projected local population changes from energy project. (From U.S. Department of Housing and Urban Development 1976, p. 8.)

private sector includes community employment, sales, income, property values, and wealth. The public sector includes all units of local government (municipal, county, special districts, and school districts). Impacts in the public sector generally fall under the heading of new or additional public revenues and new or additional public services or expenditures.

The linkage between private sector and public sector impacts involves many feedbacks, and the direction of influence is not always one way (Bender and Stinson 1984, pp. 64–67; Caroll and Sacks 1962; Cummings and Mehr 1977; Hirsch 1961b; Leistritz and Murdock 1981, pp. 105–54; Shaffer and Tweeten 1974; Summers et al., 1976, pp. 72–105). For example, the construction of a new building or addition to a plant adds to the local property tax base, which helps pay for water and sewer services. Coincidentally, the availability of excess water treatment capacity influences the decision to expand locally.

Dynamic adjustments in the community and the surrounding region influence public sector impacts (Branch et al. 1984, pp. 24–30; Cummings and Mehr 1977; Smith et al. 1971). Perceptions of the quality of public services and life in the community alter population (size and/or composition) over time. Furthermore, investments in public services tend to be lumpy and exhibit some economies of scale. This leads to a situation where an increase in population is insufficient to cause new public service investments even though costs increase and/or the quality of the service declines. In other situations, or for different services in the same community, the population increase will permit capturing economies of scale and will reduce costs. The key is the existing capacity of particular public services, the nature of the average costs, and the degree to which new users' consumption affects prior users.

Uncertainty also affects public sector impacts (Bender and Stinson 1984, pp. 63–64; Smith et al. 1971). If the community makes public infrastructure investments in anticipation of the development event and its associated secondary effects, residents may find themselves unnecessarily burdened with the costs of those investments if the event does not occur as scheduled, or in the magnitude planned, or if the local spin-offs fail to occur. Fear of this outcome can lead to a decision behavior of delay rather than anticipation.

The type of taxes collected by local government influences the degree to which additional local governmental revenues accrue (Caroll and Sacks 1962; Hirsch 1961b; Shaffer and Tweeten 1974). If fees are levied on sewer hook-ups and installations, etc., local government will begin collecting revenues immediately from new commercial, industrial, or residential construction; if the costs of installation are paid through property tax assessments there will be a delay in payment. If the community has a sales tax, some of the benefits from additional local private consumption accrue to local government. (If the state has a sales tax that is partially returned to the point of origin, the community will also capture some of the increased local spending effects, although they will be delayed.) If the community relies heavily upon property taxes (and especially if there is some form of property tax forgiveness), there will be a lag of as much as two years from the time the investment occurs, is assessed, and the taxes it generates are received.

Public sector impacts also have a primary and secondary dimension. An economic development event that increases family incomes and local consumption (primary impacts) leads to secondary impacts such as additional sales taxes and other forms of local revenues (e.g., a general increase in housing values).

Secondary impacts such as the need for additional services typically involve streets, water lines, sewage treatment, police and fire protection, or schools (Murdock and Leistritz 1979, pp. 209–45; Summers et al. 1976, pp. 72–105). If there is sufficient service capacity and it is located in appropriate areas of the community, additional public service investments will be minimized (Cummings and Mehr 1977; Hirsch 1961b), yet operating costs will rise because more water is pumped, more sewage is treated, and more students are enrolled (Hirsch 1961b). Costs are more difficult to estimate than revenues but are essential to know, especially operating costs. The implicit assumption is that revenues collected from the new residences and businesses will at least equal the costs of servicing them. While this may be true in some cases, it need not be, especially if any form of tax forgiveness is allowed.

Another potential problem for local government is the lag between expenditures and tax revenues (Bender and Stinson 1984, p. 61), especially if the community must install infrastructure and finance it through the property tax. Figure 10.5 indicates a seven-year lapse before additional annual tax revenues finally equal the additional expenditures required by a major coal-fired electrical generating plant. Over the lifetime of the project, the tax revenues exceed the costs of the public services provided, but the first few years stress local government.

A somewhat hidden aspect of municipal service impacts is the change in quantity and/or quality of public services delivered (Cummings and Mehr 1977; Murdock and Schriner 1979). It is quite possible for both quality and quantity to change, and the change may be for the better or for the worse. For example, the increase in the quantity of police protection provided a new industrial park may occur at the expense of patrols in residential areas. This need not always be the case, but there is no reason to believe that municipal service quantity and quality will consistently vary in the same direction or that both will improve as a result of an economic development event.

Two other influences on local public sector impact are the size and rate of population change and its permanency (Bender and Stinson 1984, pp. 60–63; Branch et al. 1984, pp. 26–27). A community with minimal population change is unlikely to incur substantial public service facility outlays other than those associated directly with the new economic development event itself. However, if the community experiences substantial or rapid population change, very intense, though temporary, shortages of public services will reduce the quality of services for both new and old residents (Greider and Krannich 1985). The dilemma confronting the community experiencing these types of shocks is that it does not know whether the

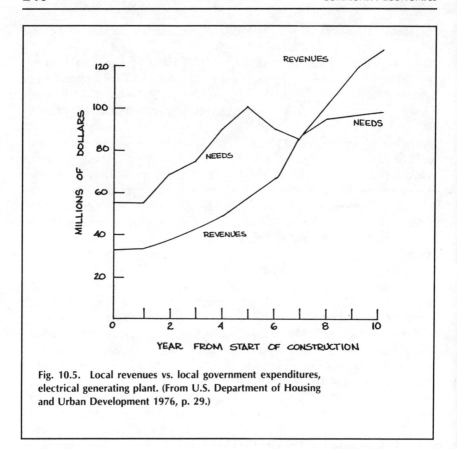

Fig. 10.5. Local revenues vs. local government expenditures,
electrical generating plant. (From U.S. Department of Housing
and Urban Development 1976, p. 29.)

change is permanent or temporary. If the change is going to last only for
two or three years, does the community wish to burden itself with major
long-term infrastructure investments, or would it prefer to suffer through
the transition period and eventually reach a more stable long-term level of
activity?[3] To a large extent the answer to this question depends upon the
availability of resources to purchase public services, certainty about future
events, and the community's attitude toward these types of changes and
deterioration of service quality.

POSITIVE AND NEGATIVE IMPACTS. An economic development event causes
both positive and negative changes in the community. There will always be
some costs associated with any change, though the benefits generally exceed
the costs. The gain in employment from an economic development event
invariably exceeds the loss of jobs because another business has been dis-

placed or people have shifted jobs and their previous jobs have not been refilled.[4]

The changes in the community often affect people and businesses very differently. Local businesses in direct competition with the economic development event (e.g., for sales or labor) find themselves affected adversely, while those not in direct competition receive the benefits of increased consumer traffic and local workers benefit from a higher wage structure. The community should not ignore the costs associated with development but rather should try to anticipate them and reduce or mitigate them.

When the question of negative impacts is raised, the community's response is frequently to attempt to mitigate them (Bender and Stinson 1984, pp. 67–73; Howell and Weber 1982; Leistritz et al. 1984). *Mitigation* means attempting to offset the negative dimensions of the economic development event so that the community can maintain its previous level of well-being or can compensate individuals or groups adversely affected by the event (Dobbs and Huff 1974). A major mitigation strategy is the creation of impact funds to pay for the costs of additional public services or for the dislocation of parties directly affected. Another strategy, especially for residential developments, is to require the developer to provide the infrastructure (e.g., streets, parks). The developer recovers these costs through raising the price of the properties. Another somewhat unique and indirect strategy is *performance mitigation*. Wisconsin now requires communities and businesses to sign performance contracts when using Community Development Block Grant funds for economic development activities. The state will support the development event, but if the promised performance, in the form of jobs created, does not occur, the community and/or private investor must reimburse the state to the extent of the shortfall.

In summary, the changes emanating from an economic development event both increase and reduce community welfare. Generally the net change is positive, but various components of the community experience different types of change. Impact analysis must identify these changes and help the community determine whether some form of policy should be initiated to amplify or mitigate them.

Community Impacts

Measuring monetary impacts across the private, municipal government, and school district sectors yields an estimate of the net gain to the community of an economic development event (Shaffer 1975; Shaffer and Tweeten 1974). The key elements in this process are: identification of community, as distinguished from total, change; estimation of both benefits and costs; and calculation of net gains. Table 10.1 presents a generalization

Table 10.1. Simplified Model for Measuring Net Gain to the Community from an Economic Development Event

Private Sector
Total private income gain in community =
  Primary income gain + secondary income gain
  (minus)
Total private income loss in community =
  Primary income loss + secondary income loss =
  (equals)
Net private income gain in community

*Local Government Sector*ᵃ
Total public revenue gain in local government =
  Primary revenue gain + secondary revenue gain
  (minus)
Total expenditure increase =
  Primary expenditure increase + secondary expenditure increase
  (equals)
Net public revenue gain in local government

Community Net Gain
Private sector net gain
+ local government sector net gain
+ school district sector net gain
= community net gain

  ᵃMunicipality and school districts.

of one integration approach. Its essence is that the community recognizes both costs and benefits associated with the development event and how changes in one part of the community affect other segments, and that the net change in one portion of the community may be at variance with the net gain over all.

Multiplie

Multipliers represent one of the forms of community change from an economic development event most frequently cited. Two important dimensions of multiplier use require elaboration here. They are the factors affecting the size of multipliers and inappropriate application of the method. Methods of estimating multipliers are discussed in the following chapter.

FACTORS INFLUENCING MULTIPLIERS. The size of the multiplier depends upon the initial stimulus and the transmission of that stimulus to other sectors inside and outside the community. Figure 10.3 displayed one likely result of the injection of autonomous expenditures into a community. The important point is that much of the original injection immediately leaks out of the community and never enters the local economy to cause a local multiplier effect (Archer 1976, p. 71; Ashcroft and Swales 1982; Little and

Doeksen 1968; Richardson 1985, pp. 616–17; Wadsworth and Conrad 1965; Wilson 1977).

A basic methodological issue in using the multiplier is identifying the direct stimulus to the local economy (Archer 1976). Since the income multiplier is the total change in household income attributable to a continuous injection of autonomous expenditures into the area, the problem is in defining that continuous autonomous injection. Is it gross payroll, take-home pay, or the change in local spending by community residents hired at the plant? Each has different implications in terms of the magnitude of direct and indirect impacts and the type of multiplier estimated. Since communities are such open economies, leakages from the plant payroll through payroll taxes, employee contributions to fringe benefit programs, and the purchase of imported goods and services by the workers and the plant must be traced. These yield the *marginal propensity to consume locally* (MPC_L) (see the discussion of equation (11.8) in the following chapter).

Other forces conditioning the size of the community's MPC_L include population, the variety of goods and services available locally, income levels, distance/access to competing retail centers, and time. While these will not all be discussed in detail, the basic principle is that for a *local* multiplier effect to occur, the spending and responding must occur within the community rather than elsewhere; see the discussion of equation (11.18) in the following chapter and "Local and Nonlocal Impacts" above.

The value of a multiplier varies directly with population size. Population is a good proxy for self-sufficiency and economies of size (Erickson 1977; Moore 1975; Oakland et al. 1971, p. 344; Smith et al. 1981, p. 21; Stewart 1959, pp. 327–28; Tiebout 1960, pp. 81–82). *Self-sufficiency* means that the community is capable of producing and sustaining the goods and services it uses. The economies of size component emphasizes the market threshold needed by a firm to produce that good or service locally at a profit (Bender 1975; Bender and Parcels 1983; Chalmers et al. 1978; Thompson 1982) (see Chapter 6 for detailed discussion). Gillis and Shahidsaless (1981) found that, in nonmetropolitan counties, for each hundred local residents added, nonbasic employment increased 14 to 17 over the next ten years. Harvey (1973) detected a similar relationship.

Another force affecting the magnitude of the local income multiplier is the spatial distribution of activities (i.e., local vs. nonlocal activities). Transactions occurring outside the community's economic boundaries reduce the impact on the community and reduce the local multiplier. Thus the spatial relationship of the community to sources of supply and consumption must be recognized.

The multiplier size varies directly with the geographic size of the area studied. The self-sufficiency argument recognizes that as community boundaries expand, imported inputs decline and leakages are reduced (Stewart 1959, pp. 327–28; Tiebout 1956b, p. 98). Thus the multiplier for any economic sector in the United States must be greater than the multiplier for a state or a community within a state. The multiplier estimates in Table 10.2 demonstrate the relationship between area (i.e., completeness of the economy) and multiplier. The cells on the diagonal are county multipliers. The off-diagonal cells represent the multiplier effect of the county in the column on the county in the intersecting row. The last row in the table is the sum of county and intercounty multipliers (i.e., the regional multiplier).

Table 10.2. Employment Multipliers by County for Changes in Final Markets, South Central Oklahoma, 1970

County	Caddo	Grady	McClain	Comanche	Stephens	Tillman	Cotton	Jefferson
Caddo	1.98	0.12	0.11	0.03	0.02	0.04	0.10	0.13
Grady	0.14	2.49	0.16	0.02	0.03	–	0.04	0.03
McClain	0.02	0.02	2.82	–	–	–	–	–
Comanche	0.09	0.05	0.01	1.95	0.06	0.07	0.18	0.11
Stephens	0.03	0.06	0.13	0.05	2.13	0.02	0.21	0.55
Tillman	–	–	–	0.01	–	2.49	0.22	0.08
Cotton	–	–	–	0.01	0.02	0.02	2.01	0.06
Jefferson	–	–	–	–	0.02	–	0.04	2.64
Total	*2.25*	*2.75*	*3.24*	*2.07*	*2.29*	*2.65*	*2.81*	*3.61*

Source: From Schreiner et al. 1972, Table 1, p. 56.

The McClain County column in the table shows that a $1.00 change in final demand causes a change of $2.82 in McClain County output, a change of $0.11 in Caddo County, a change of $0.16 in Grady County, a change of $0.01 in Comanche County, and a change of $0.13 in Stephens County. The differences in the intercounty multipliers arise from differences in economic linkages among the counties. The total change in output in the eight-county region resulting from a $1.00 change in final demand in McClain County is $3.24.

A countervailing force to the expansion of the community's economic boundaries is access to nonlocal sources of goods and services (Bender 1975; Erickson 1977; Harvey 1973, p. 471). If individuals can reach nonlocal sources of consumer goods and services (in terms of time and distance) with ease, spending will be drained away from the community's economy, thus reducing the multiplier. Richardson and Gordon (1978, pp. 310–12) found that the magnitude of the spillover from an exogenous stimulus declined with distance.

An implicit assumption in multiplier analyses is that the ratio between the basic and nonbasic sector is stable over time. This assumption permits the use of historical data to estimate multipliers. But ratios expressing the relationships of total to export sectors or of nonexport to export sectors are not constant through time.[5] It is therefore important to use time series data to estimate the multiplier. The major fallacy in using data from only one time period is that they may capture the community's economy in disequilibrium and thus the ratio estimated may be neither representative nor useful for projecting. Furthermore, the use of a single data point does not permit the full effect of the change to work itself through the economy (see Figure 10.7).

The income multiplier of a community seldom remains constant: the community experiences income growth because of changes in propensity to consume locally (MPC_L) and because conversion of local spending into local income (PSY) alters the multiplier; see (11.15) in Chapter 11 (Boehm and Pond 1976; Erickson 1977; Stewart 1959, pp. 328–31). Tiebout (1962, pp. 65–67) suggests that the critical question regarding stability of the marginal propensity to consume locally is how the change in community income occurs.[6] Work by Bender and Parcels (1981) indicates that conditions in the local economy preceding the export base change also affect the multiplier.

A community can experience three types of income change (Tiebout 1962, pp. 65–68). The first type, sometimes labeled *extensive income change,* occurs when more people are attracted to the community. Eventually the community passes a market threshold and the income multiplier increases because local consumption increases, as seen in line (*2*), Figure 10.6 (Ashcroft and Swales 1982; Boehm and Pond 1976; Erickson 1977; Friedly 1965, p. 62; Silvers 1970, p. 189). A second type of income change, labeled *intensive income change,* represents increases in per capita income of existing residents, occurring without any change in community population. Because people now have a higher per capita income, they purchase an increased proportion of their goods and services nonlocally; their taxes and savings increase; and the ratio of local consumption to income (MPC_L) declines as income increases, as seen in line (*3*) Figure 10.6 (Friedly 1965, p. 61). The third type of income change is a combination of extensive and intensive income growth (i.e., more people and more income per person), as seen in lines (*2*) and (*3*) of Figure 10.6. It is important to recognize that only line (*1*) in the figure represents the export base assumption of a constant relationship between local consumption and income.

The multiplier varies inversely with the level of local economic specialization (Harvey 1973). As the local economy becomes increasingly specialized, it becomes less likely to capture the increasing variety of goods and services that households desire (Sirkin 1959, p. 427; Stewart 1959, pp. 328–31). Hirschl and Summers' (1982) study of 176 nonmetropolitan counties found that after correcting for other socioeconomic factors each point of increase in a Gibbs-Martin index of industrial diversity yielded three addi-

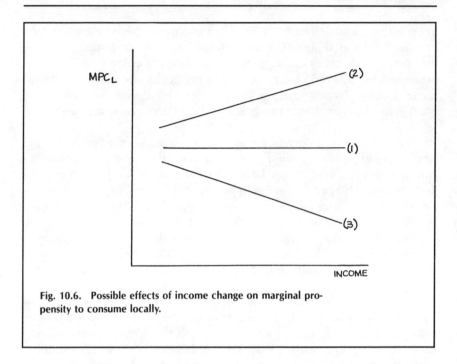

Fig. 10.6. Possible effects of income change on marginal propensity to consume locally.

tional nonbasic jobs in the county. Table 10.3 provides estimates of multipliers related to employment levels. Employment here proxies diversity in the local economy.

It is important to remember that average and marginal multipliers are likely to differ, especially when a new economic sector appears in the community. The community multiplier after a new activity has started will change because of shifts in shopping patterns, appearance of different support services, and other changes. Any attempt to estimate multipliers must take into account the location of labor and input suppliers and the speed with which adjustments occur. The analyst must anticipate adjustments in business and labor linkages in order to estimate the ancillary local employ-

Table 10.3. Employment Level and Size of Multiplier, 375 Appalachian Counties

County Employment	Average Multiplier	Probable Range[a]
1,000–2,999	1.7	1.5–1.9
3,000–4,999	1.8	1.5–2.0
5,000–9,999	1.9	1.6–2.1
10,000–19,999	2.0	1.8–2.2
20,000–49,999	2.2	2.0–2.4
50,000 and above	2.2	2.0–2.5

Source: Gadsby 1968, p.47

[a]There is a 70 percent probability that individual multipliers will be included within these ranges.

ment and investments. Another reason for differences in average and marginal multipliers is that all businesses in the export sector do not affect the local economy in the same manner. Some businesses use local labor to a greater extent than others; some pay higher wages than others; some have almost no linkage at all with the local economy.

Simple economic base ratios or aggregated input-output multipliers neglect differences in the interindustry linkages among local economic sectors. The export base approach typically yields an aggregated multiplier for all businesses in the export sector. It is undifferentiated with respect to the component of the export base initiating change. The only way to change secondary impacts in the community is to change the size of the stimulus, not its source (Garnick 1970, p. 35). Because the export base multiplier is an aggregate across a wide variety of economic sectors, it understates the multiplier of those export industries near the advanced end of the raw-materials-processing continuum if their extraction and earlier processing is done locally, while it overstates the multiplier of those industries in the extracting and earlier processing stage (Garnick 1970, p. 38).

While multiplier effects begin as soon as the first exogenous dollar is spent in the community, the total effect will not be instantaneous (Garnick 1970; Gerking and Isserman 1981; Lever 1974; McNulty 1977; Sasaki 1963). It requires time for the spending and respending to occur, and thus it may take years for the multiplier effect in the community to be fully felt. In particular, secondary investments are slow to respond to the initial stimulus. Figure 10.7 shows the influence of time on the magnitude of the multi-

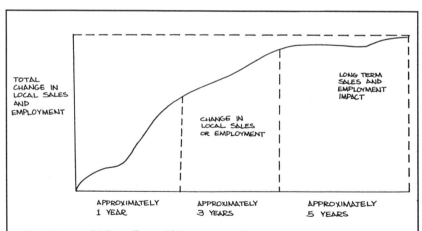

Fig. 10.7. Multiplier effect within a community over time. (From Dorf and Hoppe 1980, p. 7.)

plier. Note that secondary investments permit the local economy to capture more of the previously leaked activity.

Instantaneous multipliers do not capture the additional investment stimulated by increased output in the community (see Figure 10.7). In particular, as local markets cross thresholds, investment in nonbasic business and the additional local consumption, employment, and income generated will not be included. This import substitution or crossing of feasibility thresholds increases the magnitude of the local multiplier. The forces changing multipliers vary with the time period in question. One short-run/long-run factor is the ability of local suppliers to adjust to the needs of the economic development event. In the short run, inability to adjust reduces the local multiplier. In the long run, as time permits adjustment in supply capabilities, the multiplier increases.

Another time phenomenon is the adjustment of consumers' geographic spending patterns (Garnick 1970). Lever's (1974) study of eight Scottish firms found that the local input and output linkages for 1966, 1968, and 1970 displayed considerable variation, with the variation of input linkages relatively greater than output. Thus the firms' local income multipliers varied over time. Lever attributed the changes in linkages to learning by management. Initially, management tried to reduce the risk of a new branch plant by using current suppliers. As knowledge of the new area increased, management began to seek and use local suppliers to reduce the transportation and other costs associated with distant suppliers.

Instantaneous multipliers fail to account for the interregional feedbacks that occur as the exports of one community change. In Figure 10.8,

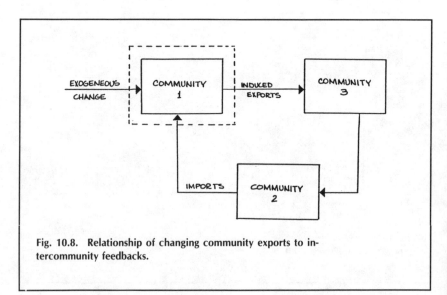

Fig. 10.8. Relationship of changing community exports to intercommunity feedbacks.

community *1* experiences an exogenous increase in its exports. As a result of this increase, it imports more inputs from community *2*. Community *2*, having experienced an increase in its exports, requires additional inputs from community *3*. Community *3* might purchase additional inputs from community *1*. Even though community *1* initiated the change, through its exports, it very quickly experiences an additional increase in its exports as the initial stimulus filters through the system of communities.

The type of worker hired also affects multiplier size. Figure 10.9 displays six different employment multipliers based on type of worker (Ashcroft and Swales 1982; Boehm and Pond 1976; Friedly 1965; Tiebout 1960). While the permanent/temporary employment dichotomy is most appropriate for a major development event such as the construction of a hydroelectric dam or mine, the distinction among local workers, in-migrant

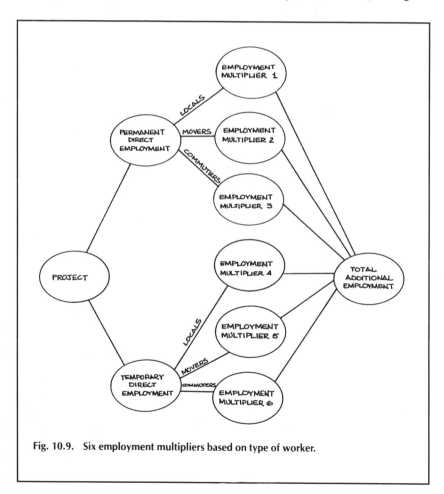

Fig. 10.9. Six employment multipliers based on type of worker.

workers, and in-commuters applies to any development event. Caution should be used when analyzing historical data from projects using a different mix of workers to estimate multipliers. The multiplier estimates reflect the residential preferences of workers for a past project, which may differ from the new development. Use of historical work force data with less in-commuting creates upward bias in the local multiplier estimated.

This compilation of factors influencing the expression of the multiplier effect is not exhaustive, but it does give a sense of the forces that accentuate or dampen secondary changes in the community. The commentary above applies to all forms of multiplier estimates (e.g., income, output, employment, pollution) and estimation methodologies (e.g., export base, input-output). Multipliers are like any other analytical tool available to the community economics analyst: while they offer insight in predicting changes, they can mislead if used in a manner that violates their conceptual foundation.

WARNINGS ABOUT THE USE OF MULTIPLIERS. There are five basic ways in which a multiplier is often misused (Lewis et al. 1979). When they are listed, the misuse becomes painfully obvious. They are: interchanging multipliers, double counting, pyramiding, confusing a multiplier with turnover, and transferring estimates among locales.

The first misuse is interchanging output, income, and employment multipliers. These multipliers tend to have similar values (i.e., higher output multipliers tend to be associated with higher income and employment multipliers). However, a moment's reflection makes it obvious that income, employment, and output are not identical measures of the same economic activity (see Table 10.4). An income multiplier differs from an employment multiplier because of differences in the wages paid for jobs in different businesses within the same economic sector or for different jobs within the same business. Thus the income multiplier may be either larger or smaller than the employment multiplier. Furthermore, both the income and employment multipliers differ from the output multiplier because of differences in capital-labor ratios, ownership of resources, etc. Although the three multipliers tend to move together and to have the same relative magnitudes, they cannot be interchanged.

The second misuse is double counting. A double counting error occurs when the total economic change occurring in the community is estimated as the direct change plus the direct change times the multiplier. The direct change has been counted twice here because the multiplier measures both the direct and indirect changes in a community. The standard procedure to avoid double counting in estimating total change is to use only direct change times the multiplier.

A third type of misuse is pyramiding. Pyramiding occurs when the

Table 10.4. Comparison of Employment and Income Multipliers

Industry	Rank	Employment	Personal Income
Transportation equipment	1	3.3858	2.8283
Fossil fuel	2	2.8447	2.5165
Stone, clay, glass	3	2.5984	1.9248
Paper	4	2.5915	2.0028
Petroleum refining and related products	5	2.4693	1.9260
Machinery	6	2.3910	1.8862
Finance, insurance, real estate	7	2.3390	2.4603
Fabricated metals	8	2.3297	1.8786
Food processing	9	2.2743	2.4908
Chemicals	10	2.1462	1.6099
Primary metals	11	1.9224	1.6835
Federal enterprises	12	1.8970	1.2413
Contract construction	13	1.8765	1.6560
Printing	14	1.8014	1.6646
Apparel	15	1.7502	1.9953
State and local government	16	1.6694	1.3563
Services	17	1.6609	1.7183
Lumber	18	1.6604	1.5718
Transport, communication, utilities	19	1.6561	1.1509
Wholesale, retail trade	20	1.4279	1.6149

Source: Saussy 1976, Table 8, p. 38.

analyst counts the changes in input supply firms more than once. Here the analyst determines the multiplier for a specific sector and works backward from the initiating sector through the local economy, adding multipliers for each linked input sector. An example is a rural community with a dairy processing plant experiencing a substantial increase in sales. The employment, income, or output multiplier for the dairy processing plant includes the change in employment, income, or output in dairy processing plus the changes in all of the locally linked economic sectors supplying that plant. In pyramiding, the analyst takes the initial multiplier and adds the multiplier for dairy farms, forgetting that the changes in dairy farming are already included in the indirect and induced effect of the dairy processing sector multiplier.

The fourth misuse is confusing a multiplier with turnover. Turnover is the number of times a dollar changes hands in a community before it escapes, which is not synonymous with the income multiplier. The difference in the value of a multiplier and turnover is seen in Figure 10.10, where the $1 of initial exports is respent or turned over five times in the community (i.e., the turnover is 5), but the multiplier is 1.66. Note that only $0.03 is involved in the last exchange, so that the last turnover does not involve the full dollar initiating the change.

The fifth misuse is transferring multiplier estimates from one locale to another. Such transferring can be done, but it requires caution. The following factors must be considered when using multipliers estimated elsewhere. First, the communities must have populations of similar size: a multiplier

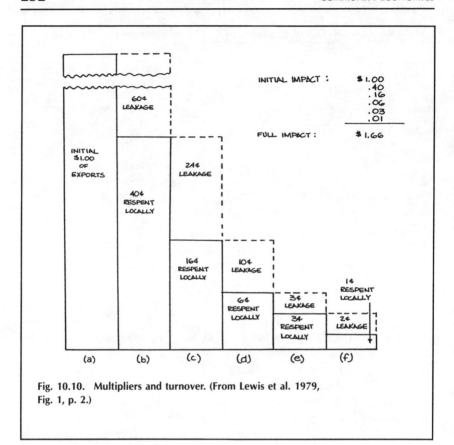

INITIAL IMPACT : $ 1.00
.40
.16
.06
.03
.01

FULL IMPACT : $ 1.66

INITIAL
$1.00
OF
EXPORTS

60¢
LEAKAGE

40¢
RESPENT
LOCALLY

24¢
LEAKAGE

16¢
RESPENT
LOCALLY

10¢
LEAKAGE

6¢
RESPENT
LOCALLY

3¢
LEAKAGE

3¢
RESPENT
LOCALLY

1¢
RESPENT
LOCALLY

2¢
LEAKAGE

(a)   (b)   (c)   (d)   (e)   (f)

Fig. 10.10. Multipliers and turnover. (From Lewis et al. 1979, Fig. 1, p. 2.)

estimated for a city of 80,000 is inappropriate for a city of 8,000. Second, the size and number of other cities (alternative trade centers) within the area should be similar. Third, the communities should be of comparable distance (in time and space) from larger trade centers—in other words, if a community is thirty miles from a larger trade center, its multiplier will probably not be the same as the multiplier of a community sixty miles from a similarly sized trade center. Fourth, the communities and their surrounding areas should have a similar economic structure (e.g., they should both be trade/commerce centers or should both be oriented toward agriculture, or manufacturing, or tourism). Fifth, the transfer of multipliers among areas requires a similar local/nonlocal residential settlement pattern for the labor force, as well as similar labor force requirements of the economic development event. The economic development events being measured should use similar production technologies and should have similar input purchase patterns, so that their initial direct impact on the local economy will be comparable. The sites should have similar propensities to consume locally and similar ratios of local income generated per dollar of local consumption. (If the propensity to consume locally is about the same at both sites, the consumer and business service sectors resemble each other.) Evidence is accumulating that for multiplier estimates to be transferred, predevelopment trends must also be similar (Bender 1975).

Summary

The discussion in this chapter has emphasized the form taken by the socioeconomic impacts of an economic development event and the forces that influence them. Because event A in community B need not always yield result C, it is important that the analyst avoid making a single or point estimate of the impacts. There are simply too many forces at work to allow the analyst to say, with any degree of confidence, that 75 new jobs will create 35 additional jobs in the community. Rather, the analyst should provide a range of estimates based on various assumptions reflecting adverse and optimal forms of change, so that the sensitivity of impacts to variations in the event or the community, or the interactions between the event and the community, can be tested. If the analyst determines that some impacts are very sensitive to certain dimensions of the project, a focused policy response can then be made.

Change is an inevitable byproduct of community economic development. However, the change that occurs is not automatic, and it is subject to manipulation. The real purpose of impact analysis is less the measurement than the identification of change and the determination of how the development event or the community can be managed to yield the desired outcomes (or, at worst, how adverse consequences can be minimized). This difficult task is complicated by the dynamic stimulus-response relationship between the development event and the community, which dramatically alters anticipated socioeconomic impacts. Figure 10.11 displays this stimulus-response feedback loop.

For the community economic analyst, multipliers are tools which are extremely efficient and easy to use, and widely accepted by noneconomists. For these reasons they are frequently misused. When they are, significant misallocation of community resources can result. For example, errors in estimating population changes can lead to incorrect estimates of housing and local government service needs and to misguided private investments.

The community multiplier is a function of the economic structure of the community and of how spending changes are allocated across various segments of that community. In other words, if a community provides the goods and services required by both workers and businesses, the multiplier will be greater than it would be if some or all of these goods and services

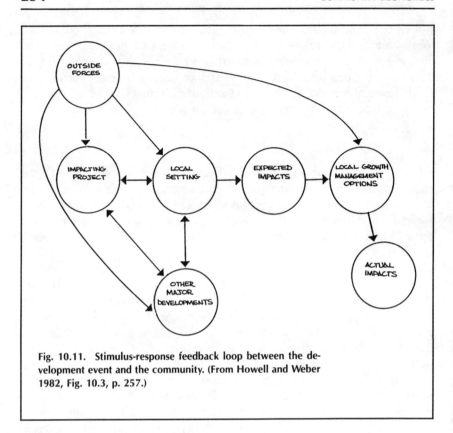

Fig. 10.11. Stimulus-response feedback loop between the development event and the community. (From Howell and Weber 1982, Fig. 10.3, p. 257.)

had to be purchased elsewhere. Likewise, different segments of the local economy have different backward linkages to other segments of the local economy. If the economic development event purchases only labor locally, its impact is different than if it also purchases utilities, transportation, and other inputs locally.

Study Questio

1. What is the difference, if any, between economic change and economic impact?

2. What is the relationship between community economic development theories and impact analysis?

3. What are the five basic impact analysis questions discussed in this chapter? Why are they important to impact analysis?

4. Why do different economic development events cause different economic impacts?

5. Why is it important to distinguish primary and secondary impacts? What is the implication for community economic development?

6. Two general and several specific factors were suggested as reducing the magnitude of community multipliers. What are they?

7. The term self-sufficiency was used in conjunction with economic impacts. What does it mean, and what is its significance to impact analysis?

8. What is the significance of time to impact analysis?

9. All community changes resulting from an economic development event are private. Evaluate the accuracy of this claim.

10. What are some of the factors affecting the incidence of local government revenues and costs?

11. Why is uncertainty particularly important to impact analysis?

12. What is the difference between public and private impacts? Monetary vs. nonmonetary impacts?

13. Why is the local vs. nonlocal distinction an important aspect of impact analysis?

14. One idea in this chapter is that there is no single number estimate of economic impact. Why not?

15. Distribution is one form of nonmonetary impact. Why is it so critical in an impact analysis?

16. Why is the identification of negative changes and costs crucial in an impact analysis?

17. What is the significance of distinguishing between measuring and managing impacts in conducting an impact analysis?

18. Discuss why the dynamic response and feedback between the economic development event and the community are important in impact analysis.

19. What are some of the factors influencing the size of the multiplier? Why are they important, and how might they influence size?

20. Can income, employment, and output multipliers be interchanged? If not, why not?

21. What factors must be considered when transferring multiplier estimates from one locale to another?

22. What is the difference between multipliers and turnover? Why is this difference important?

23. The export base multiplier is described as an aggregate multiplier. What does this mean, and why is it significant?

Economic Base and Input-Output

11

THIS CHAPTER REVIEWS THE REASONS for conducting a study of a community's economic base and examines schemes to classify economic sectors and various measures of economic activity; the discussion then moves to determining community income, the estimation of the export base, and its implications for multiplier analysis. The second half of the chapter reviews input-output, its major assumptions, and the calculation of income, employment, and output multipliers. The discussion of input-output analysis does not focus on technical details but rather emphasizes how input-output information provides a better understanding of a community and its economic activities.

Economic Base Studie

Why undertake an economic base study of the community? The most obvious reason is to acquire a better understanding of its economic structure (i.e., to improve understanding of business sectors such as manufacturing, trade, or construction). A second reason is to understand what is happening in the community's economy (i.e., to understand the markets it sells to and the linkages among various businesses within it). A third reason is to anticipate potential problems in the local economy (i.e., to expose community constraints or limitations). These reasons are not mutually exclusive.

There are four essential components to any economic base study. The first is an inventory of the economic resources in the community. This includes human, man-made, and natural capital currently used or potentially available and the resultant income and employment from the use of resources. The second is an investigation of the structure of the local economy by grouping business establishments into various categories. The third component is integration of the various local/nonlocal markets available to local businesses and identification of the relationship between the businesses serving local and nonlocal markets. The fourth component is an analysis of the nonlocal markets available to the community. The third and fourth components provide insight into the effects on the community of changes in internal and external economic forces. The first component is commonly called social accounts.

SOCIAL ACCOUNTS OF THE COMMUNITY. Any comprehensive community economic analysis starts with a compilation of background data on the community. Social accounts organize community data for the specific purpose of facilitating decision-making (Barnard 1969, p. 109; Bendavid 1974, pp. 29–78; Czamanski 1972; Hewings 1983, pp. 187–912; Hirsch 1961a; Hirsch 1962; Leven 1961; Perloff 1961; Perloff 1962). These accounts record economic activity for the community and represent the aggregation of individual households and businesses. The rudiments of a social accounting system must precede any community economic analysis, but it is not necessary to prepare a complete set of accounts.[1]

The elements of a social accounting system depend upon the questions asked, the form of analysis conducted, and data availability. Problems with data collection include the difficulty of assigning values to the many nonmarket elements included in a social accounting scheme; failure to collect information at the community level to permit comparisons among communities and over time, and the inability to distinguish between local and nonlocal economic forces. While these factors complicate assembling data, they do not preclude the usefulness of social accounts.

Social accounts represent several different economic dimensions of the community (Perloff 1962, p. 361). They measure stocks of resources (e.g., land, man-made capital) and flows of economic activity (e.g., income, sales, investment).

Table 11.1 outlines one simplified system of accounts. The population account tabulates the number of people, their age, education, sex, health status, family status, and needs for special public services. The human resources account includes the number of workers, their skills (both possessed and actually being used), stability of jobs, and sectors of employment. The income account records information on the type of income (e.g., wages and salaries, rents, transfers), local/nonlocal sources, the economic sector providing the income, its amount, and its distribution. The capital account is composed of data on natural, man-made, private, and public resources. The amount of resources available, the amount used, their transferability to other uses, and ownership or control of the resource are possible data elements. The public sector account measures amounts and sources of public revenues and expenditures as well as public infrastructure investment. Many of the important nonmarket forces are collected in the atti-

Table 11.1. Summary of the General Social Accounts

Account 1. Population and Human Resources
Population
Number of people
  Age
  Sex
Sources of change in population
  Natural
  Migration
Household characteristics
Place of residence
Labor force/employment
  Total
  Skills
  Training
  Sector of employment
Unemployment
  Skills
  Duration
Job vacancies
Labor participation
Work week
Labor attitudes
Labor commuting

Account 2. Income, Capital and Investment
Income
  Level
  Distribution
  Change
Physical resource stocks
  Private plant and equipment
Natural resources
  Private

Account 2—(cont.)
  Public
  Undeveloped land
Investment
  Private
  Public
Financial wealth

Account 3. Attitudes
Private sector aspirations
Private sector evaluation of performance
Public sector aspirations
Attitudes toward financing public programs
Attitudes of community leaders

Account 4. Public Revenues and Expenditures
Sources of funds
Current expenditures
Capital expenditures
Tax base

Account 5. Flow of Funds
Industry indicators
Output
Distribution of output
  Factor purchases
  Purchases from outside the region
  Industrial organization
Areawide indicators
  Net output produced
  Income produced
  Productivity

tudes account. The flow of funds account depicts the economic transactions within the community and with the rest of the world. This latter flow typically appears as a balance of payments account.

The theoretical concepts used to analyze community economic development questions determine the major elements and structure of social accounting systems. The supply-oriented growth theories reviewed in Chapter 2 outline the critical elements in the resources account. Labor markets (Chapter 8) and capital markets (Chapter 7) also contribute to the resources account. Chapters 2 and 8 provide the framework for the human resources account. Chapter 6 suggests important components in the population and flow of funds accounts. The discussion of income analysis in Chapter 10 aids in determining the elements of the income account. The flow of funds, business, employment, income, and output accounts all have a close relationship with the input-output analysis discussed later in this chapter.

SECTORAL COMPOSITION OF THE COMMUNITY'S ECONOMY. A community economic analysis provides little insight if it treats all economic actors (e.g., businesses, labor, households) as indistinguishable. This section reviews ways of distinguishing among various businesses.

There is no unique method of delineating the economic sectors of the community. The mechanism chosen largely depends upon the analytical questions addressed and data availability. The goal of any classification scheme is to establish typographies of relatively homogeneous economic units with similar behavioral characteristics.

One typology classifies businesses by their use of similar technology. An example of this might be Bessemer, Siemens-Martin, Kaldo, Tysland-Hole, L. D. Processes, and electric arc furnace steel mills. A more aggregated typology based on similar technology is the relative proportion of labor vs. capital used in the production process (i.e., labor- vs. capital-intensive).

A second classification uses the similarity of response to business cycles. Businesses sensitive to the national business cycles (e.g., construction) react differently than businesses less dependent upon national economic activities (e.g., food processing).

A third typology classifies businesses according to their major location needs (e.g., near their markets—retail shopping centers—or near a resource—mines).

A fourth typology characterizes business units by size, such as employment (i.e., fewer than 10 workers, 11–25, 26–50, etc.) or gross sales (i.e., less than $200,000, $201,000–500,000, etc.).

A fifth classification scheme uses the market to which businesses sell (e.g., local vs. nonlocal markets). A variant of the market-oriented classifying mechanism is classification by type of customer (e.g., households, other businesses, or government). Customers can be further delineated according to local/nonlocal residence.

A sixth scheme classifies businesses according to the type of product produced. This scheme typically starts with a goods vs. services dichotomy. Goods are further divided into durable (lasting for three or more years) and nondurable. Services are further divided into business services and consumer services. A detailed method of classifying economic activity according to what is produced is the Standard Industrial Classification (SIC) code, which generates a five-digit number grouping a business with other businesses that produce a similar product. Table 11.2 displays the SIC system and gives an indication of its detail.

The SIC code categorizes community economic data universally across the country. Therefore, it permits comparing economic activity among states, regions, or communities. Despite the widespread use of the code, it suffers some limitations. First, it relies on arbitrary judgments about how to classify multiproduct firms. Typically the method used is to classify by major product (in terms of sales), but that is not always a clear choice. Why not use employment or investment? Furthermore, the major product produced may change over time. This problem is more visible at the three- or four-digit level of classification. Second, the system is based on the product produced; thus it does not distinguish between firms using different technology to produce the same product. If the concern is types of resources and labor used, the system fails to distinguish differences.

Although the SIC scheme is frequently used to classify the economic sectors of a community, it may not be the most appropriate classification scheme for a particular concern facing the community. Thus, it is important to remember the other classification schemes mentioned, and to use the scheme most appropriate for the question addressed.

MEASURING A COMMUNITY'S ECONOMY. The choice of units to measure economic activity is guided by the question(s) asked and the availability of the data desired relative to the cost of acquiring it (Andrews 1970d; Bendavid 1974, pp. 29–80; Blumenfeld 1955, pp. 260–62; Tiebout 1962, pp. 45–46).

One measurement unit is the number of businesses and households in the community. While this measure has utility for some questions, it does not generate the detail required for in-depth analysis because it equates a business employing five workers with a business employing five hundred workers.

A second unit of measure is sales. Sales record the total economic transactions occurring in the community. The problem with sales is the double counting of intermediate product sales among firms within the community, inflating the final figure. The desire to avoid double counting lo-

Table 11.2. Example of Detail in Standard Industrial Classification System

General No.	Description
36	ELECTRIC AND ELECTRONIC EQUIPMENT
Group No.	
361	ELECTRIC TRANSMISSION AND DISTRIBUTION EQUIPMENT
3612	Power, Distribution, and Specialty Transformers

Establishments primarily engaged in manufacturing power, distribution, instrument, and specialty transformers. Establishments primarily engaged in manufacturing radio frequency or voice frequency transformers, coils, or chokes are classified in Industry 3677, and resistance welder transformers in Industry 3623.

Airport lighting transformers
Autotransformers, electric (power transformers)
Ballasts for lighting fixtures
Control transformers
Current limiting reactors, electric
Distribution transformers, electric
Doorbell transformers, electric
Electric furnace transformers
Feeder voltage regulators and boosters (electric transformers)
Fluorescent ballasts
Generator voltage regulators, electric induction and step type
Ignition transformers
Instrument transformers, except portable
Lighting transformers, fluorescent
Lighting transformers, street and airport
Line voltage regulators

Luminous tube transformers
Machine tool transformers
Ratio transformers
Rectifier transformers
Regulators, transmission and distribution voltage
Signaling transformers, electric
Specialty transformers
Street lighting transformers
Toy transformers
Transformers, electric power
Transformers, for electronic meters
Transformers, reactor
Tripping transformers
Vibrators, interrupter
Voltage regulating transformers, electric power
Voltage regulators, transmissions and distribution

Source: Office of Management and Budget, *Standard Industrial Classification Manual, 1972* (Washington, D.C.: Executive Office of the President).

cally purchased inputs leads to the use of value added as a measure of economic activity. Value added is defined as the dollar value of final sales less the cost of materials purchased. Value added includes the income to nonlocal owners of resources, which leaks out to those owners but is not deducted from the community value added. Value added does not include returns to local resource owners from the nonlocal use of their resource (e.g., capital or labor).

A third unit of measure is income, which includes wages and salaries; proprietor's income (i.e., profits); property income (i.e., rents, dividends, and interest payments); and transfer payments. This measure excludes income to nonlocal resource owners but includes the income generated from the nonlocal use of the community's resources, whether capital or labor. Income is the best measure of the economic activity within a community, but it is a very difficult concept to measure, and price changes within the community obfuscate individual income changes.

The final measure of economic activity is employment, frequently used because of ease of measurement and greater consistency among data series over time and among communities. But, despite its almost universal use as a standard measure of economic activity, this yardstick has some very definite limitations. The first is the problem of individuals holding more than one job at a time (e.g., two part-time jobs). The second is the definition of a standard unit of employment: Is it a 40-hour week, a 35-hour week, or what? Part-time jobs and jobs not fully using the worker's skills are counted and presumed to be equal to full-time jobs using workers' skills to their full potential. A third consideration is whether business owners and unpaid family workers are included. In most unemployment-insurance-derived databases they are not. Yet the employment of a community is broader than an administratively determined measure created to meet the legal requirements of unemployment insurance laws. Fourth, to count just the number of people employed over time ignores the implications of changes in productivity. For example, a community may experience an increase in the productivity of its export sector and an increase in external sales, but there may be no increase in export employment, or it may even decline. Yet the export sector is generating additional local economic activity (i.e., purchase of local nonlabor inputs). The fifth limitation of employment as a measure is that all jobs are treated as if they paid the same wage. The generation of ten jobs paying $15,000 per year creates the same community income as fifteen jobs paying $10,000 per year, yet employment measures suggest that the fifteen jobs have a greater impact on the local community. While that may be true, it is not likely that the impact of fifteen jobs would be 50 percent greater than the impact of ten. Finally, the employment measure of economic activity does not capture the effects of the flow of funds into a community from external sources, such as interest and dividends, social security payments, pensions, and public assistance. Nor does employment data measure the intracommunity flow of rents and profits.

There is thus no single comprehensive measure of a community's economic activity. The analyst should use several measures, but the choice will be constrained by cost, data availability, and question(s) being asked.

ECONOMIC BASE MULTIPLIERS. The fourth component of an economic base analysis of a community is how external forces affect the local economy. The spending and respending of the exogenous injection of income results in a total change in community income exceeding the original change. Rather than trace this spending and respending process for each change in exogenous income, multipliers provide a short cut.

The traditional Keynesian approach to income determination demonstrates how multipliers work within a community.[2] Income is the sum of consumption, exports, imports, investment, and government expenditures, as shown in (11.1). Total consumption is driven by total income, as shown in (11.2). The level of income influences the level of imports; see (11.7). Local consumption is defined as the difference between total consumption and imports, as shown in (11.3). Savings and investments are usually defined as being equal, as are governmental expenditures and taxes, as shown in (11.4) and (11.5):

$$Y = C + X - M + I + G \qquad (11.1)$$
$$C = a + cY \qquad (11.2)$$
$$C_L = C - M \qquad (11.3)$$
$$I = S \qquad (11.4)$$
$$G = Tx \qquad (11.5)$$
$$X = \overline{X} \qquad (11.6)$$
$$M = b + mY \qquad (11.7)$$

where Y is income or output, C is total consumption, C_L is local consumption, I is investment, S is savings, G is government expenditures, Tx is taxes, X is gross exports, and M is gross imports.

In (11.1) exports, investments, and government expenditures are exogenously determined in the short run. Thus, the community income level is a function of local consumption and exports because the influence of the other factors is negated. How changes in exports and local consumption affect the local economy becomes obvious by substituting (11.2) and (11.7) into (11.1), performing the algebra and solving for income (Y):

$$Y = \frac{a - b + X + I + G}{1 - (c - m)} \qquad (11.8)$$

Differentiating (11.8) with respect to exports (X) shows how a change in exports influences income. The reasoning is identical if (11.8) is differentiated with respect to investment or government, but current assumptions do not permit those values to change:

$$\frac{dY}{dX} = \frac{1}{1 - (c - m)} \tag{11.9}$$

where c is the marginal propensity to consume, m is the marginal propensity to import, and $c - m$ is the marginal propensity to consume locally. Thus the change in local income in response to a change in exports depends upon local consumption.

Equation (11.9) and the export base multiplier are identical, since the ratio of nonbasic income to total income is a proxy for the propensity to consume locally (Pleeter 1980, pp. 12–14). Thus:

$$\frac{dY}{dX} = \frac{1}{1 - \dfrac{\text{nonbasic income}}{\text{total income}}}$$

$$= \frac{1}{\dfrac{\text{basic income}}{\text{total income}}} = \frac{\text{total income}}{\text{basic income}} = k \tag{11.10}$$

Equation (11.10) indicates that the multiplier for the economy is the ratio of total income to basic income. This ratio can occur in two forms. The first form is called an *average multiplier* (total income divided by basic income). The second form is called a *marginal multiplier* (change in total income divided by change in basic income). A marginal multiplier is more appropriate because it measures change over time as a result of change in the basic sector. The equality, often implicitly assumed, between the two ratios is purely coincidental.

Equation (11.9) suggests that local consumption is the crucial variable in the change in income, but every dollar of local consumption does not yield a dollar of local income (Tiebout 1962, pp. 58–60; Wilson 1977, p. 45). Some local consumption dollars are siphoned out of the community to pay for such things as imported inputs, nonlocal taxes, or returns on local investments by nonlocal investors. Consumption, investment, or government expenditures generate local income in two steps. First, consumption, investment, or government expenditures must occur in the community. Second, these expenditures must be converted into local income, as shown here:

$$Y_T = X' + C_L' + I' + G' \tag{11.11}$$

where Y_T is total income in the community, X' is local income from community exports, C_L' is local income from consumption within the community, I' is local income from investment within the community, and G' is local income from expenditures by nonlocal government within the community. Each income source (X', C_L', I', G') is the product of the respective expenditure occurring locally and the proportion of those expenditures which becomes local income. The proportion of income per dollar of expenditure varies by type of expenditure.

The transformation of (11.11) into a statement of income change is straightforward:

$$\Delta Y_T = \Delta X' + \Delta C_L' + \Delta I' + \Delta G' \qquad (11.12)$$

Equation (11.12) can be simplified into

$$\Delta Y_T = \Delta Y_B + \Delta Y_{NB} \qquad (11.13)$$

where ΔY_B is change in basic sector income, $\Delta X' + \Delta I' + \Delta G'$, and ΔY_{NB} is change in nonbasic sector income, $\Delta C_L'$. The change in nonbasic income comes from the change in local consumption and its conversion into income:

$$\Delta Y_{NB} = \Delta C_L' = \Delta Y_T \, (MPC_L) \, (PSY) \qquad (11.14)$$

where MPC_L is the proportion of income change spent locally (marginal propensity to consume locally) and PSY is the proportion of local consumption expenditures that becomes local income. Recognition of the income-from-expenditures process leads to refining the earlier multiplier formulation, (11.9), into:

$$k = \frac{1}{1 - (MPC_L) \, (PSY)} \qquad (11.15)$$

Equation (11.15) demonstrates that variations in either MPC_L or PSY can alter the value of the multiplier. Research by Gordon and Mulkey (1978) and Wilson (1977) demonstrates the importance of the value of marginal propensity to consume locally (MPC_L) and the conversion of that spending into local income (PSY) for smaller communities. Gordon and Mulkey estimate that the marginal propensity to consume locally varies from 0.2 to 0.8, with the most likely value being 0.3 to 0.6. Furthermore, they estimate that the local income per dollar of local consumption ranges from 0.25 to 0.75. Using the best and worst scenario for a community creates a range of multipliers. In the best situation, where the maximum amount of income is consumed locally and the maximum amount of local consumption becomes local income, a local income multiplier of 2.5 occurs:

$$k = \frac{1}{1 - (0.8)\,(0.75)} = \frac{1}{0.4} = 2.5 \tag{11.16}$$

In the worst case, where a minimal amount of local consumption is generated from changes in income, and a minimal amount of local consumption becomes local income, a local income multiplier of only 1.05 occurs:

$$k = \frac{1}{1 - (0.2)\,(0.25)} = \frac{1}{0.95} = 1.05 \tag{11.17}$$

Returning to (11.11), three factors determine local income changes from exogenous expenditures: (1) the type of exogenous expenditures change (e.g., ΔX, ΔI, or ΔG); (2) the proportion of exogenous expenditure that creates local spending; and (3) the proportion of local spending that becomes local income (Tiebout 1962, p. 61). Equation (11.18) explicitly incorporates all three considerations:

$$\Delta Y_T = \frac{\Delta X + \Delta I + \Delta G}{1 - (MPC_L \times PSY_C + MPI_L \times PSY_I + MPG_L \times PSY_G)} \tag{11.18}$$

where MPC_L represents marginal propensity to consume locally, MPI_L represents marginal propensity to invest locally, MPG_L represents marginal propensity for nonlocal government expenditures to occur locally, and PSY represents proportion of respective local expenditures that becomes local income.

The only exogenous change in the short run is exports. The short-run value for ΔI is zero because investment does not change in the short run, since it is a function of past, not current, economic activity. The short-run change in nonlocal government expenditures (ΔG) is exogenous and is assumed to be zero. In the short run, ΔG, ΔI, MPG_L and MPI_L are zero.

In the long run, the changes in investment (ΔI) and in government expenditures (ΔG) need not be zero. Investment becomes a function of local economic activities and is not solely determined by previous decisions or outside forces. Rather, long-run investment arises from existing economic growth and internal forces. Furthermore, government expenditures vary with local income. In the long run, investment, government expenditures, and taxes are variable. Equation (11.18) translates into a long-run multiplier when it is recognized that the numerator (ΔX, ΔG, and ΔI) represents the product of 1, as illustrated in (11.15), and ΔX, ΔG, and ΔI.

This section demonstrates the importance of local consumption, local government spending, and local investment to the estimation of the simple economic base multiplier. Furthermore, the significance of converting local spending into local income is recognized. Finally, the simple ratio of total to basic sector as an estimate of the multiplier highlights the importance of accurate estimates of the basic sector.

DELINEATING THE ECONOMIC BASE. A critical step in any economic base analysis is allocating economic activity to either the basic or the nonbasic sectors.[3] There are both direct and indirect methods of making this allocation (Andrews 1970a; Bendavid 1974, pp. 106–13; Isserman 1980a; Isserman 1980b; Richardson 1985, pp. 611–16; Tiebout 1962, pp. 46–56).

Direct methods include an actual survey in the community to determine the flow of economic activity (Tiebout 1962, pp. 50-55). An example is measuring the physical flow of goods and services to markets outside the community. Problems with this approach include selection of the sample (e.g., firms, timing of study to avoid seasonal variation), the cost of doing the survey, and the conversion of physical units into uniform dollar units. A second direct approach measures the flow of funds into the community, rather than the physical flow of products from the community. Businesses are asked to divide their sales and purchases according to geographic location (local vs. nonlocal). Tracing checks and credit card slips from customers of businesses in the community is one way to collect this information. Individual households are asked to report total income, where it is earned, and where (geographically) it is spent. Again, the problem is cost, time, and the representativeness and accuracy of the responses.

Indirect measures of the export base provide inexpensive and relatively accurate estimates of the basic/nonbasic sectors. The three major *indirect measures* are the assumption approach, the location quotient approach, and the minimum requirements approach.[4]

With the *assumption approach,* the analyst simply assumes that certain economic sectors produce for the export market (Tiebout 1962, pp. 46–47). Typically, agriculture, forestry, mining, and manufacturing are assumed to be export sectors. The assumption approach is the simplest approach available, but it possesses three major sources of error. First, in many communities the trade sector performs an export function by serving nonlocal markets (e.g., tourists and regional shopping centers). Second, the assumption approach underestimates the export sector by excluding indirect exports.[5] Third, the assumption approach forces the analyst to allocate a specific economic sector to either export or nonexport. There is no provision to produce for local and nonlocal markets simultaneously. Yet some manufacturing is locally oriented (e.g., bakeries, some printing and publishing), and some retail and service businesses are export-oriented (e.g., insurance companies and shopping centers). The assumption approach probably is adequate for small, simple economies with minimal cross-hauling (simultaneous export and import of the same good or service).

Location quotients, another indirect measure of exports, measure specialization. The idea is that a community that is highly specialized in a given sector is exporting that good or service. A location quotient is computed in the following manner:

$$LQ = \frac{\text{percent of local employment in sector } i}{\text{percent of national employment in sector } i} \tag{11.19}$$

Location quotients indicate self-sufficiency (Isserman 1980a, pp. 34–35; Mayer and Pleeter 1975, pp. 344–47). The logic of self-sufficiency becomes more obvious with (11.20):

$$X_{ir} = \left[\frac{E_{ir}}{E_{in}} - \frac{E_r}{E_n}\right] E_{in} \tag{11.20}$$

where E is employment, i is the sector or product, r is the community, and n is the nation. The proportion of national employment in sector i located in the community (E_{ir}/E_{in}) measures the community's production of product i, assuming equal labor productivity. The proportion of national employment in the community (E_r/E_n) is a proxy for local consumption, assuming equal consumption per worker. The difference between local production and consumption represents an estimate of production for export (i.e., production greater than consumption). Equation (11.20) converts export production into export employment (X_{ir}).

Three important location quotient values derive from the self-sufficiency interpretation of location quotients. A location quotient of 1 means that the community has the same proportion of its employment in sector i as the nation or whatever economic aggregate is used as the denominator in (11.19). The community just meets local consumption requirements through local production of the specified good or service. If the location quotient is less than 1, the community is not producing enough to meet local needs. This becomes a key indicator for an import substitution strategy (see "Introducing New Goods and Services," Chapter 6). If the location quotient is greater than 1, the community has a larger proportion of its employment in sector i than does the nation. This excess proportion is for export purposes. If the location quotient is 3, then the community has two-thirds of its sector i employment devoted to export production. The following formulas estimate the proportion of employment in a particular sector used for export:

$$\text{percent of export employment} = \left(1 - \frac{1}{LQ}\right)100 \qquad (11.21)$$

$$\text{no. of export employees} = \left(1 - \frac{1}{LQ}\right) \text{employment in sector } i$$

$$(11.22)$$

Table 11.3 displays the location quotients for some communities performing similar economic functions and with similar population bases. Examining the automotive dealers sector of retail trade (SIC 55), we see that three communities (*A, D,* and *E*) have a relatively larger share of employment in this activity than does the national economy (a location quotient greater than 1), suggesting that they are exporting auto sales. Two communities (*B* and *C*) hire relatively fewer workers than the national and local average. This implies that if demand and productivity for auto dealers in B and C is similar to national averages, there is a potential to increase local employment in this sector.

Table 11.3. Location Quotients for 5 Communities with Similar Economic Functions and Population Bases

		Community				
Retail Trade Sector	SIC	A	B	C	D	E
Food stores	54	2.00	.965	1.037	1.338	.795
Automotive dealers and gasoline service stations	55	1.22	.783	.769	6.045	1.553
Furniture, home furnishing, and equip. stores	57	.60	.574	1.102	1.121	.739

Some caveats about the use of location quotients are necessary (Carroll 1981; Isserman 1980a, pp. 40–53; Leigh 1970; Richardson 1985, pp. 611–13; Tiebout 1962, p. 48). The location quotient expresses the degree of specialization and dependency of a community's economy upon a given sector. This figure can be misleading, however. Location quotient analysis assumes identical local and national demand and supply functions; variations in tastes and preferences, different marginal propensities to consume locally, different income levels, different economies of size and employment efficiency, and different production practices and technologies are not allowed (Greytak 1969; Isard 1960, pp. 125–26; Mayer and Pleeter 1975, pp. 344–52).

A location quotient greater than 1 implies that the community's economy is specialized, but that does not necessarily mean that it is exporting. Differences in demand (e.g., income, tastes and preferences) may lead to relatively more production and employment than the national average just to meet unique "excessive" local requirements. Thus the specialization implied by a location quotient greater than 1 may just fill local needs. The location quotient implicitly assumes no differences in productivity. If local productivity exceeds the national average, relatively fewer people are required to meet local needs, and the community could be exporting more than the location quotient implies. If local productivity is less than the national average, a location quotient greater than 1 implies that the community is exporting, even though it may just be meeting local needs. If local and national productivity differ greatly, the interpretation of the location quotient becomes suspect.

Location quotient values vary because of data aggregation (Isserman 1977, pp. 35–36). For example, SIC Code 37 denotes transportation equipment manufacturing; SIC Code 3732 denotes the manufacture of pleasure boats. A community location quotient of 1 or less at the two-digit SIC code level suggests no exports. But when the data are disaggregated to the four-digit SIC code level the location quotient is substantially greater than 1, indicating that the community has a major export sector. This highlights a need for every analyst to examine those dimensions of the local economy not reported in official statistics. Any analyst visiting the small community in this example and noting a pleasure boat manufacturer should anticipate that those boats are exported, even though the location quotients, derived from the reported data, did not indicate exports. If an on-site visit is impractical, the data must be disaggregated to avoid this problem.

Another problem with location quotients, as with other methods of indirect export base determination, is *cross-hauling* (Isserman 1980a, pp. 34–35). As noted above, cross-hauling occurs when a community produces goods and services for export while simultaneously importing the same goods and services for local consumption (Blumenfeld 1955). An accurate estimate of a community's export sector requires an estimate of gross export activity. In other words, the estimated volume of exports presumes that local needs are met first; no allowance is made for meeting local needs by importing the same goods that are exported. Equation (11.20) estimated gross exports as total local production less local consumption. If local consumption is completely supplied by local production, then the difference estimated in (11.20) would be gross exports. But since some local consumption comes from the import of goods and services also exported, more local consumption is deducted from local production than is justified. Rather than estimating gross exports, the equation estimates net exports (gross exports less imports of that product). Cross-hauling causes an upward bias in the multiplier estimate because the export sector is underestimated. The bias occurs because of data limitations. Location quotients presume gross export activity, but the data really measure net export activity.

Equation (11.20) demonstrates cross-hauling bias. For example, a community has 12 percent of the national employment in sector i, i.e., (E_{ir}/E_{in}) and 8 percent of total national employment, i.e., (E_r/E_n). Since (E_{ir}/E_{in}) measures local production and (E_r/E_n) measures local consumption, the difference measures the net flow of good i into or out of the community. In this case, 4 percent is the amount of national employment in sector i located in community r engaged in export production (i.e., 12 percent − 8 percent). In community r, one-third of the local employment in sector i (i.e., 4 percent/12 percent) is for export. This presumes that the balance of sector i's local employment is for local consumption of product i. However, if 60 percent of the local consumption of product i is imported, then more of sector i's employment is for export production than (11.20) indicates. In this example, the proportion of sector i's employment located in community r engaged in export activities is 12 percent − (40 percent)(8 percent) = 8.8 percent. Over 73 percent (73.3 percent = 8.8 percent/12 percent) of sector i's employment is for exports from community r. Cross-hauling causes an underestimate of the export sector and inflates the multiplier estimate.

These caveats must be emphasized since location quotients are subject to misuse because they are inexpensive, relatively easy to use, rely upon readily available data, and capture indirect exports.

The *minimum requirements approach* is another indirect method of determining a community's export base (Isserman 1980a, pp. 35–37; Moore 1975; Moore and Jacobson 1984; Pratt 1968; Richardson 1985, pp. 613–15; Ullman 1968; Ullman and Dacey 1960). The minimum requirements approach assumes that the community exports nothing until local consumption needs are met. The question becomes one of estimating production for local consumption needs. The procedure starts with the selection of a group of similar-sized communities. Next, the distribution of employment by economic sector is calculated for each community. Third, the communities are ranked from highest to lowest on the basis of the proportion of their total employment in a given sector. The community with the lowest percentage of its total employment in a given sector determines the percentage of employment required to serve local market needs. Other communities with a higher proportion of their employment in that economic sector devote the difference to export production. This process is repeated for all economic sectors, until the total economic base is determined.

Table 11.4 displays five communities. The proportion of total employ-

Table 11.4.   Hypothetical Minimum Requirements Analysis, 5 Communities

Community	% Employment in Ind. i	−	Min. %	=	Basic Employment	×	Total Comm. Employment in Ind. i	=	Basic Employment
A	35		7		28		200		56.0
B	23		7		16		80		12.8
C	17		7		10		150		15.0
D	14		7		7		80		5.6
E	7		7		0		55		0.0

ment in industry i varies from 7 to 35 percent. All of the communities with more than 7 percent of their total employment in industry i (i.e., the minimum percentage) are assumed to have the excess in basic employment.

The minimum requirements approach entails four critical assumptions: (1) that consumer tastes, income, and demand are identical among all communities; (2) that production and supply functions are identical among all communities; (3) that local consumption demand is met with local production; and (4) that every community satisfies its own local consumption needs with a minimum share of its labor force devoted to a particular activity (Isserman 1980a, pp. 35–37; Pratt 1968, pp. 120–23). The first three assumptions are the same as for location quotients; only the last assumption is an additional restriction, but is comparable to assuming that national employment distribution represents self-sufficiency.

The minimum requirement and location quotient approaches assume no cross-hauling. While the bias created can be adjusted for with the location quotient approach, it cannot be eliminated from the minimum requirements estimates. The minimum requirements approach leads to a situation in which it is assumed that every community meets its consumption needs (i.e., minimum requirements) and all communities (except those with just the minimum) export some portion of their output. A paradox occurs because the assumption of no cross-hauling means that no community imports product i (Pratt 1968, pp. 119–20; Ullman 1968, p. 368).

Another problem inherent with the minimum requirements approach is how the analyst selects the cutoff or minimum point (Pratt 1968, pp. 120–21). While it is typically assumed that the smallest percentage is the minimum point (i.e., the proportion of local employment needed for local consumption needs), there is no theoretical justification for this choice. An equally legitimate choice is just above the tenth lowest community. There is little reason to believe that the minimum-percentage city is a "pure nonexporter" (i.e., no cross-hauling) and that other cities do not have larger or smaller proportions of their employment in industry i producing for local consumption (Isserman 1980a, p. 37).

Another problem with the minimum requirements approach is that too much data disaggregation yields numerous SIC categories with zero or small proportions of total employment (Pratt 1968, pp. 121–23; Ullman 1968, p. 367). Thus a very small percentage (e.g., zero) becomes the minimum requirement, implying that a considerable amount of local employment is for export. While this may be true in some communities, it need not be universal. This problem appears as the implicit assumption that every city must have some employment in every sector, even though that sector's market may be larger than the city being analyzed. Thus the minimum requirements approach should not be used for sectors that require markets larger than the smallest city being analyzed (Pfister 1980, p. 55).

SUMMARY. A standard tenet of economic base analysis is that the export sector of a community is homogeneous and that all its components behave in a similar fashion. This ignores some very important issues. First, it implicitly assumes that earnings from jobs in separate export sectors are roughly equivalent. Second, it assumes that different parts of the export sector have similar backward linkages into the community. Third, it assumes that none of the local consumption of products being exported is met by importing that product (i.e., no cross-hauling). It is widely recognized that earnings and linkages among economic sectors in fact vary greatly. A tool that avoids some of these limitations is input-output analysis, described later in this chapter.

Analysis of the "accuracy" of indirect methods of dividing the export and nonexport sectors gives reason for concern about indiscriminate use of the analytic techniques described above. The differences between export base estimates derived from surveys and from indirect methods can be substantial (Gibson and Worden 1981; Isserman 1980a, pp. 46–51). The minimum requirements approach yields smaller errors than location quotients, but both tend to underestimate the export base. Since there is no systematic correction factor, the analyst should not rely on one set of estimates, but rather should compare results from several approaches coupled with a good working knowledge of the community's economy in order to arrive at the "best" estimates (Isserman 1980a, pp. 52–53).

The minimum requirements approach attempts to measure the local consumption coming from local production, but there is no theoretical reason to believe that the minimum percentage actually is that measure. The location quotient approach underestimates the export base because it uses net rather than gross measures of local consumption, but this can be corrected. The method yields the greatest underestimate of the export sector, so it should be viewed as a baseline figure (Isserman 1980a, pp. 52–53). It appears to be more appropriate for estimating import substitution potential (i.e., LQ less than 1) than for estimating the export base (see "Introducing New Goods and Services" in Chapter 6). The minimum requirements method tends to yield more accurate estimates of the export base, but the errors do not lead themselves to systematic correction (Isserman 1980a, p. 52).

Input-Output Analysi

This section reviews the basic assumptions of the input-output model and how the model structure relates to a community's economy. A simplified example will then be used to calculate some multipliers.

Viewing input-output analysis as a tool to generate employment, income, or output multipliers is far too limiting and fails to recognize other insights that the technique offers the community economic analyst. Input-output provides a framework in which to collect, categorize, and analyze data on the interindustry structure and interdependencies of the community's economy.

While input-output can account for economic activity and existing interrelationships, it is not strictly comparable to traditional economic accounting systems. Conventional accounting of economic activity measures the total output of the economy as the value of all final products or all final sales. If a community produces $100 million of output, that number includes the cost of all the inputs and intermediate products used in the production process. Input-output, on the other hand, measures the value of each transaction (sale) that occurs (Miernyk 1965, p. 15). The result exceeds the value of output derived through conventional accounting methods by the value of all intermediate products included in the accounting total but counted separately in the input-output approach. Inclusion of the flow of intermediate goods and services among economic sectors is the heart of the input-output approach.

Input-output includes the flow of intermediate goods and services between economically separate buyers and sellers, intrafirm transfers, and net additions to inventory. The first form represents traditional market activities among economic units. Intrafirm transfers are also general phenomena but are usually not reported publicly. An example is a utility company that owns a coal mine and transports its coal on the utility's railroad to its final use in its electrical generating plant. This represents three transactions: mining, transportation, and electrical generation. Each of these could be reported in an input-output table even though they all occur in the same company.[6] The inclusion of net additions (positive or negative) to inventory is for internal consistency and represents changes in business output with no corresponding final sales transaction occurring in the same accounting period. The net addition to inventory could be for final sales or further processing; regardless, the effect is the same because no further processing occurs during this accounting period.

CRUCIAL ASSUMPTIONS. Use of input-output analysis requires some crucial assumptions (Bendavid 1974, pp. 163–68; Miernyk 1965) that must be recognized and understood if the results are to be useful. The most obvious assumption is that the industry production function is linear, homogeneous, and has constant returns to size. The linear and constant returns to size assumptions mean that doubling inputs doubles output. Constant returns also means that there are no external economies or diseconomies associated with any changes in production: Increases in output neither create a shortage of skilled labor (i.e., external diseconomy) nor generate an improved distribution or financial system (i.e., external economy) that further alters output. The homogeneous production function assumption means that each economic sector produces only one product and produces it in a unique fashion with a single production process. The implication is that no multi-product firms exist or that their production can be separated. A community with several similar firms combined into the same economic sector requires assuming that they all use a similar production process. For example, a furniture manufacturer and iron foundry represent separate manufacturing sectors, but an input-output model with only one manufacturing sector considers them to be the same. Clearly this is not the case, but when individuals use an input-output table from another study, they will make this error.[7]

The second basic assumption of input-output analysis is that the production technology is known and fixed. This means that the proportions of various factors used in the production process do not change, at least over the time period of the analysis.[8] The importance of this assumption appears when data used to construct an input-output table are not recent. Current data need not always be obtained, but care must be exercised in using data that do not reflect current production technologies. A recent example is the implications of efforts to conserve energy on the energy/output coefficients for the 1980s versus the early 1970s.

A related assumption in input-output analysis is that changes in relative factor prices will not affect the proportion of factors used. The only way more or less of a given factor or intermediate product will be used is though a change in final demand.

This section has reviewed some of the basic assumptions of input-output. While they tend to be quite restrictive, the major difficulty is failure by the analyst to recognize their significance to the results generated. The next section examines the components of an input-output model.

TRANSACTIONS TABLE. The basic components of the input-output model are the transactions table, the direct requirements table, and the total requirements table. The *transactions table,* the foundation for the other two tables, displays the flow of goods and services among suppliers and purchasers in a specific locale for a specific time (typically a year) (Bendavid 1974, pp. 143–48; Miernyk 1965, pp. 8–21). The data in the transactions table represent the total sales (output) of every unit in the local economy for that study period.

The transactions table gives a complete accounting of the flows of goods and services within the economy. Before discussing some transformations that increase the analytical usefulness of the transactions table, let us examine the main components of the table and extract their analytical value.

The simplified transactions table shown in Figure 11.1 divides into four quadrants, *A, B, C,* and *D.* Quadrant *A* is the interindustry or processing sector. This quadrant shows the sales by local industries (suppliers) to other local industries (users). It displays the local economy and the interrelationships within itself. The processing sector is the prime concern here and represents all the sales and purchases undergoing further use by local economic units within the accounting period being studied.

Quadrant *B* is the final demand, or final sales, or final users quadrant. It includes all the output destined for economic sectors that will not process it further in this time period or in this locale. It contains both local and nonlocal users, but most will be nonlocal users. Some local users are households, sales for local investment (gross and net), and sales to local government. Investment by local processing sectors is considered a final use because the product experiences no further processing, nor is it resold in this

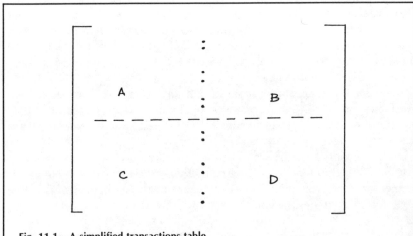

Fig. 11.1. A simplified transactions table.

time period. Sales to local households are considered a final sale if households consume the output and do not process it further. If households alter their consumption patterns they will be included in the processing sector.[9] Local government is part of the final demand sector, on the assumption that it does not process local inputs into outputs or that its level of output is invariant to local economic activity.

Some nonlocal users in the final demand sector are nonlocal households, nonlocal businesses, and central government. The sales to nonlocal businesses can be for further processing, investment, or final use. It makes no difference which because the further use occurs outside the local economy represented by the processing sector (quadrant A). The final segment of most final demand sectors is the net addition to the inventory of local businesses. It represents no further processing of the good or service in the current accounting period (i.e., a final use).

Quadrant C represents final payments or primary inputs, the result of sales by primary input suppliers to local processing sectors. The composition of the primary inputs sector depends on the analytical questions asked. The two major variations are whether local households and local governments are included as primary inputs or as part of the processing sector.[10] Final payments to households includes wages, salaries, proprietor income, property income, and other sources of personal income. Other final payments can be to local and nonlocal suppliers, including gross business savings,[11] payments for imported goods and services, and taxes to local and nonlocal government.[12] For small communities, the purchase of imported inputs is a major portion of the primary inputs sector. These imports are the difference between total inputs needed and what is supplied locally.[13]

Quadrant D represents the final payment to the final demand sector. This section of the transactions table records total sales by suppliers to purchasers (i.e., volume of total transactions).

When the primary inputs and final demand sectors are added to the processing sector, an equivalency of total inputs and outputs occurs. In other words, the economy must generate enough output to use all the inputs purchased during the period under study, or the economy purchases only enough inputs to produce the outputs generated during the time studied.

The preceding discussion of input-output is one way of examining the elements of the transactions table. Another way is to divide the table into the two basic economic actors it represents, suppliers and purchasers (Bendavid 1974, pp. 128–29). Quadrants A and C represent suppliers. The rows in quadrant A are the intermediate supply sectors. They represent local producers who purchase and transform inputs into products sold to other economic sectors (intersecting columns of the row) for further processing or final use. These rows represent the economic sectors in the community using local and nonlocal inputs to produce goods and services for further production or final use.

Quadrant C represents primary suppliers who produce inputs not requiring the purchase of intermediate goods and services from the local processing sector in this time period to generate those inputs. Payment for these inputs is a final payment and generates no further economic transactions in the local economy. In some studies, local households are considered a primary input supplier (i.e., labor), and payments for labor do not generate changes in consumption by community households.

Quadrants A and B in the table represent the purchasers. Quadrant A represents both suppliers and purchasers because the interpretation of the data changes depending upon how the table is read. Reading across a row in quadrant A gives an indication of the distribution of sales (i.e., a supplier). Reading down a column gives an indication of what inputs the economic sector acquires for its production.[14] The columns of quadrant A report the purchases of intermediate goods and services for further processing.

Quadrant B represents the final users who purchase outputs from the processing sector in their final form and for their final use. The "rest of the world" determines the level of final demand for the local economy. At this simple level, input-output is similar to export base analysis. This analogy is strengthened if the production of goods and services to meet final demand is the force generating all the interindustry transactions occurring in the processing sector. The input-output approach, however, is not as simplistic as the export base approach, since the export (final demand) and nonexport (processing) sectors are analyzed in much greater detail.

Delineating the supplier-purchaser elements of the transactions table highlights the interrelationships in the table. Intermediate suppliers and purchasers (i.e., the processing sector) are in the same economic sectors (e.g., retail trade, agriculture, manufacturing, transportation). The sales and purchases among these economic sectors are interrelated because the purchase of inputs depends upon the sector's sales. Primary suppliers and final purchasers need not be the same economic parties, although they can be, because of nonlocal purchasers and suppliers. Households are the major economic sector included in both the primary input and final demand sectors. They supply the primary input, labor, and also purchase goods and services for final consumption. Even though the households may be identical, they or any other identical economic sector included in both the primary inputs and final demand sectors are treated as if their demand and supply decisions are independent.

Additional information can be gleaned from the transactions table by triangularization (Bendavid 1974, pp. 168–70; Bromley 1972). Triangular-ization simply means rearranging the rows in the processing sector on the basis of the number of linkages with (sales to) other local economic sectors. This procedure clearly demonstrates the level of interdependence among the various elements of the processing sector and clarifies the role that any economic sector plays with the rest of the local economy, as measured by its degree of economic interconnectedness.

A variation of triangularization is to rank each sector, including the final demand (primary supply) sector, according to the portion of sales (inputs) that go to (come from) the processing sectors and final demand (primary suppliers) sector. The ranking of processing sectors according to the proportion of sales to either further processing or final demand indi-cates how sensitive a given sector is to local vs. nonlocal demand forces. The ranking of each sector's purchases from other local businesses or as imports also indicates the dependence upon local vs. nonlocal suppliers. Both insights help the community economic analyst to determine the rela-tive importance of external and local forces to a particular sector.

DIRECT REQUIREMENTS TABLE. The first modification of the transactions table for input-output analysis yields the direct inputs required for the output of any processing sector (Bendavid 1974, pp. 148–49; Miernyk 1965, pp. 21–24). The ratio of direct inputs to output, called the technical coefficient, measures the technical relationship between inputs and outputs in an economic sector. Every business is familiar with these numbers be-cause they adjust their purchases of materials and labor as sales change. Dividing each number in a processing sector column by the total output produced by that sector computes the technical coefficients in the process-ing sector (quadrant A in Figure 11.1). This calculation is not performed for the economic sectors in the final demand sector because sales to final demand do not represent sales to other local firms for further local process-ing in this accounting period.

TOTAL REQUIREMENTS TABLE. The next transformation computes the total requirements table. Total requirements sums the direct and indirect input requirements per unit of output. This calculation recognizes that if output for final demand increases not only must purchases of direct inputs in-crease, but purchases of inputs by firms supplying those direct inputs must also increase. Thus the total requirements table displays the additional pro-duction (i.e., input supply) increases responding to the initial stimulus.

The calculation of total requirements requires matrix algebra, and an excellent discussion can be found in Bendavid (1974, pp. 150–61) and Miernyk (1965, pp. 24–28).

Tables 11.5 through 11.7 give a simple numerical example of the transactions table, direct requirements table, and total requirements table.

Table 11.5, a simplified input-output transactions table, indicates that this economy's total output was $14,012 during the accounting period under study. Reading across the Agriculture row of the table, we see that $741 of output was sold in the following manner: $202 to other local agricultural producers; $182 to manufacturers; $10 to trade businesses; $12 to local service businesses, $100 to households and $235 to nonlocal users. Thus, over half ($406) of the agricultural production went to other local businesses for further local processing and uses, and households consumed $100. Reading down the Agriculture column of the table, we see that over half ($374) of the total inputs required to produce the agricultural output came from households ($200) and imported inputs ($174); of the balance, $32 came from manufacturing firms, $47 came from trade firms, and $86 came from service firms.

Table 11.5. Simplified Input-Output Transactions Table

	Agriculture	Manufacturing	Trade Businesses	Local Service Businesses	Households	Nonlocal Users	Total Output
Agriculture	$202	$182	$ 10	$ 12	$ 100	$ 235	$ 741
Manufacturing	32	68	2	26	39	300	467
Trade businesses	47	35	991	334	$1,200	172	2,779
Service businesses	86	59	565	561	1,500	262	3,033
Households	200	40	205	1,250	1,698	100	3,493
Imported inputs	174	83	1,006	850	333	1,053	3,499
Total inputs	741	467	2,779	3,033			14,012

Table 11.6 displays the direct requirements or technical coefficients.[15] The technical coefficients for the Agriculture column are computed in the following manner:

Sector	Computation	Technical Coefficient
Agriculture	$202/741	$0.27
Manufacturing	32/741	0.05
Trade	47/741	0.06
Service	86/741	0.12
Households	200/741	0.27
Imported inputs	174/741	0.23

Table 11.6 and the text table above show that every dollar of agricultural production requires $0.27 of inputs from other agricultural firms and $0.06 from trade firms.

The computations above show how the local economy responds to a change in final sales of a particular sector. A dollar increase in agricultural sales for final demand causes a direct increase in agricultural production of

$1.27, or $1.00 + .27 (see Table 11.6) This increase means that additional local inputs must be purchased to permit an increase in production, calculated from Table 11.6 as follows:

Sector	Direct Output Change in Initiating Sector		Direct Requirements		Direct Output Change in Other Sectors
Manufacturing	$1.27	×	$0.05	=	$0.064
Trade	1.27	×	0.06	=	0.076
Service	1.27	×	0.12	=	0.152
Total					$0.292

The $0.292 represents the amount of additional output generated in other sectors of the local economy to produce the $1.27 change in agricultural output. However, this figure does not include the effects on other sectors because manufacturing increased its output by $0.064, etc. Table 11.7 shows the total effect (direct and indirect).

The total requirements table represents all of the repeated increases in output and input purchases. Rather than repeat the technical math and matrix algebra, the reader is referred to Bendavid (1974) and Meirnyk (1965) for further details.

INPUT-OUTPUT MULTIPLIERS. The most obvious result of an input-output analysis is the multiplier estimate. The three types of multipliers generally estimated are output, income, and employment (Richardson 1972, pp. 31–52). Other types of multipliers linking output to community characteristics are possible (e.g., solid waste, energy, suspended particulates) (Johnson and Bennett 1981; Schreiner et al. 1973).

Table 11.6. Direct Requirements Table

	Agriculture	Manufacturing	Trade	Service
Agriculture	$0.27	$0.39	$0.00	$0.02
Manufacturing	0.05	0.15	0.00	0.01
Trade	0.06	0.07	0.36	0.15
Service	0.12	0.13	0.20	0.17
Households	0.27	0.08	0.07	0.41
Imported inputs	0.23	0.18	0.36	0.24
Total inputs	1.00	1.00	1.00	1.00

Table 11.7. Total Requirements Table

	Agriculture	Manufacturing	Trade	Service
Agriculture	$1.44	$0.68	$0.04	$0.12
Manufacturing	0.12	1.26	0.05	0.16
Trade	0.21	0.29	1.67	0.34
Service	0.28	0.37	0.42	1.33
Output multipliers	2.05	2.60	2.18	1.95

The basic multiplier estimated with input-output analysis is the output multiplier, since the data in a transactions table are gross sales (output) data. The output multiplier indicates the total output change in all processing sectors in an economy resulting from a dollar change in the final demand for the output of a specific sector. It is computed by summing the total (direct and indirect) coefficients in the processing sector only (see Table 11.7).

The income multiplier is the total change in local income resulting from a dollar change in output for a specific sector (Miernyk 1965, pp. 42–57). The basic assumption is that a change in output for a processing sector results in a local income change that is some fraction of the output change. The direct income change is the direct (technical) coefficient of the household row intersecting with the column representing the processing sector that is experiencing the initial change in output. This direct coefficient is the wages, salaries, proprietors income, etc., per dollar of output (Table 11.6). The indirect income change is the conversion of indirect output changes into household income; in other words, as output of intermediate producers changes to meet the change in final demand, some proportion of these indirect output increases are income for workers and proprietors.

The direct income effect is the row of household coefficients in Table 11.6 For example, if agricultural production increases by $1.00, direct household income will increase by $0.27. The direct change in agricultural household income as a result of the $1.00 change in final demand for agricultural products is $0.39. The total requirements table indicates that each dollar increase in final demand increases total (direct and indirect) agricultural output by $1.44. This $1.44 increase in agricultural production generates $0.27 of household income for each dollar change in output:

Total Change in Output for Sector		Direct Income Coefficient for Sector		Income Change for Households in Sector
$1.44	×	$0.27	=	$0.39

But the increase in agricultural production (output) also affects the output of other economic sectors and the households (workers) in those sectors. Table 11.7 indicates that a $1.00 increase in agricultural output causes a $0.12 increase in output of the manufacturing sector, a $0.21 increase in the output of the trade sector, and a $0.28 increase in the output of the service sector. These supply the total output stimulated ($1.44) in the agriculture sector. The household row of the direct requirements table indicates how much income is created in each sector of the local economy as a result of changes in their output. This row indicates that households in the respective sectors receive the following amounts of income from each $1.00 increase in output for that sector: manufacturing, $0.08, trade, $0.07, and services

$0.41. Using this information, we compute the indirect income change from the $1.44 change in agricultural output as $0.14:

Sector	Total Output Change		Direct Income Coefficient		Indirect Income Change
Manufacturing	$0.12	×	$0.08	=	$0.010
Trade	0.21	×	0.07	=	0.015
Services	0.28	×	0.41	=	0.115
Total					$0.140

The total income change from the $1.00 change in the final demand for agricultural output is $0.53. The total income change is the sum of the direct and indirect income changes ($0.39) in the initiating sector (agriculture) and the income changes from the indirect output effects ($0.14). The income multiplier in this case is not 0.53 but 1.963, and is computed as follows:

$$\frac{\text{total income change}}{\begin{array}{c}\text{direct income change}\\\text{in initiating sector}\end{array}} = \text{income multiplier}$$

$$\frac{\$0.53}{\$0.27} = 1.963$$

The employment multiplier measures the total change in employment due to a dollar change in final demand in a specific economic sector. The measure used is typically jobs or man-years. The basic assumption is a linear relationship between man-years of employment and dollars of output generated. An increase in output leads to a linear and proportional increase in the labor required to produce the additional output. The household row in Table 11.6 becomes man-years of labor supplied rather than income received. The procedure for estimating the employment multiplier parallels the income multiplier.

USES OF INPUT-OUTPUT. Input-output offers several advantages in community economic analysis. An input-output model disaggregates changes into individual economic sectors of the local economy. Both the effect of a change in a specific sector on all other sectors and the effect of a change in the output of all sectors on a specific sector can be examined. The approach distinguishes direct changes; indirect changes, and, if the model is closed, induced changes.[16]

The most obvious disadvantage of input-output analysis is that it requires an immense amount of data to detail the interrelationships within an economy (Richardson 1972, pp. 85–110). These data require considerable time to generate and are very expensive to assemble. A subfield within input-output studies has therefore developed to shortcut the data collection requirements (Davis 1976; Harrigan et al. 1980; Miernyk 1976; Morrison and Smith 1974; Richardson 1972, pp. 111–29; Richardson 1985; pp. 618–31; Round 1983; Schaffer and Chu 1969). These semi-survey and nonsurvey methods assume production techniques in the community and the nation to be identical. Thus the locally observed technical coefficient is a community trade coefficient and a community import coefficient,[17] represented in the following fashion: $a_{ij} = r_{ij} + m_{ij}$, where a_{ij} represents the national technical coefficient for row i and column j of the input-output matrix, and r_{ij} represents the community trade coefficient for row i and column j and must always be less than or equal to $a_{ij} \times m_{ij}$, which represents the import coefficient for row i, column j.

Czamanski and Malizia (1969, p. 65) note four types of differences between national and community technical coefficients: differences in the industrial mix of the two economies, differences in the relative importance of the foreign trade or intercommunity trade sector, differences in production technologies, and differences in the relative prices of inputs, which can cause substitution.

Differences in industrial mix mean that the same business types are not present in the local and national economies. For example, if nationally the textile manufacturing sector includes both natural and man-made fibers, then the textile manufacturing sector in the local economy should too. If not, an error is introduced in the local interindustry relationships. Disaggregating the national economic sectors to permit more "accurate" combining of economic sectors avoids this error. Differences in foreign trade mean that inputs not available locally alter the interindustry relationship in the locale compared with the national economy. The change appears as using a substitute, or relatively more imports. Differences in production techniques mean that local firms use different technologies than national firms, causing different levels and types of inputs to be purchased for the same volume of output. This error is particularly troublesome because the national data reflect an average of several types of technology. Differences in relative factor prices cause local firms to combine labor, capital, and intermediate inputs in proportions different than national averages, even when using the same general technology.

These factors force the analyst to be sensitive in transferring input-output models and their associated multipliers from one locale to another.

SUMMARY. Input-output analysis offers the community economic analyst a powerful tool to examine the community's economy. In its simplest descriptive form, it concisely presents an enormous amount of quantitative information on the interindustry relationships in the local economy and highlights the strategic importance of various sectors to the local economy.

The most obvious use of input-output analysis is to calculate the output, income, and employment multipliers in order to evaluate the total effects of various development options. While the direct coefficient of the households row gives some idea about the direct income (employment) effect of development options, the income (employment) multiplier measures direct and indirect (total) changes. Recently, the concept of multipliers has been expanded to measure physical changes (e.g., waste, pollution, energy).

The total requirements table gives the analyst insight into several community economic development questions. It permits (1) simulation of the effects of a change in total final demand on a specific processing sector, (2) simulation of the effects of a change in a specific portion of final demand on all processing sectors, and (3) simulation of the effects of changing technology (technical coefficients) for a specific processing sector on the rest of the local economy. The first allows examination of the effects on a particular sector as total community output changes. The second permits analysis of changes in output of a particular local sector on all other businesses in the community. The third allows tracing the impacts if one sector of the local economy adopts new technology or of a new economic sector is introduced. These calculations permit anticipating the supporting business and manpower needs from a development event.

Study Questions

1. What are the basic components of an economic base study, and why should such a study of a community's economy be undertaken?

2. Why is it important to generate a typography or classifying system for the components of a community's economy?

3. What are some of the possible units of measure of community economic activity and the positive and negative reasons for using each of them?

4. What does a multiplier represent?

5. In a multiplier analysis, why is it important to recognize the difference between income from consumption and consumption?

6. What are the implications of leakages to multiplier analysis? Be sure to consider both local and nonlocal dimensions.

7. Why is it important to estimate the export base accurately?

8. What are location quotients, and how are they used to estimate the export base?

9. What is the minimum requirements approach, and how can it be used to estimate the export base?

10. What does the processing sector represent in the input-output model?

11. How is the processing sector read to give an indication of the demand and supply aspects of the local economy?

12. The total requirements table measures what? Why is it important to have this measure?

13. What is the reasoning and significance of including households in the processing sector?

Notes

CHAPTER 1

1. While the definition presented earlier implies a strong physical-geographic connotation, there are two extremes to this perspective. The first would be a community which has no physical setting (e.g., a community of scholars). The second would be a community which consists of only its physical setting, such as a community intended for human settlement but temporarily vacant (e.g., a platted subdivision prior to the building of the first home).

CHAPTER 2

1. Harry Richardson (1969b, p. 322) notes that even if individual communities maintain a constant growth rate, and growth rates vary among communities, the system growth rate would increase over time. Thus setting growth rates equal to a constant ensures a dynamic equilibrium.

2. Proponents of the neighborhood and hierarchical effects suggest that space and time are crucial to the diffusion of innovation. They are important, but alone they are insufficient to bring about diffusion. Yehoshua Cohen (1972, p. 13) argues that "space and time are elements that are external to the diffusion process, while social, economic, cultural, psychological, or other behavioral factors are the endogenous causes of acceptance, rejection, and spread of innovations."

3. There is often a tacit assumption among policymakers that "all" people in less developed communities need improved incomes. Underdeveloped communities, however, often exhibit an extreme maldistribution of resource ownership and income.

4. Charles Leven (1966, p. 80) suggests that one way of distinguishing export and nonexport businesses is to see whether they can exhaust economies of scale within the local market. If they can be met by the local market, then the business is nonexport-oriented.

5. "Political" is interpreted to include citizen groups with quasi-government status (e.g., the local development corporation); the word does not exclude individual households and businesses acting to achieve their own economic goals.

CHAPTER 3

1. For the adventurous, this technique can be extended to the selection of numerous raw material and labor sources, but that complexity does not alter the basic form of analysis presented here.

2. The shape of the isosale line depends upon the relationship between transportation and nontransportation costs.

3. This is sometimes referred to as CIF pricing or cost, insurance, and freight pricing.

4. Parr and Denike (1970) explicitly recognize that the quantity:distance relationship in *Stage 1* is derived from an individual's downward-sloping demand curve, which compares FOB price and quantity. Ignoring transportation costs, at any given FOB price all individuals within the market will demand the same amount of the product. Customers next to the factory, where distance is zero, will demand that amount. However, customers farther away will demand proportionately less because the effective (delivered) price is increased by transportation costs. Firms using CIF pricing will have lower net prices and receive less profit on sales to more distant markets. Eventually, zero profits will discourage the firm from expanding sales.

5. Excess profits exist because the firm's average revenue curve exceeds the average cost curve at the quantity sold; see Figure 3.10.

6. Although not explicitly recognized, each level of output mentioned represents the profit-maximizing point of $MR = MC$.

7. There is concern about production levels only when average costs are increasing because the firm will increase production as long as average costs decline.

8. Decisionmakers have a tendency to repeat prior successful decisions. For communities, this means that businesses continue to use the same production technique or location rather than trying new ones (Lloyd and Dicken 1977, p. 412; Rees 1974, p. 198). Townroe (1974, pp. 287–90) describes three management conditions associated with location decisions: (1) lack of experience with the type of decision and no precedents to follow; (2) ignorance of all the relevant location possibilities; and (3) uncertainty about what decision criteria to use. Location decisions are made in a dynamic environment in which the firm and community affect each other. This learning and adaptation process is continuous. It may take the form of altered production scheduling and processes, reduced sales and profits, or relocation or closure. Townroe argues that the adjustment/adaptation process occurs because there were unforeseen circumstances at the time of the initial decision, because inadequate information was sought and used, because critical factors for operation were not fully accounted for, and, finally, because poor judgment was used initially.

9. The work by Rees (1974) indicates that the generalized process described in Figure 3.14 varies with the specific type of location decision (e.g., in situ expansion vs. relocation). North (1974) also detects differences in the decision process based on the type of location decision being made.

10. Muller and Morgan (1962) note that a location decision to remain at the original site appears to be due to inertia, importance of established business contacts, familiarity with the existing locale, and the cost and uncertainty of relocation.

11. Proximity as a location factor appears to be declining (Garnick 1984, p. 262). Technological change in transportation (e.g., interstate highways, air freight) coupled with structural shift to information/services industries (e.g., telecommunications) makes physical transportation relatively less significant. Furthermore, the increased proportion of workers with skills and increased mobility relaxes that form of locational constraint.

12. The basic elements of the location decision process are similar regardless of the type of decision, but the critical information varies among types of location decisions.

CHAPTER 4

1. Examination of the weights (size and sign) of the specific components of the community's socioeconomic welfare function distills down to questions of what types of gains or losses occur and who are the gainers and losers from the economic development event. If the socioeconomic well-being function is a linear function, we have typically assumed all the coefficients to be positive. A positive coefficient would indicate a gainer, and a negative coefficient would indicate a loser. All positive coefficients mean that an economic development event had no losers or, at worst, that there were nongainers (i.e., a coefficient not significantly different from zero). We now know that the gainers and losers are often different individuals, and that the net effects may be quite different than originally anticipated (Shaffer 1979; Summers et al. 1976). See Chapter 10 for more discussion.

2. A common misconception in community economic development efforts is that secondary effects will flow naturally from the primary effect. With the increased mobility and intraorganizational linkages in today's economy, there is no reason to believe that the hoped-for secondary effects will unquestionably occur.

3. A typical but generally unjustified assumption is that the cost of resources must reflect this foregone output; if not, this use of the resources could not bid them away from other uses. The problem is that market imperfections prevent the resource price from reflecting foregone output, and it fails to capture the value added when this resource is combined with other resources.

4. A continuing evaluation dilemma is time. The evaluation should not occur so early that the program has not had a chance to affect investment and production decisions. Yet evaluation cannot be postponed so long that opportunities to make minor corrections or even the decision to cancel are foregone.

CHAPTER 5

1. A third source is formal analysis of secondary data that is discussed in greater detail in Chapter 11.

2. Some suggest using portfolio analysis as a mechanism to guide the selection of alternative employment sources (see "Targeting" and "Diversification" later in this chapter for more detail).

3. If the local linkages are on the product side, this could be called an "additional local value added" strategy. If the linkage is on the input side, this could be called an "input substitution" strategy. The demarcations between strategies are not firm.

4. Community brochures should contain three basic elements: (1) a catchy opening sentence to capture the reader's attention (e.g., "Increase your profits by 20% in Community X"); (2) a brief summary of community attributes likely to be important to the business; (3) name, address, and phone number of the individual to contact for more information.

5. As an indication of the competition a community faces in its economic development efforts, a 1978 study claims that the fifty states spent an estimated $28 million in advertising to attract industry, or an average of $560,000 per state. Nationwide, the author found 7,500 local industrial development groups who pursue 750 major industrial relocations each year (Ted M. Levine, "States Spend Big To Sell Themselves," *Advertising Age* 28 [March 1979]:50–52).

CHAPTER 6

1. While the concept of city hierarchy is generally accepted, some suggest that it violates fundamental economic principles (Henderson 1972).

2. Variations in the central functions performed by members of a tier will be fewer than the variations in the functions performed by members of different tiers.

3. This community influence is often expressed as external economies or economies of agglomeration, which shift the firm's average cost curve (see Figure 6.5) and shift its demand curve (see Figure 6.6).

4. Free entry is characterized by a minimal number of restrictions such as licenses, permits, large capital requirements, or exclusive franchises.

5. There are two measures of the range of a good or service. The *ideal range* is represented by the definition. The *real range* is less than the ideal range because competition from other suppliers will enable the consumer to buy at a lower price from a closer source (Parr and Denike 1970). This means that the presence of a competitor in some directions from the firm/community causes a "shorter" range in that direction while the range will be greater in other directions. The end result is noncircular and nonhexagonal market areas.

6. For a review of these concepts, the reader is referred to the discussion of Figure 3.10 in Chapter 3.

7. This same type of shift in demand curves occurs with the loss of population in the central place and its tributary area.

8. In contrast, Rushton (1971) modeled a system allowing consumers to have spatial preferences. Consumers derive psychic gain from the shopping experience, and so balance effective price against the excitement of shopping. The selection and style of merchandise, together with the physical attributes of the shopping environment, constitute the major qualities of the shopping experience in this model.

9. Bacon (1984) demonstrated that minimizing aggregate transportation costs requires a shopping strategy mixing single and multipurpose trips. Consumers must vary their supply points for the same function, making the shopping location choice conditional on other goods or services purchased concurrently. By sharing transportation costs, a place's effective price differential for a function may be negated completely.

10. An associated phenomenon would be the larger market allowing the firm in the higher-order center to capture more economies of size (e.g., the movement from Q_2 to Q_3 or Q_4 in Figure 6.5).

11. This formulation is reached by recognizing that the distance between places A and B or D_{AB} is fixed, thus $D_B = D_{AB} - D_A$. This can be substituted into equation (6.6) and then solved for D_A.

12. Location quotients are a measure of local specialization and are discussed at length in Chapter 11. This discussion of an import strategy is appropriate only for consumer trade and service activities.

13. The reason why municipal and not trade area population is used is because of the difficulty in consistently estimating total population and employment over numerous trade areas. Using municipal population assumes the same population density around communities.

CHAPTER 7

1. Public capital markets are not limited to government. They have two other important characteristics. First, their securities are standard and homogenous and therefore can be easily traded. Second, there is wide dissemination of relatively inexpensive information about companies trying to sell their securities in the market. In private capital markets, contractual terms vary and information is harder to obtain, requiring negotiations between the supplier/demander over the investment terms (e.g., commercial bank loan terms, direct placement of incorporate debt with pension funds) (Litvak and Daniels 1979, pp. 38–39).

2. Guarantees are a mechanism to reduce risks to financial intermediaries while reducing the demand or need for information about borrowers. The reduced demand for information reduces information costs because there can be some economies of size in delivering that information and because the guarantee itself yields some information (Litvak and Daniels 1979, p. 69). Loan guarantees standardize financial instruments, thus facilitating the trading of such loans on secondary markets.

3. Each bank, whether it has a federal or state charter, is limited in the amount of loans that it can make to any one individual or business. This lending limit is typically 10 percent of the bank's capital base.

4. In many cases, smaller banks and in particular rural banks are at a disadvantage because the local capital market is undiversified and small, so that they are highly exposed to cyclical changes in the local market. Furthermore, when they wish to sell or to pool risk by selling loans in a secondary or national money market, they are hampered because of uncertainty about their ability to judge risk, because of uncertainty about the quality of collateral pledged, etc. The end result is an impediment in the flow of capital into those markets (Mikesell and Davidson 1982, p. 182).

5. Regulation Q is a Federal Reserve regulation governing the amount of interest banks can pay on savings and checking deposits.

CHAPTER 8

1. One must recognize, of course, that in many other countries the possession of a job is even more important than it is in the United States, as demonstrated by attempts by both public and private actors abroad to ensure that full employment is achieved, rather than permitting it to be a coincidental outcome of private market forces.

2. Clark (1983, pp. 165–71) argues that contract theory applied to the market between laborer and employer suggests that the adjustment is not in wages, but rather appears as employment changes with minimal wage changes.

3. This distinction between place of work and place of residence is important when examining secondary data on labor markets. Some secondary data reports employment on the basis of residence (e.g., the U.S. Census of Population). While looking at employment by place of residence gives the analyst some perspective on the labor force skills present in that locale, it does not give an accurate picture of its economic structure. Likewise, looking at employment by place of work gives the analyst a better picture of the economic structure of the local economy, but biases estimates of the profile of the local labor force.

4. The short-run demand for labor is conditioned by a given quantity of capital and land. Changes in the price of these resources can alter the demand for labor. If the firm added more capital to the production process or workers became more productive, the demand curve for labor would shift up and to the right in Figure 8.1. The new equilibrium conditions would yield more labor hired and higher wages. In the long run, when the quantity of fixed resources is also allowed to vary, the demand for labor incorporates differences in amounts of other factors of production.

5. Some contend that laborers and firms do not bargain wages but that firms set a wage and labor either agrees to work for it or seeks other work (Clark 1983, p. 169).

6. In this situation the economy would increase employment and output by shifting labor to a competitive market (Fleisher 1972, p. 162).

7. A continuing concern in labor market analysis is *labor market exploitation,* which occurs when labor is paid less than its *VMP* (Kreps et al. 1974, pp. 249–50). The firm maximizes profits by equating *MR* and *MC.* Since the firm's demand for labor is $W = VMP_L = MPP_L \times P_o$ in a competitive market, exploitation (in a pure economic sense) occurs

whenever $W < VMP_L$. The most likely case is when the firm faces a less than competitive product market and $MR_o < P_o$. Thus, $W_{nc} = MPP_L MR_o < MPP_L P_o = VMP_L = W_c$. The extent of labor exploitation is the degree that $W_{nc} < VMP_L$. This does not deny the possibility that exploitation (in the popular sense) can arise from other sources.

8. The traditional model suggests that the supply of labor within the existing population base depends upon individuals' willingness to exchange nonwork time for work time. This is far too simplistic because it does not capture the interactions within the family unit (Becker 1965) and ignores the implications of spatial and occupational frictions which reduce the capacity of workers to move between jobs and places or to trade off work and nonwork activities. Thus to examine a community's true labor supply requires an analysis not only of the community's population characteristics but also of the population characteristics of nearby surrounding areas and the ability of those people to move on a daily basis to jobs available in the community. It also requires recognition of family structures rather than just the socioeconomic characteristics of individuals (Beck and Goode 1981, p. 46).

9. An important element which makes the supply of labor different from the supply of other factors of production is that labor typically is supplied by a family or household unit. The complications of the individual who substitutes formal and informal work are amplified by family members who may substitute involvement in the formal work force among themselves. A general increase in wages may cause the family member who supplies the majority of time to the formal work force to maintain or even reduce his/her time, while the spouse and other family members may increase their time. Thus the individual who was previously working may now substitute more nonwork in the face of an increasing wage rate (Kreps et al. 1974, pp. 218–22).

10. A major criticism of neoclassical theory is its failure to recognize how ageism, sexism, racial discrimination, and other social characteristics affect mobility (Clark and Gertler 1981, p. 13). Job mobility can be labeled *job hopping*. Job hopping can be viewed as a positive or negative phenomenon, negative if the individual cannot become socialized into the work force or find a job to match skills, positive if the individual uses this as an informal way of acquiring information about the quality of various jobs and working conditions.

11. While applicants tend to have some information about wage rates and job availability, they have only minimal information about the other forms of compensation (Kreps et al. 1974, p. 27). Current employees, however, can compare employment opportunities based on personality of the foreman, friendliness of fellow workers, and nature of the work surroundings.

12. Showing up for work on time, staying for the allotted time, not consistently having blue Mondays and blue Fridays, etc., are socialization skills typically acquired over time through family, cultural, and prior job experiences.

13. The term "irreducible minimum" to characterize frictional unemployment is actually a misnomer. The "irreducible minimum" varies with society's choices among unemployment, inflation, idle human resources, and public programs to aid labor mobility (Stevens 1977, p. 75). It is the joint output of social preferences and institutional features, as reflected in the concept of a natural rate of unemployment, which is the long-run rate of unemployment if price expectations prevail.

14. Labor mobility has high economic and social costs, however, not only to the individual but to the firm (Lester 1966, p. 143). The individual pays the traditional psychic costs, but the firm also experiences costs in the form of lost investment in training and on-the-job experience and worker knowledge of value to that particular firm and its production processes or clients. These costs tend to reduce labor mobility under changing conditions.

CHAPTER 9

1. It is critical to remember that the migration of resources can occur between uses in the same community as well as among communities.

2. An always-present option that perhaps should be exercised more often is not to intervene at all: the market may be functioning adequately, government may be unable to do anything effective, or its actions, if taken, may be too late to be of importance. For the purposes of this discussion, it is assumed that government action is felt to be appropriate and potentially useful.

3. Several of these approaches require the federal government to create the program. However, local government often performs the critical role either of making use of the program itself or of encouraging the local private sector to do so.

4. All training programs must be sensitive to creating the skills required (to the demand for labor) rather than just working on the labor supply function. See Chapter 8 for more detail.

5. The private costs to the firm may also be insignificant, but one of the purposes of regulations is to make the firm account for some of its externalities (to dispose of, and pay for the disposal of, its effluent discharge, for example).

6. The enormous volume of information required to utilize freight rates to obtain minimal transportation costs makes it difficult to use the freight rate structure as a general instrument of public policy directed toward economic development.

7. It is assumed in this argument that the cause of the economic depression within the community is a stagnated industry, not a lack of resources or limited access to markets or resources. If the latter is the case, public efforts of the sort discussed here will not alleviate the situation.

8. The increase in MPP_L could be achieved through capital investment shifting the demand for labor outward. For further discussion, see "Which Type of Subsidy?" below and "Demand for Labor" in Chapter 8.

9. A critical element, from the community's perspective, is the danger of over-subsidization, which occurs when the community provides more incentives than required to influence a decision or when it gives inappropriate or noncritical subsidies.

10. A variation of this type of subsidy is a Norwegian program to reduce a firm's employment tax, which is 20 percent of the annual wage bill, if it relocates in designated areas.

11. An adjunct concern is that the subsidization program will yield an uneconomic distribution of economic activity, in terms of both use and space. However, such a distribution can occur as a result of factors other than subsidy programs, and the concern should not dominate the decision about their use.

12. One long-run effect of subsidy programs is the tendency for firms to bid up the cost of the factors used with the subsidized factor, thereby eliminating the cost advantage created by the subsidy. Often the policy response is to increase the original subsidy, setting off another round of linked factor price increases, or to expand the subsidy to other factors.

13. If the community finances an incentive program from local resources only, it must draw upon the secondary benefits of the development to do so; if it does not, it either reduces the effective incentive given or worsens the economic situation of existing residents and businesses. Our increased awareness of the secondary effects of such programs suggests that they are seldom of the magnitude anticipated and that they take time to manifest themselves. The only primary benefits available to finance an incentive program are the gains in net income of existing residents or the gains in gross income of new residents.

14. While new firm start-ups are eligible to participate in many incentive programs, most programs do not target them specifically.

CHAPTER 10

1. "Economic development event" refers to any form of economic change that alters community income, employment, sales, or wealth. It includes any of the five generic strategies discussed in Chapter 4 plus closure and contractions.

2. It should be noted that the community experiences no net employment change if the previous job is not refilled, and that it gains only the difference between the old and new wage level, not the total of the new wage, if the old job is not refilled.

3. This represents a classic distinction between change and impact. There will be a change in the use and quality of public services. The issue is whether permanent or temporary residents or the economic development event itself will bear the burden through increased taxes and fees or through a decline in quality of services (i.e., an impact issue).

4. This generalization ignores the distributional consequences among community groups.

5. The analysis by Shahidsaless et al. (1983) demonstrated that multiplier values changed over a twenty-year period in nonmetropolitan counties. However, the study did not determine whether the multiplier values were stable for shorter time periods. The analysis by Garnick (1970) also demonstrated the variability of the service to base ratio over time.

6. There is a very definite relationship between marginal and average propensity to consume. It allows us to estimate the income elasticity of various products and to allocate changes in income to different economic sectors or different goods and services. It can be used to adjust average propensity to consume into marginal propensity to consume. If

$$APC = C/Y,$$

and

$$\epsilon = \frac{\Delta C}{C} / \frac{\Delta Y}{Y} = \frac{\text{percent change in consumption}}{\text{percent change in income}}$$

then

$$MPC = \frac{\Delta C}{\Delta Y} = \frac{C}{Y} \frac{\Delta C}{C} \frac{Y}{\Delta Y} = APC \times \epsilon.$$

CHAPTER 11

1. The framework outlined in Czamanski's work in Nova Scotia gives an idea of how extensive and complex a social accounting system can be (Czamanski 1972, Chapters 2 and 3). The conceptual work reported by Isard (1960, Chapter 4) is also useful reading before a community social accounting system is developed, to demonstrate why it is necessary. Both Czamanski and Isard show that most communities cannot afford the time and cost of such an effort, but the absence of social accounts does not prevent useful analysis of the community's economic situation. Bendavid (1974, Chapters 3 and 4) presents a much less comprehensive system but one still beyond that required for most communities.

2. The following presentation will use income. Employment could be the unit of measure, but the discussion would become excruciating.

3. An overestimation of the export base causes an underestimation of the multiplier, or vice versa.

4. The econometric approach is also available but is not discussed here (Mathur and Rosen 1976).

5. An example of indirect exports would be a vegetable processing plant in a small community whose direct export is canned vegetables. However, a can manufacturing plant in the community sells cans to the vegetable cannery. It is an independent operation but has only one customer, the cannery. Since it is serving the export sector, it could be considered a nonbasic activity. However, the can manufacturer is so closely tied to the export business that it is difficult to classify. The production of cans can be called indirect exports. As industrial organizations become more complex and specialized, there is an increasing tendency to subcontract parts of the production process to other divisions of the same firm to capture economies of scale. This subcontracting of production can confuse the distinction between direct and indirect exports.

6. Conventional accounting methods would include the value of mining and transportation in the value of the final output—electricity.

7. A variant issue is how multi-product firms are separated. For example, how is a firm producing and wholesaling a product divided into those sectors?

8. Input-output analysis should not be used for long-run predictions without relaxing this assumption. Conway's (1977) analysis indicates that the variation in multiplier estimates over time due to changes in technical coefficients is smaller than anticipated. The problems arise from other sources.

9. The issue of whether households and/or local government are included or excluded from the processing sector depends on the questions analyzed and assumptions made. The elements in the various quadrants will vary somewhat among studies because of the analytical questions posed. A major difference among input-output studies is which sectors are included in the processing sector and the final demand/payments sector. The most frequent difference is whether households and local government are in the processing sector or the final demand/ payments sector. If households are included in the processing sector, the model is a closed input-output model and will generate larger multipliers because more transactions are permitted to occur in the local economy (Miernyk 1965, p. 43). These multipliers are frequently referred to as Type II multipliers. Closing the input-output model permits induced changes in the consumption/spending patterns of households and generally represents longer-run multiplier effects.

10. If included as primary inputs, they will be included in the final demand sector.

11. Gross business savings includes capital consumption allowances, which generally are depreciation but need not be.

12. Taxes to local government will be included in the primary inputs sector only if sales to local government are included in the final demand sector.

13. An implicit assumption is that local production will be used as local intermediate inputs before any selling to nonlocal markets occurs (i.e., final demand).

14. The distinction between quadrant A inputs and quadrant C inputs can be local vs. nonlocal suppliers.

15. For this example, households are assumed to be part of the primary inputs sector, not the processing sector.

16. "Closed" means that the household sector is included in the processing sector; "open" would mean that the household sector was included as part of the final demand and primary inputs sectors.

17. A community trade coefficient represents the purchases of inputs from local suppliers; a community import coefficient represents the purchases from nonlocal suppliers.

References

Advisory Commission on Intergovernmental Relations. 1967. *State-Local Taxation and Industrial Location.* ACIR Report A-30. Washington, DC: By the Commission.

Allen, Kevin, Chris Hull, and Douglas Yuill. 1979. "Options in Regional Incentive Policy." In *Balanced National Growth,* ed. Kevin Allen, 1–34. Lexington, MA: Lexington Books.

Alyea, Paul E. 1967. "Property Tax Inducements to Attract Industry." In *Property Taxation, USA,* ed. Richard W. Lindholm, 139–58. Madison, WI: UW Press.

Anderson, F. J. 1976. "Demand Conditions and Supply Constraints in Regional Economic Growth." *Journal of Regional Science* 16 (Aug.): 213–23.

Andrews, Richard B. 1970a. "General Problems of Base Identification." Reprinted in *The Techniques of Urban Economic Analysis,* ed. Ralph W. Pfouts, 81–96. West Trenton, NJ: Chandler-Davis.

_____. 1970b. "Mechanics of the Urban Economic Base: The Problem of Terminology." Reprinted in *The Techniques of Urban Economic Analysis,* ed. Ralph W. Pfouts, 39–50. West Trenton, NJ: Chandler-Davis.

_____. 1970c. "Mechanics of the Urban Economic Base: Special Problems of Base Identification." Reprinted in *The Techniques of Urban Economic Analysis,* ed. Ralph W. Pfouts, 97–116. West Trenton, NJ: Chandler-Davis.

_____. 1970d. "The Problem of Base Measurement." Reprinted in *The Techniques of Urban Economic Analysis,* ed. Ralph W. Pfouts, 65–80. West Trenton, NJ: Chandler-Davis.

Appelbaum, Eileen, 1983. "Alternative Labor Market Strategies," In *Manpower Programs: A Survey of Theory and Extension Opportunities,* ed. Dennis U. Fisher, 27–38. College Station, TX: National Extension Manpower Task Force, Extension Commission on Organization and Policy, Texas A & M University.

Archer, R. B. 1976. "The Anatomy of a Multiplier." *Regional Studies* 10 (1): 71–78.

Arrow, Kenneth. 1973. "Higher Education as a Filter." *Journal of Public Economics* 2:193–216.

Ashcroft, Brian. 1979. "The Evaluation of Regional Economic Policy: The Case of the United Kingdom." In *Balanced National Growth,* ed. Kevin Allen, 231–96. Lexington, MA: D. C. Heath-Lexington Books.

_____. 1982. "The Measurement of the Impact of Regional Policies in Europe." *Regional Studies* 16 (Aug.): 287–306.

Ashcroft, Brian, and J. K. Swales. 1982. "The Importance of the First Round in the Multiplier Process: The Impact of Civil Service Dispersal." *Environment and Planning* 14 (Apr.): 429–44.

Averitt, Robert T. 1968. *The Dual Economy: The Dynamics of American Industry Structure.* New York: W. W. Norton.

Bacon, Robert W. 1984. *Consumer Spatial Behavior: A Model of Purchasing Decisions over Time and Space.* Oxford: Clarendon Press.

Bain, John S. 1984. "Transfer Payment Impacts in Rural Markets." *Regional Science Perspectives* 14 (1): 3–15.

Barnard, Jerald R. 1969. "A Social Accounting System for Regional Development Planning." *Journal of Regional Science* 9 (Apr.): 109–15.

Barsh, Russell, and Jeffrey Gale. 1981. "United States Economic Development Policy–The Urban-Rural Dimension." *Policy Studies Journal* 10 (Dec.): 248–71.

Bartels, Cornelius P. A., William R. Nicol, and Jacob J. van Duijn. 1982. "Estimating the Impact of Regional Policy: A Review of Applied Research Methods." *Regional Science and Urban Economics* 12 (Feb.): 3–42.

Barth, James, John Kraft, and Philip Wiest. 1975. "A Portfolio Theoretic Approach to Industrial Diversification and Regional Employment." *Journal of Regional Science* 15 (Apr.): 9–16.

Batty, M. 1978. "Reilly's Challenge: New Laws of Retail Gravitation Which Define Systems of Central Places." *Environment and Planning A* 10 (Feb.): 185–219.

Baumol, William J. 1965. *The Stock Market and Economic Efficiency.* New York: Fordham University Press.

Bearse, Peter. 1979. "Influence Capital Flows for Urban Economic Development: Incentives or Institution Building?" *Journal of Regional Science* 19 (Feb.): 79–91.

Beck, E. M., Louis Dotson, and Gene F. Summers. 1973. "Effects of Industrial Development on Heads of Households." *Growth and Change* 3 (July): 16–19.

Beck, Roger, and Frank Goode. 1981. "The Availability of Labor in Rural Communities." In *New Approaches to Economic Development Research in Rural Areas,* ed. Roger Beck, 39–61. Ithaca, NY: Northeast Center for Rural Development.

Becker, Gary S. 1965. "A Theory of the Allocation of Time." *Economics Journal* 75 (Sept.): 493–517.

———. 1985. *Human Capital.* New York: National Bureau of Economic Research.

Bell, Thomas L.. 1973. "Central Place as a Mixture of the Function Pattern Principles of Christaller and Losch: Some Empirical Tests and Applications." Ph.D. diss., University of Iowa.

Bendavid, Avrom. 1974. *Regional Economic Analysis for Practitioners.* Rev. ed. New York: Praeger.

Bender, Lloyd D. 1975. *Predicting Employment in Four Regions of the Western United States.* U.S. Dept. of Agriculture, Economic Research Service, Technical Bulletin no. 1529. Washington, DC: USDA.

Bender, Lloyd D., Bernal L. Green, and Rex A. Campbell. 1971. "Trickle-Down and Leakages in the War on Poverty." *Growth and Change* 2 (Oct.): 34–41.

Bender, Lloyd D., and Larry C. Parcels. 1981. "Economic Adjustments in Small Rural Economies: An Exploratory Analysis." Paper presented at the annual meeting of the Western Regional Science Association, Northport Beach, CA, February.

———. 1983. "Structural Differences and the Time Pattern of Basic Employment." *Land Economics* 59 (May): 220–34.

Bender, Lloyd D., and Thomas F. Stinson. 1984. "Mitigating Impacts of Rapid Growth on Local Government," *Journal of the Community Development Society* 15 (1): 59–74.

Berry, Brian J. L. 1967. *Geography of Market Centers and Retail Distribution.* Englewood Cliffs, NJ: Prentice-Hall.

Berry, Brian J. L., and William L. Garrison. 1958a. "A Note on Central Place Theory and the Range of a Good." *Economic Geography* 34 (Oct.): 304–11.

_____. 1958b. "Recent Developments in Central Place Theory." *Proceedings of the Regional Science Association* 4: 107–21.

Bessire, Howard D. 1970. *The Practice of Industrial Development.* El Paso, TX: Hill Printing Co.

Blair, John P., and Robert Premus. 1987. "Major Factors in Industrial Location: A Review." *Economic Development Quarterly* 1 (Feb.): 72–85.

Blomnestein, H., P. Nijkamp, and W. Van Veenendaal. 1980. "Shopping Perceptions and Preferences: A Multidimensional Attractiveness Analysis of Consumer and Entrepreneurial Attitudes." *Economic Geography* 56 (Apr.): 155–74.

Bluestone, Barry, W. M. Murphy, and M. Stevenson. 1973. *Low Wages and the Working Poor.* Ann Arbor: Institute for Labor and Industrial Relations, University of Michigan.

Blumenfeld, Hans. 1955. "The Economic Base of the Metropolis." Reprinted in *The Techniques of Urban Economic Analysis,* ed. Ralph W. Pfouts, 227–77. West Trenton, NJ: Chandler-Davis.

Boehm, William, and Martin T. Pond. 1976. "Job Location, Retail Purchasing Patterns and Local Economic Development." *Growth and Change* 6 (Jan.): 7–12.

Borchert, John R. 1963. "The Urbanization of the Upper Midwest: 1930–1960." *Upper Midwest Study.* Urban Report no. 2. Minneapolis: Department of Geography, University of Minnesota.

Borts, George. 1971. "Growth and Capital Movements among U.S. Regions in the Postwar Period." In *Essays in Regional Economics,* ed. John F. Kain and John R. Meyer, 189–217. Cambridge, MA: Harvard University Press.

Borts, George, and Jerome L. Stein. 1964. *Economic Growth in a Free Market.* New York: Columbia University Press.

_____. 1968. "Regional Growth and Maturity in the United States: A Study of Regional Structural Change." In *Regional Analysis,* ed. L. Needleman, 159–97. Baltimore, MD: Penguin Books.

Bramley, Glen, Murray Steward, and Jack Underwood. 1979. "Local Economic Initiatives: A Review." *Town Planning Review* 5 (Apr.): 137–47.

Branch, Kristi, Douglas Hooper, and James Moore. 1984. "Decision-Making under Uncertainty: Public Facilities and Services Provision in Energy Resource Communities." In *Resource Communities: A Decade of Disruption,* ed. Don D. Detomasi and John W. Gartrell, 23–40. Boulder, CO: Westview Press.

Bridges, Benjamin. 1965. "State and Local Inducements for Industry, Part II." *National Tax Journal* 29 (June): 175–92.

Britton, John N. H. 1974. "Environmental Adaption of Industrial Plants: Service Linkages, Locational Environment and Organization." In *Spatial Perspectives on Industrial Organizations and Decision Making,* ed. F. E. I. Hamilton, 363–92. New York: John Wiley and Sons.

Bromley, Daniel W. 1972. "An Alternative to Input-Output Models: A Methodological Hypothesis." *Land Economics* 48 (May): 125–33.

Buchanan, James M., and John E. Moes. 1960. "A Regional Countermeasure to the Minimum Wage." *American Economic Review* 50 (June): 434–38.

Buck, T. W., and M. H. Atkins. 1976. "Capital Subsidies and Unemployed Labor, a Regional Production Function Approach." *Regional Studies* 10 (June): 215–22.

Bucklin, Louis P. 1967. *Shopping Patterns in an Urban Area.* Berkeley: Institute of Business and Economic Research, University of California.

_____. 1971. "Retail Gravity Models and Consumer Choice: A Theoretical and Empirical Critique." *Economic Geography* 47 (Oct.): 489–97.

Buhr, Walter. 1973. "Toward the Design of Intra-Regional and Infrastructure Policy." *Papers of the Regional Science Association* 31: 213–40.

Cadwallader, Martin. 1975. "A Behavioural Model of Consumer Spatial Decision-Making." *Economic Geography* 51 (Oct.): 339–49.

Cain, Glen. 1976. "The Challenge of Segmented Labor Market Theories to Orthodox Theory: A Survey." *Journal of Economic Literature* 14 (Dec.): 1215–57.

Cameron, Gordon C. 1970. *Regional Economic Development: The Federal Role.* Baltimore, MD: Johns Hopkins Press for Resources for the Future, Inc.

Carlburg, M. 1981. "A Neo-classical Model of Interregional Economic Growth." *Regional Science and Urban Economics* 11 (May): 191–203.

Caroll, John J., and Seymour Sacks. 1962. "The Property Tax Base and the Pattern of Local Government Expenditures: The Influence of Industry." *Papers of the Regional Science Association* 9: 173–90.

Carroll, J. Douglas, Jr. 1955. "Spatial Interaction and the Urban-Metropolitan Regional Description." *Proceedings of the Regional Science Association* 1: D1–D14.

Carroll, Richard R. 1981. "Analyzing Growth Potential of Regional Industry using Location Quotients." *AEDC Journal* 15 (Fall): 5–18.

Carrothers, Gerald A. P. 1956. "An Historical Review of the Gravity Potential Concept of Human Interaction." *Journal of the American Institute of Planners* 22 (2): 94–102.

Cary, Lee J., Jr. 1970. *Community Development as a Process.* Columbia, MO: University of Missouri Press.

Cebula, R. J., and M. Zaharoff. 1975. "Interregional Capital Transfers and Interest Rate Differentials: An Empirical Note." *Annals of Regional Science* 8:87–94.

Cecchette, Steven G., Daniel H. Saks, and Ronald S. Warren, Jr. 1981. "Employment and Training Policy and the National Economy." In *The Federal Interest in Employment and Training*, 19-42. 7th Annual Report of the National Commission for Employment Policy. Washington, DC: By the Commission.

Chalmers, James A. 1977. "The Role of Spatial Relationships in Assessing the Social and Economic Impacts of Large Scale Construction Projects." *Natural Resources Journal* 17 (Apr.): 209–22.

Chalmers, James A., Eric J. Anderson, Terrance Beckhelm, and William Hannigan. 1978. "Spatial Interaction in Sparsely Populated Regions: An Hierarchial Economic Base Approach." *International Regional Science Review* 3 (Fall): 75–92.

Chesire, Paul C. 1979. "Inner Areas as Spatial Labour Markets: A Critique of the Inner Area Studies." *Urban Studies* 16 (Feb.): 29–44.

Chisholm, Michael. 1976. "Regional Policies in an Era of Slow Population Growth and Higher Unemployment." *Regional Studies* 10 (2): 201–13.

Cho, Dong W., and Allen C. Schuermann. 1980. "A Decision Model for Regional Industrial Recruitment and Development." *Regional Science and Urban Economics* 10: 259–73.

Ciriacy-Wantrup, S. V. 1969. "Natural Resources in Economic Growth: The Role of Institutions and Policies." *American Journal of Agricultural Economics* 81 (Dec.): 1314–24.

Clapp, John M. 1980. "The Intrametropolitan Location of Office Activities." *Journal of Regional Science* 20 (Aug.): 387–400.

Clark, David B. 1973. "The Concept of Community: A Reexamination." *Sociological Review* 21 (Aug.): 397–416.

Clark, Gordon L. 1983. "Fluctuations and Rigidities in Local Labor Markets. Part I: Theory and Evidence." *Environment and Planning A* 15 (Feb.): 165–86.

Clark, Gordon L., and Meric Gertler. 1981. "Local Labor Markets, Theories and Policies in the U.S. During the 1970's." Discussion Paper D81-2, Urban Planning, Policy Analysis and Administration. J. F. Kennedy School of Government, Harvard University, June.

Clark, Gordon L., and J. Whiteman. 1983. "Why Poor People Do Not Move: Job Search Behavior and Disequilibrium amongst Local Labor Markets." *Environment and Planning A* 15 (Jan.): 85–105.

Cohen, Mark W. 1976. "A Look at Process: That Often Ignored Component of Program Evaluation." *Journal of the Community Development Society* 7 (Spring): 17–23.

Cohen, Saul B., and George K. Lewis. 1967. "Form and Function in the Geography of Retailing." *Economic Geography* 43 (Jan.): 1–42.

Cohen, Yehoshua S. 1972. "Diffusion of an Innovation in an Urban System." Research Report no 140. Department of Geography, University of Chicago.

Colwell, Peter F. 1982. "Central Place Theory and the Simple Economic Foundations of the Gravity Model." *Journal of Regional Science* 22 (Nov.): 541–46.

Connelly, F. J. 1978. "The Industrial Development Bond as a Financial Attraction Device." In *Proceedings of the National Tax Association–Tax Institute of America, 70th Annual Conference; Louisville, KY, November.* Louisville: By the Association.

Conrad, Jon M., and Barry C. Field. 1975. *Rural Development: Goals, Economic Growth, and Community Preferences.* Agricultural Experiment Station Bulletin 634. Amherst, MA: University of Massachusetts.

Conroy, Michael E. 1975a. *The Challenge of Urban Economic Development.* Lexington, MA: D. C. Heath-Lexington Books.

_____. 1975b. *Regional Economic Diversification.* New York: Praeger.

Converse, Paul D. 1949. "New Laws of Retail Gravitation." *Journal of Marketing* 14 (Oct.): 379–84.

Conway, R. S. 1977. "The Stability of Regional Input-Output Multipliers." *Environment and Planning A* 9 (Feb.): 197–214.

Conway Research, Inc. [Atlanta, GA]. 1966–76. *Industrial Development.* Nov.-Dec. issues.

Cornia, Gary C., William A. Testa, and Frederick D. Stocker. 1978. *State-Local Fiscal Incentives and Economic Development.* Urban and Regional Development Series no. 4. Columbus, OH: Academy for Contemporary Problems.

Cortese, Charles. 1979. "The Social Impacts of Energy Developments in the West: An Introduction." *Social Science Journal* 16 (Apr.): 1–7.

Cortese, Charles, and Bernie Jones. 1977. "The Sociological Analysis of Boomtowns." *Western Sociological Review* 8 (1): 76–90.

Cumberland, John. 1971. *Regional Development Experiences and Prospects in the United States of America.* Paris: Mouton and Co.

Cumberland, John, and Fritz Van Beek. 1967. "Regional Economic Development Objectives and Subsidization of Local Industry." *Land Economics* 43 (Aug.): 253–64.

Cummings, Ronald G., and Arthur F. Mehr. 1977. "Municipal Investments for Social Infrastructure in Boomtowns." *Natural Resources Journal* 17 (Apr.): 223–40.

Curry, Leslie. 1967. "Central Places in the Random Spatial Economy." *Journal of Regional Science* 7 (Winter): 217–38.

Czamanski, Stan. 1972. *Regional Science Techniques in Practice: The Case of Nova Scotia.* Lexington, MA: D. C. Heath-Lexington Books.

Czamanski, Stan, and Emil Malizia. 1969. "Applicability and Limitations in the Use of National Input-Output Tables for Regional Studies." *Papers of the Regional Science Association* 23: 65–77.

Daniels, Belden H. 1978. "Capital Is Only Part of the Problem." In *Mobilizing Capital for Economic Development,* ed. Peter J. Bearse, 2–19. New Brunswick, NJ: Center for New Jersey Affairs, Rutgers University.

_____. 1979. "The Mythology of Capital in Community Economic Development." Policy Note P79-2. Department of City and Regional Planning, Harvard University.

Daniels, Belden H., Nancy Barbe, and Beth Seigel. 1981. "The Experience and Potential for Community Based Development." In *Expanding the Opportunities to Produce,* ed. Robert Friedman and William Schweke, 176–85. Washington, DC: Corporation for Enterprise Development.

Davies, R. L. 1977. "Store Location and Store Assessment Research—The Integration of Some New and Traditional Techniques." *Transactions of the Institute of British Geographers,* N.S. 2 (2): 141–57.

Davis, H. Craig. 1976. "Regional Sectoral Multipliers with Reduced Data Requirements." *International Regional Science Review* 1 (Fall): 18–29.

Davis, Lane E., and Douglass C. North. 1971. *Institutional Change and American Economic Growth.* New York: Cambridge University Press.

Davis, M. LeRoy, Donald Sorensen, and Forrest Walters. 1975. "Industrial Development in Rural Colorado." *Journal of the Community Development Society* 6 (Fall): 57–63.

Dean, Robert D. 1972. "Plant Location Decision Process." *Review of Regional Studies* 3 (Fall): 1–13.

Deaton, Brady J., and Dan Gunther. 1974. "The Influence of Community Characteristics on Industrial Plant Location and Expansion: A Preliminary View." *Tennessee Farm and Home Science,* July–Sept., pp. 34–36.

Deaton, Brady J., and Maurice R. Landes. 1978. "Rural Industrialization and the Changing Distribution of Family Incomes." *American Journal of Agricultural Economics* 60 (Dec.): 950–54.

Dobbs, Thomas L., and Charles E. Huff. 1974. "Analyzing Reimbursement Mechanisms for Resource Development Projects." *Water Resources Research* 10 (Dec.): 1061–69.

Doeringer, Peter B., and Michael J. Piore. 1971. *Internal Labor Markets and Manpower Analysis.* Lexington, MA: D. C. Heath-Lexington Books.

Dominguez, John R. 1976. *Capital Flows in Minority Areas.* Lexington, MA: D. C. Heath-Lexington Books.

Dorf, Ronald J., and Robert A. Hoppe. 1980. *An Input-Output Model for the Upper Minnesota Valley Regional Development Commission.* Special Report 82. Agriculture Extension Service, University of Minnesota.

Dresch, Stephen. 1977. "Human Capital and Economic Growth: Retrospect and Prospect." In *U.S. Economic Growth from 1976 to 1986: Prospects, Problems and Patterns.* Vol. 11, *Human Capital,* U.S. Congress, Joint Economic Committee, 95th Cong., 1st sess., May, 112–53.

Due, John F. 1961. "Studies of State-Local Tax Influences on the Location of Industry." *National Tax Journal* 14 (June): 163–73.

Edwards, Clark. 1976a. "The Political Economy of Rural Development: Theoretical Perspectives." *American Journal of Agricultural Economics* 58 (Dec.): 914–21.

_____. 1976b. *Strategies for Balanced Rural-Urban Growth.* U.S. Department of Agriculture, Economic Research Service, Agricultural Information Bulletin no. 391. Washington, DC: USDA.

Ehrenberg, Ronald G., and Robert S. Smith. 1985. *Labor Economics: Theory and Public Policy.* 2d ed. Glenview, IL: Scott Foresman and Co.

Engle, Robert F. 1974. "Issues in the Specification of an Econometric Model of Metropolitan Growth." *Journal of Urban Economics* 1 (Apr.): 250–67.

Erickson, Rodney. 1977. "Sub-Regional Impact Multipliers: Income Spread Effects of a Major Defense Installation." *Economic Geography* 53 (July): 283–94.

Fernstrom, Richard. 1974. *Bringing in the Sheaves.* Corvallis: Cooperative Extension Service, Oregon State University.

Fleisher, Belton M. 1972. *Labor Economics Theory and Evidence.* Englewood Cliffs, NJ: Prentice-Hall.

Fleisher, Belton M., and Thomas J. Kneisner. 1984. *Labor Economics: Theory, Evidence and Policy.* 3d ed., Englewood Cliffs, NJ: Prentice-Hall.

Foust, Brady J., and Anthony R. de Souza. 1977. "The Wisconsin Urban System: Functional

Size, Trade Area Size, and Nesting." Unpubl. manuscript. Department of Geography, University of Wisconsin, Eau Claire.

Foust, Brady J., and Edward Pickett. 1974. "Threshold Estimates: A Tool For Small Business Planning in Wisconsin." Unpubl. manuscript. Department of Geography, University of Wisconsin, Eau Claire.

Frederickson, George. 1975. "Strategy for Development Administration." *Journal of the Community Development Society* 6 (Spring): 88–101.

Freilich, Norris. 1963. "Toward an Operational Definition of Community." *Rural Sociology* 33 (June): 117–27.

Freudenburg, William R. 1982. "Impacts of Rapid Growth on the Social and Personal Well-Being of Local Community Residents." In *Coping with Rapid Growth in Rural Communities,* ed. Bruce Weber and Robert Howell, 137–70. Boulder, CO: Westview Press.

Friedly, Philip. 1965. "A Note on the Retail Trade Multiplier and Residential Mobility." *Journal of Regional Science* 6 (Summer): 57–63.

Gadsby, Dwight M. 1968. "Current Procedures Used in Evaluating Resource, Conservation and Development Projects." In *Secondary Impacts of Public Investments in Natural Resources.* U.S. Department of Agriculture, Economic Research Service, Miscellaneous Publication 1117. Washington, DC.

Garnick, Daniel. 1970. "Differential Regional Multiplier Models." *Journal of Regional Science* 10 (Apr.): 35–47.

———. 1984. "Shifting Balances in U.S. Metropolitan Area Growth." *International Regional Science Review* 9 (Dec.): 257–74.

Gerking, Shelby D., and Andrew M. Isserman. 1981. "Bifurcation and the Time Pattern of Impacts in the Economic Base Model." *Journal of Regional Science* 21 (Nov.): 451–66.

Gibson, Lay James, and Marshall A. Worden. 1981. "Estimating the Economic Base Multiplier: A Test of Alternative Procedures." *Economic Geography* 57 (Apr.): 146–59.

Gillis, William R. 1983. "Achieving Employment Objectives in the Nonmetropolitan North Central Region." Unpublished Ph.D. diss., Department of Agricultural Economics, University of Wisconsin-Madison.

Gillis, William R., and Ron Shaffer. 1985. "Targeting Employment Opportunities Toward Selected Workers." *Land Economics* 61 (Nov.): 433–44.

Gillis, William R., and Shahin Shahidsaless. 1981. "Effects of Community Attributes on Total Employment Change in Nonmetropolitan Counties." *North Central Journal of Agricultural Economics* 3 (July): 149–56.

Gleave, D., and D. Palmer. 1980. "Spatial Variations in Unemployment Problems: A Typology." *Papers of the Regional Science Association* 44 (1980): 57–74.

Goeken, Wayne R., and Thomas L. Dobbs. 1982. *Rural Manufacturing Development . . . What Influences It?* Agriculture Experiment Station Bulletin B683. Brookings, SD: South Dakota State University.

Goffman, Irvin J. 1962. "Local Subsidies to Industry: Comment." *Southern Economic Journal* 29 (Oct.): 111–14.

Goldstucker, Jac L., Danny N. Bellenger, Thomas J. Stanley, and Ruth L. Otte. 1978. *New Developments in Retail Trading Area Analysis and Site Selection.* Atlanta, GA: College of Business Administration, Georgia State University.

Gordon, David. 1972. *Theories of Poverty and Underemployment: Orthodox, Radical and Dual Labor Market Perspectives.* Lexington, MA: D. C. Heath-Lexington Books.

Gordon, John, and David Mulkey. 1978. "Income Multipliers for Community Impact Analysis—What Size Is Reasonable?" *Journal of the Community Development Society* 9 (Fall): 85–93.

Gotsch, Carl H. 1972. "Technical Changes and the Distribution of Income in Rural Areas."

American Journal of Agricultural Economics 50 (May): 326–40.

Gray, Ralph. 1964. "Industrial Development Subsidies and Efficiency in Resource Allocation." *National Tax Journal* 17 (June): 164–72.

Greenhut, Melvin L. 1956. *Plant Location in Theory and Practice.* Chapel Hill, NC: University of North Carolina Press.

_____. 1963. *Microeconomics and the Space Economy.* Chicago: Scott Foresman and Co.

Greider, Thomas R., and Richard S. Krannich. 1985. "Perceptions of Problems in Rapid Growth and Stable Communities: A Comparative Analysis." *Journal of the Community Development Society* 16 (2): 80–96.

Greytak, David. 1969. "A Statistical Analysis of Regional Export Estimating Techniques." *Journal of Regional Science* 9 (Dec.): 387–95.

Griliches, Zvi. 1969. "Capital-Skill Complementarity." *Review of Economics and Statistics* 51 (Nov.): 465–68.

Grossman, Gene M., and Carl Shapiro. 1982. "A Theory of Factor Mobility." *Journal of Political Economy* 90 (Oct.): 1054–69.

Grzywinski, Ronald A., and Dennis R. Marino. 1981. "Public Policy, Private Banks and Economic Development." In *Expanding the Opportunity to Produce,* ed. Robert Friedman and William Schweke, 243–56. Washington, DC: Corporation for Enterprise Development.

Guedry, Leo, and Eugene Rosera. 1979. *Economic Impact of Industrialization on a Rural Louisiana Economy: La Salle Parish.* DAE Report 558. Baton Rouge: Department of Agricultural Economics, Louisiana State University.

Guenther, Harry P. 1981. *The Impact of Bank Regulation on Small Business Financing.* Washington, DC: Interagency Task Force on Small Business Finance, Small Business Administration.

Gurwitz, Aaron. 1978. "The Economic Effects of Property Tax Abatement for Industry." Paper presented at the 70th annual meeting of the National Tax Association-Tax Institute of America, Philadelphia, November.

Hägerstrand, Torsten. 1966. "Aspects of the Spatial Structure of Social Communications and the Diffusion of Information." *Papers of the Regional Science Association* 16: 127–42.

Haggard, Joel. 1982. "Commercial Bank Lending and Attitudes Toward Risk and Community Service: The Case of Rural Wisconsin Bankers." Master's thesis, Department of Agricultural Economics, University of Wisconsin-Madison.

Hamermesh, Daniel, and James Grant. 1979. "Economic Studies of Labor-Labor Substitution and Their Implications for Policy." *Journal of Human Resources* 14 (Fall): 518–42.

Hamilton, F. E. Ian. 1974. "A View of Spatial Behaviour, Industrial Organizations and Decision Making." In *Spatial Perspectives on Industrial Organizations and Decision-Making,* ed. F. E. I. Hamilton, 3–46. New York: John Wiley and Sons.

Hansen, Derek. 1981a. *Banking and Small Business, Studies in Development Policy.* Vol. 10. Washington, DC: Council of State Planning Agencies.

_____. 1981b. "Expansion–A Program Policy Guideline (Part Two)." In *Expanding the Opportunity to Produce,* ed. Robert Friedman and William Schweke, 217–42. Washington, DC: Corporation for Enterprise Development.

Hansen, Richard W., and Gary M. Munsinger. 1972. "A Prescriptive Model for Industrial Development." *Land Economics* 48 (Feb.): 76–81.

Harmston, Floyd K. 1979. "A Study of the Economic Relationships of Retired People and a Small Community." Paper presented at the annual meeting of the Mid-Continent Section of the Regional Science Association, Minneapolis, MN, June.

Harrigan, F. J., J. W. McGilvray, and I. H. McNicoll. 1980. "Simulating the Structure of a Regional Economy." *Environment and Planning A* 12 (Aug.): 927–36.

Harrison, Bennett, and Sandra Kanter. 1978. "The Political Economy of States' Job Creation Business Incentives." *Journal of the American Institute of Planners* 44 (Oct.): 424–35.

Harvey, Andrew W. 1973. "Spatial Variation of Export Employment Multipliers: A Cross Section Analysis." *Land Economics* 49 (Nov.): 469–74.

Harvey, David. 1971. "Social Processes, Spatial Form and the Redistribution of Real Income in an Urban System." In *Regional Forecasting,* ed. Michael Chrisholm, Alan E. Frey, and Peter Haggett, 267–300. London: Butterworth.

Haveman, Robert H. 1976. "Evaluating the Impact of Public Policies on Regional Welfare." *Regional Studies* 10 (4): 449–63.

Haveman, Robert H., and Gregory B. Christiansen. 1978. "Public Employment and Wage Subsidies in Western Europe and the U.S.: What We're Doing and What We Know." Discussion Paper 522-78. Institute for Research on Poverty, University of Wisconsin-Madison.

Haveman, Robert H., and Burton A. Weisbrod. 1975. "Defining Benefits of Public Programs: Some Guidance for Policy Analysis." *Policy Analysis* 1: 169–96.

Henderson, J. V. 1972. "Hierarchy Models of City Size: An Economic Evaluation." *Journal of Regional Science* 12 (Dec.): 435–41.

Hewings, Geoffrey J. D. 1977. *Regional Industrial Analysis and Development.* New York: St. Martins Press.

_____. 1983. "Design of Appropriate Accounting Systems for Regional Development in Developing Counties." *Papers of the Regional Science Association* 51: 179–96.

Hildreth, R. James, and W. Neill Schaller. 1972. "Community Development in the 1970's." *American Journal of Agricultural Economics* 54 (Dec.): 764–73.

Hillery, George A. 1955. "Definitions of Community Areas of Agreement." *Rural Sociology* 20 (June): 111–23.

Hirsch, Werner Z. 1961a. "A General Structure for Regional Economic Analysis." In *Design of Regional Accounts,* ed. Werner Hochwald, 1–32. Baltimore, MD: Johns Hopkins University Press.

_____. 1961b. "Regional Fiscal Impact of Local Industrial Development." *Papers of the Regional Science Association* 7: 119–32.

_____. 1962. "Design and Use of Regional Accounts." *American Economic Review* 52 (May): 365–73.

_____. 1973. *Urban Economic Analysis.* New York: McGraw-Hill.

Hirschl, Thomas A., and Gene F. Summers. 1982. "Cash Transfers and the Export Base of Small Communities." *Rural Sociology* 47 (Summer): 295–316.

Ho, Yan ki. 1978. "Commercial Banking and Regional Growth: The Wisconsin Case." Ph.D. diss., Department of Agricultural Economics, University of Wisconsin-Madison.

Honadale, Beth Walter. 1982. "Defining and Managing Capacity-Building Considerations for Research and Action." *Journal of the Community Development Society* 13 (2): 65–74.

Hoover Edgar M. 1937. *Location Theory and the Shoe and Leather Industries.* Cambridge, MA: Harvard University Press.

_____. 1948. *The Location of Economic Activity.* New York: McGraw-Hill.

Howard, Dick, ed. 1972. *Guide to Industrial Development.* Englewood Cliffs, NJ: Prentice Hall Inc.

Howell, Robert E., and Bruce A. Weber. 1982. "Impact Assessment and Rapid Growth Management." In *Coping with Rapid Growth in Rural Communities,* ed. Bruce A. Weber and Robert E. Howell, 243–68. Boulder, CO: Westview Press.

Huff, David L. 1961. "Ecological Characteristics of Consumer Behavior." *Proceedings of the Regional Science Association* 7:19–28.

_____. 1964. "Defining and Estimating a Trade Area." *Journal of Marketing* 28 (July): 34–38.

Hunker, Henry L. 1974. *Industrial Development: Concepts and Principles,* Lexington, MA: D. C. Heath-Lexington Books.

Hustedde, Ron, Ron Shaffer, and Glen Pulver. 1984. *Community Economic Analysis: A How*

To Manual. Ames, IA: North Central Regional Center for Rural Development, Iowa State University.

Isard, Walter. 1975. "A Simple Rationale for Gravity Model Type Behavior." *Proceedings of the Regional Science Association* 35:25–30.

Isserman, Andrew M. 1977. "Location Quotient Approach to Estimating Regional Economic Impacts." *Journal of the American Institute of Planners* 43 (Jan.): 33–41.

―――. 1980a. "Alternative Economic Base Bifurcation Techniques: Theory, Implementation, and Results." In *Economic Impact Analysis: Methodology and Applications,* ed. Saul Pleeter, 32–53. Boston, MA: Martinus Nijhoff.

―――. 1980b. "Estimating Export Activity in a Regional Economy: A Theoretical and Empirical Analysis of Alternative Methods." *International Regional Science Review* 5 (Winter): 155–84.

Isserman, Andrew, and John Merrifield. 1982. "The Use of Control Groups in Evaluating Regional Economic Policy." *Regional Science and Urban Economics* 12 (1): 43–58.

Jacobs, Jerry. 1979. *Bidding for Business: Corporate Auctions and the 50 Disunited States.* Washington, DC: Public Interest Research Group.

Johansen, Harley E.. and Glenn V. Fugitt. 1984. *The Changing Rural Village in America: Demographic and Economic Trends since 1950.* New York: Ballinger Press.

Johnson, Kenneth M. 1982. "Organization Adjustment to Population Change in Nonmetropolitan America: A Longitudinal Analysis of Retail Trade." *Social Forces* 60 (June): 1123–39.

Johnson, Manuel H., and James T. Bennett. 1981. "Regional Environmental and Economic Impact Evaluation: An Input-Output Approach." *Regional Science and Urban Economics* 11 (May): 215–30.

Kahne, Hilda, and Andrew I. Kohen. 1975. "Economic Perspective on the Roles of Women in the American Economy." *Journal of Economic Literature* 13 (Dec.): 1249–92.

Kalachek, Edward D. 1973. *Labor Markets and Unemployment.* Belmont, CA: Wadsworth Publishers.

Kalleberg, Arne L., and Aage B. Sorensen. 1974. "Matching of Men to Jobs: Mechanism and Consequences for Organizations and Individuals." Discussion Paper 212-74. Institute for Research on Poverty, University of Wisconsin-Madison.

―――. 1979. "The Sociology of Labor Markets." *Annual Review of Sociology* 5: 351–59.

Kerr, Clark. 1982. "The Balkanization of Labor Markets." In *Readings in Labor Economics and Labor Relations,* ed. Lloyd G. Reynolds, Stanley H. Masters, and Collete Moser, 61–70. 3d ed. Englewood Cliffs, NJ: Prentice-Hall.

Kesselman, Jonathan R., Samuel H. Williamson, and Ernest R. Berndt. 1977. "Tax Credits for Employment rather than Investment." *American Economic Review* 67 (June): 339–49.

Kieschnick, Michael. 1981a. "The Role of Equity Capital in Urban Economic Development." In *Expanding the Opportunity to Produce,* ed. Robert Friedman and William Schweke, 373–87. Washington, DC: Corporation for Enterprise Development.

―――. 1981b. *Taxes and Growth: Business Incentives and Economic Development.* Washington, DC: Council of State Planning Agencies.

Kieschnick, Michael, and Belden Daniels. 1979. *Development Finance: A Primer for Policymakers.* Washington, DC: National Rural Center.

Kimball, William J. 1978. "Understanding the Community." *Intensive Training for Nonmetropolitan Development Conference.* Ames, IA: North Central Regional Center for Rural Development.

Kivell, P. T., and G. Shaw. 1980. "The Study of Retail Location." In *Retail Geography,* ed. John A. Dawson, 95–155. New York: John Wiley and Sons.

Klaasen, Leonardus K. 1967. *Methods of Selecting Industries for Depressed Areas.* Paris: Organization for Economic Cooperation and Development.

Koneya, Mele. 1975. "Toward an Essential Definition of Community Development." *Journal of the Community Development Society* 6 (Spring): 2–12.

Krannich, Richard S. 1979. "A Comparative Analysis of Factors Influencing the Socio-Economic Impacts of Electric Generating Facilities." *Socio-Economic Planning Sciences* 13 (1): 41–46.

Kreps, Juanita, Gerald G. Somers, and Richard Perlman. 1974. *Contemporary Labor Economics: Issues, Analysis and Policies.* Belmont, CA: Wadsworth Publishing.

Krueckeberg, Donald A., and Arthur L. Silvers. 1974. *Urban Planning Analysis: Methods and Models.* New York: John Wiley and Sons.

Kruger, Daniel H. 1983. "Social Intervention and Employment and Training Programs." In *Manpower Programs, a Survey of Theory and Extension Opportunities,* ed. Dennis U. Fisher, 70–77. College Station, TX: National Extension Manpower Task Force, Extension Commission on Organization and Policy, Texas A & M University.

Krumm, Ronald J. 1983. "Regional Wage Differentials, Fluctuations in Labor Demand, and Migration." *International Regional Science Review* 8 (June): 23–46.

Krutilla, John. 1955. "Criteria for Evaluating Regional Development Programs." *American Economic Review* 45 (May): 120–32.

Kubursi, A. A. 1974. "Evaluating the Economic Impact of Government Expenditures by Department, an Application of Input-Output Analysis." *Socio-Economic Planning Sciences* 8 (Apr.): 101–8.

Kuehn, John A., Lloyd D. Bender, Bernal Green, and Herbert Hoover. 1972. *Impact of Job Development on Poverty in Four Developing Areas, 1970.* U.S. Department of Agriculture, Economic Research Service, Agricultural Economics Report no. 225. Washington, DC: USDA.

Laird, William E., and James R. Rinehart. 1967. "Neglected Aspects of Industrial Subsidy." *Land Economics* 43 (Feb.): 25–31.

———. 1979. "Economic Theory and Local Industrial Promotion: A Reappraisal of Usual Assumptions." *Journal of the American Industrial Development Council* 14 (Apr.): 33–49.

Ledebur, Larry C. 1977. *Issues in the Economic Development of Nonmetropolitan United States.* U.S. Department of Commerce, Economic Development Administration, Economic Research Report.

Leigh, Roger. 1970. "The Use of Location Quotients in Urban Economic Base Studies." *Land Economics* 46 (May): 202–5.

Leistritz, F. Larry, John M. Halstead, Robert A. Chase, and Steve H. Murdock. 1984. "A Systems Approach to Impact Management." In *Resource Communities: A Decade of Disruption,* ed. Don D. Detomasi and John W. Gartrell, 137–52. Boulder, CO: Westview Press.

Leistritz, F. Larry, and Steve H. Murdock. 1981. *Socioeconomic Impacts of Resource Development: Methods for Assessment.* Boulder, CO: Westview Press.

Lester, Richard T. 1966. *Manpower Planning in a Free Society.* Princeton, NJ: Princeton University Press.

Leven, Charles L. 1961. "Regional Income and Product Accounts: Construction and Application." In *Design of Regional Accounts,* ed. Werner Hochwald, 169–80. Baltimore, MD: Johns Hopkins University Press.

———. 1965. "Theories of Regional Growth." In *Problems of Chronically Depressed Rural Areas.* Raleigh, NC: Agricultural Policy Institute.

———. 1966. "The Economic Base and Regional Growth." In *Research and Education for Regional and Area Development.* Ames, IA: Iowa State University Press.

———. 1985. "Regional Development Analysis and Policy." *Journal of Regional Science* 25 (Nov.): 569–92.

Lever, W. F. 1974. "Changes in Local Income Multipliers over Time." *Journal of Economic Studies* N.S. 1: 98–112.

_____. 1980. "The Operation of Local Labor Markets in Great Britain." *Papers of the Regional Science Association* 44: 37–56.

Levitan, Sar. 1983. "Doing the Impossible—Planning a Human Resource Policy." In *Manpower Programs: A Survey of Theory and Extension Opportunities,* ed. Dennis U. Fisher, 14–21. College Station, TX: National Extension Manpower Task Force, Extension Commission on Organization and Policy, Texas A & M University.

Lewis, Eugene, Russell Youmans, George Goldman, and Garnet Premer. 1979. "Economic Multipliers: Can a Rural Community Use Them?" Coping with Growth Series. WREP 24. Corvallis, OR: Western Rural Development Center.

Lewis, William C. 1972. "A Critical Examination of the Export Base Theory of Urban-Regional Growth." *Annals of Regional Science* 6 (Dec.): 15–25.

Little, Charles H., and Gerald Doeksen. 1968. "Measurement of Leakage by the Use of an Input-Output Model." *Journal of Farm Economics* 50 (Nov.): 921–34.

Litvak, Lawrence, and Belden Daniels. 1979. *Innovations in Development Finance.* Washington, DC: Council of State Policy and Planning Agencies.

Lloyd, Peter E., and Peter Dicken. 1977. *Location in Space: A Theoretical Approach to Economic Geography.* 2d ed. New York: Harper and Row.

Longbrake, David, and James F. Geyler. 1979. "Commercial Development in Small Isolated Energy Impacted Communities." *Social Science Journal* 16 (Apr.): 51–62.

Lösch, August. 1954. *The Economics of Location,* tr. W. H. Woglom. New Haven, CT: Yale University Press.

Madden, Janice F. 1977. "An Empirical Analysis of the Spatial Elasticity of Labor Supply." *Papers of the Regional Science Association* 39: 157–74.

Malecki, Edward J. 1983. "Towards a Model of Technical Change and Regional Economic Change." *Regional Science Perspectives* 13 (2): 51–60.

Mandelbaum, Thomas A., and David L. Chicoine. 1985. "The Appropriate Time Frame in Economic Base Analysis." Paper presented at the annual meeting of the American Agricultural Economics Association, Ames, IA, August.

Massey, Doreen. 1975. "Approaches to Industrial Location Theory: A Possible Spatial Framework." In *Regional Science: New Concepts and Old Problems,* ed. E. L. Cripp, 84–108. London: Pion.

Mathur, Vijay K., and Harvey S. Rosen. 1974. "Regional Employment Multiplier: A New Approach." *Land Economics* 50 (Feb.): 93–96.

Mayer, Wolfgang, and Saul Pleeter. 1975. "A Theoretical Justification for the Use of Location Quotients." *Regional Science and Urban Economics* 5 (Aug.): 343–55.

McGuire, M. C., and H. A. Garn. 1969. "The Integration of Equity and Efficiency Criteria in Public Project Selection." *Economic Journal* 79 (Dec.): 882–93.

McNulty, James E. 1977. "A Test of the Time Dimension in Economic Base Analysis." *Land Economics* 53 (Aug.): 359–68.

Mellor, I., and R. G. Ironsides. 1978. "Incidence Multiplier Impacts of Regional Development Programme." *Canadian Geographer* 22 (3): 225–51.

Meyer, D. R. 1977. "Agglomeration Economies and Urban Industrial Growth: A Clarification and Review of Concepts." *Regional Science Perspectives* 7(1): 80–92.

Michelson, Stephen. 1981. "Community Based Development in Urban Areas." In *Expanding the Opportunity To Produce,* ed. Robert Friedman and William Schweke, 534–39. Washington, DC: Corporation for Enterprise Development.

Miernyk, William H. 1965. *The Elements of Input-Output Analysis.* New York: Random House.

_____. 1976. "Comments on Recent Development in Regional Input-Output Analysis." *International Regional Science Review* 1 (Fall): 47–55.

Mikesell, James, and Steve Davidson. 1982. "Financing Rural America: A Public Policy and Research Perspective." In *Rural Financial Markets: Research Issues for the 1980's.* Chicago, IL: Federal Reserve Bank of Chicago.

Miller, E. Willard. 1977. *Manufacturing: A Study of Industrial Location.* University Park, PA: Pennsylvania State University Press.

Miller, James. 1980. *Nonmetropolitan Job Growth and Locational Change in Manufacturing.* U.S. Department of Agriculture, Economic Research Service, RDRR-24. Washington, DC: USDA.

Minshall, Charles W. 1979. *The Identification of Feasible and Desirable Industries: The Screening Concept.* Columbus, OH: Batelle Institute.

Moes, John E. 1961. "The Subsidization of Industries by Local Communities in the South." *Southern Economic Journal.* 28 (Oct.): 187–93.

———. 1962. *Local Subsidies to Industries.* Chapel Hill, NC: University of North Carolina Press.

Molle, Willem. 1982. "Technology Change and Regional Development in Europe." *Papers of the Regional Science Association* 52: 23–38.

Moomaw, Ronald L. 1983. "Spatial Productivity Variations in Manufacturing: A Critical Survey of Cross Sectional Analysis." *International Regional Science Review* 8 (June): 1–22.

Moore, Craig L. 1975. "A New Look at the Minimum Requirements Approach to Regional Economic Analysis." *Economic Geography* 51 (Oct.): 350–56.

Moore, Craig L., and Joanne M. Hill. 1982. "Interregional Arbitrage and the Supply of Loanable Funds." *Journal of Regional Science* 22 (Nov.): 499–512.

Moore, Craig L., and Marilyn Jacobson. 1984. "Minimum Requirements and Regional Economics, 1980." *Economic Geography* 60 (July): 217–24.

Moriarty, Barry M. 1980. *Industrial Location and Community Development.* Chapel Hill, NC: University of North Carolina Press.

Morrison, W. I., and P. Smith. 1974. "Nonsurvey Input-Output Techniques at the Small Area Level: An Evaluation." *Journal of Regional Science* 14 (Apr.): 1–14.

Morss, Elliott R. 1966. "The Potentials of Competitive Subsidization." *Land Economics* 42 (May): 161–69.

Moses, Leon N. 1958. "Location and Theory of Production." *Quarterly Journal of Economics* 72 (May): 259–72.

Mottershaw, B. 1968. "Estimating Shopping Potential." *Planning Outlook M. S.* 5 (Fall): 40–68.

Muller, Eva, and James N. Morgan. 1962. "Location Decisions of Manufacturers." *American Economic Review* 52 (May): 204–17.

Murdock, Steve H., and F. Larry Leistritz. 1979. *Energy Development in the Western United States.* New York: Praeger.

Murdock, Steve H., and Eldon Schriner. 1978. "Structural and Distributional Factors in Community Development." *Rural Sociology* 43 (3): 426–49.

———. 1979. "Community Service Satisfaction and Stages of Community Development: An Examination of Evidence from Impacted Communities." *Journal of the Community Development Society* 10 (Spring): 109–24.

Murray, James M., and James L. Harris. 1978. *A Regional Economic Analysis of the Turtle Mountain Indian Reservation: Determining Potential for Commercial Development.* Minneapolis, MN: Federal Reserve Bank of Minneapolis.

Muth, Richard. 1968. "Differential Growth among Large Cities." In *Papers in Quantitative Economics,* ed. James P. Quirk and Arvid M. Zarley, 311–58. Lawrence, KS: University of Kansas Press.

Nadler, Paul S. 1973. *Commercial Banking and the Economy.* New York: Random House.

Nelson, Glenn L. 1979. "Distributional Issues in Community Growth Impact Models." In

Proceedings of Ex Ante Growth Impact Models Conference, ed. George Morse and LeRoy Husak, 17–42. Ames, IA: North Central Regional Center for Rural Development.

———. 1984. "Elements of a Paradigm for Rural Development." *American Journal of Agricultural Economics* 66 (Dec.): 694–700.

Nelson, J. Russell, and William Rudelius. 1972. "The Search for Industry: Identifying Regional Manufacturing Opportunities." *California Management Review* 14 (Summer): 52–62.

Nicol, W. R. 1982. "Estimating the Effects of Regional Policy: A Critique of the European Experience." *Regional Studies* 16 (June): 199–210.

Nicol, William, and Reinhart Wittman. 1979. "Background Notes to Restrictive Regional Policy Measures in the European Community." In *Balanced National Growth,* ed. Kevin Allen, 157–230. Lexington, MA: D. C. Heath-Lexington Books.

Niedercorn, J. H., and B. W. Bechdolt. 1969. "An Economic Derivation of the Gravity Law of Spatial Interaction." *Journal of Regional Science* 9 (Aug.): 273–82.

Nishioka, H., and G. Krumme. 1973. "Location Conditions, Factors and Decisions: An Evaluation of Selected Location Surveys." *Land Economics* 49 (May): 195–205.

North, David J. 1974. "The Process of Locational Change in Different Manufacturing Organizations." In *Spatial Perspectives on Industrial Organization and Decision Making,* ed. F. E. I. Hamilton, 213–44. New York: John Wiley and Sons.

North, Douglass C. 1955. "Location Theory and Regional Economic Growth." *Journal of Political Economy* 63 (June): 243–58.

———. 1956. "A Reply." *Journal of Political Economy* 64 (Apr.): 170–72.

———. 1961. *The Economic Growth of the United States 1790–1860.* Englewood Cliffs, NJ: Prentice-Hall.

North, Douglass C., and Robert Thomas. 1970. "An Economic Theory of the Growth of the Western World." *Economic History Review,* 2d ser., 23:1–17.

Oakland, William H., Frederick T. Sparrow, and H. Louis Stettler III. 1971. "Ghetto Multipliers: A Case Study of Hough." *Journal of Regional Science* 11 (Dec.): 337–45.

Olsson, Gunnar. 1966. "Central Place Systems, Spatial Interaction, and Stochastic Processes." *Proceedings of the Regional Science Association* 18: 18–45.

Palander, Tord. 1935. *Beitrage zur Standortsthorie.* Uppsala, Sweden: Alquist and Wiksells.

Papi, G. U. 1969. "The Role of the State in Mixed Economies." In *Public Economics: An Analysis of Public Protection and Consumption and Their Relationship to the Private Sector,* ed. J. Marglois and H. Guitton, 1–21. New York: St. Martin's Press.

Parr, John B. 1973. "Structure and Size in the Urban System of Losch." *Economic Geography* 49 (3): 185–212.

———. 1981. "Temporal Change in a Central Place System." *Environment and Planning A* 13 (Jan.): 97–118.

Parr, John B., and Kenneth G. Denike. 1970. "Theoretical Problems in Central Place Analysis." *Economic Geography* 46 (Oct.): 568–86.

Parsons, Ken H. 1964. "Institutional Innovations in Economic Growth." In *Optimizing Institutions for Economic Growth.* Raleigh, NC: Agricultural Policy Institute.

Peirce, Neal R., Jerry Hagstrom, and Carol Steinbach. 1979. *Economic Development: The Challenge of the 1980's.* Washington, DC: Council of State Planning Agencies.

Perloff, Harvey S. 1961. "Relative Regional Growth: An Approach to Regional Accounts." In *Design of Regional Accounts,* ed. Werner Hochwald, 38–65. Baltimore, MD: Johns Hopkins University Press.

———. 1962. "A National System of Metropolitan Information and Analysis." *American Economic Review* 52 (May): 356–64.

Perloff, Harvey S., and Lowdon Wingo, Jr. 1961. "Natural Resources Endowment and Regional Economic Development." In *Natural Resources and Economic Growth,* ed. Joseph

J. Spengler, 191–212. Washington, DC: Resources for the Future, Inc.

Pfister, Richard. 1976. "Improving Export Base Studies." *Regional Science Perspectives* 6: 104–16.

――――. 1980. "The Minimum Requirements Technique of Estimating Exports: A Further Evaluation." In *Economic Impact Analysis: Methodology and Applications,* ed. Saul Pleeter, 59–67. Boston, MA: Martinus Nijhoff.

Piore, Michael J. 1973. "Fragments of a 'Sociological' Theory of Wages." *American Economic Review* 63 (May): 377–84.

Pleeter, Saul. 1980. "Methodologies of Economic Impact Analysis: An Overview." In *Economic Impact Analysis: Methodology and Applications,* ed. Saul Pleeter, 7–31. Boston, MA: Martinus Nijhoff.

Potter, Robert B. 1982. *The Urban Retailing System: Location, Cognition and Behaviour.* Aldershot, England: Gower Publishing Co.

Pratt, Richard T. 1968. "An Appraisal of the Minimum Requirements Technique." *Economic Geography* 44 (Apr.): 117–24.

Pred, Alan R. 1967. *Behavior and Location: Foundations for Geographic and Dynamic Location Theory.* Lund Studies in Geography, Pt. 1. Uppsala, Sweden: Lund University.

――――. 1974. "Industry, Information and City System Interdepencies." In *Spatial Perspectives on Industrial Organizations and Decision Making,* ed. F. E. I. Hamilton, 105–39. New York: John Wiley and Sons.

Pryde, Paul L. 1981. "Human Capacity and Local Development." In *Expanding the Opportunity to Produce,* ed. Robert Freidman and William Schweke, 521–33. Washington, DC: Corporation for Enterprise Development.

Pulver, Glen C. 1979. "A Theoretical Framework for the Analysis of Community Economic Development Policy Options." In *Nonmetropolitan Industrial Growth and Community Change,* ed. Gene F. Summers and Arne Selvik, 105–18. Lexington, MA: D. C. Heath-Lexington Books.

Pulver, Glen C., Arne Selvik, and Ron Shaffer. 1984. "The Impact of a Major Economic Development Event on Community Income Distribution." In *Resource Communities: A Decade of Disruption,* ed. Don D. Detomasi and John W. Gartrell, 71–84. Boulder, CO: Westview Press.

Rees, John. 1972. "Organization Theory and Corporate Decisions: Some Implications for Industrial Location Analysis." *Regional Science Perspectives* 2 (2): 126–35.

――――. 1974. "Decision-Making, the Growth of the Firm and the Business Environment." In *Spatial Perspectives on Industrial Organizations and Decision Making,* ed. F. E. I. Hamilton, 189–211. New York: John Wiley and Sons.

Reich, Michael, David M. Gordon, and Richard C. Edwards. 1973. "A Theory of Labor Market Segmentation." *American Economic Review* 63 (May): 359–65.

Reilly, William J. 1931. *The Law of Retail Gravitation.* New York: Knickerbocker Press.

Reiner, Thomas A. 1971. "A Multiple Goals Framework for Regional Planning." *Papers of the Regional Science Association* 26: 207–39.

Richardson, Harry W. 1969a. *Elements of Regional Economics.* Baltimore, MD: Penguin Books.

――――. 1969b. *Regional Economics: Location Theory, Urban Structure, Regional Change.* New York: Praeger.

――――. 1972. *Input-Output and Regional Economics.* New York: John Wiley and Sons.

――――. 1973. *Regional Growth Theory.* New York: John Wiley and Sons.

――――. 1978a. *Regional and Urban Economics.* New York: Penguin Books.

――――. 1978b. "The State of Regional Economics." *International Regional Science Review* 3 (Fall): 1–48.

――――. 1985. "Input-Output and Economic Base Multipliers: Looking Backward and

Forward." *Journal of Regional Science* 25 (Nov.): 607–62.

Richardson, Harry W., and P. Gordon. 1978. "A Note on Spatial Multipliers." *Economic Geography* 54 (Oct.): 309–13.

Rinehart, James R., and William E. Laird. 1972. "Community Inducements and Zero Sum Game." *Scottish Journal of Political Economy* 77 (Feb.): 73–90.

Roberts, R. Blaine, and Henry Fishkind. 1979. "The Role of Monetary Forces in Regional Economic Activity: An Econometric Simulation Analysis." *Journal of Regional Science* 19 (Feb.): 15–30.

Robock, Stephen H. 1966. "Strategies for Regional Economic Development." *Papers of the Regional Science Association* 17: 129–41.

Robson, Brian. 1973. *Urban Growth: An Approach*. New York: Barnes and Noble.

Romans, J. Thomas. 1965. *Capital Exports and Growth among U.S. Regions*. Middletown, CT: Wesleyan University Press.

Round, Jeffrey I. 1983. "Nonsurvey Techniques: A Critical Review of the Theory and the Evidence." *International Regional Science Review* 8 (Dec.): 189–212.

Rushton, Gerard. 1971. "Postulates of Central-Place Theory and the Properties of Central Place Systems." *Geographical Analysis* 3: 140–55.

Ruttan, Vernon W. 1978. "Institutional Innovation." In T. W. Schultz, ed., *Distortions of Agricultural Incentives*, 290–304. Bloomington, IN: Indiana University Press.

———. 1984. "Social Science Knowledge and Institutional Change." *American Journal of Agricultural Economics* 66 (Dec.): 549–59.

Sanders, Irwin T. 1966. *The Community: An Introduction to a Social System*. New York: Ronald Press.

Sasaki, Kyohei. 1963. "Military Expenditures and Employment Multipliers in Hawaii." *Review of Economics and Statistics* 45 (Aug.): 298–304.

Saussy, G. A. 1976. *The Fiscal Impact of Energy Resource Depletion on Louisiana*. Final Report to Conservation Department, State of Louisiana. Baton Rouge, LA: By the Department.

Schaffer, William A., and Kong Chu. 1969. "Nonsurvey Techniques for Constructing Regional Interindustry Models." *Papers of the Regional Science Association* 23: 83–104.

Schmenner, Roger W. 1979. "How Corporations Select Communities for New Manufacturing Plants." Paper presented at the Federal Trade Commission Conference on the Economies of Firm Size, Market Structure, and Social Performance, Rosslyn, VA, December.

———. 1982. *Making Business Location Decisions*. New York: Prentice-Hall.

Schmid, A. Allan. 1972. "Analytical Institutional Economics: Challenging Problems in the Economics of Resources for a New Environment." *American Journal of Agricultural Economics* 54 (Aug.): 893–901.

Schreiner, Dean F., George Muncrief, and Bob Davis. 1972. "Estimating Intercounty Economic Linkages in a Multi-County Development District." *Southern Journal of Agricultural Economics* 4 (July): 53–58.

———. 1973. "Solid Waste Management for Rural Areas: Analysis of Cost and Service Requirements." *American Journal of Agricultural Economics* 45 (Nov.): 567–76.

Schultz, T. W. 1968. "Institutions and the Rising Economic Value of Man." *American Journal of Agricultural Economics* 50 (Dec.): 1113–27.

Schumpeter, Joseph A. 1961. *The Theory of Economic Development*. New York: Oxford University Press.

Scott, Loren C., Lewis H. Smith, and Brian Rungeling. 1977. "Labor Force Participation in Southern Rural Labor Markets." *American Journal of Agricultural Economics* 59 (May): 266–74.

Shaeffer, Peter. 1985. "Human Capital Accumulation and Job Mobility." *Journal of Regional Science* 25 (Feb.): 103–14.

Shaffer, James D. 1969. "On Institutional Obsolescence and Innovation—Background for

Professional Dialogue on Public Policy." *American Journal of Agricultural Economics* 51 (May): 245–67.

Shaffer, Ron E. 1974. "Rural Industrialization: A Local Income Analysis." *Southern Journal of Agricultural Economics* 6 (July): 97–104.

———. 1975. "Measuring the Economic Impact of New Industry." *Journal of the American Industrial Development Council* 10 (July): 37–65.

———. 1979. "The General Economic Impact of Industrial Growth on the Private Sector of Nonmetropolitan Communities." In *Nonmetropolitan Industrialization,* ed. Richard E. Lonsdale and H. L. Syler, 103–18. Washington, DC: V. H. Winston and Sons.

Shaffer, Ron E., and David Fischer. 1981. "Evaluating Local-National Impacts from Landing Stratfjord Gas." Arbeidsrapport no. 41. Bergen, Norway: Industriøkonomi Institutt.

Shaffer, Ron E., David Fischer, and Glen C. Pulver. 1982. "Capturing Secondary Benefits of Economic Development." In *Energy Resource Communities,* ed. Gene F. Summers and Arne Selvik, 121–40. Madison, WI: MJM Publishing.

Shaffer, Ron E., and Luther G. Tweeten. 1974. "Measuring Net Economic Change from Rural Industrial Development: Oklahoma." *Journal of Land Economics* 50 (Aug.): 261–70.

Shahidsaless, Shahin, William Gillis, and Ron Shaffer. 1983. "Community Characteristics and Employment Multipliers in Nonmetropolitan Counties, 1950–1970." *Land Economics* 59 (Feb.): 84–93.

Shapero, Al. 1981. "The Role of Entrepreneurship in Economic Development at the Less-Than-National Level." In *Expanding the Opportunity To Produce,* ed. Robert Friedman and William Schweke, 25–35. Washington, DC: Corporation for Enterprise Development.

Shepard, Eric S. 1980. "The Ideology of Spatial Choice." *Papers of the Regional Science Association* 45: 197–213.

Shepard, I. D., and C. J. Thomas. 1980. "Urban Consumer Behaviour." In *Retail Geography,* ed. John A. Dawson, 18–94. New York: John Wiley and Sons.

Siebert, Horst. 1969. *Regional Economic Growth: Theory and Policy.* Scranton, PA: International Textbook Co.

Silvers, Arthur L. 1970. "The Structure of Community Income Circulation in an Incidence Multiplier for Development Planning." *Journal of Regional Science* 10 (Aug.): 175–89.

Simmons, Peter L. 1973/74. "The Shape of Suburban Retail Markets: Implications from a Literature Review." *Journal of Retailing* 49 (Winter): 65–78.

Sirkin, Gerald. 1959. "The Theory of the Regional Economic Base." *Review of Economics and Statistics* 59 (Nov.): 426–29.

Smith, Courtland L., Thomas C. Hogg, and Michael J. Reagan. 1971. "Economic Development: Panacea or Perplexity for Rural Areas." *Rural Sociology* 36 (June): 173–86.

Smith, David. 1966. *Industrial Location: An Economic Geographical Analysis.* New York: John Wiley and Sons.

1971. *Industrial Location.* New York: John Wiley and Sons.

Smith, Eldon B., Brady Deaton, and David Kelch. 1980. "Cost Effective Programs of Rural Community Development." *Journal of the Community Development Society* 11 (Spring): 113–24.

Smith, Eldon B., Merlin Hackbart, and Johannes Van Veen. 1981. "A Modified Regression Base Multiplier." *Growth and Change* 13 (July): 17–22.

Smith, Ralph E. 1981. "Groups in Need of Employment and Training Assistance." In *The Federal Interest in Employment and Training.* 7th Annual Report of the National Commission for Employment Policy. Washington, DC: By the Commission.

Smith, Steve M. 1978. *Wisconsin State Government Employment and Spending: Their Role in State and Regional Development.* Research Report R2952. College of Agriculture and Life Sciences, University of Wisconsin-Madison.

Smith, Steve M., and Glen C. Pulver. 1981. "Nonmanufacturing Business as a Growth Alternative in Nonmetropolitan Areas." *Journal of the Community Development Society* 12 (Spring): 33–48.

Sorensen, Aage, and Arne Kalleberg. 1974. "Jobs, Training and Attitudes of Workers." Discussion Paper 204–74. Institute for Research on Poverty, University of Wisconsin-Madison.

Spence, Michael. 1974. *Market Signalling: Informational Transfer in Hiring and Screening Processes.* Cambridge MA: Harvard University Press.

Stabler, J. C., and P. R. Williams. 1973. "Changing Structure of the Central Place Hierarchy." *Land Economics* 49 (Nov.): 454–58.

Stafford, Howard A. 1974. "The Anatomy of the Location Decision: Content Analysis of Case Studies." In *Spatial Perspectives on Industrial Organization and Decisionmaking,* ed. F. E. I. Hamilton, 169–87. New York: John Wiley and Sons.

Stern, Irving. 1975. "Industry Effects of Government Expenditures: An Input-Output Analysis." *Survey of Current Business* 55 (May): 80–89.

Stevens, David W. 1977. "Labor Market Considerations in Economic Development Planning." In *Human Resources and Regional Economic Development,* ed. Paul V. Braden, 59–110. Economic Development Research Report. Washington, DC: Economic Development Administration, U.S. Department of Commerce.

Stewart, Charles B. 1959. "Economic Base Dynamics." *Land Economics* 35 (Nov.): 327–36.

Stinson, Thomas F. 1968. *The Effects of Taxes and Public Financing on Local Industrial Development: A Survey of the Literature.* U.S. Department of Agriculture, Economic Research Service, Agricultural Economics Report 133. Washington, DC: USDA.

Stöhr, Walter, and Franz Todtling. 1977. "Spatial Equity—Some Anti-Theses to Current Regional Development Strategy." *Papers of the Regional Science Association* 38: 33–54.

Stokey, Edith, and Richard Zeckhauser. 1978. *A Primer for Policy Analysis.* New York: W. W. Norton.

Stone, Kenneth E., and James C. McConnon. 1983. "Analyzing Retail Sales Potential for Counties and Towns." Paper presented at the American Agricultural Economics Association annual meeting, Iowa State University, Ames.

Straszheim, Mahlon R. 1971. "An Introduction and Overview of Regional Money Capital Markets." In *Essays in Regional Economics,* ed. John F. Kain and John T. Meyer, 218–42. Cambridge, MA: Harvard University Press.

Stutzer, Michael. 1985. "The Statewide Economic Impact of Small Issue Industrial Revenue Bonds." *Quarterly Review [of the Federal Reserve Bank of Minneapolis]* 9 (Spring): 2–13.

Summers, Gene F., Sharon D. Evans, Frank Clements, Elwood M. Beck, Jr., and Jon Minkoff. 1976. *Industrial Invasion of Nonmetropolitan America: A Quarter Century of Experience.* New York: Praeger.

Summers, Gene F., and Thomas A. Hirschl. 1986. "Community Economic Development Efforts in 44 Wisconsin Cities and Villages." Paper presented at the Seventh Conference on the Small City and the Regional Community, University of Wisconsin-Stevens Point, March.

Sweet, David C. 1970. "An Industrial Development Screening Matrix." *Professional Geographer* 22 (May): 124–27.

Temple, George S. 1979. "The Spatial and Temporal Distribution of Activities among Small Rural Areas." Paper presented at the Western Regional Science Association annual meeting, San Diego, CA, February.

Thomas, Morgan D. 1964. "The Export Base and Development Stages of Regional Economic Growth: An Appraisal." *Land Economics* 40 (Nov.): 421–32.

Thompson, James H. 1962. "Local Subsidies for Industry: Comment." *Southern Economic Journal* 29 (Oct.): 114–19.

Thompson, John Scott. 1982. "An Empirical Note on the Compatibility of Central Place Models and Economic Base Theory." *Journal of Regional Science* 22 (Feb.): 97–104.

Thompson, Wilbur R. 1965. *A Preface to Urban Economics*. Baltimore, MD: Johns Hopkins University Press.

_____. 1973. "The Economic Base of Urban Problems." In *Contemporary Economic Issues,* ed. N.W. Chamberlain, 1–48. Homewood, IL: Richard D. Irwin.

_____. 1975, "Internal and External Factors in the Development of Urban Economies." In *Regional Policy Readings in Theory and Application,* ed. John Friedman and William Alonso, 201–20. Cambridge, MA: MIT Press.

_____. 1978. "The Urban Development Process." In *Small Cities in Transition,* ed. Harrington Bryce, 95–112. Cambridge, MA: Ballinger.

Thorngren, B. 1970. "How Do Contact Systems Affect Regional Development." *Environment and Planning* 2: 409–27.

Thurow, Lester C. 1975. *Generating Inequality: Mechanism of Distribution in the U.S. Economy.* New York: Basic Books.

Tiebout, Charles M. 1956a "Exports and Regional Economic Growth." *Journal of Political Economy* 64 (Apr.): 160–69.

_____. 1956b. "The Urban Economic Base Reconsidered." *Land Economics* 31 (Feb.): 95–100.

_____. 1960. "Community Income Multipliers: A Population Growth Model." *Journal of Regional Science* 2 (Spring): 75–84.

_____. 1962. "The Community Economic Base Study." Supplementary Paper 16. New York: Committee for Economic Development.

Tinbergen, Jan. 1967. *Development Planning.* New York, McGraw-Hill.

Tornquist, Gunnar. 1977. "The Geography of Economic Activities: Some Viewpoints on Theory and Application." *Economic Geography* 53 (Apr.): 153–62.

Townroe, Peter M. 1974. "Post Move Stability and the Location Decision." In *Spatial Perspectives on Industrial Organization and Decision Making,* ed. F. E. I. Hamilton, 287–307. New York: John Wiley and Sons.

_____. 1979. "Design of Local Economic Development Policies." *Town Planning Review* 5 (Apr.): 148–63.

Turner, R., and H. S. D. Cole. 1980. "The Estimation and Reliability of Urban Shopping Models." *Urban Studies* 17 (June): 140–50.

Tweeten, Luther G., and George Brinkman. 1976. *Micropolitan Development.* Ames, IA: Iowa State University Press.

Ullman, Edward L. 1968. "Minimum Requirements after a Decade: A Critique and an Appraisal." *Economic Geography* 44 (Oct.): 364–69.

Ullman, Edward L., and Michael F. Dacey. 1960. "The Minimum Requirements Approach to the Urban Economic Base." *Papers of the Regional Science Association* 6: 175–94.

U.S. Department of Housing and Urban Development. 1976. *Rapid Growth from Energy Projects.* Washington, DC: HUD.

Vander Muellen, Allen, Jr., and Orman H. Paananen. 1977. "Selected Welfare Implications of Rapid Energy Related Development Impact." *Natural Resources Journal* 17 (Apr.): 301–23.

Vaughan, Roger J. 1977. *The Urban Impacts of Federal Policies.* Vol. 2, *Economic Development.* Report R-2028-KF/RC. Santa Monica, CA: RAND Corporation.

_____. 1979. *State Taxation and Economic Development.* Washington, DC: Council of State Planning Agencies.

_____. 1985. *The Wealth of States: The Political Economy of State Development.* Washington, DC: Council of State Planning Agencies.

Vaughan, Roger J., and Peter Bearse. 1981. "Federal Economic Development Programs: A Framework for Design and Evaluation." In *Expanding the Opportunity to Produce,* ed. Robert Friedman and William Schweke, 307–29. Washington, DC: Corporation for Enterprise Development.

Vietorisz, Thomas, and Bennett Harrison. 1973. "Labor Market Segmentation: Positive Feedback and Divergent Development." *American Economic Review* 63 (May): 366–75.

Wadsworth, H. A., and J. M. Conrad. 1965. "Leakages Reducing Employment Multipliers in Labor Surplus Rural Areas." *Journal of Farm Economics* 47 (Dec.): 1197–1202.

Wagner, William B. 1974. "An Empirical Test of Reilly's Law of Retail Gravitation." *Growth and Change* 6 (July): 30–35.

Wallace, Luther T., and Vernon W. Ruttan. 1961. "The Role of the Community as a Factor in Industrial Location." *Papers of the Regional Science Association* 7: 133–42.

Walpin, Kenneth I. 1977. "Education and Screening." *American Economic Review* 67 (Dec.): 949–58.

Weber, Alfred. 1929. *Alfred Weber's Theory of Location of Industries,* translated by C. J. Friedrich from *Uber den Standort der Industrien* (1909). Chicago, IL: University of Chicago Press.

Weisbrod, Burton A. 1977. "Collective Action and the Distribution of Income: A Conceptual Approach." In *Public Expenditure and Policy Analysis,* ed. R. H. Haveman and J. Margolis, 117–41. Chicago, IL: Rand-McNally.

Weitzell, E. C. 1969. *Planning for Rural Industry.* U.S. Department of Agriculture, Cooperative Extension Service, PA-894. Washington, D.C.: USDA.

Williams, James, Andrew Sofranko, and Brenda Root. 1977. "Industrial Development in Small Towns: Will Social Action Have Any Impact?" *Journal of the Community Development Society* 8 (Spring): 19–29.

Williamson, Robert B. 1975. "Regional Growth: Predictive Power of the Export Base Theory." *Growth and Change* 6 (Jan.): 3–10.

Wilson, J. Holton. 1977. "Impact Analysis and Multiplier Specification." *Growth and Change* 8 (July): 42–46.

Wisconsin, State of, Department of Development. 1967. "Factors in Wisconsin Plant Location." Unpubl. manuscript. Madison, WI.

Wisconsin, State of, Department of Revenue. 1977. *Wisconsin Mining Impact Study.* Madison, WI: By the Department.

Index

Agglomeration costs, 50–52
Assumption approach, 267–68

Banks
   correspondent, 165–66
   role in community economic
       development, 172–74
Basic sector. *See* export base
Behavioral approach
   to consumer shopping decisions, 149–51
   to location decisions, 66–69
Behavioral matrix, 68
Benefit/cost assessment, 99–100
Boundaries
   community, 4
   economic, 231–32, 243–44
   labor market, 180
   market, 60–63
   trade area, 147–49
Business climate, 226–27

Capacity building, 211
Capital
   accumulation, 15
   deficiency, 17–18
   demand, 159–61
   imports, 163–64
   share of income, 15–16
   share of output, 14
Capital markets
   correspondent banking, 165–66
   defined, 158–61
   demand, 162–64
   failure, 166–72, 174–75
   information, 169
   institutions, 162–64
   loan guarantee, 164–65

mobility, 167–69
   regulations, 37, 162, 171–72
   secondary, 164–65
   segments, 161–62
   supply, 162–64
Capital-output ratio, 14, 16–17
Capital subsidies, 216–18
Career ladder, 193
Central place
   defined, 126
   hierarchy, 126–33
Central place theory
   central function, 126, 129
   demand threshold, 59, 133–39
   range of good/service, 133, 143
   tributary area, 126, 128
Community
   boundaries, 4
   defined, 3–4
   development, 5
   economic analysis, 1, 8–9
   economic development
       ecological factors, 117–18
       social action and initiative, 118
       strategies, 81–82, 94–97
       theory, 41–44
   indifference curve, 85–88
   inventory, 114–15
   preference function, 85–88
   resources, 5
   satisfaction level, 85–86
   studies
       boundaries, 4
       ecology, 4
       economics, 4
       ethnographic, 4
       qualitative factors, 4
       sociological, 4
   vitality, 6

Compensating balances, 165–66
Consumer shopping decisions, 149–51
  behavioral approach, 149–50
  ecological approach, 150–51
Core firms, 194
Cost factors of location, 64–65
Credentialing theory. *See* signaling/
  screening theory
Cross hauling, 270–71
Customer survey, 144

Debt capital, 161
Decision-making
  capacity, 35–36, 211–12
  consumer, 132, 149–51
  location, 70–72
Demand
  for capital, 159–61
  derived, 181
  final, 276
  for labor, 181–84
  threshold, 59, 133–39
  changes in, 135–39
Demand-oriented development theory, 27–
  35
  export base thoery, 28–34
  policies, 28
Desirability matrix, 120–23
Development
  defined, 5–8
  economic, 7–9
  event, 228–31
  growth, 7–8
Direct requirements table, 279
Discouraged workers, 187
Distribution effects
  of development, 36, 233, 240–41
  of policy, 85–88, 205, 233
Diversification, 123
Dual labor market theory, 194–95

Ecological approach
  to community study, 4
  to retail trade analysis, 150–51
Economic approach to community study, 4
Economic base
  delineating, 267–73
    assumption approach, 267–68
    location quotients, 268–71
    minimum requirements, 271–73
  multipliers, 263–67
  theory, 28–34
Economic development
  defined, 7–8
  event, 228–29

goals, 82–88
  objectives, 82–88
  organizations, 118
  policy model, 89–94
  theory, 41–44
Economic size of community, 236
Efficiency vs. equity, 87–88, 92–93, 103,
  204
Employment tax credit, 217
Entrepreneurship, 24–25, 35, 38–40
  constellation of events, 39
  culture, 39–40
  personal characteristics, 38–39
  skills, 39
Equity
  capital, 161
  vs. efficiency, 87–88, 92–93, 204
Ethnographic approach to community
  study, 4
Export base
  base theory, 28–34
  change in, 30–31
  defined, 29–30
  external demand, 28
  linkages, 29
  sector of economy, 29–30, 267
Externalities, 24

Feasibility matrix, 123
Final payments, 277
Final sales. *See* Demand, final
Financial
  capital, 161
  expertise, 211
Firm/business
  orientation, 73
  typology, 73, 259–60
Free on board, 58
Functional units, 126
Funds, flow of, 259

Goals and objectives
  hierarchy, 84, 112
  relationship, 84–85
  time, 88
Government expenditures, 204, 211
Gravity models, 144–46. *See also* Reilly's
  law
Growth
  defined, 7–8
  function, 13–17

Hexagonal market areas, 126–29. *See also*
  Market area

distortion in, 63, 139
formation of, 58–59
Hierarchy of goals/objectives, 84, 112
Human capital
    investments, 190–91
    theory, 190–92

Immobility, 20, 24, 167–69, 179, 195–96, 199–200
Impact
    community, 241–24
    demographic, 228
    economic, 228
    fiscal, 228
    local, 231–32
    location, 234–36
    monetary, 232–34
    municipal, 236–39
    negative, 240–41
    nonlocal, 231–32
    nonmonetary, 232–34
    physical, 228
    positive, 240–41
    primary, 234–36. See also Multipliers
    private, 236–40
    public, 236–40
    secondary, 234–36. See also Multipliers
    social, 228
    time, 236
Impact funds, 241
Import substitution, 34, 119, 154–56, 273
Incentives/subsidies, 208, 210
    effective rate, 217
    employment tax credit, 217
    justification, 212–16
    reservations about, 221–26
    types, 216–18
Income
    effect, 185–86
    type of change, 245
In-commuters, 188
Indifference curve, 85–88
Indirect change. See Export base, Input-output, Multipliers
Induced changes. See Input-output
Informal labor markets, 184
Information
    behavioral approach, 68
    in capital market failure, 166, 169
    imperfect, 24, 68–69, 166–67, 169
    in labor market failure, 198–99
In-migrants, 188
Innovation, 21
Input-output
    direct inputs, 279
    direct requirements, tables, 279

final demand, 276
final payments, 277
indirect inputs, 279
multipliers, 281–83
    employment, 283
    income, 282–83
    output, 281–82
nonsurvey, 284
purchasers, 278
semi-survey, 284
suppliers, 278
technical coefficients, 279, 284
transactions table, 275–79
triangularization, 278–79
total requirements table, 279–81
Institutional capacity, 36, 118
    change, 37–38
    strategies for, 37–38
    factors in location, 53–55
Institutions, 35–41
    capacity building, 118, 211
    defined, 35–37
Interdependence. See Input-output
Interest rate, 14, 167–70
Interindustry. See Input-output
Internal labor markets. See Dual labor market theory
Invention, 21
Investment diversification, 171
Isodapanes, 49–50
    critical, 50

Job competition theory, 193–94
Jobs
    appropriate, 179
    families of, 193
    good/bad, 189
    quality, 188–89
Joint ownership, 210–11

Labor
    cost, 49–50
    demand, 181–84
    derived, 180
    sources of, 183
Labor force
    defined, 184–87
    growth, 15–17
    mobility, 199
Labor market
    boundaries, 180
    community issues, 195–200
    defined, 179
    demand, 181–84
    external, 194–97

Labor market (*cont.*)
    formal/informal, 184
    information, 198–99
    institutions, 188–89
    segmentation, 179–80
Labor market theories
    demand oriented, 192–95
    credentialing, 192–93
    dual labor market, 194–95
    job competition, 193–94
    screening, 192–93
    signaling, 192–93
    supply oriented, 190–92
    human capital, 190–92
Labor share of income, 14
Labor subsidies, 216–17
Labor supply, 179, 184–88
    backward bending, 185–86
    elasticities, 186–87
    sources of, 184–85, 187–88
Leakages in economic boundaries, 232,
    243–44
Least cost location, 47–56
Loan guarantees, 164–65
Loan selling, 164
Locational interdependence approach. *See*
    Location theory
Location decision process, 70–72
Location factors, 72–77
Location quotients, 154, 268–71
    cross hauling, 270–71
Location theory
    behavioral approach, 66–69
    demand maximization, 56–63
    least cost, 47–56
    locational interdependence, 56–63
    profit maximization, 63–65
    significance to community, 46–47

Marginal product
    of capital, 14, 167
    of labor, 14, 181–82
Marginal propensity
    to consume locally, 30, 243, 264–67
    to import, 264
Marginal workers, 187
Market
    area. *See also* Trade area
        analysis, 116, 142–57
        formation of, 58–59
        hexagonal, 58–59, 63
        boundaries, 60–63, 143–44, 147–50
        freight rate structure, 61
        production costs, 60
    expansion, 211
    failure, 22–25, 203

    power, 24, 56–58
Matching job/worker requirements, 195–97
Measurement of economic activity
    of business, 260
    of employment, 262
    of income, 262
Minimum requirements approach, 271–73
Mitigation, 240–41
Mobility
    capital, 167–69
    labor, 188, 190, 199–200
Movement imagery, 133
Multipliers
    average, 246–47, 264
    economic base, 263–67
    employment, 250, 283
    export, 263–65
    factors influencing, 242–50
    income, 245, 250, 282–83
    input-output, 281–83
    instantaneous, 248
    investment, 263, 266
    marginal, 246, 264
    output, 250, 281–82
    pyramiding, 250–51
    turnover, 251

Neighborhood effect, 22
Net mill price, 56
New entrants, 187
Nonbasic sector, 28
Nonexport sector, 28

Objective tree, 82
Overtraining. *See* Underemployment

People vs. places, 92
Performance failure, 23
Peripheral firms, 194
Physical capital, 161
Place vs. people, 92
Policy
    distribution, 85–88
    goals and objectives, 82–88
    model, 89
    questions, 80–81
    strategy, 81–82, 91–97
    targeting, 94
    time, 93–94
Policy evaluation, 97–102
    methods of, 99–102
        actual vs. expected, 99
        ad hoc assessment, 99
        benefit costs, 99–100

meeting predetermined goals, 99
Policy goals, 82–88
  complementary, 84–85
  conflicting, 84–85
  hierarchy of, 84
  independent, 84–85
  mixed, 84–85
  time, 88
Policy philosophy, 92–94
  equity-efficiency, 92–93
  people-places, 92
Population-employment ratios, 154–55. *See* Market area analysis
Population growth, 17
Portfolio
  analysis, 123
  diversification, 171
Positive impact, 240–41
Preference function
  individual, 85–86
  weighing of, 86–87
Price subsidies, 216
Primary inputs. *See* Final payments
Private effects of investment, 168
Process, 7
Processing sector. *See* Input-output
Production function, 13–14
Productivity theory, 17–19
Profit maximization approach, 63–65
Profit rate, 14
Program inputs and costs, 98
Prospecting, 119
Public sector intervention approaches, 209–12
Public sector involvement
  mechanisms of, 205–9
  reasons for, 203–5
Pyramiding, 250–51

Qualitative approach to community study, 4

Random survey, 144
Range of good/service, 133, 143
Regulation, 161–62, 171–72, 208, 210
Reilly's law of retail gravitation, 147–49
  Converse's adaptation, 147
Residentiary sector. *See* Nonexport sector
Resource
  defined, 5
  endowment theory, 19–20
  immobility, 20, 24, 167–69, 179, 195–96, 199–200
  requirement/availability analysis, 116
Retail business
  coincidental, 156

generative, 156
shared, 156
Returnees, 187
Risk, 170–71
  default, 170
  inflation, 170
  interest rate, 170
  liquidity, 170
  strategies, 170–71

Sales, 260
  potential, 151–52
  retention, 151–52
Screening matrix system, 120–23
Secondary markets, 164–65
Sectoral composition, 259–60
Segmentation
  of capital markets, 161
  of labor markets, 179–80
Self-sufficiency, 236, 243, 268
Semi-survey. *See* Input-output
Shopdoor survey, 144
Signaling/screening theory, 192–93
Skills, 190–91
  discrepancies, 196
  entrepreneurship, 39
Social accounts, 257–63
  composition of, 259–60
  measures of, 260–63
Social effects of investment, 168
Socioeconomic welfare function, 89
Sociological approach to community, 4
Space cost curves, 53
Spatial monopoly control, 56–58, 141
Standard industrial classification code (SIC), 260
Strategy
  defined, 81–82
  for economic development, 91–97
Structural failure, 23
Subsidies. *See also* Incentives/subsidies
  capital, 216–18
  effects of, 218–20
  labor, 216–17
  price, 216
  self-limiting, 221-22
Substitution effect, 185–86, 219
Supply-oriented development theories
  dynamic, 25
  equilibrium growth, 14–17
  growth function, 13–17
  policy, 17

Target efficiency, 98–99
Targeting, 94, 119–23

322

Targeting (*cont.*)
  feasibility matrix, 123
  rifle approach, 120
  screening matrix, 120–23
  shotgun approach, 119
Technical coefficients, 279, 282, 284
Technological change
  adoption of, 20–22
  effect of, 16–17, 183
  hierarchical effect, 22
  innovation, 21
  invention, 21
  neighborhood effect, 22
Technological progress, 15–16
Threshold
  analysis, 156
  demand, 132–39
Total requirements table, 279–81
Trade area
  capture, 152–53
  defined, 143
  delineated, 143–50
Trade environment, 150–51
Training, 190–92, 196
Transactions table, 275–79
Transportation costs, 47–49, 52–53, 169
Tributary area, 126
Turnover, 251
Typology
  local vs. nonlocal markets, 259
  product, 260
  size, 259
  technology, 259

Uncertainty, 66–68, 238
Underemployment, 187
Unemployment
  demand deficient, 197
  frictional, 198
  hidden, 187
  structural, 197

Value added, 262
Value, marginal product of labor, 181–82
Vitality, 6–7

Wages, 181, 198
  differential, 199
  income effect, 185
  substitution effect, 185
Welfare
  function, 89–91
  human, 7
Well-being
  group, 90
  human, 7
  individual, 89–90
  measures, 90–91

Zero sum, 102–6
  conditions for, 104–6
  efficiency, 103
  public/private, 104
  socioeconomic group, 104
  spatial, 103